IMPRINT and TRACE

# Imprint and Trace

Handwriting in the Age of Technology

Sonja Neef

REAKTION BOOKS

*For Martin, Jonas and Vera*

Published by Reaktion Books Ltd
33 Great Sutton Street
London EC1V 0DX, UK
www.reaktionbooks.co.uk

This book was first published in 2008 by Kulturverlag Kadmos Berlin as
*Abdruck und Spur: Handschrift im Zeitalter ihrer technischen
Reproduzierbarkeit.*

First published in English in 2011.

English language translation by Anthony Mathews

English language translation copyright © Reaktion Books 2011.
The translation was funded with the aid of the Faculty of Media,
Bauhaus-University Weimar.

Printed and bound in Great Britain
by CPI Antony Rowe, Chippenham, Wiltshire

British Library Cataloguing in Publication Data
Neef, Sonja.
Imprint and trace : handwriting in the age of technology.
1. Penmanship – History.
2. Writing – Materials and instruments – History.
3. Written communication – Technological innovations.
I. Title
652.1'09-dc22

ISBN: 978 1 86189 653 7

# Contents

# . . . before Aleph

Then we begin with the **A** of ABC.

It has always been at the very start of things.

It is the first letter of our **A**lphabet

and likewise the first letter of the Greek alphabet.

The first letter of the Hebrew alphabet is *Aleph*.

The first letter of the Arabic alphabet is *Alif*, and they both represent the number 1.

When the book-keepers and traders of Mesopotamia across the
Arabian peninsula as far as Egypt did their counting and inventories,
they were confronted with the problem of indicating that something
was whole and complete, and that it was to be treated as one thing in
clear distinction to other quantities – duality, trinity, etc. For this they
chose the sign Aleph. They carved it on their tablets of dried clay or
wrote it on papyrus. For the first day of the calendar, as also for the
first verse of a sacred text, the letter-number Aleph was used in the
ancient kingdoms of Judaea and Israel.[1] And even though the Arabic
number script appears to follow its own system, called *Huruf Al-Jumal*
('calculation of the sum with the help of letters'), the Arabic Alif also
counts as one.[2]

The letter **A** has always been the first letter sign in the ancient
Hebrew and in Aramaic script and also in the Syrian, Greek and
Etruscan. Not only does **A**leph, as a letter number, signal the
mythological beginning of all existence but it must be taken as
the first pictogram and the first logogram of our written culture.
And over and above this it can be taken as the very first letter of all.
This is how it is generally described by historians of writing.

At one time Aleph stood as a sign for an ox. It symbolized
power and life, the Ur-energon; it was the **A**rchi-sign of an **A**grarian
society and the first monument of human memorializ**A**tion. Around
1500 BC, Aleph was adopted by Semitic immigr**A**nt workers during
their exile in the Arabian peninsula of Sinai from their Egypti**A**n
hosts. In its use in Semitic writing the concept gradually faded in
relation to the image, and the archaic iconogr**A**m soon turned into
a phonogram; from now on the sign no longer corresponded to
a concept, but to a unit of sound. Strictly speaking, this sound
correspondence was acrophonic, i.e., the sign of the ox-head stood
for the first sound, the onset of the word 'Aleph', meaning 'ox' in
Semitic. The first phonographic letter was born.[3] It formed the basis
for the idea of Alpha and Beta, of writing and the alphabet and their
very conditions.

When one says ['alef], even before one pronounces the [a],
one produces that non-sound that linguists call the *glottal stop* and
note as [ʔ], that 'unheard' sound that in speaking is linked to a vowel.
A glottal stop arises when the airstream is blocked in the larynx and
then released 'explosively'. This sound preceding a vowel, as it were

introducing the voicing, is itself barely perceived. In the Roman alphabet it is not even written. Only that other, aspirated way of saying the vowel, is marked by a letter: <H>. It indicates the flow of breath rasped as a fricative in the larynx and expelled out of one's mouth even before one's breath is voiced and the vowel itself strikes in. When articulation starts with a glottal stop [ʔ], one only needs to write the vowel, however; the non-aspirated onset is invisible as regards writing.

In the ancient Sinaitic alphabets, by contrast, the glottal stop was written instead of the vowel. Thus, in fact, A stands at the beginning of the phonographic alphabet, it is the first 'sound' sign, but at the same time it is itself silent in its origin. A substitute resonates barely audibly in its place:

At least until such time as the Greeks adopt the sign. They take over Alpha from the Phoenicians and change its use from the sign for the glottal stop to the sign for the vowel. From now on, **A** does not signify an 'empty' noise made by the breath [ʔ] any more but a fully voiced breAth: [a]: *aazô* means 'breathe' in Greek; *anima, Atem, adem* and *âme* are all related in this sense, likewise *asthma*. With this re-evaluation from [ʔ] to [a] the Greek alpha heralds the birth of the first complete alphabet. Complete, for the reason that the alphabet now represents, not only consonants, but also vowels. Formerly in an earlier, proto-Sinaitic form, the **A** of 'Arche' – the origin, the ox, along with the **A**rchive of writing – had been annihilated, it had snuffed out the voiced breath, as it doesn't signify the vowel to which it is assigned, just as in Arabic and Hebrew the vowel sound is not fully written. Instead aleph announces the breath as something that is not actually present in this place but that is nevertheless to come.[4]

Like A, **E** is also the 'first' vowel of our alphabet. Another first.

E is actually the first letter to wear out on the keyboard as it is the most used.

In the Greek alphabet the sound [e] is written not only as epsilon but also with the letter eta (<H>, <η>). This eta is a remarkable letter.

From the perspective of the history of writing it displays a similar dual logic to aleph. The classical philologist Alfred Schmitt describes the history of the letter H (eta) in Greek as follows:

> The letter that represents the aspirate sound in the Roman alphabet, has in Greek the sound ē. The textbooks give the following explanation for this peculiar fact: The letter was originally called heta in Greek and represented the aspirate sound. In Eastern Greek, however, the aspiration was soon lost; the name of the letter thus became eta, and accordingly the eastern Greeks then used the sign to write ē. In Western Greek, in the *Motherland*, the aspiration was retained and with it also the value h for the sign heta. The Romans took over their script from a Western Greek alphabet mediated by the Etruscans. Therefore the letter had for them as well the sound h, and this sound value has won international favour through the Roman alphabet. For the Greek world, on the other hand, the Eastern Greek rule has been crucial through the widespread reception of the Ionic alphabet.[5]

In our alphabet eta – like A – has incontestably the status of the principal, 'first' bearer of sound in the great Archive of writing. At the same time, however, the Greek h/eta, transformed into a Roman sign, stands for the aspirate sound [h], for the *pneuma*, the pure, voiceless breath, the spiritus, this 'almost Nothing' of a lightly rasped stream of air.

The fates of alpha and h/eta run parallel and coincide at moments when the Greeks graphematically transform the sign of the aspirate sound into the sign of a vowel sound and the Romans similarly transform the vowel sign into a sign for the aspirate sound. On the threshold of these transcriptions, the onset of the voice is determined as aspirate or inaspirate pneuma. Aleph signifies *before* this act of transcription and eta *after* it for the pure and voiceless breath; in each case the voice is audible beyond this threshold. In the Greek alphabet the aspirate sounds are not written again until later in the shape of what remains of the letters deformed into diacritics: the front half of the letter <H>, abbreviated to a vertical bar, provides the spiritus, the supplemental sign marking an aspirate sound in the classical Greek alphabet. Italicized, i.e., slanting towards the right, with the bar looking like an *accent grave* in French, it is referred to as spiritus asper; it indicates that a vowel is aspirated at the beginning of a word. Later the Alexandrine grammarians invented in addition spiritus lenis, looking like an *accent aigu* and indicating that a vowel at the beginning of a word is to be started with a glottal stop, in other words not aspirated.[6]

It is not accidental that E forms in association with A the binary pair that Jacques Derrida uses to demonstrate the basic principle of writing: 'différance'. The difference between 'différence' and 'différance', writes Derrida,

> this graphic difference (a instead of e), this marked difference between two apparently vocal notations, between two vowels, remains purely graphic: it is read, or it is written, but it cannot be heard.[7]

When Derrida argues that this difference, *différance*, remains 'a silent sign' and bases his euro- and phonocentric critique on this, I should like to add that A and E as well from the perspective of the history of writing have from the start carried within themselves the erasure of the vowel. The 'unheard-of' *différant* of Aleph is H/Eta, both resounding aloud:

[A], [E]

and at the same time almost nothing, either a silent, pneumatic mini-explosion in the larynx of the speaker:

[ʔ]

or an unvoiced breath of air:

....[hhhhhh]....

But all this concerns the domain of the voice and thus – as has often been argued – does not affect writing. What is the situation then as regards the letter, the GrAph?

The stone-mason setting up the original letter on its two feet, stabilizing it with a diagonal stroke as the most mAjestic of all mAjuscules, placing the vowel, chiselling it in, his stone writing body, as Hegel argues in his *Encylopaedia*, adopts the form of an Egyptian pyrAmid. The monument of the pyrAmid is, however at the same time, the grAve of the phAraoh which, as Derrida writes, 'remains silent as a tomb'.[8]

In this respect, erasure stands at the origin of the monument, and inscription and erasure prove to be two aspects of the same operation. The archive, writes Derrida, suffers from one evil (one *Mal d'archive*), i.e. a destructive drive or even a death drive which, as it always works in silence, never leaves its own archive behind. At the moment of inscription, the archive erases its traces and destroys itself as an *archē*, an origin. The archive, Derrida writes, is 'archiviolitic'.[9] Even if historians of writing prefer to enquire into how letters and alphabets have developed and how the one has derived from the other, one could on the other hand equally emphatically ask what there was *before* Aleph.

Before Aleph was Aleph, Aleph, Al . . .

Besides, if one takes seriously the graphic form of <A> in its physical materiality as a *différAnt*, another difference appears. Because <A> also occurs with an inaudible difference as <a>. And also as

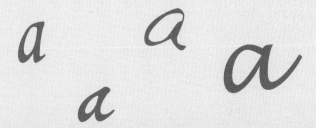

**A** = 0000 0000 0100 0100 = U+0041 = LATIN CAPITAL LETTER A

# Introduction: *Manus ex machina*

At present, here and now, there is something material – visible but
scarcely readable – that, referring only to itself, no longer makes a
trace, unless it traces only by losing the trace it scarcely leaves
– that it just barely remains
– but that is just what he calls the trace, this effacement.
Jacques Derrida, *Cinders*[1]

## Thinking handwriting, from the perspective of the screen

Writing these days is a highly technical business. And our writing tools are getting more and more remarkable. Anyone wanting to express themselves in writing, whether for private or public consumption, usually does it with the aid of the electric and electronic equipment of the new media age. We compose our *manu*scripts with the aid of a word processor; we can deal rapidly with our post via e-mail or text messaging, with more speed and efficiency than with the *manus ministra* of shorthand typists and secretaries. We write our diaries as blogs; we check off the goods on our shopping lists with the click of a mouse and toss them into virtual shopping trolleys. We now no longer initiate our relationships by entrusting handwritten love letters to carrier pigeons; instead we make dates in internet chatrooms and meet on Facebook and MySpace. Where once there was a blackboard and both teachers and students developed the movement of thought according to the real-time choreography of the act of writing, there is now a multimedia centre playing back pre-programmed sounds and images in multiple formats; in addition, through access to networks – wireless and un-restricted – we can tap into a universe of data. Using terminals, mouse and keyboard we direct the multimedia performance, project images onto screens and scroll texts down the screen. In this technical process of writing we inevitably lose something relating to the physical dimension of the '*ductus*', i.e., the 'movement' of the hand leading a pen (*ducere*). Instead, the writing strikes us as the product of a matrix of zeros and ones on screens and other surfaces. Electronic writing is produced – at least at first glance – not as the trace of our (hand)-writing, but by algorithms. According to the latest opinion in media studies, we too are disappearing along with our (hand)writing by being reduced to the function of end-users. As such we are faced with a totally 'standardized interface' and lacking both a body and a right to decision-making. This seems to be the conclusion in view of the fact that this interface is no longer open to perception.[2]

Anyone doubting the blissfulness of technology may not be able to resist the impulse to reach for the last piece of chalk left lying in a drawer of a seminar room. On the look-out for a good old blackboard they find their eye caught by one of those easy-to-overlook stickers placed at the bottom right-hand corner of the board on which there is a small pictogram, a 'Please do not' notice, in the style of a 'No smoking' notice, showing a hand in the act of writing crossed through by a red line warning the writer: 'No handwriting on the projection screen please'. The long-held suspicion that digital equipment and handwriting cannot coexist seems to be confirmed here for good and all. The sticker openly demonstrates the supremacy of electronic writing.

Nowadays writing with chalk or a pen is getting rarer and rarer. And as the letters do not flow directly from a hand, they do not flow at all. As a rule they are produced by tapping a key and transmitting them to a processor by means of an electronic impulse using the binary code by which they are finally made visible as alphabetical signs on a screen. This is a quick and tidy process. No ink blots, no blunt pencils, no chalk squeaking or scraping on the board, no dust, no 'real' at all, gets in the way between writer and symbolic order. In addition, the computer – as Kittler pointed out – can not only store data (like stone tablets) and transmit data (like carrier pigeons and couriers), but also process data: like a wax tablet, on which data can be deleted without destroying the medium, and which in addition can be written on again and again without the loss of the earlier data.[3] More than ever in the history of writing, in our time handwriting seems to be a doomed cultural practice. Its means of material production is too time-consuming, too slow and too expensive, for it to meet the needs of efficient communication. Handwriting at best appears to owe its survival to its aura of nostalgia reminding us of a historic past in which human beings were still human beings and authentic in a physical sense, free of organic spare parts or technical extensions of their senses. Nowadays, it seems, at best we still write by hand in the same way that we ride in a carriage: as a pleasant relaxation, only to rush off the next minute by high-speed rail.

This then seems to be where we are at now as regards handwriting. But only at first sight. This book tells another story and history of writing. The aim of this book is not so much to set up writing by hand in opposition to the technical modes of writing, but more to make use of this binary scheme in order to differentiate just what handwriting is and how it operates in the field of media and culture. The mechanical or digital copy or the standardized imprint (*empreinte*) of handwriting brings into question once more issues of autography, of the trace of the physical, unique and authentic act (*hand*ling) of writing. My argument is that there is no definitive dichotomy between printed script in the sense of mechanical, technical or digital writing techniques on the one hand, and handwriting in the sense of an individual, unique and singular trace on the other, but that the principles of 'imprint' and 'trace' are always historically and systematically bound up with one another. In this book I attempt to illustrate how these media opposites have an impact on one another and influence each other without ever at the same time giving up their specific polarity or even just starting to reduce it. 'Imprint' and 'trace' then represent the two basic principles of handwriting, conceptual opposites facing each other diametrically but both nevertheless always affecting the practice of handwriting.

### New Roman Times

In keeping with its reputedly marginal position in the field of writing techniques, handwriting is absent even from discussions of the sciences of written and literary language. '*The* Story of Handwriting', a definitive historical and systematic study of handwriting, has yet to be written. There is much talk about writing: writing, its use and system, from the perspective of archaeology, palaeontology, pedagogy and linguistics. From Plato's *Kratylos* through Saussure's *Course in General Linguistics* up to the current paradigms of linguistics, writing – Jacques Derrida has analysed this Western school of argument in detail in his work *Of Grammatology* – is conceived as external to language.[4] In turn the essential characteristics of language are seen as independent from their performance as media. Language has a referential structure, and the relation between signifier and signified is considered arbitrary. Language is a system of differences, and the theoretically limitless possibilities of selection and combination make this system productive to such an extent that a finite set of signs can create an infinite number of articulations. In general, the way language is represented in terms of classical linguistics is marked by a 'desensualization of language' – as Sybille Krämer very nicely characterizes it.[5] Even for the linguistics of written language, which is concerned with the transcription of sound (or more precisely phonological representations) into graphic constructs – graphematics and orthography are its central objects of study – a difference such as that between handwriting and printed writing is of hardly any importance.[6]

Furthermore, palaeography possesses a certain degree of authority in the study of handwriting in its concern with the materiality of writing instruments and writing surfaces – the study of epigraphs with chiselled inscriptions, papyrology and parchmentology with the corresponding writing materials and so on. Palaeography has nothing to say, however, in relation to contemporary developments of handwriting techniques, concerned as it is with the '*palaios*', the 'ancient' or primitive era of writing. For that reason, the blank space produced by an ink eraser, or a copying machine, or – in combination – the photocopy of handwriting erased by an eraser pen, hardly brings delight to the heart of a palaeontologist, even though making visible the invisible traces of writing at the deepest levels of palimpsests constitutes one of his central objects of study; though the letter forms of the Roman alphabet which we still use nowadays – manually, mechanically, electrically or electronically – cannot be thought of but in relation to the historical techniques of writing on mud, sand, wax, wood, stone, papyrus, parchment, paper, canvas, slate-tablet, writing pad and so on and passed on across millennia through the changes of media. Nevertheless, for the contemporary alphabet we have ceased to relate letter fonts back to writing technologies, since the difference between Times New Roman (with serifs that the stone-mason added with his chisel to embellish the frayed line-beginnings) and Arial (the uniform sans serif of the World Wide Web) seems to make no difference. Altogether, the examination of handwriting has become a specialist interest: the case of the eraser pen is a concern only for the student of forensic investigation of documents; the didactics of handwriting purely a matter for primary school pedagogy and what it says about character is the territory of grapho-psychology. But as a whole area of cultural technology to be looked at from an interdisciplinary perspective, handwriting remains a blank on the canvas of the great and significant cultural practices of the West.

Only with the arrival of the young discipline of media studies is there a bringing together of considerations of the materiality, functionality and structurality of writing and writing culture. But so far media studies has not shown much interest in *hand*writing. It prefers to see its main object of research in the technical innovations that are continually being renewed with every change of media, particularly so in this digital age. So handwriting easily gets left out of the picture. Compared with the spectacular acts on the stage of our contemporary media culture, handwriting comes over as an anachronistic leftover, a relic of a pre-technical age.

The claim is often made that handwriting represents a moribund cultural technology. With the advent of the age of the typewriter, Friedrich Kittler already announced its demise. The argument heralding the death of handwriting arises from the thesis that culture and technology have been becoming generally less manual since the onset of industrialization and the advent of mass media. To say that this development bodes ill for humanity is an equally widespread myth. In the end the hand figures as a neuromotor 'dispositif', not only for the genealogy of writing but for the evolution of the human race as such. This paleontological perspective is the one argued by André Leroi-Gourhan in his monumental work on *Gesture and Speech*, in which he studies the hand, from Archanthropians up to modern man, as the main motivator in the evolution of mankind. According to his theory, walking upright frees the hand from its mobility function. For its part, the hand now being free frees the lips from the task of supplying food and so sets language free. The hand becomes a tool and itself soon picks up a tool; in cooperation with a short face, the hand develops graphism. From now on, the face adapts to reading and the hand adapts to painting. For Leroi-Gourhan, a free hand along with an upright walking position and a short face is one of the main characteristics of mankind.

The development of the precision of the hand, discussed by Leroi-Gourhan (who goes into detail on all facets of the question), covers a considerable period of time – from the fish to *Homo sapiens* – a seemingly never-ending process that suddenly took a sharp turn in the course of evolution:

> Originally [the hand] was a claw or pincer for holding stones; the human triumph was to turn it into the ever-skillful servant of human technical intelligence. From the Upper Paleolithic to the nineteenth century, the hand enjoyed what seems like an interminable heyday. It still plays an essential role in industry, a few

skilled toolmakers producing the operative parts of machines to be operated by crowds of workers requiring no more than a five-fingered claw to push the buttons ...

The dwindling importance of the makeshift organ that is our hand would not matter a great deal if there were not overwhelming evidence to prove that its activity is closely related to the balance of the brain areas with which it is connected. 'Being useless with one's fingers,' 'being ham-fisted,' is not a very alarming thing at the level of the species as a whole; a good number of millennia will pass before so old an organ of our neuromotor apparatus actually regresses. But at the individual level the situation is very different. Not having to 'think with one's fingers' is equivalent to lacking a part of one's normally, phylogenetically human mind. Thus the problem of regression of the hand already exists today at the individual if not the species level.[7]

Taking Leroi-Gourhan at his word, in the distance one can make out ominous signs on the horizon of our highly technological civilization. What is to become of us, of our hand, of our writing? Is there life for thought beyond the hand, and if so, what shape will such ways of thinking take for a hand-retarded species? Exaggerating a little in the spirit of Kittler's media-consumer deprived of his right to decide: are we going to hell in the same handcart as our handwriting?

This and other questions in relation to handwriting as an important Western cultural practice have not yet been discussed so far in any coherent way. And even this book will not make up for the lack. At best it marks a chapter in 'The Story of Handwriting', i.e., the last chapter – for the time being – the one in which handwriting is supposed to be disappearing. After all, this book deals with handwriting in the very aftermath of the great revolutions of the printing press, typewriter and the digital media: the age that since Benjamin has been dubbed the age of mechanical reproduction. This book pursues handwriting into its last refuges and darkest recesses, and tracks it down, not only in school classrooms; it states that our contemporary media culture is full of handwriting. In spite of digital writing equipment, handwriting holds its own within the bastions of private and personal correspondence – as formal condolences or (even still) as intimate love-talk – as also in the manifold practices of signing, from signing one's name in an autograph, via the engraving or tattooing of one's skin as a mark of authenticity, through to spraying on walls: everywhere it is a matter of establishing or maintaining one's unique identity. Now as much as in the past, handwriting – alongside the digital remediations mentioned above – remains the means of writing for the *aide mémoire*: one's diary, shopping list and a quick note on the phone.

The role of this book is neither to carry out an inquisition against contemporary developments in the media and culture, nor to do a conservation job at rescuing handwriting (and by extension at rescuing humanity). Beyond genealogism and evolutionism – of both humanity and the media – I am more concerned with looking at the manual *in* the digital: the fingerprint on the touch-screen, the stylus on the writing pad of the tablet PC; in short: with thinking handwriting from the perspective of the screen.

Because surprisingly, handwriting often turns up precisely where we least expect it: in those very areas where we think it is at a disadvantage in competition with the new media. Whether etched, photographed, filmed, facsimiled or scanned, it comes to us in printed reproduction in the form of artistic calligraphy, on microfiche in microscopic reduction, in a serial letter as the relief facsimile of a signature or in e-mail correspondence as a pre-programmed font on our PC screens that now once again function as a writing pad, just like the slate-tablet of ancient times. A screen and handwriting do not rule each other out. On the contrary, the technical innovations of the visual media since photography and xerography offer the means of reproduction of what was hitherto limited to a unique and absolutely singular act of writing: handwriting. In this book it is just such areas thought to be free of handwriting that will be explored, areas in which technical reproduction makes previously unique, original works of art into repeatable, palpable and permanently available instant replays.

The aporia of handwriting only becomes truly apprehensible in its contest with the other media, since this is where the very particularity of handwriting as a medium and as a cultural practice comes to the fore. It is only in this difference that we can see what handwriting is really like and how it functions in the field of media and culture. Through detailed analysis of a large number of media phenomena and cultural practices, this book investigates the systematic nature of the intermedial relations of handwriting as a 'hypermedium' that mediates between the voice and the hand. In the movement of the hand, both the voice (*'die Stimme'*) and the spirit, atmosphere or mood (*'die Stimmung'*) as a highly individual, ephemeral and irreducibly physical *'pneuma'* or breath (to refer to what 'aura' literally means in Greek) takes on a shape as writing and as image. This book proceeds by detailed analysis of what N. Katherine Hayes terms the 'inscription technologies' of handwriting in the age of the new media. Inscription technologies refer to the specific inscriptions of the text in different medial modes. 'To count as an inscription technology, a device must initiate material changes that can be read as marks.'[8] The basic operation of inscription consists for Hayles in the act of 'translation', something she closely identifies with the idea of a 'material metaphor', a metaphor in the sense of a vehicle (*meta-ferein*: to carry across), the idea of 'traffic' or of 'interfaces' between the ungraspable side 'beyond' the skull and the here and now of the visible surfaces.[9]

Handwriting is just such a sort of 'device', or interface, just like a 'typewriter' in the sense of Kittler's writing tools. After all, it moves thoughts on by the movement of the hand and records the trace of the passing 'hand jive' as a readable, that is, not just permanent but also repeatable, coded (new) inscription of the written signs or their imaginary imprints. And it does this using its own particular technologies. One example of these is the fact that handwriting – more than 'normal' mechanical writing – works as a hybrid (or even: 'hyper-') medium combining word (speech), writing and image. Although handwriting as an alphabetical script is spellable, nevertheless it can only be reproduced under certain conditions, that is, with the aid of such techniques of reproduction or forgery, for which handwriting's visual performance is essential. Like no other writing, handwriting makes claims as to its authenticity and uniqueness and gains, now more than ever, its cultural significance from that claim. This insistence on a historical materiality sometimes shrouds handwritten texts in the aura of nostalgia, such that it is in danger of tempting one into a fetishistic ideologizing, whereby the past becomes stylized into a freely accessible object.

Against this, employing precisely the logic inherent to handwriting itself, one could object that handwriting, although it makes an emphatic claim to originality, is never just singular but paradoxically always iterable, given that its basic operation consists in copying a pre-prepared ideal type (an imprint). Handwriting is thus based on the capability of repeating the original type or (and I shall return to this repeatedly in this book) of forging it. In addition, the writing produced in this way is never just a re-presentation, but also a performative act, since the repetition or quotation of the collective norm (the way one learns to write at school) – to borrow from Derrida's legendary essay 'Signature Event Context' – in principle contains within it the possibility of the rupture of this norm. In the interplay between cultural norm and teratological deviation, what we understand by 'individuality' comes to the fore. This idea of individuality is precisely the origin of the myth that one's handwriting reveals the writer's character.

All these characteristics and myths make handwriting a remarkable special form of writing that promises either less or more than the 'dead' letters of mechanized writing standardized for communication purposes. This 'added value' becomes particularly vivid and at the same time problematic whenever handwriting is represented in a second medium in which what is considered to be physical, authentic and unique – the hand – emerges from a machine.

## Ashes and Fire

Just as it is in the process of disappearing, handwriting is a particularly interesting subject to be looking at, not only in the sense of giving it the last rites before its final demise but for the reason that, right on the verge of being forgotten, handwriting blazes its trail anew. Even before the advent of the great emphasis on hypertext fashionable in the media studies of the 1980s and the related claim about an 'end of the book', Jacques Derrida described the 'beginning of writing'.[10] And the same goes for the latest multimedia technical equipment: it convulses writing and because of this, writing may – perhaps – disappear. But not without leaving any remains behind. And out of these remains writing is restored anew. Because, as Michael Wetzel says about the often proclaimed (plural) 'ends of the book':

precisely because writing is always confronted with its demise, it can arise anew. Its demise is not in the Other of writing, but in the writing itself. For that reason its realm is less in the visible forms of its epoch-making monuments than in its ashes, i.e. in that which remains without remaining.[11]

It is not by accident that Wetzel invokes here the image of fire. After it has been extinguished, either by the burning of libraries or book-burning – in Germany we know all about this – or by the switch to new writing and reading technologies, writing lingers on as that which persists when there is nothing left besides ashes. As in the fable of the phoenix, that mythological bird that sets fire to itself every five hundred years on its nest of sweet-smelling spices and then arises anew from the ashes, writing moves on as the 'trace of the ashes', according to Wetzel, 'to rise again in the dark ashes of xerography'.[12]

It is just these ashes that are the subject matter of this book. It does not, however, see the mere survival as a lingering vestige of the hand in the age of the new media for new, *handicapped* writing cultures. Instead it is aimed at understanding the structure of its repetition – and ashes and fire – and at comprehending the grammar of its reincarnation as the interplay of imprint and trace.

## Before a Stele

Before the library of Celsus in the ancient necropolis of Ephesus in
Asia Minor, the modern-day Aegean, there stands an unusual stele.
The Austrian Archaeological Institute in Vienna records it as a 'letter'
in stone of the Byzantine emperor Mauricius from 11 February 585.
The stele carries an inscription in two paragraphs, both chiselled, but
produced by two distinct styles of writing or *ductus*. The upper part
that ends with a cross as a punctuation mark is chiselled in well
preserved Greek capitals:

> . . . ΑΛΛΑ/ΤΑC/ΗCΥΧΙΑC/ΑΠΑΝ
> [ΤΑΣ/]ΑΓΕΙΝ/[ΚΑΙ/]Ε Ι/ΤΗC/ΠΑΡΑ/ΤΑΥ
> ΤΑ/ΔΙΑΓΕΕΓΟΝΕΝ/ΕΙ/ΚΕ/ΑΙ
> [Ν/]ΥΣΤΕΡѠ/ΔΙΑΓΕΝΗΤΑΙ/
> [ΤΟΥ]ΤѠΝ/CΥΝΛΑΒΕCΘΑΙ/
> ΠΟΙΝΑC/ΤΕ/ΕΙΡΙΘΕΠΙΝΕ/ΑΥΤѠ/
> ΤΑC/ΤѠΝ/ΠΑΡΑΝΟΜѠC/ΒΙŎΝ
> ΤѠΝ/ΑŽΙΑC †

> *. . . but all are to keep quiet; and if anyone should behave differ-*
> *ently or if he does it later, he is to be seized and made to suffer the*
> *punishments that are appropriate for people who live unlawfully.*[1]

Given the Greek alphabet that has come down to us, we find some
of the written signs in this paragraph strange. For example, the way
the rounded sigma is written looking like a Latin C strikes one.
In addition, some of the letters are written in minuscule alongside
majuscule letters: the omega, the theta and in the last line the xi. In
'ΒΙΟΥΝ' omicron and upsilon are combined together as one ligature.
This is not unusual for writing on stone as the material for writing
on is valuable and chiselling is hard work. All together, however, this
Greek square writing presents a uniform caption which is legible
because it copies, or 'imprints', the prototype of the letter sign.

In contrast to this, the lower inscription looks totally different.
Its curved forms and fluid *ductus* remind one less of the technique of
using a mallet and chisel than of the gliding stroke of a *calamus* or a
pen applying ink swiftly onto a writing surface. Were it not that the

Edict of the Byzantine Emperor
Mauricius (Flavius Mauritius
Tiberius, 539–602) of 11 February
AD 585, excavation at Ephesus,
Turkey.

archaeologists draw attention to the fact that this inscription is
written in Roman letters, as a habitual user of Roman script one
would be standing before the stele like an illiterate:

> datu[m]/III/Idus/februar[ias]/co
> nstantinupo[li]/imp[er]a[toris]/
> d[omini]/n[ost]ri [▢▢▢▢▢▢▢▢] [[Mauricii T-]]
> iberi/P̊[r]P̊[tui]/aug[usti]/ann[o]/III
> et/post/cons[ulatum]/eius[dem]/
> ann[o]/I †

> *Given on the third day of the Ides of February in Constantinople,*
> *in the third year of the Emperor, our Lord, . . . [Mauricius]*
> *Tiberius, who is still Augustus, and in the first year after*
> *his consulate.*

The cryptic nature of this inscription arises, on the one hand, from the number of odd specific signs for abbreviations and ligatures which admittedly speed up the writing becoming tachygraphy, but which make reading more difficult. Actually, the cursive, 'lapidary' writing style of this lapidary script looks totally 'unlapidary'. The traces of correction besides give the impression of handwriting, sketchy as in a personal note, for example in the third to last line, where a double P is crossed out using a full slash and a double e is written above it. And also the line above it looks as though the stone-mason has reached for the eraser pen. From the historical point of view, the deletion of the letters indicates less a mistake in writing than that nomoclastic practice whereby the scar in the stone stands as a sign for the fall of the ruler: the name Mauricius was chiselled out after he was deposed by Phokas.

But even looked at in that light, the lower inscription remains peculiar. The archaeologists presume that the Greek stone-mason was not familiar with the script of the Roman colonizer and that he 'chiselled down' the handwritten note from the Imperial scribal chancelry exactly as it was written along with the cursive *ductus* and short forms. The trace of this writing was certainly not intended for or suited to chiselling in stone. It is precisely in the contravention of the norm of the inscription technologies which classically strictly distinguishes the engraving of impressions and imprints from that other way of writing, that is, the drawing of a line or a trace in a free, 'flowing', curvilinear stroke of the hand, that the two basic principles of writing appear in all their clarity: the writing at the top shows an imprint, the one at the bottom shows a trace. Or more exactly – and this reveals the shocking nature of the contravention of the norm: the imprint of a trace.

# 1 Exergue: Imprint and Trace

To make an imprint (*empreinte*): to produce a mark by pressing a body onto a surface. The corresponding verb imprint (*empreindre*, in German *prägen*) describes the process of impressing something *onto* something or *into* something to produce a shape ... Often the word 'imprint' – perhaps in contrast to the trace, but this would have to be investigated further – refers to the fact that the result of the process survives, that the gesture results in a 'permanent mark'.

Georges Didi-Huberman, *Ähnlichkeit und Berührung*[1]

In 1717 Johann Heinrich Schulze, an all-round man of science of the Baroque, by profession a doctor and at the time an up-and-coming scientist in the early days of the Academia Fredericiana Halensis, laid a milestone in the history of experimental chemistry. On the basis of the chemical-physical knowledge that was up until that time still quite unsystematic, he experimented with the light sensitivity of photo-active substances. He soaked chalk powder in *aqua fortis* (acid of salt-petre diluted with water) containing silver nitrate, and filled a glass container with the mixture. He had previously carefully prepared the glass container:

> [I covered] most of the glass with dark bodies ... but [exposed] a small part to the entry of light. Thus I frequently wrote names or whole sentences on paper and carefully cut out the parts marked with ink using a sharp knife; with wax I stuck the paper pierced in this way onto the glass. Before long, the sun's rays wrote those words or sentences on the deposit of chalk, in the places where they met the glass through the openings in the paper, so precisely and clearly that I caused many curious people who did not know the experiment to attribute the whole thing to some kind of trick.[2]

The trick is none other than what was to be called later on 'photography'. Schulze describes his experiment in his essay later published under the title 'Scotophorus pro phosphoro inventus' (discovered a conveyor of darkness instead of a conveyor of light) with the subtitle 'seu experimentum curiosum de effectu radiorum solarium' (or: remarkable experiment on the effect of the sun's rays).[3] Schulze was not as yet a photographer. But his discovery contributed to what was to lead to the invention of photography, preparing the way up to the cross-roads where chemistry (light sensitive substances) and optics (*camera obscura*) meet.[4]

Schulze's experiment is effective in two respects: because of the way in which it not only plays a role in the invention of photography – and just *en passant* it does this like so many experiments literally through the template of writing – but also invents writing anew. Strictly speaking Schulze is orchestrating an experiment in writing, a sort of *écriture automatique*, written by the rays of the sun, the words

Johann Heinrich
Schulze (1687–1744),
the 'discoverer of
photography'.

*Dr. Johann Heinrich Schulze*
geboren 1687, gestorben 1744

appearing as out of nowhere as darknesses against a light background: by and by in *stages* but not as usual *one after another*; not letter for letter and word for word, but as a whole simultaneously in a new kind of temporal sequentiality of becoming visible. Perhaps this is the first time in the history of writing that writing is written 'archeiropoetically', not by a hand; nor is it printed or stamped by a machine.

Just as once the printing press reproduced pre-prepared, standardized letters, photocopying and soon after its 'dry' variant, xerography (which is produced without a developing tank) now opens up to duplication that which was previously considered to be absolutely unique and inimitable: the stroke of individual handwriting as a line, drawn or traced by a physical hand with an unmistakeable *ductus*. Photography literally makes handwriting chemically and physically cloneable. When it is photographed, handwriting then appears in a different light. Previously a line or trace, it becomes an imprint. Or more precisely: an imprint of a trace.

## Icon and Index

Photography, at least apart from the case of (digital) manipulation, records the trace of the visible appearance. It has its base in a chemical and physical relation to that which Roland Barthes, in his now classical work *Camera Lucida*, describes, still using a structuralist expression, as the 'photographic referent': the necessarily real thing placed before the lens and without which there could be no photography. This relation is an affirmation: '*The thing has been there*'.[5] Long before Barthes, Charles Sanders Peirce described photographs as an indexical sign,

> because we know that they are in certain respects exactly like the objects they represent. But this resemblance is due to the photographs having been produced under such circumstances that they were physically forced to correspond point by point to nature.[6]

Handwriting is just such an indexical sign since, unlike printed writing, it points its finger at a ground, or originator. The legal argument behind the signature is based on precisely this indexicality, since the claim of an authentic and physical presence of the originator in the act of writing survives intact even and, in particular, when it is no longer present – as the instrument of a last will and testament.[7]

It is not by chance that in identity documents signatures and passport photos together form a system in which two physical symptoms mutually legitimize each other. The success of the identification then indeed depends on the fact that the passport holder 'looks like' the person in the passport photo and their signature in addition 'looks like' the original signature in the passport. In this respect, the indexicality of photographs, as of the signature, is based on still another characteristic – its likeness – which makes it 'an *icon* [of the object]'.[8] Photos, like signatures and handwriting in general, need not just that physical 'ground' of originality, but they are not considered to take effect until they become readable for a reader or observer, until therefore the writing/image produced 'looks like' its referent.

Handwriting often falls at this hurdle. For example, take the case where an addressee gets a postcard, of which they can deduce – indexically – from the image of the writing who the sender is but of which they cannot decipher the message because the curvilinear trace of the writing is too idiosyncratic, deviating too much from the normal copy or imprint of the letters to which it bears hardly any iconic relation of similarity. Cy Twombly's scribbles are examples of such indexical writing: they employ the inscription technologies of handwriting as chalk on slates and carry out the trace of their curvilinear *ductus*. As writing they are not successful, however, because they do not display any symbolic imprints.

Reading means – I shall be talking about this again later on – recognition. In the digital realm: 'Optical Character Reading'. The advantage of print letter fonts lies in the economy of their legibility, as they consist of perfect imprints of a pre-programmed, iterable type. In contrast to handwriting, whose individual trace points its finger at its originator, its indexical potential is however rather questionable. Handwriting is both – here it differentiates itself from mechanized writing. On the one hand, it follows the logic of the imprint in the way in which even in a photographic portrait the physiognomic facial motions 'rub off' on one another. On the other hand, the motion of the hand produces a unique line, which like the photographic portrait indexically points to an unmistakeable ground or origin and to its presence, even and precisely when it is past, so that in doing this it occasionally, as Barthes put it, 'entered into Death backward'.[9] Handwriting also involves the physical absence of its referent that it belatedly 'almost' touches.[10]

In the next four chapters, headed 'Exergue', 'Preamble', 'Prolegomenon' and 'Fore-Word', I should like to attempt an approach to a concept of handwriting using both these poles derived from photography: as icon and index, as imprint and trace. From the vantage point of photography I should like to make use of its wide-focus lens to range over the distant landscapes in which handwriting occurs from its first beginnings and in its confrontation with the technical, prevailing new media – speaking in leaps and bounds: the hand, the stylus, the pen, then the art of printing, leading to the typewriter, finally electric and electronic equipment: the Xerox copying machine, the fax machine, the digital scanner and the tablet PC. In all these forms handwriting is continually invented anew, always undecided between its trace and imprint, by constantly restructuring the principles of similarity and contiguity and interweaving them into one another according to the process of reading described by Paul de Man, who saw the logical tensions between metaphor and metonymy as a mutual enfolding, as the 'rhetoricization of grammar' and the 'grammatization of rhetoric'.[11]

In the course of the rest of the book my particular interest will be directed towards that area where the panoramic view becomes all-round: on the interstice where the very new and the very ancient meet. There is no break, no barrier across this area. Rather, it is the place where Then and Now blend into one another, where fragments of Leonardo da Vinci's manuscript are displayed on T-shirts, where Albert Einstein's chalk scrawls adorn the opening captions of scientific and cultural television programmes, where the Phaistos disk, once probably the most mysterious writing, preserved on just a single clay tablet, the only one of its type and without a bilingual version, has become the stencil of a moulding for thousands of casts, available at a considerable price in the museum shop at Heraklion as a 'unique' souvenir for every enthusiast. At this point of intersection the *tour d'horizon* turns into a helter-skelter ride through the system of coordinates without any stable Before and After and Above and Below. Here we find the latest fingerprint by which the super-modern man communicates with a computer via a touch-screen next to the earliest human hand-imprint, and here slate tablet, mystic writing pad and tablet PC meet. Then we shall see that handwriting is not on the point of dying out. It has not been petrified into *Lucida Handwriting*, *Rago-Italic* or *Edwardian Serifs*. Rather, its distinctive line or trace continues unabated to form a personal hieroglyph, whose unique aura is *imprinted* thousandfold in the Here and Now of the medial prisma.

Yet in these introductory chapters my overview proceeds initially in a linear, chronological order. I shall begin therefore by zooming into the most distant eras.

## Resemblance and Touch

The thesis that in the beginning of writing – *before* Aleph – was the hand – hand-writing – is widely held. In terms of human history there was a long way to go before the activation of the hand. A large number of theories and myths have taken off from the question of the origin of writing. Such a myth is described by Carlo Ginzburg in his essay on traces and evidence *Spurensicherung*, in which the *search for knowledge* occasionally proceeds on the same track as the *search for writing*, that is, at the moment when the tracker-reader Ginzburg alights upon that archaic ur-scene of human history, when the hunter – for his part – picks up the trail of his prey. Writing comes into play, according to Ginzburg, at the moment, when the hunter begins to 'read', when he learns,

> to reconstruct, from traces in the mud, from broken twigs, pieces of dirt, tufts of hair, matted feathers and left-over smells, the kind, the size and the trail of prey. He learned to conjecture, perceive, interpret traces as fine as spiders' webs.[12]

Precisely this ability to comprehend a presence as the sign of an absence and in addition to draw conclusions from the kind of sign as to the nature of the thing that is absent, according to Ginzburg, led in the course of a long historical process to the invention of writing. Ginzburg describes a comparable scenario using a Chinese myth 'that attributes the invention of writing to a high dignitary who had observed the footprints of a bird in the sandy bank of a river.'[13] Even if this 'ur-writing' lacks a grammar in the strict sense, nevertheless it features some characteristics that approximate to what we understand by writing. It consists of a contingent of familiar signs which are meaningful for the reason that the footprint of the bird 'looks like' the foot of the bird, because therefore it is *iconic*. And because the imprint has an iterable form distinguishing it equally from the imprints of other birds, it is readable, just as letters are also readable, because they enjoy a relation of similarity to their ideal form and are different to the other letters.

If in this sense the beginning of writing and the beginning of history – the term 'historiography' refers to the writing of history as much as to the history of writing – is preceded by the historic footprint and this again is preceded by the animal imprint of a claw or paw, then in this series of presuppositions there appears another aspect of writing. Because, as a sort of writing, the imprint of a bird's foot in the sandy river-bank is also namely a sign that a bird has passed this way leaving a track by its foot being pressed into the sand. The imprint is not only an *icon* of a species, but at the same time an *index* of the bird. It was *previously* touched by the bird's foot and it belatedly touches it itself by metonymy. The imprint only becomes significant, that is, readable writing, subsequently to the foot being raised from the sand; only then does it appear as an icon and an index at all. Not until the *ab*sence of the bird does its *pre*sence take shape. Georges Didi-Huberman characterizes the imprint in this sense as '*the touch of an absence*' and compares its anachronistic structure with 'the spectral effect of "ghosts", of an *afterlife* . . . of something that has gone and yet stays with us, haunts us giving us a sign of its absence'.[14] The imprint reveals itself as writing, particularly in respect to this *belatedness of touch*, as writing that will be readable for a future reader and thanks to that double quality that Didi-Huberman characterizes using the dual concept of *similarity* and *touch*. The imprint – and literally also the photographic print – is in this sense an iconic index or similar touch.

## In the Beginning Was the Hand

'In the beginning' – if there ever was such a state – 'was the word'. That at least is what it says in the most famous of 'fore-words', the ultimate first 'ex-ergue': in the prologue to St John's gospel: 'and the word was with God, and God was the word'.[15] The genesis of humankind starts with the Logos; it is its alpha and omega. However, if some key characteristics of writing are already starting to emerge in the footprint of a bird on a beach, then writing was long before the first word. And if the first readable writing was provided by the *imprint* of a bird's claw, then the question arises whether the first *hand*-writing started with a hand-*imprint*.

But in comparison with a foot or a paw, the hAnd marks a considerable difference. Because from the point of view of human history the imprint of the hand requires those motor skills that only come with walking upright. André Leroi-Gourhan also pursues this argument, in his modern study, based on evolutionary theory, of the archaeology of the human race with the both monumental and 'handy' title *Gesture and Speech*, to which I have already referred:

> The situation of the human, in the broadest sense, thus appears to be conditioned by erect posture. The phenomenon would seem incomprehensible were it not one of the solutions to a biological

problem as old as the vertebrates themselves, that of the relationship between the face as bearer of the organs of nourishment
and the forelimb as an organ not only of locomotion but also
of prehension.[16]

According to Leroi-Gourhan, acquiring the use of two feet has a double
effect: it leads, not only to a change in function of the front extremities,
but it also frees the face, raises it from being a snout down on the ground
into becoming a civilized head. With this dual polarity arises the
conditions for a new ordering of the relation between the face and the
hand: the face is from now on devoted to language, the hand to the tool.
Thereby both poles are very closely bound up with one another. Modern
linguistics by another route also comes to the recognition of the fact
'that the hand sets language free',[17] by arguing anatomically that walking
upright led to the lowering of the larynx, as a result of which the human
speech organs could for the first time develop precision in the articulation of extremely varied phonetic expressions.[18]

This definition of the hand as being that which characterizes
mankind goes back a long way.[19] Aristotle describes it as the 'organ of
organs' in *On the Soul* (432a). Here his anthropology belongs decidedly
to the philosophy of technology, as he details in his essay *On the
Parts of Animals*: 'now the hand would appear to be not just one single
instrument but many, as it were an instrument that represents many
instruments (ὄργανον πρό ὀργανων)'(687a). This merging of a hand-
tool and thoughttool Aristotle derives from Anaxagoras of Clazomenae,
who, like Leroi-Gourhan, saw walking upright, freeing of the hand,
intelligence and language as closely interlinked.[20] Aristotle, however,
proceeds in the opposite direction down the evolutionary causal chain:

> And since man stands upright, he has no need of legs in front;
> instead of them Nature has given him arms and hands. Anaxagoras
> indeed asserts that it is his possession of hands that makes man the
> most intelligent of the animals; but surely the reasonable point of
> view is that it is because he is the most intelligent animal that he has
> got hands. Hands are an instrument [ὄργανον]; and Nature, like a
> sensible human being, always assigns an organ to the animal that
> can use it (as it is more in keeping to give flutes to a man who is

already a flute-player than to provide a man who possesses flutes with the skill to play them) . . .[21]

Aristotle concludes: 'it is not true to say that man is the most intelligent animal because he possesses hands, but he has hands because he is the most intelligent animal' (687a 16–23), and thereby formulates an essentialistic definition of that which is an a priori of man: a flute-player who is master of his instrument before he picks it up in his hands for the first time.

A prominent recent thinker who discusses a definition of the essence of man is Martin Heidegger who, in his much-quoted lecture on Parmenides (1942/43) characterizes the hand – like Aristotle, only infinitely more cryptically – as that which essentially distinguishes man from an animal and in so doing describes the 'work of the hand' as an intelligible action (*Hand*lung). I again quote:

> Man himself acts [handelt] through the hand [Hand]; for the hand is, together with the word, the essential distinction of man. Only a being which, like man, 'has' the word (μῦτος)(λόγος), can and must 'have' 'the hand'. Through the hand occur both prayer and murder, greeting and thanks, oath and signal, and also the 'work' of the hand, the 'hand-work', and the tool. The handshake seals the covenant . . . No animal has a hand, a hand never originates from a paw or a talon.[22]

Hand and word are, for Heidegger, inseparably bound up with one another: whoever has the word, has a hand serving then as a medium for prayer, greeting, oath-taking etc.

The causal linkage of hand and word to writing is obvious here. Leroi-Gourhan argues from a palaeontological perspective that, like language, the birth of symbolic graphism also results from the bipolar technicity of hand and face: the hand is devoted to the tool, the face to language, then 'the sense of vision holds the dominant place in the pairs "face/reading" and "hand/graphic sign"'.[23] Heidegger also orientates the connection of hand – man – word directly towards the concept of writing:

> Man does not 'have' hands, but the hand holds the essence of man, because the word as the essential realm of the hand is the ground of the essence of man. The word as what is inscribed and what appears to the regard is the written word, i.e. script. And the word as script is handwriting.[24]

The elements of this conceptual chain each constitute a monumental pillar of Western thought: the hand – man – the word – writing. Henceforth they are associated together metonymically, finally culminating in a kind of super-symbol of 'Being': handwriting. For Heidegger, handwriting represents the dawn of humanity, and this is true both diachronically in its evolutionary difference to the animals and also synchronically in the systematicity of its 'essential being'.

## Two Left Hands

Leroi-Gourhan as well as Aristotle and Heidegger – however divergent their epistemic frameworks and their ways of argumentation may be – agree in this connection indicated by the short and simple title of Leroi-Gourhan's book *Gesture and Speech*. When theorizing the concept of the hand, all three theories – each within their own framework of discussion – appear to refer, however, without making it explicit, less to the hand as such and certainly not to the left hand. When Aristotle talks about the intelligence of man and, in so doing, consistently refers to the hand in the plural – man 'has hands because he is the most intelligent animal', he is here suppressing the predominance of the right hand, to which the authority of technicity, of skill and of any civilized activity (*Hand*eln) is ascribed. And Leroi-Gourhan too, who discusses the cognitive development of *Homo sapiens* in great detail, remains silent on the question of the evolutionary superiority of the right hand.

Heidegger, for his part, deals with the hand in the singular. But he too does not address the question of the right/left hierarchy; instead he takes for granted that the 'right extremity' is 'all right'.[25] This is demonstrated by the examples that Heidegger cites as the 'work' of the hand: murder, greeting and thanking, taking an oath and waving, i.e. 'handcraft', and using a tool. Here it is not a question of *pairs* of hands and certainly not of the left hand. *Heidegger's hand*: Jacques Derrida has tracked it down and identified it as an organ whose (monstrous) vocation is 'to show (*montrer*)' and 'to give (not to grip)'. And when Heidegger for once talks of the hand in the plural referring to praying hands, then he is concerned not with the awkward, wild, non-literate left hand; prayer, as Derrida observes, is rather 'the gesture, in which the two hands join together (*sich falten*) to make themselves one in simplicity (*Einfalt*)'. And Derrida develops his critique of Heidegger: '*On the other hand*, nothing is ever said of the caress or of desire. Does one make love, does man make love with the hand or the hands?'[26] Directly following on from this there is also then the question in respect to the technique of writing and writing tools: 'Does one write with the hand or the hands?'

For Heidegger the singular hand predominates over a pair of hands, and from this there follows automatically the superiority of the right hand, conceived of as radically singular, over the left hand. In precisely this hierarchical binary structure man emerges as a non-animal, of whom the most evident characteristic is handwriting. It is the product of an intelligible action (*Hand*lung), and it makes the essence of man *mani*fest, that is, literally 'visible', 'capable of being *han-d*led'. The *hand*ling has nothing in common with the intuitive gestures of the body. Everything that is physical, sexual, the gesture of touching and the associated tactile sensation of touch Heidegger excludes from his concept of handwriting.

Without doubt, in the writing conventions of our RomAn alphabet, handwriting is a skill of the right hand. Writing runs towards the right, the letters tilt towards the right, the ligatures tend towards the right as also the kinetic interplay of main shaft and attribute shaft (the so-called 'hasta and coda principle' that will be discussed later in this book). If Heidegger's (right) hand is dedicated to the moral and the intelligible ('prayer and murder, greetings and thanks, taking an oath and waving', the 'work' of the hand, the 'handwork'), then the left hand is left as the amoral and non-literate; it is literally *sinister*: an extremity of the primitive lower depths of the body.

A theory that runs 'as if on wheels' we could call this using Derrida's compelling formulation.[27] At least, the dextral theory would run smoothly were it not for the archaeological discoveries of handprints in the caves of El Castillo (Santander) and Gargas (Hautes-Pyrénées) that revealed another, more complex picture.

As a cultural practice the handprint has survived for thousands of years, from the images in prehistoric caves to that neo-religious ceremony on the Walk of Fame in Los Angeles, where the gods and godesses of the media society – namely Harrison Ford, Mel Gibson, Tom Hanks, Robin Williams, Arnold Schwarzenegger, Eddie Murphy, Meryl Streep, Whoopi Goldberg, Al Pacino or Michael Douglas – kneel down on Hollywood Boulevard in order to press their hands into the wet cement and then to sign the imprints with a long stylus, leaving a personal message plus an autograph. From the first appearance of the handprint, one can make out in principle two basic types. Firstly, in the case of a positive imprint a hand is dipped in paint and then pressed onto a hard surface as with a stamp. Secondly, in the case of a negative imprint the hand is placed with fingers spread out onto the surface and its outline is stencilled on, either – opinions differ within archaeology – by dabbing or spraying dry colour pigment, or by spraying on liquid colour by mouth or through a blowpipe.[28] In this the positive imprint resembles, in terms of the gesture of its production, Ginzburg's Chinese bird track, as both of them result from a part of the body being imprinted into or onto a writing surface. The negative imprint functions differently. Because its production requires a technical process that can not result from an unconscious or accidental action. In this case, if not before, we cannot help seeing an intellectual act (*Hand*lung) at work.

In the light of the right-hand cultural norm widespread in the West, it is not surprising that the technical achievement of the prehistoric handprint is in palaeontology normally attributed to the right hand. Just *en passant*, as though the difference between left and right were marginal to evolution, Leroi-Gourhan describes the error of such a 'right-hand' theory likewise running 'as if on wheels'. And identifies what is archaeologically 'right':

> The [palaeontologist] Abbé Breuil discovered long ago at Gargas and El Castillo that nine out of ten hands seemed to be left hands; this suggested that the owner was right-handed and put the palm of his left hand against the wall, using his right to surround it with color.[29]

The attribution here by Breuil of the act of writing to the right hand arises from the no doubt universally valid and cognitively based recognition that the right hand is more skilful than the left. His attribution proves, however, to be premature (as so often, when one tries to explain cultural behaviour biologically). Leroi-Gourhan refers to the fact that

> [a]nalysis of the imprints . . . also identifies right hands whose backs were placed against the wall; that also explains the fact that many of the imprints occur in concave sections where one could not place the palm of one's hand.

According to this, it would be possible to envisage scenarios of painting where the left hand is the agent by carrying out the negative imprint on the outline of the right hand, or where two right hands are involved working on one another. The relationships between left and right in no way follow that strict binary order which in the West has given rise to a real pedagogical witch-hunt against everything on the left for being 'gauche', 'maladroit' and sinister.[30] Rather, handwriting operates – the writing of Hebrew, Arabic or Japanese indicate this very clearly – outside of this binary scheme, as it links sense and sensitivity, physical materiality and symbolic literacy, making one the condition for the other.

## Dactylography

Another thing that strikes one about the handprints in Gargas is that, in the interplay of left and right, forms arise in contact with one another that are no longer complete biometric hand-icons. Leroi-Gourhan discusses them as follows:

> At Gargas, a considerable number of hands seem to have had fingers cut off or deformed. This has been explained as the result of 'ritual' mutilations. But here again, closer scrutiny suggests that the person who put the back of his hand against the wall bent one or two fingers; the reason for this is not clear, but it did not have mutilation as its cause. In certain cases we can even see that the fingers, originally long, were later retouched to shorten them.

Finger markings made in
the moist clay that oozed from
the walls in the cave at Gargas,
Hautes-Pyrénées, dated to
30,000–15,000 BCE.

At Gargas and Pech-Merle rows of thumbs or fingers, bent to
form hooks, are found near the hands.[31]

The absence of individual limbs, sometimes even whole fingers,
produces in each case a different deviation from the norm, and precisely in this incompletion of the natural, biometric imprint there
arises a *differentiation* of the sign producing something like a writing
system: *dactylography* (Greek *daktylos* = 'finger'; *graphein* = writing).[32]
The method of functioning of this writing is remarkable, not only
in that in the gesture of the imprint it derives from the individual
matrix of the hand a set of signs based on the principle of difference,
but that the 'disabled imprints' thus produced occur over and over
again: just in the caves of Gargas there are over two hundred, and they
are also found outside of the Pyrenees in the caves of Niaux, Santi-
mamie and Altamira, as repetitions of individual deviations from the
norm. These imprints can be understood as writing in so far as every
imprint follows and repeats the principle of difference.

In addition, amongst the prehistoric imprints there are also occasionally some that are not just *made*, but *copied*. The subtle difference
between the '*made imprint*' and the '*copied imprint*' is discussed by Didi-
Huberman as follows:

> The archaeologists were not surprised to find bears' claw marks
> on the walls in the Magdalenian caves; it was more surprising
> for them to discover *copied* bears' claw marks, engravings made
> by men or finger drawings.[33]

The copying of animal imprints proves to be just as shocking as the copying or forging of the (human) signature. Both operations count as equally complete cultural achievements to the extent that the 'forger' makes use of the original structure of the sign as an iterable uniqueness.

The *copied* prehistoric bears' claw marks are not just simple repetitions, however, because in the *copying* of the animal print the paint was spread on the background using fingers, and, in the gesture of spreading the paint, forms were created that deviated from the physiognomy of the human hand. In this gesture of mimetic painting and spreading the paint then there arises what we understand by a 'trace'. The 'finger drawings' produce pictures with meandering lines and traces that are to be found everywhere on the cave walls of the Pyrenees. In Pech-Merle, not without reason, they have famously been dubbed the 'hieroglyph ceiling'. Whereas the writing quality of Ginzburg's hunter's track was limited to its readability, the handprints and finger-lines of Gargas perhaps reveal the first 'writable' writing.

## Stylus

Already in the Gargas caves the iconography of the hand had not been reduced to pure biometry. All the more then the hand was soon emancipated from its function as a writing tool when it itself took up a tool. With this tool, not only can a mark be impressed or stamped but a broad range of writing techniques also start to take shape. *Scribere*: literally, score, scratch, notch. One takes a stylus in one's hand, and with it engraves on wood, clay or stone. The Babylonians cut reed-pens (*calami*) and shaped the soft clay from their river banks into writing tablets on which they engraved their cuneiform signs. Likewise using a stylus, this time made of metal, the Egyptians carved their hieroglyphs on stelae. Later, with a wedge-like instrument the writers of antiquity cut Phoenician, Greek and Latin letters on wood or wax tablets, and Archimedes of Syracuse drew his indisruptible circles in the fine sand.

According to the legend, a stylus was also used by Dibutades, the Corinthian potter's daughter, when she drew her beloved before he departed for battle. In order to do this, she outlined his shadow projected onto the wall using a wand. The movement of the wand

Joseph-Benoît Suvée, *Dibutades'
Daughter, or the Invention of
Painting*, 1791.

produced a line, literally drawn, *tracé*, by the girl's hand. In this trail or
*trace* Jacques Derrida sees the quintessence of *écriture*:[34]

> She who traces, holding, handling, now, the wand, is very close
> to touching what is very close to being the other *itself*, close by a
> minute difference; that small difference – visibility, spacing, death
> – is undoubtedly the origin of the sign and the breaking of
> immediacy . . .[35]

The movement of the wand copies the shape of the beloved true
to life, paints an iconic line of its object, of which it is a likeness and on

whose presence it is based – like a portrait photo. Eckhardt Schumacher has more closely identified this mythical unity with a resounding minimal pair: 'presence and present'.[36] But like a photograph the silhouette is not limited to its iconicity. Rather for Derrida, the gist of this scene of painting is precisely that the sign is absent from the body, that this absence is already announced by the rupture of the 'almost' of touch, that the beloved even in the present of his presence 'incorporates death'. Michael Wetzel underlines this idea: 'In the moment of re-presentation observation already turns into recollection, looking into recording, perception into apperception, becoming as it were that paradoxical effect called *déjà vu*.'[37] If Derrida sees writing as trace, as a line drawn, forming it is true an iconic facsimile of a presence, this is only because the trace *always already* defers presence as the movement of difference and delay. The French word *trace* does not only signify literally, as in English, 'trace' or 'line', but it gives rise to the German word 'Trasse', English 'track', referring amongst other things to the railway and also literally to the lines on which a train – even in the moment of passing by – has also always already gone past. In writing by hand this trace, that anticipates absence, and death, is produced by the hand holding the stylus. The basic movement of this hand is pulling and scratching, but also incising and engraving. The reed-pen/stylus: a stiletto,[38] every piece of handwriting is always a testament; at the same time the marking of a body on a surface, i.e. imprint/touch, and the stroke of the stick, i.e. trace/resemblance.

These binary principles – imprint and trace, index and icon, resemblance and touch – can be observed again and again in the history of writing and handwriting. The imprint is the basic act of any mechanized form of writing: cuneiform script, seal, woodcut, lithography, movable type, typewriting and any keyboard whatsoever. A trace on the other hand indicates a continuously moving stroke, such as is created typically by a pen, be that the 'electronic pen' of a seismograph or of a cymograph, recording movements on continuous paper as indicative diagrams,[39] or of other curvilinear drawing equipment. Typically, however, this stroke is generated by a hand.

A trace is drawn: a line ————
An imprint on the other hand is placed, engraved or printed: a point.

## Before a Line

Before one draws a line, this is how it is explained by the young Gerardus Mercator Rupelmondanus (*b* 1512 in Rupelmonde in East Flanders, where the river Rupel flows into the Scheldt; *d* 1594 in Duisburg, Germany), who was to become famous years later as a cartographer, toolmaker and calligraphist; before one draws a line, then, one must take some precautions. What these are exactly, he describes in his tractatus *Literarum Latinarum, quas italicas, cursoriasque vocant, scribendarium ratio* (How one writes the Latin letters that are called italic or cursive). This tractatus is written, like the style of writing that it deals with, in humanistic cursives: 52 sides altogether that were first printed and published as woodcuts in the printing offices of Rutgerus Rescius in Louvain (Leuven) in 1540, later in Antwerp and elsewhere.

Before one draws a line, then, one provides oneself with technical aids: literally the *arma scriptoria* (the writing tools being referred to also as military hardware), consisting of *circinus* (compass), *regula* (ruler) and *calamus* (reed pen).[1] These are absolutely necessary, irrespective of whether one is going to draw a coastline on a map

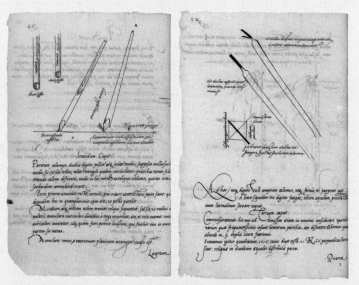

Two folios from Mercator's *Literarum Latinarum* manuscript now in Madrid's Bibliotheca Nacional.

or carry out a piece of writing. To write with a beautiful humanistic hand, before one writes one draws parallel lines onto paper with these '*arma*'. Then one chooses a quill; it should be transparent, not too hard and not too soft, and cuts it into shape, not too wide, not too sharp so that it takes up just enough ink and also dispenses it again equally (see illus. 6). The position of the hand is important then: the quill should be held between thumb and index and the other fingers lying on one another in such a way that the whole hand is supported only on the little finger. The hand itself should remain free and flexible; it should be connected to the forearm and by extension to the upper arm as with a hinge.

The remarkable thing about this description – for this distinguishes Mercator's tractatus from the other important European writing primers, even if these often refer back to his – how much attention he gives to the *ductus* of writing itself: '[T]he pen should be held invariably in such a position that its broadest stroke would join the opposite angles of a square (*i.e. at an angle of 45°*)'.[2] The correct pen-hold allows various line widths, the widest from top left to bottom right, as broad as the pen-nib itself; the thinnest hairline opposed to this. The sketch of the square on the recto shows this very graphically. The elegance and clarity of the writing that all penmen strive for is pursued by Mercator in the variation of the line and this he determines with geometric accuracy. for example he 'calculates' the proportions of the letter *y* in Chapter 3 of his tractatus:

> So let us take a square *abcd*, the two perpendicular sides of which are *ac* and *bd* respectively, and let the other two sides be divided into twelve equal parts. Take away a quarter of the whole square, *ef* being the dividing line. The remaining quadrilateral will contain the letter *y*. Then let a line be drawn from angle *c* to the first division of the line *ab* and, parallel to this, another from the second division of the line *ab* to the first division of the line *cd*. These lines form the boundaries of the first downstroke of the above-mentioned letter.
>
> Similarly, let a line be drawn from the ninth division of the line *ab* to the eighth of *cd*: this will eventually be prolonged below in the same direction, but just how far I will explain in

the following chapter. Let another parallel line be added from the eighth division of line *ab* to the seventh of *cd*, and these two will be the boundaries of the second downstroke of the letter *y*.

Now let a line, connecting the two outlines already made, be drawn from angle *c* to *b* [sic!]. This we shall call the narrow diagonal ['*tenuissimam*': that which is very finely, most finely drawn], not that it is the thinnest stroke that can be made but because, of all the strokes used to make the letters, it approximates most nearly to this. It is, in fact, to the line which connects the angles *c b* that this term properly belongs.

The measurements of the remaining letters of the alphabet should be derived from the proportions of this letter.[3]

This number of lines are (at least virtually) necessary for Mercator before the first real line can be drawn. Amongst the lines imagined one stands out in particular: the 'narrow diagonal' since it lies at the basis of all letters, if only hidden within their deep structure. In it the optimal proportion of the letters is defined, as it limits them in their extension. As a diagonal drawn from top right to bottom left, it produces a very fine hairline; admittedly this is not the '*linea revera tenuissima*' (truly thinnest line), but this one comes 'nearest' to it. Which line, one may well ask, can then be even finer than the almost finest? Which one tops this one for fineness? Which one is even more drawn out, or torn/*tracé*?

The various lines are categorized by Mercator according to their *ductus* as narrow, broad and medium strokes. Depending on whether they are executed straight or curved, convex or concave,

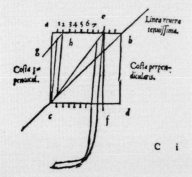

A folio from Mercator's *Literarum Latinarum* showing a facsimile of the woodcut *ex officina Rutgeri Rescii*, Louvain 1540.

as vertical downstrokes or diagonally, these lines may adopt various degrees of thickness (illus. 8).

*Elementorum aliud*: other elements
*Tenuissimum*: ultra narrow line
 (diagonal)
*Latissumum*: ultra broad line
 (diagonal)
*Mediocre aliud*: other medium lines
*Rectum*: straight
*Curvum*: curved
*Descendus*: downstroke
*Transversum*: cross-stroke

From Mercator's *Literarum Latinarum*.

The distance *ad* – for right-handers, it must be added – always results in the broadest line, and accordingly the distance *cb* results in the narrowest line, i.e. the one that is even narrower than the afore-mentioned narrow diagonal. The distance *cb* is the narrowest possible hairline; Mercator therefore refers to it even in the superlative: *linea revera tenuissima*, literally: the one that is longest sustained, most gossamer-like, finest and most exact. This line is ultra-thin, a geometric hair, or if you like, the 'breath' (or 'aura') of a winding line.

Before Mercator had, however, defined the same distance *cb*, now referred to as the truly ultimately thin line, as that narrow diagonal and emphasized that this is not 'the thinnest stroke that can be made', but he refers to it as such, 'because, of all the strokes used to make the letters, it approximates most nearly to this'. When first quoting it, I already added a 'sic' to this distance *cb* emphasizing that it is really written there 'so': *cb* and not, if you accurately think it through, the true diagonal: *ce*. The English translator of Mercator's *tractatus* also noticed this 'mistake' since he remarks in a footnote that actually *ce* is meant rather than *cb*: 'this is surely an error for *c* to *e*.'[4]

In the general context of Mercator's argument this is clear since a few pages later he himself deals with the difference between a 'broadest stroke' (*ductus latissimus*) and an 'even thicker' one:

'hic ductus re vera lattisimus': 'this line is actually the thickest';
likewise between the 'thinnest' (*linea tenuissima*) and absolutely
the thinnest line (*linea definite tenuissima*). In this respect then,
in the passage above where Mercator defines *cb* as an admittedly
thin line, but not the 'thinnest stroke', it must have been a case of
a *lapsus pennae*.

If we read this section *à la lettre*, as it really is written *sic!*, *so!*,
and interpret, as Harold Bloom proposes in *On Misreading*, the
*mis*scription as scription, other interpretations and even illogical
and false readings suggest themselves perhaps throwing up more
questions rather than providing answers and so, *sic!*, accounting for
the aporia of the line. In the process of misreading the distance *cb*
appears ambivalent, or even illogical, i.e. as a line which is not
really the thinnest line but is at the same time the *linea definita
tenuissima* which is even thinner than the *linea tenuissima*. If we
take the misscription seriously as writing, then the diagonal *cb*
appears to us to be a line which is less than and simultaneously
more than itself, i.e. a line which is not quite in place, which is
not identical with itself. *cb* or *ce*: As non-phonic *différants* they
create a difference that is significant, since in this triangle *ceb*
Mercator identifies the surface which, when separating the top
right part *efb* from it, forms the second 'coda line' of the letter *y*.

This 'coda line' begins in that angle *c* forming the intersection
of the distances *ce* and *cb*, i.e. where the narrow diagonal *ce* is both
broader and also narrower than the *linea tenuissima* (*cb* and/or *ce*).
In this point *c*, even if it is ultra-small, the two *différants* meet and
cross each other. Within it there lies invisibly this final difference,

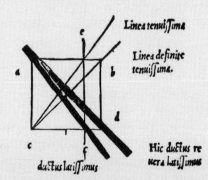

From Mercator's *Literarum
Latinarum*.

this ultra-thin difference between the thinnest and the absolutely thinnest line to which Mercator attaches the ideal proportions of the letter *y*.

According to the representation, all midpoint values are possible between the ultra-broad and the ultra-thin lines. In the following chapters of the *Literarum Latinarum* Mercator then develops a prescriptive guide how to perform the *ductus* of writing by measuring the individual letters of the alphabet against these ideal proportions of the letter *y* and analyzing them according to his categorization of the line types into elements ('hastae' and 'codae'), all of which, however crooked they may be, can always be accurately calculated. The cursivization of the hastae, the ligature of the letters by means of hairlines and the spaces separating the letters are most precisely covered by his rules. Mercator lays down for every individual line-execution whether and to what extent it corresponds to the governing rule and the norms for its calculated imprint.

It is not surprising that this man brought the same precision with which he calibrated handwriting by applying geometry also to his measuring of the world, representing coastlines, river-courses and highways as graphically exact lines, their loops and bends having nothing random about them but giving the most accurate iconic imprints of reality. He had acquired the habit of fine line-drawing for his cartographic work in his student days in Louvain from the Antwerp copperplate engravers that he visited again and again. Along with his atlases and maps and his globes of the earth and the heavens, his particularly beautiful and pin sharp cursive script became widely known, and continued up to the nineteenth century to be the model handwriting for maps.

The script was literally pin sharp, by reason of the fact that the *Literarum Latinarum* was cut in wood before it was printed in the offices of Rutgerus Rescius.[5] The *very fine* difference between the *linea tenuissima* and the *linea definite tenuissima*, which Mercator greatly developed by the technology of quill, ink and paper, and for which in addition an exactly defined manual *ductus* is a prerequisite, this *very fine difference* was created by Mercator in his *Literarum Latinarum* with the writing tools of a wood carver: scoring and notching with a burin, gouge, scauper and contour knife he sets the loops and bends of the trace into the wood-block. The wood-block acquires the matrices of the lines, however idiosyncratic and convoluted they may be, and it retains the ultra-fine differences of the lines, and it reproduces them to a hair, or better '*to a y*' in the printing workshop.

# 2 Preamble: Scribing On

We cannot think of a line without drawing it in thought.

Immanuel Kant, *Critique of Pure Reason*[1]

## What is Handwriting?

Handwriting – in the context of our Western writing culture along with its precursors and near relatives – is not, as one might at first glance suppose, writing written by hand.[2] There is other script produced by hand, such as the marks scratched onto bones and wood, Babylonian cuneiform signs engraved on clay and hieroglyphs stamped by hand from the Mesopotamian writing culture which also produced the famous Phaistos disk. Even alphabetic *printed* letters can be *hand*-written. And yet these writings still do not qualify as handwriting. Nor does the Roman *capitalis* chiselled by hand. It is not by chance that its graphic form survived over two thousand years with still the same imprint before evolving, firstly via the rotary press as Times New Roman, later via digital methods to become the standard font preferred by daily newspapers and text-processing. Along with serifs and various broad shafts that originate from the fact that the stone-mason applied the stylus at different angles, the *capitalis* is in our time engraved into the binary code just as it was before in marble.[3] From the beginning this writing technique was tailored to the economy of standardization and serial production, and its main principle was and is its ability to copy the imprint producing unity of form and thereby legibility. All these scripts were admittedly written *by hand* and produced without mechanical instruments. For them to count as handwriting, however, they lack the trace.

What then makes for handwriting?

In the middle of July 1799 an officer of Napoleon's *Grande Armée* in the Western Nile delta near Rashid (or for Europeans: Rosetta) discovered a mysterious granite stone engraved with an inscription in two languages – Egyptian and Greek – but in three different scripts: the top 14 lines in ancient Egyptian hieroglyphs, the middle 32 in demotic script, and the bottom 54 in ancient Greek script. Casts were taken and presented to the most eminent French writing experts for deciphering. In 1822 the linguist Jean-François Champollion (1790–1832), after many years' study, succeeded in deciphering the ancient Egyptian hieroglyphs on the Rosetta Stone with the help of its Greek parallel text.

By counting, Champollion established that the number of written signs in the hieroglyphic text far exceeded that of the words in the

The Rosetta Stone: hieroglyphs, demotic script and Greek script.

Greek parallel text. Then he compared the signs in the cartouches with the names of kings and pharaohs in which he recognized individual signs as being constants: on the Rosetta Stone, on the Philae obelisk and on the Casati papyrus as well as in various temple inscriptions. Reading from right to left, he finally spelled out: 'Ptolemy', 'Kleopatra' and 'Ramses' in a kind of writing functioning according to phonetic principles, with only the signs for vowels missing. Here he was

overturning the ancient mythology that had surrounded the hieroglyphs since the government of Egypt under Greco-Roman rule by the
Greeks, who were unable to read the writing.[4] According to them,
hieroglyphs had in general been interpreted as ideographic and, partly
also cryptographic, symbolic writing which, as Porphyry (234–301)
says in his *De vita Pythagorae* (pp. 11–12), designates 'the meaning by
representation (kata *mimesin*) [and the] symbolic by certain allegorical
riddles (*kata tinas aignigmous*)'.[5] In its very ancient form, as for example in the tombs of the kings and the books of the underworld, we are

# TABLEAU

### DES

## HIÉROGLYPHES PHONÉTIQUES

#### AVEC LES

### SIGNES HIÉRATIQUES CORRESPONDANTS

#### ET

#### LEUR VALEUR EN LETTRES COPTES.

Conversion table
of hieroglyphs and
hieratic signs (after
Champollion).

in fact dealing with a sacred writing ritual and, into the bargain, with keeping this secret. In this respect, it is not surprising that the Greeks even in the post-Pharaonic state gave the beautiful, strange script a name which was to become a *stigma sacralis*: ἱερός γλυφεῖν (*hieros glyfein*), which literally means 'sacred engraving'.[6]

Champollion distinguished between these *hiéroglyphes purs* and the *hieroglyphes linéaires* that was a book- and all-purpose script and could be both applied with a brush onto papyrus and engraved on wood, metal or stone. According to Champollion, from this script derived via a further stage of abbreviation the *signes hiératiques de la seconde classe*: hieratic script.[7] It is worth noting then that Champollion recognized that hieroglyphic writing was not purely ideographic. Rather, he divided the characters into three categories: the 'mimetic or figurative characters', the 'tropical or symbolic characters' and – and this is the most remarkable – the 'phonetic characters' or 'sound signs'.

Whereas Champollion's deciphering of the hieroglyphs was highly celebrated, the middle, demotic inscription on the Rosetta Stone hardly received any attention, but it is of vital interest for the question of handwriting concerning us. Already Napoleon's writing experts, Jean-Joseph Marcel and Remi Raige, had correctly identified this middle piece of writing as early as 1799 in Cairo. Like the upper inscription with the hieroglyphs, however, this writing also remained unreadable for them at first. 'Demotic' means literally epistolographic: *zS n Sot*: 'epistolary script'.[8] This script is certainly the culmination of the hieratic that for its part already made fluid the graphically complex, 'slow' full forms of the hieroglyphic script and, within a process that lasted for a millennium in writing culture, changed it into a cursive, functional script. Written with ink and a brush or calamus on papyrus, the demotic script, with its abbreviations and ligatures that was used for administration, communication and other secular purposes, functioned as the 'fast' variant of the hieroglyphic 'full form' of writing.

Although King Psammetich 1 had declared demotic to be the governmental script of the empire in 643 BC, it was still regarded for a long time as an inferior secretarial script, particularly since the beautiful, mysterious hieroglyphs continued to hold their own in sacred texts.[9] Thus Clemens of Alexandria in his writings from the second and third centuries AD (Chap. 4, 20.3) describes the demotic script as a

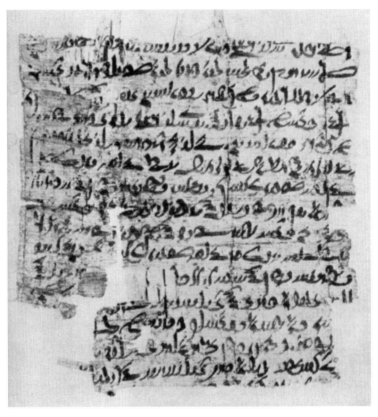

Demotic script on papyrus.

functional script for everyday communication, falling far short of the sacred hieroglyphs of the official and religious texts. In his description of the curriculum of an Egyptian apprentice scribe (*Stromata*, Book 5) he then also recommends dealing with the epistolary script first in the teaching of writing as it represented the lowest grade of writing.[10] It is not surprising then that Western writing experts in their studies of the Egyptian writing culture should have concentrated principally on the hieroglyphs ever since, and up to the Renaissance regarded these as epitomizing the Egyptian mysteries. Even after Champollion's revelation of the hieroglyphs as phonographic, consonantal writing they were still interpreted as images of wisdom; Hegel still saw in them the 'archetypes of signs'.[11]

The unequal twins of hieroglyphic writing and demotic writing reveal two basic operations of the stylus. The gesture of the first writing technique is the scoring, scratching or engraving of *in*scriptions with a stylus im*pressing* itself (again: γλυφεῖν = score). The other – and this is the moment where the trace of the handwriting comes into play – applies writing fluid onto a writing surface and thereby writes, as it were, '*on*scriptions' ('*Auf*schriften'). The fact that the binary concept of *in*scription and '*on*scription' is extremely significant for the history of media is pointed out by Vilém Flusser in *Die Schrift*. The object of his analysis is the current crisis of writing, and he discusses this by contrasting precisely these two writing techniques that he pinpoints as 'painting' and 'chiselling':

> One paints with a brush instead of chiselling in order to be able to write with less effort and faster. The speed of writing is the basic difference between inscription and 'onscription' [*Inschrift* and *Aufschrift*]. One reaches for the brush or the feather (this natural brush) in order to write, 'featheredly', gaining wings, as it were taking flight. Then one turns the feather round and writes with the tip of the feather in order to write even faster . . . From the quill pen one then reaches for faster and faster writing instruments: the ballpoint pen, the typewriter, the word processor – in other words faster and faster feathered pens. Western writers are birds of the feather. Inscriptions are painstaking, slow and therefore considered ('monere' = consider). 'Onscriptions' are writings thrown hastily onto surfaces.[12]

Handwriting as trace, it clearly follows, belongs to 'onscriptions'. These do not, however, replace inscriptions, as Flusser seems to suggest, but they always complement them. Whereas the inscriptions of the pyramids, temples and grave sites admittedly survive for long periods of time – Flusser therefore also calls them 'permanent traces' – comparatively ephemeral 'onscriptions', of which writing surfaces used range from leaves, bark and papyrus up to paper and parchment, serve chiefly as media for the processing of data. And as light and ephemeral writings are better suited than static monuments to overcome space, 'onscriptions' besides function as media of data transmission – via (flying) messengers, mounted couriers, post or e-mail.

## Currere

*Currere* means literally 'to flow' and refers to water and rivers as well as to handwriting in the sense of cursive, that is literally 'current'. Harold Adam Innis, the 'planning engineer' of the channels of media culture, has stated this in no uncertain terms:

> The flow of the long Nile river to the north and dissipation of its regular floods in the numerous channels of the delta provided a background for the development of artificial canals and dykes by which the valley might be widened and the water held at the height of the flood for irrigation.[13]

In the ancient kingdom of the pharaohs, according to Innis, the pyrAmids, those eternal burial places of the mummified dead, stood as powerful signs of sovereignty over military hordes and armies of workers. The central control governing time extended to a decentred power governing space at the time when the leading scribes of the bureaucracy turned hieroglyphic writing into the fluid hieratic. In the course of the five centuries between the sixth and the twelfth dynasty, they developed a system of uniform spelling, for which they used papyrus. Moreover, by employing horses and chariots (in about the reign of Ahmosius I, 1580 BC), they improved the channels of communication.[14] In this respect, *currere* means on the one hand, the flowing of the long river; its flowing on down does not leave any trace but it just keeps right on flowing, pouring away, so channelling its trace.[15] On the other hand, *currere* means literally 'to run' – as in 'courier' – meaning therefore the mailrun, the sending of messages and likewise transmission or translation.

Translation is just such a kind of channel (or river). Its work does not only begin with translation between languages but from the very moment when language itself – or more precisely thought *per se* – is transmitted, when concepts make their way from one place to another. Here the notion of the channel or the river can not be emphasized enough, because it illustrates the distinction between a classical theory of representation (of 'constatives') and a theory of cognition (of 'performatives'). Such a distinction is anticipated by Johann Georg Hamann when he conceives of 'poeisis' literally as 'doing' (pre-Romantically prefiguring the thesis of language as activity in the sense of a performative practice):

> To speak is to translate – from an angelic language into a human language, that is, to translate thoughts into words – things into names – images into signs, which can be poetic or curiological, historical or symbolical or hieroglyphic – and philosophical and characteristic.[16]

So writing is also a postal system, or a sort of channel. Unlike the engineered channel straightened out for economic reasons, with its almost stationary water, whose objective is always to take the shortest route and thus optimize communication, the case of handwriting as 'current' and 'cursive' is more like the idea of a river: a lively, flowing, meandering river. Like the Nile flowing from South to North and thus carrying the edicts of the kingdom of Thebes down to Memphis, writing seeks to go in one direction and at the same time is always going round bends, its diversions, twists and branches 'overflowing', 'dispersing' or 'disseminating' its 'nomos' or law.

In this respect, media cultures are – according to Flusser – neither consecutively occupied in processing, transmitting or storing data; nor are they specialized in one of these functions, as Harold Innis suggested.[17] Instead, these basic operations of the media overlap and coexist. This is also largely what is indicated by the above mentioned 'stone letters', the stele of the Byzantine Emperor Mauricius in Ephesus and the Rosetta Stone of the Egyptian King Psammetich I. Firstly, both pieces of writing are a permanent memory thanks to their material construction. Secondly, before they were chiselled in stone, they were, however, planned as handwritten rough-notes, as 'aerial writing', so to speak, or 'pneumatic dispatches', transferring thought from beyond the skull to the here and now of writing, as it were. Thirdly, as both of the stones served to proclaim the law of the respective ruler as a 'solid' edict in the distant, colonial province, they are also postings in the sense that they function as media of data transmission.

The message of Emperor Mauricius from Byzantium cleared all these hurdles. It only came unstuck when it got into the hands of the

Greek stone-mason in Ephesus who, as in a defective handover, relayed the writing not in the planned standard code of the Roman capital but 'chiselled down' the cursive trace of handwriting stroke by stroke – blow by blow – and thereby took the wrong transmission channel.

This is proof of the fact that, if the posting is to succeed, the trace of a handwritten text must be likewise also inscribed as an imprint, acting as an interchange to the reader. This is true particularly when writing is to enforce at the receiving end a law signed by the ruler renewing an already established matrix of power. The remarkable thing about the communication system of power then is that the nomos draws its authority from the structure of the writing itself, which succeeds as a performative precisely when the ruler or colonizer in the foreign country does not trace his laws back to an 'original' authority, but im*prints* his sovereignty in the act of signing.[18] The signature at the bottom of the posting is probably the most successful imprint.

## A

Writing cultures have always made use of *in*scriptions as well as '*on*scriptions'. They store worthwhile thought up for eternity on written monuments, they proclaim laws in epigraphic script, they rule and administer in official and documentary script, do business in trade script and discover new ways of thinking by sketching them out in cursive script that, if successful, is copied for purposes of publication in fancy book script. All these scripts are produced over the millennia by hand. But not necessarily in handwriting.

This is also the context to mention the fact that many writings occur as real digraphs. What the demotic script was for hieroglyphs was in the case of the Roman alphabet the later Roman cursive for the *Capitalis Monumentalis*. But in still another respect the Roman alphabet is di-graphic: it contains majuscules as well as miniscules.

The road to this digraphic alphabet is long. It led, as historians of writing argue, from the Egyptian hieroglyphs via Sinaitic, Phoenician, Greek and Etruscan script.[19] In the course of this journey the letters were passed through many hands by which not only the sound value of the signs changed, as I discussed at the beginning of this

Later Roman cursive, second half of 6th century.

An example of *capitalis quadrata* written in pen on parchment in imitation of Roman inscriptions, here in a codex of Virgil's poetry, *c.* AD 500.

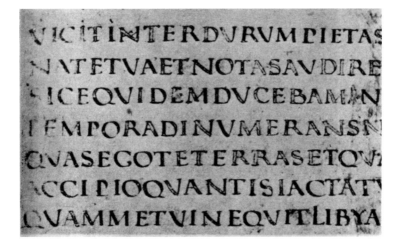

book in relation to Aleph and H/Eta, but also the physiognomy of hands and writing techniques affected the graphic form of the letters.[20] The key element here was largely the direction of the writing. For example, the α appears still in its recumbent form on the threshold from the Phoenician to the Greek alphabet, the tails sometimes pointing to the left and sometimes to the right according to the direction of the writing.[21] The Phoenicians wrote mostly from right to left, i.e.

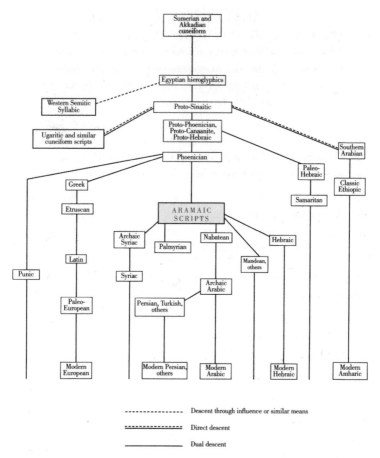

Genealogical tree showing the development of alphabetic writing from cuneiform script to modern forms.

sinistrograde, while the writing programme within the letter was dextral. But it also happened that the scribes, writing on metre-long papyrus rolls, began a new line where the old one ceased. The roll was scrolled back alternately from right to left and from left to right in a constant back-and-forth. In this way, the readers too were able to find the start of the new line without difficulty amidst the closely packed lines. Even nowadays, or now once more, we find this movement of the act of reading when we scroll on the computer screen with the mouse; we move left and right along the scrollbar back and forth and with the scroll wheel of the mouse up and down. By scrolling, the computer screen becomes for us a rotulus.

When the scribes wrote in boustrophedon, i.e. 'following a furrow' 'as the ox ploughs', it occasionally also happened that the letters changed their vectoral orientation with every turn of the line: in dextrograde writing direction, the internal orientation of the letters was dextral, in sinistrograde direction it was sinistral, so that individual signs received a mirror-image twin. When the scribes engraved on wood, clay or wax tablets and in so doing sometimes simply turned their tablets round after every line, the flow of the text appeared as 'snake writing', in which at the turning of the line of writing the letters were left hanging *capo volto* (headfirst). All these hands turned and twisted the letters in all directions for such a long time that Aleph finally got up on its feet and found its final form as a capital letter; it was stabilized, as mentioned before, its body took on the form of a pyrAmid. Just like Alpha other letters were also oriented vertically: Delta, Mu, Nu, Pi.

At the time when Alpha arose, Western alphabets positioned themselves against the flow of Oriental alphabets, against which they went on to impose themselves not only on the basis of their right-handed direction but whose reserve over the writing of vowels they categorised linguistically with the *terminus technicus* of 'defective alphabet'.[22] From now on Europe was to write 'against' the 'other' writing. In the beginning of the Western alphabet there was a 'contra'-vention ('Zu*widerhand*lung'). The politics of this culture clash is demonstrated not just by the persecution and annihilation of Hebrew in the burning of synagogues in Europe, but it has recently taken on a subtle form when in our TV news bulletins the ticker on the screen from left to right flows in the reverse – or 'perverse' – direction for reading. On this 'counter-movement', the cultural stereotypes of the

| Egyptian | Cretan (linear) | Phoenician | Stele from Byblos |
|---|---|---|---|
| | | | |

From Aleph to A.

'Other' are based; they become manifest in their hand, their signature. The 'other' hand has always been the wrong one, the Alien, cack-handed one, the sinister one, either in the form of the left hand's contravention of the norm in Europe, or in the form of irritation on the part of the Roman alphabet reader at writing that runs towards the left, making all sinistrograde script and particularly Arabic look to the television viewer like a terrorist media event. This is also what A does.[23]

a

In the rightward flow of writing in Roman majuscules there asserts itself in the course of time a line that is designed less for the engraving and scoring of inscriptions than for the rapid application of ink on parchment or papyrus and which, in addition, is suited to the movement of the hand tending to the right. This writing movement gives to the letters, according to Herbert Brekle, the so-called 'Hasta-Coda' scheme: a vertical main shaft, the 'hasta', is joined in the writing and reading direction by one or several 'identifying shafts', the coda/e: K, P, R, D, F, E, B.[24]

In respect to writing technology, minuscule signs function in a fundamentally different way. According to Brekle, they are not, as has often been asserted in palaeontology, 'further developments' of the square writing designed for writing on stone material but instead result from a completely different grapho-kinetic writing program.[25] Its *ductus* consists less in building the letters out of individual strokes than in avoiding 'air strokes' and linking writing strokes by means of ligatures, so that the writing becomes more fluent, i.e. *cursivized*. Whereas the capital letters are set out in an abstract, rectangular surface in a two-line system, the minuscules transform the originally free 'hasta' of the majuscule letters (the part of the letter that is free of the 'coda'-parts, e.g. the lower shaft of the P or the vertical shaft of the L) into arcs or loops that form upper and lower prolongations and now replace a two-line system with a four-line system. The ascenders and descenders serve at the same time not only as optical points of fixture making reading easier – as cognitive reading research argues – but they also facilitate the *ductus* of writing.[26]

The flowing line of the minuscules provides that which gives to our Western alphabet writings the 'aura' of handwriting, drawn by a decidedly physical act (*Hand*lung), still concealing within itself the play of an individual deviation from the norm. The majuscules, on the other hand, provide the essence of the imprint. It is not by chance that there are only majuscules on the keys of our keyboards; the minuscules are derived from them 'by shift key' as secondary signs; they are the special signs of type-writing. The first typewriters did without them completely, all the more because they found themselves freed at last from the vestiges of the laborious and slow way of handwriting.

The shift key, switching between majuscule and minuscule, between imprint and trace, is a key characteristic of our Roman alphabet. Arabic script with its rounded flowing shapes, whose ligature cursives occupy a whole four-line area, does without majuscules. In this respect, it is always handwriting, its trace having a flourish, even if it is written on a keyboard. Hebrew script, on the contrary pure block writing in a two-line system, uses neither minuscules nor ligatures. For this reason it never displays the aesthetics of handwriting, even when it has been done by hand as a unique act of writing.[27]

## Carolingian

Long before the typewriter, however, the minuscules were the ones that made the writing process fluid and speeded writing up into a hitherto unknown 'tachygraphy' (τάχος = fast). For our Roman script the minuscule was perhaps the most important invention of media technology in the Middle Ages as regards the simplification of text production and functionality of documents, to a certain extent comparable to the invention of printing in the early modern period or to the typewriter at the time of industrialization (but that would of course need closer examination). The 'greatness' of the small letters reached a high point when the Anglo-Saxon cleric Alcuin of York (around 730 to 804) adopted them. The Emperor Charlemagne had summoned him from England as a scholar of reform and a personal counsellor to the Palace school in Aachen, of which Alcuin became head from 782. After all, Charlemagne's *renovatio imperii* had set out to renew the education of the clergy and monastic life, to cultivate science and art and revive the

Carolingian minuscule, end of the 8th century.

cultural heritage of Late Antiquity. To this end, Charlemagne ordered probably the greatest project for the copying of ancient texts that resulted in both the normalization of (Medieval) Latin and a reform of writing: in the unified Frankish Empire writing was, from now on, to be uniformly in Carolingian minuscules. The major exponents of the reform were the scriptoria of the writing academies, the Imperial chanceries of Godescalc and Dagulf and the royal monasteries, above all Corbie and Saint-Martin de Tours. Starting out from these centres of writing, the new script spread from the Pyrenees to the Elbe, from the North Sea to the Danube valley.[28] The pyrAmid of the Frankish Empire was the minuscule.

The Carolingian is a remarkable style of script. Not only does it stand out amongst the multiplicity of forms in medieval writings by reason of its clear legibility, its pleasing proportions, its natural flow and the regular design of the individual letters, but also, from the point of view of kinetic gesture, it is an ideal type of handwriting in the sense described above. It differentiates itself from the uncial script that preceded it, like ancient monumental writing strictly constrained within a two-line system, and from the Gothic (or blackletter) script

Uncials,
8th century.

TIBI UNUM ET
MOYSI UNUM
ET hELIAEU NUM
NON ENIM SCIE
BAT QUIO OICERET
ERANT ENIM TIMO
RE EXTERRITI
ET FACTA EST NUBES
OBUMBRANS EOS
ET UENIT UOX OE
NUBE OICENS
hIC EST FILIUS ME
US CARISSIMUS
AUOITE ILLUM
ET STATIM CIR CUM

that succeeded it, 'breaking' the curved lines within a letter in angular
strokes and at the same time providing shafts with decorative serifs
and finials, for which downstrokes have to be partly redrawn by an
upstroke. Altogether several strokes and as many air strokes are necessary for a letter to be written.[29]

The Carolingian minuscule has everything that makes for handwriting: it is an 'onscription' with strong cursivization, it executes letters
with a flowing *ductus*, often – following the ergonomy of the right hand
– with the angles tending to slant towards the right in a four-line system
whose ascenders and descenders in the course of time form ligatures.

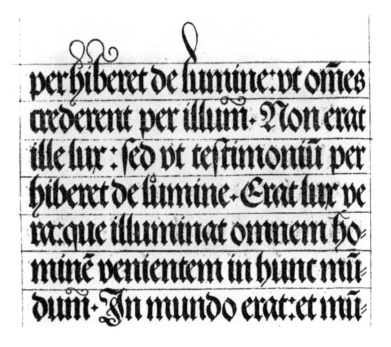

Gothic black letter (*Fraktur*), in Emperor Maximilian I's prayer book.

The copyists of the monasteries, along with the secretaries and bookkeepers of the royal chanceries, were instructed by the writing masters to carry out this kind of 'running hand'. For example, the mentor from the abbey of Melk on the Danube in a late-medieval copy book of penmanship gives the instruction to form the letters flowingly and with few strokes of the pen. The 'littere manuales minus principales' ('the less big handletters') – meaning a, i, m, n, and u – 'and all letters following them can be continued with one stroke, and this by an upward movement of the lower hairlines'.[30]

It is remarkable then that this ideal type of handwriting at the same time laid the basis for the first mass writing style, since the scriptoria establishing the norm practised the cursive trace of writing in an instant replay as a copyable imprint. Acting as an economic conveyor-belt of writing, the Carolingian was at the same time an efficient script for copying; the first copying machine consisted of a goose quill and parchment.

In this context Flusser's distinction between lapidary inscriptions and painted 'onscriptions' seems premature, because strictly speaking the Codices also belong to 'onscriptions' – this goes for the functional books turned out at great speed under the piece-work system as much as for the artistically painted *libri illuminate* with their exquisite calligraphic work. Flusser himself concedes that the difference between permanent, monumental (*monere* = consider) inscriptions and hastily produced, documentary (*docere* = instruct) 'onscriptions' is

> not always clear. When the Romans scored their wax tablets with their styli [*mit Griffeln*], the important thing for them was to capture [*im Griff halten*] their ideas. They wanted to document. And when the monks painstakingly, and with consideration, applied one sacred letter after another onto parchment with their quills, the important thing for them was to contemplate the godhead, to set up a monument to it. One cannot help feeling that it would have been better if the Romans had applied the brush and the monks had chiselled.[31]

In this respect, the writing in medieval books is handwritten, it is true, but it does not necessarily constitute handwriting. Flusser's image of the 'chiselled' uncials, Carolingian minuscules or 'Gothic' (blackletter, *Fraktur*) brings their fluctuation between trace and imprint nicely into focus. It is true that, as we have seen, the Carolingian contains more trace than the scripts preceding or succeeding it, but not without fashioning the gesture of the hand as a normalized imprint.

## *Itera*

From the point of view of the history of writing, handwriting – that which constitutes handwriting, its trace, its *ductus*, its *currere* – appears to be a sort of exception to the official or sacred, permanent, lapidary writing styles from which it is derived as tachygraphic documentary and administrative writing, making its calligraphic forms more fluid and shortening its full forms into abbreviations and ligatures, just as the demotic script did with the hieroglyphs and the Roman cursive with the *capitalis*, i.e. in all the places where fast writing occurs as parallel script alongside the 'official', 'eternal' script. In all these forms the cursive script was always a script for copying.

It is worth noting that its suitability for copying also creates the basic structure of writing beyond any historical perspective. This is precisely where there arises, alongside the historical question, the systematical dimension of the concept of writing. The aporia of writing, the question of what we understand by it and what not, is quite often posed as a question of demarcation, in which one considers the relation of the (copyable, readable) writing and the (non-copyable, visual) image. For example, Claude Lévi-Strauss in *Tristes Tropiques* raises this sort of question in relation to notches on the gourds of the Nambikwara Indians. Roland Barthes too puts the question like this in his reflexions on the scribbles in Cy Twombly's *Untitled* cycle in the 1970s and also in his book on Japan, *Empire of Signs*. According to Derrida's *Of Grammatology*, however, all myths of the beginning, origin or categorical boundaries of the alphabetical writing system should be measured against the sign character of writing itself. And writing only becomes a matter of a sign – Derrida describes this in detail in his legendary essay 'Signature Event Context' – when it can function by repetition as writing, that is, when it will be readable for a future reader or when it can be copied by another writer:

> in order for my 'written communication' to retain its function as writing, i.e. its readability . . . [my] communication must be repeatable – iterable – in the absolute absence of the receiver or of any empirically determinable collectivity of receivers.[32]

'Iterability' is for Derrida the key characteristic of writing. And, I should like to add, it is at the same time the basic principle of handwriting: the repeatability of readable form.

'Iterability' does not, however, concern only the imprint. From the present-day perspective – looking back from the tablet PC – handwriting only really begins to be handwriting when its trace not only copies, imprints, repeats, iterates the norm accurately, but when at the same time the trace of its present performance is 'other' than its ideal imprint. Handwriting only comes into being with the deviation from the standardized official script on the part of a practised notary and from the writing practice using a four-line system on the part of first-year pupils; in other words, when a wobbly hand gives a face to a scribe or a wayward *ductus* affected by attention deficit disorder rebels against the four-line system of the school writing textbook.

This 'other'-ness of the sign along with its readability and repeatability is summed up by Derrida as constituting iterability:

> Such iterability – (*iter*, again, probably comes from *itara*, *other* in Sanskrit, and everything that follows can be read as the working out of the logic that ties repetition to alterity) structures the mark of writing itself, no matter what particular type of writing is involved (whether pictographical, hieroglyphic, ideographic, phonetic, alphabetic, to cite the old categories).[33]

It is precisely in the binary logic of this polarity that we find what is special about handwriting: it is always unique and at the same time it nevertheless repeats the ideal type of readable imprint. To sum up: it is simultaneously an iterable imprint and a singular trace: singular iterability, iterable singularity.

## 'Ceci tuera cela'

> Technology in any case does not mean – does not only mean –
> 'progress' and 'novelty': it points in all temporal directions.
> Didi-Huberman, *Ähnlichkeit und Berührung*[34]

Victor Hugo's historical novel *Notre-Dame de Paris* (1831) takes place in the year of Our Lord 1482. Quotations are often made from the passage in the fifth book where an event is recounted that we would nowadays see as a media-cultural shock. The archdeacon, a Late Gothic scholar figure, has studied medicine, astrology and alchemy. His main achievement, however, has been his ability to decipher stone structures, statues and gravestones, pyramids and temples, the façades and portals of churches and hospices, as if they were written in secret code. He can literally read the 'marble letters of the alphabet, the granite pages of the book'. But now there lies on his desk the first printed book, a folio from the famous press in Nuremberg. He glances up uncomfortably from the open book to look through the open window towards the mighty Gothic cathedral, *Notre-Dame de Paris*, standing out in silhouette against the starlit sky and he murmurs the ominous words of insight into the change of media taking place before him: 'Ceci tuera cela'. 'Alas! This will kill that.' The age marked by sacred, monumental architecture will be followed by the era of Gutenberg.[35] And, one could add, handwriting will also be destroyed along with the cathedral.

The development of handwriting in fact has repeatedly gone through rough periods. With every new writing device and every new writing material there have arisen again and again possibilities for trying out and perfecting a writing *ductus* with highly sophisticated movements, until in the early modern period printing literally took the pen out of the hands of the copyist.[36] There really was an ink-eraser at work. But handwriting as such, I should like to argue, was not destroyed but got into difficulties, particularly its 'chiselled', architectonic, marble form. In Victor Hugo's opinion the printed book will replace – and outlast – the monumental, epigraphic styles of writing as the medium for storing the human memory: 'The book will kill the building'. It stands to reason that from now on the culture of handwriting will not remain unaffected. Scribes will in future devote themselves less to copying – the typesetter will take over this role. Relieved in this way, the hand will concentrate on its 'documental' activity: as a drawing instrument it will design the architecture of thought, draw the construction plans of knowledge and, in Flusser's sense, 'document' onscriptions. From now on it will act less as a storage medium than as a processor.

The consensus view is that, with the invention of printing, the information society takes off; a society in which knowledge is no longer restricted to relatively small circles in isolated workshops and auditoria but is now produced typographically and distributed by the new mass medium. But handwriting was not thereby 'erased' by any manner of means. Not only due to the fact that there was always a mAnuscript prior to the printing process, but in addition the *nova forma scribendi* required that the printed incunabala themselves looked like handwriting. For his world-famous 42-line Bible, Johannes Gensfleisch von Gutenberg cast movable letters after the fashion of the contemporary *hand*written book script, Gothic *Textura*. To achieve a harmonic block setting, he prepared different forms of every type with varying letter widths and ligatures. With the repertoire of types produced in this way consisting of 290 signs he created a type-token relationship that resembled more the variety of forms of handwriting than that of standardized print.[37]

Once upon a time copyists prepared *Textura* using artistic handcraft. With a pen cut diagonally towards the left they pushed hairlines in the upstroke and pulled broad strokes in the downstroke. In a hard and fast sequence of loose penstrokes they formed sharp corners and pointed angles and thus they 'broke' the letters – stroke by stroke – letter by letter – day by day. With the printing press the letters were placed with one stamp onto the paper as an imprint, along with spindle-like 'hastae' and multiple broken 'codae' with invariable perfection, but with a new kind of serial sequentiality of pulling, breaking and pushing. 'The mechanization of the scribal art was probably the first reduction of any handicraft to mechanical terms', is how Marshall McLuhan sums up the work of the machine, 'it was the first translation of movement into a series of static shots or frames'. In this respect, print was 'the first uniform and repeatable "commodity" [and] the first assembly line'.[38] The possibilities for deviation, or an 'otherness' within such standardized repetition have of course a different quality than in the strokes of a hand made individual by body, breath, concentration, etc., and yet this iteration – as I will later show in detail – is not indifferent.

And this is true by the mere fact alone that the 'calligraphic writing machine' ('Schönschreibmaschine') – as Giesecke calls the printing press – could not do without manual work. In larger printing works the individual stages of the book production were supervised by a corrector who patched up or marked any technical and orthographic defects *by hand*, in which process he carried out a censorious authority appropriate to handwriting to this day. To finish off the printed form, the work of illuminators and rubricators was needed, decorating the 'bald' print with miniatures and flourishes and adding coloured initials as navigation aids for the reader.[39] To the uninitiated eye, Late Gothic illuminated handwriting is hardly distinguishable from a high quality print production. Handwriting and printing stand in relation to one another less as predecessors and successors than as joined

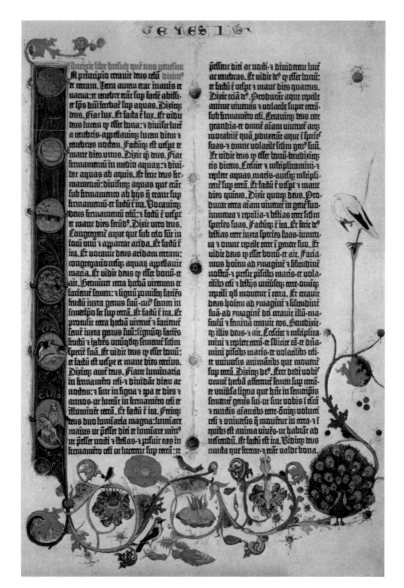

A folio from the *Gutenberg Bible*, printed at Mainz in 1453/55.

technologies. If Giesecke's credo for printing is 'reproduction creates new originals', then one can counter this using the same argumentative rhetoric by saying that the 'ancient' handwritten 'originals' had always already – *déjà* – been reproductions: imprints of traces.

After all, the products of Gutenberg's workshop are not only the magnificent Bible but also the so-called 'bread writings' or indulgences. These printings only gained their validity as receipts when the name of the donor was written in the blanks along with the place and date and the document was then certified by a seal or a seal plus signature.[40] Here too handwriting – literally – fills a niche worth consideration, because up until the current age of the form, handwriting has been, at the same time, the equal partner of the printed form and its greatest opponent. Not for nothing are the writers required to limit their trace when it says on the top of the form: 'Block letters only please'.

## The Calamus of Erasmus

Half a century after the death of Gutenberg at the Wartburg in 1521, Martin Luther set out to shake the sacred structure of dogma to its foundations ('to kill this with that') and to translate the Bible into the language of the people; he reached not for the powerful, new medium of writing – the printing press – but for the goose quill pen as before. His adversary Erasmus of Rotterdam, meanwhile, in his choice of writing instrument preferred the calamus following the fashion of the Humanist Renaissance and of classical Antiquity.[41] At least this was how he had himself painted in the portrait by Hans Holbein the Elder: with a writing instrument whose form more resembles a (vegetable) reed than an (animal) bird's quill.[42]

Erasmus's calamus is a Janus-headed writing instrument. In a reverse direction it looks back to the ancient culture of writing, in a forwards direction it sets its sights on a future that is in the hands of writers to come. Erasmus bequeathes his reed-pen to one such writer: 'Erasmus Roterodamus Guilielmo Neseno calamum dono dedit cum hoc epigrammate. Calamus loquitur' (Erasmus of Rotterdam presented his calamus to Wilhelm Nesen with this epigram), as it says in his poem in praise of the calamus (1516):

*Tantillus calamus tot, tanta volumina scripsi*
*Solus, at articulis ductus Erasmiacis.*
*Aediderat Nilus, dederat Reuchlinus Erasmo,*
*Nunc rude donatum me Gulielmus habet.*
*Isque sacrum musis servat, Phoeboque dicatum,*
*Aeternae charum pignus amicitiae,*
*Ne peream obscurus, per quem tot nomina noscet*
*Posteritas, longo nunquam abolenda die.*

Little reed pen that I am, I wrote so many
large volumes all by myself, though I was
guided by the finger joints of Erasmus.
The Nile produced me, Reuchlin gave me to
Erasmus, and now, honourably discharged,
I belong to Wilhelm. And he preserves me as
sacred to the Muses and dedicated to Apollo,
a dear token of eternal friendship, lest I, who
made so many names known to posterity,
names never to be wiped out in the long
course of time, should perish in obscurity.[43]

By going from hand to hand – from Reuchlin to Erasmus to Wilhelm Nesen – the little calamus, every time it is handed on, transmits the names of the past to the future and thus becomes a highly effective instrument of inscription of the human archive. In this process the reed anticipates the future not just at the time of writing itself but it selects from this future point of view *ex post* those names that will be saved from the obscurity of amnesia, so that they will – later – be known. As a tool of remembrance the calamus in Erasmus's hand draws its trace of writing in both temporal directions, blazes its trail for a journey through time and into the great Western [**A**]rchive that as it were writes the past along with the future – or: posterity.

Erasmus's calamus is not just, however, a tool *for writing*, but it is itself *written on*. Here the writing instrument also always includes within the highly singular, physical gesture of the writer here-and-now the hand of the other, that is, the one who is always writing *with* the writer, even if at the actual time of writing he is already a writer of the

Hans Holbein, *Erasmus of Rotterdam*, 1523, tempera on paper mounted on pinewood.

past. In this respect, the calamus of Erasmus exemplifies the ideal type of that historiographic poetics for ever inherent within every writing instrument: it de*scribes* a 'medial historiography' (a history of the media as much as the mediality of history): both a history written by the calamus and a calamus as a device manufactured by historical processes in writing culture.

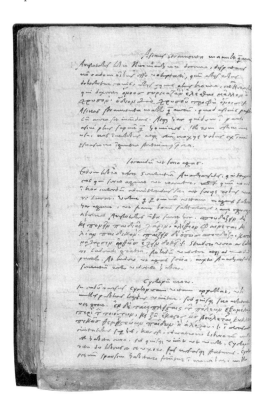

A sheet of writing by Erasmus dating from 1523.

## Loops, Curves and other Preposterous Lines

The concept of medial historiography manages exactly to combine these two irreconcilables by linking the inseparable touch of the self with the abandoning or dissemination of the *graphe* in the act of writing. Because 'medial historiography', as in Lorenz Engell and Joseph Vogl's coining of the term, concerns itself above all with the circumstance

> that all history writing is for its part dependent on the media. Without media of examination, archiving, sorting, deduction, without media of coding and representation in images, words and numbers, without media of distribution after all history writing (and along with it history at all) is not possible. The media are therefore not only the object of historical observation, coding and representation, rather they themselves condition

historical examination, coding and representation. Thus there is always an – unspoken, but needing to be revealed – concept of the historical that is specific to the respective medium, be it of a scriptorial or pictorial, filmic or photographic, literate or electronic nature.[44]

For handwriting, conceived of as a medium – or better, as a 'hypermedium' (as simultaneously 'scriptorial' and 'pictorial', simultaneously 'filmic' in the sense of temporal and moving as much as 'photographic' in the sense of the copying processes of reprint and imprint, finally also 'literate' and 'electronic' [at least potentially]) – the 'specific concept of the historical' has its basis not the least in its graphic line. Even if the flow of the line takes its course chiefly from left to right, nevertheless in its kinetic program it always provides for interruptions and new beginnings as well, along with curves, loops and cross-overs. At one moment the line rushes on fleeting and thin, the next moment it builds up expansive and sluggish. The trace of handwriting takes its course in which medial historiography does not steer teleologically towards a pre-defined destination, rather it makes its way using steeply sloping, straight or undulating patterns, one moment extending it, the next moment abbreviating it, in which process in particular the reverse movements characterize the development of 'progress'.

Like the tablet PC that 'remediates' the writing slate, Erasmus's calamus also marks the join described above where Then and Now infiltrate one another. The process of medial historiography specific to handwriting is here committed to a conception of historicity that blends the temporal levels and thereby occasionally also 'reverses' the linear logic of causality so that the line of writing in its temporal course runs 'against the flow', 'widdershins', maybe even 'twisting the wrong way round'. In its movement the line of handwriting does not simply seek to go forwards; it is more intent on the deviations and the winding detours than on tracing a fast way to cover the distance. Its *first line* of interest is in turning or twisting, in looping or curving, in other words, essentially the baroque figures of the curlicue, the furl or the fold. 'Baroque' (Port.: *barroco*) originally referred to an irregular pearl and means literally (not only as a style description) 'ornate', 'overdone', likewise 'bizarre' and 'grotesque'. Or even, as T. S. Eliot describes it, 'preposterous'. Here he is absolutely suggesting a historiographical concept: 'Whoever has approved the idea of order . . . will not find it preposterous that the past should be altered by the present as much as the present is directed by the past.' 'Preposterous history': Mieke Bal characterizes it following Eliot as the (baroque) idea of convolution, of the curl, of the loop, of the 'stilted' and portrays it at the same time as a 'twisted', 'preposterous' conception of historicity. 'Preposterous history' means for Bal a revision of the events, 'which puts what came chronologically first ("pre-") as an aftereffect behind ("post") its later recycling'.[45] It is precisely in this sense that handwriting is 'preposterous' writing: a historiography whose timeline twists and turns back and forth.

## Litterae antiquae

Just as Luther and Erasmus differed in their writing instruments, so they also wrote in different hands. Luther wrote in the German cursive (*Kurrent*), the typically German handwriting, that Johann Neudörffer ('Anweysung einer gemeinen hanndschrift', 'instruction on a common handwriting', Nuremberg, 1519) placed alongside black-letter (*Fraktur*) as a decorated and at the same time fluid script.[46] Erasmus meanwhile wrote after the new fashion of the *litterae antiquae*, the Humanistic minuscule: the European Latin script that starting with the Italian Renaissance began to replace the broken Gothic script that was difficult to read and to write. Rightly the cursive script then soon came to be known in England as *italic writing*.[47] The accompanying assumption that the writing of the Renaissance not only derived geographically from Italy, but also historically from Antiquity, was utterly wrong, however. It is true that the Humanistic minuscule was in fact a 'new old' style of writing, only its 'preposterous' shift related less to Antiquity than to the Frankish Empire. Basically, its *stilus graphicus* took up the kinetic program of the Carolingian minuscule, in which each letter was written with only one or two strokes of the pen, though now carried out with a an even more fluent, more 'cursive' trace.[48] It is also in this sense that the 'new *antiqua*' is preposterous, with its curvilinear movement forming, instead of loose pen-strokes, flowing loops and curves with only rare breaks.

The attribution of the Humanistic *litterae antiquae* to Antiquity came about in the context of a general secularization of writing. Whenever writing masters then had to discipline the hand of a noble pupil instead of the hand of a secretary, they preferred to make reference to the *gramme* of the renowned Ancients, for example harking back to the instructions of the Roman Emperor Augustus which prohibited the scribe from allowing the writing to be prolonged above the line. 'The noble line is a noble line', is how Goldberg describes the fine distinction that constitutes the Humanistic cursive.[49]

The conception of a preposterous writing does not simply reverse a fixed, mono-linear chronology but truly sends its trajectory spinning off in contradictory and multi-linear directions. When Mieke Bal talks of 'recycling' in the sense of bringing into circulation older cultural practices in a historically more recent present, then she means by that neither the traditional concept of the present being influenced by the past nor a strict reversal of it. Rather she uses, as the linchpin of analysis, quotation that can encompass multiple relationships in the universe of artifacts. And as quotation is a performative practice, its iteration always also makes a difference (*itera*): '[preposterous] revisions of . . . art neither collapse past and present, as in an ill-conceived presentism, nor objectify the past and bring it within our grasp, as in a problematic positivist historicism.'[50]

In the context of such preposterous twisting and turning one can see a genealogy of the media taking shape, in which book printing does not simply take over the letter forms of letters used in manuscripts as in a one-way street but has, at the same time, produced them itself. After all, the inscription technologies of scriptography have to a great extent affected those of book printing and, vice versa, the typecase has in its turn changed writing by hand; not only in that the *ductus* of writing – in both Latin and German script – became more fluid as a result of the economic time-pressure of mechanical and technical competition in the ways of writing, but altogether the writing masters set their calligraphically improved handwriting in pattern sheets and in copy books of penmanship, which they then put into the hands of punch-cutters, type-founders and book-printers so that they could make the 'new trace' multiply imprintable with the aid of woodcut and printing press. Vice versa – or, if you like, twisted the other way –

handwriting imprinted its mark on the printed script, to the extent that the 'new old' Humanistic script passed on its harmonic and clear writing-image onto a new printed writing: A*ntiqua*. The staccato action of mechanical writing by key of the types and the continually flowing trace of the manual cursive in the new, mechanized age have mutually 'remediated' one another.[51] Handwriting, being simultaneously imprint and trace, has finally also emerged out of the machine: *mAnus ex mAchina*.

### Before a Cookery Book

The cookery album, bound in pale green linen covers, the title
engraved in gold letters: 'Cooking recipes' is inscribed with joined-up
writing, its capital letters ornamented with multiple coiled squiggles
(in German called 'elephants' trunks'), the minuscules shaped in one
continuously flowing hand. The writing is underlined with a flourish
like a double-knotted clef as though transferring the symbolic
dimension of writing into musical notation. The book is an old
exercise book, more beautiful than all the poetry albums of one's
childhood; the opening of it commands respect. Inside, the card-
board fly-leaf is patterned with pale green foliage. After it there
comes the actual exercise book with lined paper and with an index,
whose tabs on the right-hand side carry respective labels in printed
German handwriting dividing the album according to headings:
'Soups, Vegetables, Fish, Meat-roasts, Sauces, Salads, Puddings,
Sweets, Cakes and Biscuits, Miscellaneous Recipes.' From the first
to the last page, the album is painstakingly filled with regular and
harmonious German current-cursive *Kurrent* script.

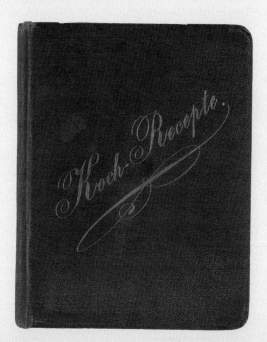

A handwritten cookery
book bound in a linen
cover, c. 1900.

In the age of instant printouts and ready-to-serve meals, this cookery book strikes one as a wonder of both culinary art and calligraphy. The handwriting is immaculate, nothing is crossed out nor are things written in above or in the margins, there are neither ink-blots nor food-stains. Instead, the writing is embellished with curves and loops, ascenders and descenders are steeply and boldly slanted at the identical angle, the bows and the wavy lines are executed in a flowing but confident hand:

> Lettuce
> Remove the green leaves, trim the lower part of the stalks, rinse the lettuce having pulled off its leaves previously, drain and toss it in vinegar, oil, pepper, salt and sugar. Allow 2 spoonfuls of oil, 1 spoonful of vinegar. Then season to taste. Best of all is lettuce with mayonnaise.

The incredible beauty of the book and the decoration of the letters stand in stark contrast to the banality of its contents. What is being revealed here are neither the secrets of an occult poison-cult nor highly refined recipes with which to captivate the senses. Instead it is just lettuce. There is the addition of a particular recommendation of mayonnaise, prepared by that nameless subject of cookery, the eternal housewife: hardworking, clean, loving order and without a name. Perhaps the writer took years to write this down; one recipe every Sunday. And yet she does not sign her name. Without a pre-considered plan for the work as a whole and having no final revision, she has written a book which will in retrospect be perfect. Day by day, penstroke by penstroke she has repeated the ritual movements with which generations of mothers and housewives prepared the food. In this way, she has created a work of copying from which there will never emerge an autonomous hand or an individual I.

This album has neither a beginning nor an end, arranged according to headings like an archive, every entry made *between whiles*: before cooking, before the *mise en cuisine*, before shopping, yes, even before one has checked the recipe for the ingredients, the dish is recorded in the archive. It is only written up, indeed, after everything has been consumed, the whole lettuce leaf by leaf, and when the table has been cleared, the washing up done, and the kitchen tidied up, before it is again time to go shopping, do the cleaning, the scrubbing, peeling and chopping up.

Perhaps the album was given as a wedding present to the daughter, destined to follow in the footsteps of her mother and repeat the daily ritual of the anonymous preparation of meals. Perhaps, however, it was intended as a journal for the writer, a permanent written testament to the activity of cooking, otherwise lost without trace. A calligraphic bottling of the store of female creative rituals. Restless journals of cooking and eating as a last memorial. Against traceless cooking.

# 3 Prolegomenon: Writing and Technology

[W]riting (especially alphabetic writing) *is a technology*, calling forth the use of tools and other equipments: styli or brushes or pens, carefully prepared surfaces such as paper, animal skins, strips of wood, as well as inks or paint, and much more.

Walter J. Ong, *Orality and Literacy*[1]

## Prometheus and Epimetheus

When it comes to deciding what 'technological' is, particularly in relation
to writing practices, handwriting tends to be classed as non- or pre-technological. Handwriting and handcraft in general are often understood
as anthropomorphic activities and thus contrasted with mechanical ones
since they date from the era *before* electricity and *before* electronics.[2]
Technological media, as Friedrich Kittler has repeatedly pointed out,
begin where analogue media (book printing, gramophone, cinematog-
raphy and the typewriter) are replaced by digital and it is no longer
only the symbolic but the unique and contingent physical real itself
that is stored, transmitted and processed.[3]

Against this canonical media studies model, I should like to pro-
pose a counter-theory by postulating that the cultural *practice* of writing by hand was a cultural *technology* right from the start. 'Practice'
(πρᾶξις) and 'techne' (τέχνη) are both associated with *hand*work and
action (*Hand*lung), also with art, skill, science and know-how – and,
to be sure, not just in line with an Aristotelian concept of technology.[4]
Accordingly, handwriting not only becomes technological with the
writing *tool*, the stylus, that first extension of the hand, and in general
its technology is not limited to being a supplement to orality, as Walter
Ong claimed. Handwriting is not, therefore, technological because it
has been considered in different epistemological contexts as respectively a prosthesis or extension to the sense of touch, a store of memory,
a supplement to the voice, etc., but in a much more fundamental sense.
This is also how Georges Didi-Huberman argues when he insists that
already prehistoric handprints must be regarded as highly technological processes. Didi-Huberman considers the imprint to be a decidedly
technological form, not just in its (post-)modern form as a frottage or
process of decalcomania, but also and especially as a 'primitive' and
prehistoric gesture:

> The fact that the imprint seems to be the 'dawning of the image',
> does not mean that it is a *simplified* kind of image, on the con-
> trary. The technological gesture of the imprint was complex from
> the start, and from the start imaginatively and symbolically over-
> determined possibilities were structured within it.[5]

With this comment, Didi-Huberman rejects the prevailing view that the imprint is 'too rudimentary, too archaic, too anachronistic' to count as 'technological' and into the bargain 'not an invention – its invention is lost in the mists of time, it was not even consciously invented' (something besides that one cannot accuse writing of). In reply to this, Didi-Huberman argues: 'Technology in any case does not mean – does not only mean – "progress" and "innovation": it points in all temporal directions.'

By putting it in this way Didi-Huberman relates the technology of the imprint to that other concept: the idea of the trace. The relation of technology and time, as Didi-Huberman argues, referring to Bernard Stiegler's *La technique et le temps*, 'contrary to the usual idea of the *development* of technology' is determined 'rather by a fundamental and "original" *disorientation*'.[6]

There is the familiar myth according to which Prometheus (Προμηθεύς), literally 'the one with forethought', formed men out of clay, taught them handwork and culture and even brought back to them the fire that Zeus had robbed them of. Out of revenge Zeus then sent onto earth the beautiful Pandora with her disastrous box. Although his brother had expressly warned him, Epimetheus (Ἐπιμηθεύς: 'the one with afterthought') accepted the gift, bringing disaster. It is precisely this error by Epimetheus, the 'inseparable disunity' between the brothers, one Προ, the other Ἐπι, in which Bernard Stiegler identifies the temporal dynamic of technology: 'the Promethean pressing on and the Epimethean delay (which is also the mistake of Epimetheus in the sense of *forgetting*) *together* form *prométheia* as foresight and *épimétheia* as wanton carelessness *and* as belated mediation.' This Epimethean error (or its paradox) represents for Stiegler the 'original *technicity*' that has always proven to be a 'failure of origin'.[7]

I would suggest that handwriting as technology must be seen in this double sense: as imprint and trace. As a technological trace, it blazes a 'preposterous' – or 'Pro- Epi- methean' – trail, the flow of which runs admittedly from left to right, in the process however, foreseeing backwards movements, new beginnings as well as loops and crossings in its kinetic programme. The work of the trace is thereby always also the work of the hand. The 'new' and future-oriented mechanical or electrically driven extensions and prostheses of the human senses that we call media, both analogue and digital, display once more the '*em*-bodied' condition of writing. Like all technologies, writing techniques are 'supplements' of humanity; they constitute an 'original supplementarity' ('*une supplémentarité originaire*'), as Bernard Stiegler writes referring to Derrida's *Of Grammatology*:

> The logic of the supplement, which is always already the *history* of the supplement, is a techno-logic, by which non-organic material is *organized*, and it affects the living organism of which it is the original supplement.[8]

In this respect, the writing body is always already technified, and as such 'dysembodied'. Technology has always influenced the relation of writing and the body, has remediated it, twisted it, turned it, or worked on it somehow with a preposterous (or 'Pro- Epi- methean') turnabout.

## Tachygraphs

> *Currant verba licet, manus est velocior illus*
> *Nondum lingua suum, dextra peregit opus.*

> Even if the words run, the hand is still faster than them.
> Before the tongue comes to rest, the right hand is already at the finish.
> Martial, AD 85[9]

When around 1800 the Western world entered the Age of Industrialization, the technology of writing, along with all *hand*work, came under a new-style pressure for efficiency. There was not only a quantitative increase in writing, so that all writing had to be accelerated, but in the wake of nationalism, colonization and globalization the written word had to be capable of being communicated more quickly as well.

Whereas the fastest way of transmitting handwritten express messages was by foot messengers and dispatch riders, the network of post, telegraph and telephone services went over to the coding of messages sent at lightning speed by electric telegraph (the first commercially run electric telegraph line between Washington DC and Baltimore was set up in 1844) or by telephone (the first telephone communication by the Bell Telephone Company took place in 1879). If the *ductus* of writing had up to now consisted of placing dots by putting pen to paper and by alternately pulling and pushing strokes upwards and downwards, thereby forming the lines of writing, the electromagnetic telegraph did not just radicalize these movements but replaced them with a completely different way of writing: the letters of the alphabet, which had been formed by the analogue movement of the hand over millennia into an interplay of 'hastae' and 'codae', now adopted the form of electrical impulses in a digital binary system. In the Morse code, a dot is a release of energy, a dash a flow of current.[10]

Apart from data transmission, i.e. before coding and decoding, it remained as before the hand itself that was responsible for data processing and storage. All the activities in trade and administration as well in the cultural field continued to be written down or written up by hand, and in addition a lot of written material for its part had to recorded, registered and stored in the archive. Writing instructors, calligraphers and civil servants then found every means available to speed up the *ductus* of the hand itself. In the course of rationalization and industrialization, new methods of writing were developed, designed to make writing quicker and easier. In the Republic of the Netherlands the *Maatschappij tot nut van 't Algemeen* had been working since 1784 on the improvement of education, and had also introduced pencils, slates and charcoal alongside pen and ink. In the first place, the teaching of writing was to be directed more at the production of clear and lively handwriting, no longer just the cultivation of a beautiful 'copper-plate'.[11] In Germany Rossberg's *Systematische Anweisung zum Schön- und Geschwindschreiben* (1796–1811), for example, pointed in the same direction,[12] and in the USA the centuries-old Victorian writing instruction gave way in the end to the 'Palmer method of penmanship', developed by the New York business man Austin Norman Palmer in his *Palmer's Guide to Business Writing* (1894) as a 'plain and rapid style', designed for the 'rush of business'.[13]

With the arrival of modern parliamentarianism there also increasingly came into use a way of writing that would keep pace with the speed of speech by means of abbreviating the graphical elements of the letters by partial representation of their strokes and by leaving out syllables or whole segments of the text: shorthand or stenography –

from *stenos*: narrow (as opposed to 'longhand'). Based on this idea, it adopted elements from ancient Egyptian syllabary by which a single grapheme represents a whole syllable, and combined it with the principles of ligature and abbreviation that had characterized Greek tachygraphy.

The capture of speech in writing that can keep pace with the speed of talking forms the basis for all politically engaged activity. It is not an accident that it was Marcus Tullius Tiro, freed slave and secretary to the consul and great orator Cicero, who laid the foundation stone for shorthand, the *Notae Tironianae* or Tironic notes that were still being used for rough work a millennium later in the scriptorial chanceries of the Merovingians and Carolingians. For a long time in ancient Rome it happened that a 'writing circle' was instituted for important speeches in the Senate, at public meetings and legal proceedings: a sort of relay race with a stylus, in which a team of expert scribes wrote in a circle one after another; each one noted as many words as he could catch on his own roll, and gave the next one along a sign when he should take over writing.[14]

In the period when the declining republic had to hold out against the rebellious Catalina, on 5 December 63 BC a new writing process came into force for the first time which seriously cut back on hand movement. Plutarch records how Cicero introduced the invention of his secretary: he taught 'those senators who were skilled in writing, signs whose small and short forms represented many letters'.[15]

The technique of the writing circle had consisted in dividing up the line of the temporal flow of speech into memorable and therefore writable sequences that as units of writing outlasted the units of speech corresponding to them. The fragmented writing subjects were then united in the figure of the circle, as if the speech had been written down by one unified and connected body that was able to delay the temporal trace of the speech as if by magic by paring down the line itself to its essentials, chopping it up and putting it back together again. The Tironic notes on the other hand followed a different principle. They did not prolong the trace but plumped for the clipping and shortening of the written signs by the imprint.

Still in the tradition of the Tironic notes, in 1602 Willis derived from Roman capitalis the stenographic word images – the 'stenemes' –

of his Early Modern 'geometric' shorthand that was imported around 1900 from the British Isles to France and the countries of the Iberian peninsula.[16] Germany, however, went its own way as regards shorthand (and writing in general). After 1817 Franz Xaver Gabelsberger, apparently unaware of the existing geometric shorthand, developed a 'cursive' stenography that he derived from the German *Kurrent* in use in the chanceries of Munich. As in German handwriting, this shorthand connects the consistently multi-stroke stenemes by upstrokes that are supposed to allow for a greater speed of writing. Gabelsberger's shorthand was taught for a while as a High School subject in Bavaria, Saxony and Austria and became the preferred script of academics and authors until it was officially adapted in 1924 into German Unified Shorthand (Deutsche Einheitskurzschrift, DEK).[17]

Whether as a geometrically reduced imprint of square majuscule letters (like Willis's) or as a cursive *Kurrent* (like Gabelsberger's), the shorthands have one thing in common: as scripts for notes, dictation or rough work they are as a rule not intended for reading by other people and therefore both need transcribing and editing into longhand. It depended and still also depends on limiting longhand itself in the extension of its trace and compressing it into printable type.

## The Script of the Nation

While Europe wrote in Humanistic cursive letters, in Germany the German *Kurrent* remained as the script in wide use. This was a cursive script designed for a (pre-)national time in the sixteenth century when it had been drawn up by Johann Neudörffer, following the tradition of *Fraktur* scripts with squiggles ('elephant trunks') and 'quadrangles' in majuscules, with double fracture of the shafts 'executed with triangular angles and also higher in the writing', as it says in his copy book of penmanship that appeared in 1538, 'Eine gute Ordnung und kurzer Unterricht' ('A good order and short tutorial').[18] Later the abundant curlicues of Neudörffer's letter forms were simplified into a script for everyday use in the chanceries by his star pupil Wolfgang Fugger in favour of faster writing.

At Martin Luther's instigation after the Homburg Synod of 1525, writing in elementary boys' schools was to be 'in German' so that

**Jeder dritte Deutsche ist Auslandsdeutscher.**

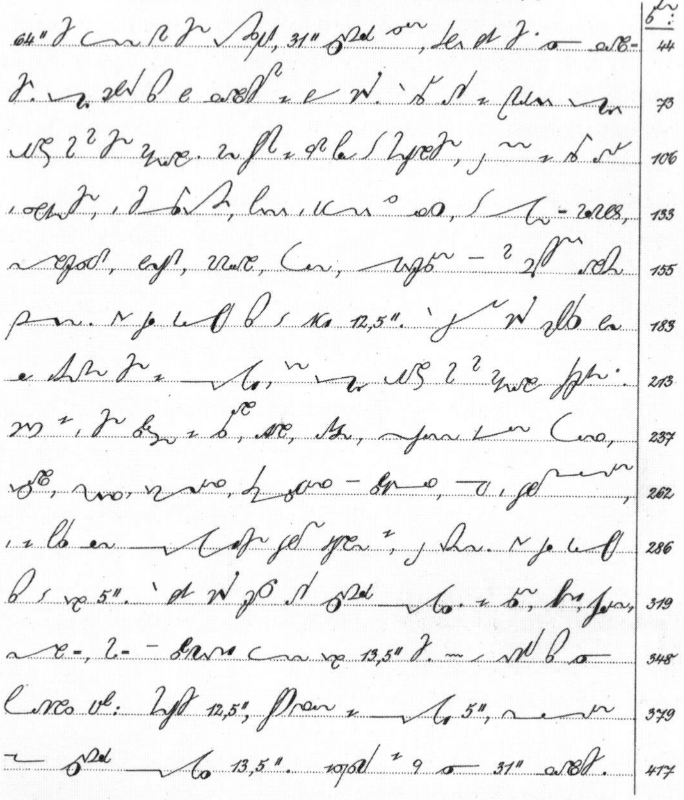

**6. Ü.:** Diese 31 Millionen | kämpfen als Pioniere für die deut||sche Kultur, sind Bahnbrecher und Vermitt||ler deutscher Wirtschaftsanbahnung, oftmals || bedroht von Willkür und Gefahr der Aus||saugung seitens anderer Völker. Wer || zählt die Millionen, die der deutschen | Heimat bereits verloren gingen zu || Nutzen und Frommen anderer Rassen, | oft verzweifelnd am deutschen Vaterland, || verbittert ob seines Undanks. | 31 Millionen auf Vorposten || im schweren Kampf. Stärker als je müssen | darum alle in der ganzen Welt ver||streuten Deutschen die gegenseitige | Verbindung aufnehmen, um dem gegen || das Deutschtum in aller Welt entfachten | Kampf erfolgreich zu widerstehen. (179 Silben)

**Prägen Sie sich die Zahlzeichen sicher ein; Sie ersparen damit unnötige Schriftzüge!**

42

The sixth exercise, from Max Maier and Karl Lang's *Lehrgang der Deutschen Schrift* (1936).

under the instruction of the reformed pastors the pupils could read the Bible in German in printed black-letter (so-called *Fraktur*) and learn to write an equally German script.[19] As the script in general use in schools, *Kurrent* outlasted the scriptorial war between the international Humanistic (or Latin) Antiqua and German script that had broken out around 1800 in German intellectual circles. In book printing Friedrich Gottlieb Klopstock, Wilhelm von Humboldt, Friedrich Nietzsche, Jakob Grimm and others were committed to the classical Antiqua. A counter-movement was initiated by Christoph Martin Wieland with his demand: 'German books better with German letters'. In this context, a symptom of this is the much quoted admonition of Katharina Elisabeth Goethe, née Textor, to her son:

> I am happy about any expression that your writings, both old and new, have not seen the light of day in those Latin letters that are so disagreeable to me; – in the *Roman Carnival*, then it might be all right – but apart from that, I beg you, stick to German, even in the letters of the alphabet.[20]

Her son, however, did not totally turn his back on the Latin script while Heine, Eichendorff, E.T.A. Hoffmann and Brentano later went back to *Fraktur* again.

As elsewhere in the first half of the nineteenth century German handwriting was 'fluidized'. In the wake of the so-called 'genetic methods' of Heinrich Stephani (1815) and Hermann Dietlein (1856) it was reformed to the effect that the influence of the physiological movement of writing on the forms of the letters was recognized and the anatomical character of the movement of writing was upvalued as against the 'mechanical' standardized *ductus*.[21] For Dietlein writing is not just pure copying in the sense of 'drawing letter forms' and 'painting characters' but also 'writing letters' and even 'writing thoughts'[22] – the latter then also in particular in respect to the cultural self-image of the nAtion:

> The nature of our nation is clearly reflected . . . in the German *Kurrent*. Our script has not been conditioned, formed and shaped by great trade and transformation, but rather by the profound

study of the sciences and arts . . . It is therefore a script of scholars, of science and of art, since it lends itself more than any other to speed writing, to the running with the pen on the paper, this is why it is called *Laufschrift* = *Kurrentschrift*, i.e. 'running hand', because it has the advantage that it can always be joined up without breaks, letter following letter, the end of one being the start of the following one.[23]

Thus special consideration must also be given to the flow of the movement of writing. Dietlein recommends that, along with the finger and hand movements forming the basic strokes of the script, one should, right from the start, also practise the locomotion of the arm tending towards the right. Within 36 to 40 lessons the pupils should learn to 'proceed tactically'. To this end the small (fast!) alphabet of German *Kurrent* is first divided according to the characteristics of a kinetic 'family likeness' and covered in teaching units of 7 to 10 lessons respectively: 1. the 'family of the upstroke and downstroke including the lower semi-curve', 2. the 'family of the left side-curve including the lower point of the loop and the left loop', 3. the 'family of the right side-curve including the upper point of the loop and the right loop, (fig. 26) and 4. the 'family of mixed loops'.[24] Within the families the

'The small alphabet of German *Kurrent*', from Hermann Dietlein's *Wegweiser für den Schreibunterricht* (1856).

'Family of the right side-curve and the upper point of the loop', from Dietlein's *Wegweiser für den Schreibunterricht* (1856).

letters are then ranked by low to high degree of complexity so that they form a 'genetic hierarchy'. For the capital letters Dietlein distinguishes the various *ductus* of the lines multifariously as wavy, snaking and flaming. The act of writing, it is clear, is an act of movement of the greatest precision. It should be rhythmic and flowing, not stiff and drilled, but like an effortless choreography.

For Stephani too writing instruction is 'a subject for the autonomous development of the intellect'. Pupils should no longer just be 'forced to copy the strokes prescribed for them until thereby they acquire a mechanical skill to *copy* them *correctly*'.[25] Rather, the trace of the letters and combinations of letters should continue to flow rhythmically; as Kittler characterizes the new school, it should 'arise . . . genetically out of the pure ego.'[26]

It is worth noting that such movements of pedagogical reform with their ideal of a child-centred education were by no means limited to Germany. Instead, one notices that the whole industrialized West completely rethought the early teaching of writing so as to promote the 'autonomous' and 'creative' abilities of the pupil by taking account of the 'formative' and 'rhythmic' dimensions of writing. In the Anglo-Saxon countries the drill and discipline of their Victorian teaching methods of writing after the fashion of Platt Rogers Spencer gave way to the time-saving speed writing method of Palmer.[27] From now on, one wrote 'in English', i.e. according to the English technique with a pointed nib (instead of the 'German' broad-pen) that was considered easier and quicker. In addition, the *ductus* was accelerated by the looping of ascenders and descenders leading to greater clarity in the maintenance of legibility, that is to say, indicating the difference to the other letters. Germany persisted in its national way of writing in the confirmed belief in the motoric and aesthetic superiority of its script, at the same time taking on board new ideas from the handicraft school movement associated with Fritz Kuhlmann and the art education movement associated with Rudolf von Larisch, who went so far as to 'reject an official norm of writing and to seek to acknowledge the individual characteristics of the writer'.[28]

In Prussia in 1915, the child-friendly, comprehensive way of writing developed by the Berlin calligrapher and calligraphy instructor Ludwig Sütterlin (1865–1917) was introduced as the basic script to be mastered in elementary school. In the 1920s it triumphed in the curriculum in all German schools – even the Catholic ones. *Fraktur* in print and *Kurrent* in handwriting were together regarded as unmistakeable signs of German culture – under the Kaisers as well as under the Nazis, who were to exploit *Fraktur* as a cultural political tool, declaring it to be the official script, until such time as it proved too unwieldy for the administration of the Reich. In 1941 it was unceremoniously banned by a decree (the so-called 'Normalschrifterlass'), dismissing it as 'Schwabach Jewish letters'. What makes one hesitate about *Fraktur* nowadays is not of course its – actually incorrect – image of being a Jewish script; owing to its National Socialist period, black-letter will for ever come over as suspiciously 'Nazi' brown.[29]

At the end of the nineteenth century handwriting was to become more than ever before a personal matter. It was a matter of simplifying and accelerating the trace by disclosing the writer's individuality, while at the same time bringing an unmistakeably nationally impressed character (or imprint) into play. An oxymoron of writing: 'ex-pression' of the nation as the most individual trace.[30] Handwriting has always oscillated between the two extremes of following the norm of the imprint and of deviation from the norm through the trace, but the awareness of this was never so sharp as in the period around 1900 when modern

Elementary school script from Ludwig
Sütterlin's *Neuer Leitfaden für den
Schreibunterricht* (1924).

disciplines like psychology, pedagogy, anthropology, ethnology and criminology began to radically affect the image of the formation of the individual. The dropping of the mechanistic *ductus* of the hand and the accompanying exact imprint of the letter in favour of the individual trace, however, of course originated also in the fact that at the end of the nineteenth century a completely different process of writing had gained admittance to the centres of writing.

## Typewriter and Carbon Paper

> The typewriter will alienate the hand of the man of letters from the
> pen only when the precision of typographic forms has directly entered
> the conception of his books. One might suppose that new systems with
> more variable typefaces would then be needed. They will replace the
> pliancy of the hand with the innervation of commanding fingers.
> Walter Benjamin, *One-Way Street and Other Writings*[31]

The typewriter represented a mechanical achievement without parallel as soon as it had been developed. Like the printing press it dissected the trace of handwriting into discrete types but which it then transferred at one go onto the paper by a simple touch on the key at a hitherto unknown speed. In so doing, it carried out the work of writer, typesetter and printer with one hand – even if it was ambidextrous. 'Industrialization simultaneously nullified handwriting and handbased work', writes Friedrich Kittler in *Gramophone, Film, Typewriter*. This book, which has achieved cult status not only with media studies specialists, deals with the protagonists of the mechanical, electric and electronic notation systems. Essentially, however, it is – willy-nilly – a book about handwriting. Even though the main task of this study consists of an appreciation of the world-shattering dawning of the (would-be) first 'technological media' as a preparation for and a heralding of the digital Turing age, and at the same time a characterization of handwriting as a backward-looking cultural practice against which the technological innovation of the typewriter is triumphant, Kittler along the way devotes so much implicit attention to this ailing beauty, this 'victim' of the typewriter, that his study occasionally comes over as a declaration of love; even if he presents this most forcefully *ex negativo*.

Kittler describes how not only whole armies of office workers fell victim to the new, mechanical writing but writers and philosophers also gave in to it. Malling Hansen's writing-ball typewriter rescues Friedrich Nietzsche with his failing eyesight who recognizes that his writing tool, not only 'works on his thoughts', but is also 'a thing like me'.[32] And Franz Kafka even (or especially) writes his love letters to the shorthand-typist Felice Bauer on a typewriter.[33] In so doing, it happened that he, the insurance agent, used to store a carbon copy in his desk drawer and so rendered the unique capable of multiple reproduction.

Whenever authors consider themselves also to be 'writers', it can happen that they turn writing itself into the subject of their writing. The list of such devotion to a writing tool is endless. The Expressionist poems that the Belgian poet Paul van Ostaijen delivered to the compositor are admittedly written by hand in a number of brightly coloured inks, almost as if they had been painted, and were also likewise published posthumously as colour facsimiles, but the first drafts of these 'calligrams' were occasionally designed by Van Ostaijen on the typewriter. Not so very far removed from these are the *Calligrammes* of Guillaume Apollinaire, who 'painted' on the typewriter.[34] With the arrival of the typewriter, even the last bastion of writing by hand now seemed to have been stormed.

When in 1874 the firm of Remington & Son, which had originally specialized in the production of weapons, put the first mass-produced typewriter on the market, all the efforts of schoolteachers and all the techniques for speeding up handwriting were finally brought to nought. After printing had already taken the pen out of the hand of the copyists, individual writing now took place typographically with hitherto unequalled graphic accuracy and at unheard-of writing speed. According to Otto Burghagen, an eyewitness, with the aid of the typewriter:

> one can complete office work in a third of the time it would take with the pen, for with each strike of a key the machine produces a complete letter, while the pen has to undergo about five strokes in order to produce a letter . . . In the time it takes the pen to put a dot on the 'i' or to make the 'u' sign, the machine produces two complete letters. The striking of the keys follows in succession with great speed, especially when one writes with all fingers; then, one can count five to ten keyboard hits per second![35]

However, the typewriter only became unbeatable with the arrival of carbon paper. Here coated paper had originally been used for the reproduction – and hence the acceleration – of various handwriting practices such as filling in delivery and order forms that in principle required a copy. Thus in 1885 in US stationery shops, 'Bushnell's Perfect Letter Copying Book' was on sale, a copying book with 150 sides of transparent, thin tissue-paper sheets under which a manila sheet and a dampened cloth were placed. Thus an original document written on with a special ink was placed with the side written on onto the tissue paper and covered with a further manila sheet. Finally the book was closed and carefully passed through a roller press applied to the book's spine. The press produced a copy of the original correspondence on the tissue paper, but this was then a mirror image and had to be read from the back of the transparent paper. A difficulty was also that this copying technique at first only allowed for a single copy. With the import of strong Japanese tissue-papers, copying books were widely distributed and after the invention of aniline dyes and inks, mainly produced in Germany, up to 15 copies of a document were possible.[36] Whole firms' archives from now on stored their bills and receipts in the form of such negative 'poor copies', mirror-image writing faded by the press or with broken lines on wafer-thin wisps of paper.

Cyanotypes also belong to the precursors of carbon paper, still known today as blueprints, used to copy technical drawings. For this, a drawing prepared on transparent paper was covered with a sheet of paper that had been treated with ferrocyanide made of potassium and iron peroxide. Under the effect of sunlight the image was transferred from the transparent paper onto the paper treated with cyanide. By rinsing off the chemicals in a water bath the image was finally captured.[37] White lines on a blue background: this is how the first wet copies appeared. And as a negative-positive process they only inverted the colouring and not the drawing itself.

Carbon paper had the distinct advantage of being dependent neither on a chemical reaction of liquid light-sensitive substances nor on pressing which is foreign to the natural *ductus* of the writing or drawing hand and has to be added to it mechanically only later. Being a dry material, carbon paper draws its writing strength from the strike of the type-bar on the platen and so it also reproduces the type in the form of the 'right' imprint on the copy. Whereas the preceding processes all served to overcome the slowness and laboriousness of writing or drawing by hand, the conjunction of carbon paper and typewriter brought together a true writing monster, combining the advantages of the 'thinking' individual hand with those of multiple printing, and thus the essential inscription technologies of handwriting and printing press. The abbreviation 'cc' that we today click on in our e-mail programs to send electronic mail to several addresses is a remediated relic from the days of carbon paper: 'carbon copy'.

## Steel-pens and electric fountain-pens

The frontal attack of what Kittler calls the 'discursive machine-gun', the typewriter, does not by any means bring handwriting as a cultural practice to a full stop.[38] This I should like to argue against the widespread claims and fears. After all, the age of mechanical reproduction has produced not only the typewriter but also revolutionized handwriting techniques by a series of innovations that have raised the achievements of handwriting to historic levels both quantitatively and qualitatively. The road to a mass writing culture is paved with a series of curiosities and inventions, not by any means just involving the mechanical media. The steel of the typewriter, with its typing that 'resembles a flying projectile',[39] is matched by those faithful to handwriting – literally – in the shape of the steel pen.

Using the same material as railway lines, steel girders and the precision mechanisms of firearms, sewing machines and typewriters, the new handwriting tools were made by the new social class of industrial workers and women workers in particular. After Peregrine Williamson of Baltimore in the USA had gained the patent for the 'metallic writing pen' in 1809, the steel pen saw a steep rise in its fortunes.[40]

Very soon after, Mason in Birmingham became the first firm in Europe, starting in the first third of the nineteenth century, to process Sheffield steel by the ton in gigantic works equipped with their steam-powered, smoking blast furnaces and enormous factory spaces. The pens are stamped out of the rolled steel with punches and then perforated. Rammers next stamp the firm's name and trade mark into the flat blanks, over and over again the same unmistakeable signature with which the manufacturers vouched for the quality of their product: Gillot, Mason, Perry and Mitchell in England, in Germany Soennecken, Heintze, Blanckertz and Brause. After being heated until they are red-hot, the pens are bent, hardened, scoured and heated one last time, then cleaned, polished and ground. Only then does the master craftsman split the nib of the pen down the middle – like a quill pen – by hand, in order to make it compliant to the hand of a future writer.[41]

It does not seem surprising then that an individual writing hand is geared to an equally individual product. The 'case' of Nietzsche for example is well known. Before going over to a typewriter, he was devoted to his favourite pen. Even on his numerous travels he sent his order to his sister in Naumburg: 'Do me the favour of having a gross of the Humbold pen Roeder's B [= No. 15; B means 'soft'] sent by Dr Romundt. It is the only pen that I can still write with.'[42]

The technical convenience of writing using the steel pen is nicely illustrated by considering, for example, how Goethe in his house on

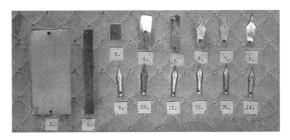

The various stages in the production of a pen, from the unworked metal sheet up to the introduction of the writing head made of iridium.

An assortment of boxed steel pens.

the Frauenplan in Weimar still set out for the poetic heights feathered
by quill pens. First he fetched writing paper, also scribbling paper and
wax candles, then seal and sealing wax, ink and blotting sand, blotter
and a piece of silk to soak up any superfluous ink, finally (several!)
goose quills and a quill knife. The quills were admittedly supplied
ready prepared, i.e. softened, dried and scoured in warm sand and
hardened. During the process of writing the quill had however to be

freshly cut to shape over and over again so that it supplied a usable trace of ink, and one had to be skilled even at this, as revealed in the instructions for the preparation of a pen in the booklet *Das aufs neue wohl zubereitete Tinten=faß* ('The newly well prepared ink-pot') (1733):

> In the case of a pen-knife it is not sufficient/ that such a thing is made of good steel and well sharpened/ although these are the two characteristics of the same thing/ but it must also have a comfortable form. Because too long and wide pen-knives cannot be handled very well/ but it is rather too great a width that is the cause/ if one tries to cut the pen a bit hollow on both sides/ before one knows what is happening; the one point of the pen goes with it.[43]

The steel pen was not only optimally cut but in addition it was essentially more durable than the quill. It was not for nothing that in 1878 the Belgian Parliament went over to using steel pens. Up until then at sittings a servant had to be employed, purely to sharpen the quills.[44]

Also from the logistical point of view, the steel pen had clear advantages. Even though the age of mechanical reproduction coincided with the age of intensified animal husbandry and mass slaughter houses, the chanceries of Europe nevertheless suffered more and more from a lack of usable goose quills. Towards the end of the eighteenth century it happened that Prussian civil servants were allocated a single quill per day;[45] one more reason why the quill gradually disappeared from the writing scene.

With the steel pen, the cultural practice of handwriting moved into the industrial age. Like the typewriter the steel pen was presented as a speed writing tool: 'Écrit 600 Mots d'une prise d'encre', is how the firm of Yankee advertises its product.[46] Another manufacturer calls its tool 'for rapid writing' after an aeroplane: 'The Aviator N° 1909' and illustrates on the label of the pen-case, not a pen, but a propeller plane described as 'John Heaths Perfection'.[47] With an 'Aviator', Charles Lindbergh undertook the first solo flight from New York to Paris in 33½ hours in 1927. The feathers of Pegasus were from now on made of steel.

Like every other technological innovation, the steel pen did not always meet with a positive reception. Victor Hugo had sworn never

A steel pen 'Plume Sergent-Major' box-label.

to use these 'needles', and Jules Janin, the leading spokesman of the French opponents to steel pens, passed the following judgement on steel pens:

> The steel pen is the true root of all evil from which society as a whole is suffering in our time. One needs to compare the steel pen that one uses nowadays with the good old quill that well served our venerable ancestors. The steel pen, this modern invention, makes an unpleasant impression upon us. It is as though one fell in love against one's will with a little, hardly visible dagger dipped in poison. Its point is as sharp as a sword, and it cuts both ways like the tongue of slanderer . . .[48]

Already Napoleon had supplied his (literate) *Grande Armée* with writing paper that had printed at the top pictures of soldiers or a portrait of Napoleon,[49] and the steel pen subsequently provided a suitable writing instrument for the dispatch of field post. Not only did the *Compagnie Française* produce so-called 'Sergent-Major' pens, advertisements blatantly dressed the steel pen in military uniform or made the analogy between a steel pen and a bayonet. 'La France militaire – Marine de l'Etat', runs the caption on the label of a steel pen-case from the firm of Baignol & Farjon of Boulogne sur Mer; another advertises 'la vraie Plume du Soldat – fabriquée spécialement pour l'armée française', even if it was made by Hinks, Wells & Co. in Birmingham.[50]

With the steel pen the modern nation states drew up their state treaties and signed trade agreements, and they founded their education systems on it.[51] If Kittler writes, 'writing as keystrokes, spacing, and the automatics of discrete block letters bypassed a whole system of education', then one can counter this by saying that, right up into the twentieth century, after the sand-table (or abax) and the writing slate, it was the steel pen and not the typewriter with which the children 'of all classes', according to the education acts, were taught to write, draw and do sums.[52] In Germany the metal pen with its multifarious presentations in addition created the preconditions for the return of the calligraphic, broken style of writing, since it made it possible to adopt the form of the broad pen and thus to carry out narrow hairlines by pushing in the upstroke and broad 'shadowlines' by pulling in the downstroke;[53] a preposterous turn, or loop, of events that was soon to be re-enacted by the printed letters.

## *Graph*ite

It is not surprising that Goethe in the moments of his greatest inspiration, as he acknowledges in *Dichtung und Wahrheit* (*Poetry and Truth*),

> preferred to take up a pencil which produced the strokes more willingly; for it had happened to me several times that the scratching and spattering of the pen roused me from my sleep-walking poetic mode, distracted me and strangled a brain wave at birth.[54]

The advantages of a pencil are obvious, and it can hold its own not just in competition with the quill. Would a day-dreaming Goethe nowadays have to start up his PC, tap in his user code, go into his word-processing program and open a file first before giving 'birth' to a brain wave? The pencil has always been the instrument of precipitate delivery.

But also for outlining, jotting down bright ideas and generally working things out 'on the back of an envelope', a pencil is just the job. A shorthand user only takes a few lightning strokes, preferably with a sharp HB pencil, to get everything down and so she can produce significant differences of meaning by means of the most minimal graphic accents – for example, raising or lowering the following sign, not pressing or pressing harder, varying the linking space or altering the size or the shape.[55]

In Antiquity the scribes shaped lead pencils for pre-drawing lines on their parchment manuscripts in the form of a sharp-edged disc, the *plumbum* or *paragraphos*, and in the medieval codices guidelines, by which the scribe oriented himself writing the durable ink uncials, were drawn using a 'silver crayon' (made of alloys of lead with tin and silver) and rubbed off with breadcrumbs after writing. The pencil came into its own in the middle of the sixteenth century when a mine in Borrowdale in Cumberland, England, was discovered to be the source of a shiny black mineral which left lead-coloured traces on paper without scratching. It was also durable and did not fade but nevertheless, if one then wanted, could be completely erased. The mineral, which was discovered later on to be chemically identical with a diamond, was called graphite – from *graphein*: to write. As with the steel pen, this media innovation again happened in conjunction with its military application since graphite also found a use in the production of crucibles for cannon balls and other military equipment.[56]

As time went by, the crude lumps of graphite acquired a pen-shape, were inserted into straws and tied with cord or set into wooden *porte-crayons*, thus accommodated to the hand. A ban on the export of English graphite obliged the continental pencil-manufacturers to extract their raw material from impure ore. Later they imported it from the rich deposits in Siberia, mixed it in variable proportions with clay and water, according to the process developed by Nicolas-Jacques Conté, and burned it to various degrees of hardness. The names of the pencil pioneers were to become famous: *crayons Conté* in Paris, in Nuremberg the works of Staedtler and Faber.[57]

When, in 1839, Freiherr Lothar von Faber took over the family business and went in for the *crayon*, he established the norms that are still valid today as regards length, diameter and degree of hardness of the pencil leads and turned the pencil into the first trademarked writing utensil.[58] By the middle of the nineteenth century, in addition to Faber-Castell, Lyra, Staedtler and Schwan-Stabilo were founded. Meanwhile, in England in 1822, the engineer Sampson Mordan patented the 'ever-pointed pencil', a pencil with a refillable lead of graphite that was so fine that it did not need to be sharpened.

An advert for Faber-Castell's 'Castell 9000' pencil developed in 1905.

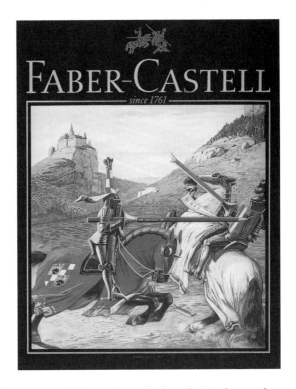

The pencil was eventually brought to final perfection by another sort of campaign. When the eraser was vulcanized from rubber, a product of colonial origin, the pencil's inscription technology now allowed for locating the search for the 'ideal' trace, not only in writing, but adding to it the possibilities of erasing, correcting and re-writing. The users of a typewriter have to laboriously return the carriage and, using the return key, hit the mistake precisely at the right spot to the very millimetre while having to struggle, as with all writing processes based on ink, with the misfortune that the ink cannot be erased easily; they will have to apply liquid paper or correction fluid to replace a black imprint with a white reprint and then to write it anew. The pencil, on the other hand, 'flies' across the paper with a lightness for a guiding tool that apart from it can only be achieved by a mouse. If, in addition to this, a rubber is attached to the end by a clip, the pencil is able to erase and re-write until such time as an ideal graphic form or wording can be achieved.

Even now the pencil is not only used by children in their first year of primary school learning to write by motorically practising the form of the letters but it is often there within reach along with scrap paper at the side of every keyboard. Its technology consists in the ability to create traces that are as durable as ink and at the same time are until the end not in their final form. At any time and in theory ad infinitum, a pencil line can be rubbed out and corrected, over and over again, until the paper gets too thin or tears. All that remains at most are the smudges, or if the pencil and the rubber are hard, ghostly strokes on or engravings in the paper like palimpsests, vestiges of writing, adopting the form of an imprint and scoring themselves more into the tactile deep structure than onto the visible surface of the written material. It is precisely in the age of reproductive writing technologies set to bring writing to a definitive form that the pencil is just coming to the top of its game. Even when it is sharpened over and over again till it is nothing but a stub, and even if the word has been printed for some time, the pencil still has something to say: whenever a reader notes something in the margin of a book.[59]

## As warm as blood: *Waterman's Ideal Fountain Pen*

> [The text] is no more than the open list of the fires of language (those living fires . . . wandering features strewn in the text *like seeds* and which for us advantageously replace the *'semina aeternitatis'* . . .
> Roland Barthes, *The Pleasure of the Text*[60]

But what about the fountain pen? It is the fetish object amongst writing instruments. Like the pencil, it functions as a writing tool of the trace, the graphic line and the free *ductus* of the hand. Unlike any other writing instrument, in this it is ideal for use by an individual hand which it faithfully serves – from the first day at school right up to writing one's will. This quality of producing script that strongly and unmistakeably expresses character has made the fountain pen irreplaceable from the moment it was introduced right up until the digital age. The fountain pen ranks as a cult object. It is not by chance that it is deployed at the great ritual moments of writing: equivalent to the blessing of the rings in church, at the register office the limited-edition fountain pen fulfils the same role.[61] Apart from the marriage register, divorce and other legal papers, trade agreements, military and peace treaties, as well as all great state treaties, are still today signed by a fountain pen which, in keeping with the majesty of the occasion, is a gold pen complete with inset rubies, clip and lid with sapphires and jewels, or like Abraham Lincoln's fountain pen, with DNA traces from the hand that writes with it.[62] As a unique object or part of a limited edition, it literally assigns to its user the insignia. It gives the writer credit and it does this even if the cheques signed by them subsequently bounce or if the marriage is a sham. The guardians of the fetish pay tribute to the fountain pen less on account of its specific quality as a writing instrument producing a legible script proof against forgery – a ballpoint pen can do this as well – than on account of the aura it gives.

But in still another quite different respect the fountain pen has the status of a fetish. Whereas the typewriter, steel pen and graphite pencil seem to march in step with the innovations of war machinery, the fountain pen seems to be walking out hand in hand with Eros. The Amsterdam writer Harry Mulisch nicely sums up this somatic metaphor, in his aut(h)o(r)-reflection, by swearing his devotion to the fountain pen, and in so doing touches on a topos that no other writing instrument can cope with: 'When one holds a fountain pen in one's hand, the ink grows warm. The ink flows as warm as blood onto the paper.'[63]

Dieser Füller aus Ebonit, Silber und Gold trägt den Namen Abraham Lincoln und würde auch gut in das Kapitel »Ungewöhnliche Modelle« passen, trägt er doch auf der Kappe, in einen Amethyst eingelassen, die DNA des Staatsmannes. Eine ähnliche Philosophie steht hinter dem Modell William Shakespeare von Krone, einem Füllfederhalter in Violett, allerdings ohne DNA.

The 'Abraham Lincoln' fountain-pen, made of ebonite, silver and gold, carrying on the lid Lincoln's DNA set into an amethyst.

It has become quite common, and Mulisch was not the first, to compare the flow of ink with the flow of other somatic juices. Take as an example, and a charmingly poetic one, the passage in which Jacques Derrida, referring back to the 'Portrait' of *Jacques Derrida* drawn by himself and Geoffrey Bennington, à propos of a blood donation in a laboratory in Algiers, reflects on the flow of blood. In this he dreams

> . . . of another language, an entirely crude language, of a half-fluid name too, there, like blood, and I hear them snigger, poor old man, doesn't look likely, not going to happen tomorrow, you'll never know, superabundance of a flood after which a dike becomes beautiful like the ruin it will always have walled up inside it, cruelty above all, blood again, *cruor, confiteor*, what blood will have been for me, I wonder if Geoff knows it
>
> . . . at the precise moment at which by the point of the syringe there was established an invisible passage, always invisible, for the continuous flowing of blood, absolute, absolved in the sense that nothing seemed to come between the source and the mouth, the quite complicated apparatus of the syringe being introduced in that place only to allow the passage and to disappear as instrument, but continuous in that other sense that, without the now brutal intervention of the other who, deciding to interrupt the flow once the syringe, still upright, was withdrawn from the body, quickly folded my arm upward and pressed the swab inside the elbow, the blood could still have flooded, not indefinitely but continuously to the point of exhausting me, thus aspirating toward it what I called: the glorious appeasement.[64]

In this period there are no grammatical or rhetorical ways out available; it flows along in phrase after phrase, like the waves of a never ending flood, a great river, a Nile that keeps on rolling along, punctuated only by commas, as constant as the flow of blood that it deals with. By variations on the word 'cru/e', written as 'cru', meaning 'crude', on the other hand as 'crue' meaning 'flood', Derrida associates the genuine blood with an original, pure or crude language, that naturally can flow following the paradoxical course of a death drive only as far as a 'glorious appeasement' by its flow extinguishing the source of its origin. Even in the Latin variation this destructive power is openly expressed. Strictly translated, *cruor* means the blood outside of the body, i.e. flowing out of the body as a result of an act of violence, in contrast to *sanguis*, which refers to the blood flowing through the body.[65]

Like no other writing instrument, the fountain pen embodies this somatic dimension of writing. The trace of ink flows evenly and continuously from the hand via the fountain pen as if it were extracting its serum directly from the artery. Against the failure of the origin, the fountain pen opposes anything that has ever been used to reveal writing as an instrument of power, symbolizing it in the ultimate sign of patriarchal potency, always having the threat of violent castration in sight against which, according to Sigmund Freud, the fetish acts as a '*stigma indelebile*' (an inextinguishable sign).[66]

Already on its first appearance at the World Exhibition in Paris in 1900, when Lewis Edson Waterman presented his 'Ideal Fountain Pen', one could not fail to see the nature of this writing instrument as a fetish. In 1884 the New York insurance broker Waterman had succeeded in developing a functional pen-holder with a metal attachable pen that could do without an inkwell, so that the flow of writing no longer needed to be interrupted by constant dipping of the pen. Admittedly, fountain pens had been on offer for some time, but Waterman's brilliant idea was the special design of the nib of the pen having grooves on the underside. When writing, ink could flow out of the ink-container through these grooves and at the same time air could flow into it. In so doing, the circulation of air and ink in a capillary action controlled the flow of ink without either too much or too little ink flowing onto the paper.

At the start of Lewis Waterman's brilliant invention, however, there was – literally – a failure, at least according to the story that Waterman told about his invention. One day he had the chance of a large deal that fell through plainly and simply because the technically underdeveloped pen that Waterman was about to sign with failed: 'And then the damned fountain pen refused to write! When ink finally flowed, it all came at once and the reservoir emptied onto the contract.'[67]

Waterman's *lapsus pennae* may in the end have led to a much greater success than the happy outcome of the deal originally sought for. Historians of technology have enjoyed pointing out this irony.[68]

At the moment of the failure of the first – unsuccessful – deal, more was at stake than a screwed-up dollar deal. Strictly speaking the lack of success of the fountain pen consisted in *two* failures: firstly it did not flow like it should have and then it came at the wrong time and out of control. In both cases it was a matter of nothing less than the narrow gap between writing and not-writing or between the sign and its erasure, evidenced equally by the failure of the ink-flow and of its excessive outflow, i.e. in the double sense of the sign that Jacques Derrida has identified, between an excess and a lack, in the process of signification as *dissémination*.

'Dissemination' means that, at the moment that the sign is placed, its meaning is divided polysemically into an infinite 'context', dispersed and in so doing through the process of *différance* is deferred. The process of signification of *écriture* thus becomes a 'délogement perpétuel', as Lucette Finas remarks in an interview with Jacques Derrida, a 'continual departure', a kind of journey with an uncertain destination, whose indecisiveness can, however, be advanced then 'with persistence' ('avec persistance'), i.e., with a large measure of decisiveness. Derrida answers Finas's observation by referring to the 'accidental similarity between '*sème*' [Gr.: σῆμα: sign] and 'semen' [Lat.: seed], between 'le sens' [sense] and 'la semence' [seed]. In this respect, the word *dissémination* possesses 'the economic power to merge . . . the question of semantic *différance* . . . and of seminal drift, of the impossible, (monocentric, paternal, familial) reappropriation of the concept and of the sperma'.[69]

Waterman's 'seed' took off. The pen boomed, the sales figures soared, the pen 'disseminated' the aura of writing throughout the world, became the mass means of writing, promoted its aura massively, in every classroom, and – something that is a bigger threat to the aura – on every second label on jam jars and beer mats by which the manufacturers suggest 'made by hand at home!'. Once Waterman's 'Ideal Fountain Pen' had overcome the teething problems of his predecessors, the fountain pen proved how, better than any other writing instrument, it enables one to make a successful signature every time, that the ink flows constantly, at the right time and with exactly the right amount needed, off the cuff. In so doing, however, with every victorious act of writing it also always carries out this '*stigma indelebile*' against failure. In writing this fountain pen always communicates the possibility of the ink stopping or leaking as a definite symptom of its technical conditions.

## Ballpoint Pen

Whereas the uncomplicated pencil that is still good for something when it is only a stub is like a (little) brother to the fountain pen, the ballpoint pen is its worst enemy, the tart of writing culture, willingly and indiscriminately passed from hand to hand. Whereas an advertisement for a fountain pen claims in down-to-earth fashion: 'Whoever writes with a particular writing instrument proclaims their own thoughts – and makes a mark for their own personal culture of writing',[70] the ballpoint pen is simply the expression of a slavish lack of culture, the epitome of which has become the ball-joint chain by which the ballpoint pen is attached at public writing counters in post offices and hotel receptions and is made available for use at any time by everyone. It is looked down on – nothing but a 'biro' or a 'bic' (or in German, a '*Kuli*', literally a coolie) – in schools as in any personal correspondence, because it spoils one's writing and is good for nothing but doodling. If writing love letters on a typewriter with its 'dead letters' seems shocking, using a ballpoint pen is looked upon as seriously lacking in style, incapable as it is of expressing anything personal and individual.[71]

The biro does not release a stream, it does not give of itself, its ink does not flow, as it does not contain any ink but a paste that in the worst cases even smears, smudges the page, turning it from a writing surface into an area full of smudges. The biro never runs out, as it dries up before the remains of the ink are finished or the pen is totally lost, replaced by another one of the millions produced. Again Harry Mulisch considers the ballpoint pen

> an inferior instrument. The ballpoint pen is just the thing for waiters who have to add up 1.23 guilders and 2.37 guilders, not for writers. With a ballpoint pen one cannot suggest the slightest nuance in the line. Not that I do calligraphy, but I should like to be able sometimes to do thick writing and sometimes to do thin writing. The ballpoint pen is always the same great three-quarter millimetre thickie.[72]

At the same time, the ballpoint pen is nothing more – and also nothing less – than the technological answer to the needs of mass writing, the expression of a wide-ranging penetration of everyday life as regards handwriting and one's omnipresent personal signature required everywhere for certifying legal documents.

The invention of the ballpoint pen goes back to the Hungarian newspaper editor Lászlo József Bíró (1899–1985). It was he who in the 1930s filled a tube with a paste-like, smoothly flowing special ink. This he contained with a ring securing an inserted freely moving ball. According to the story, the sight of the smooth, continuous movement of the rotating rollers of the printing presses of his newspaper had inspired the invention of his writing instrument, an appliance producing a line always of identical thickness independently of the *ductus*, pressure and speed of writing. In 1938 he patented his 'Fountain Pen for Pulpy Ink'.[73]

When Bíró was forced to flee from the Nazis going via Paris to Argentina, the French manufacturer of fountain pen parts Baron Marcel Bich acquired the rights to the patent and in 1950 he launched the first throw-away ballpoint pen on the market with the name – now known throughout world – of *bic* (*Biro Crayon*). From 1965 it replaced the fountain pen in schools and contributed by the million to worldwide literacy.[74] People do not learn to write on a keyboard, neither Western alphabets nor ideographic or logographic scripts, and not with a fountain pen either.

The ballpoint pen, however, still conceals another kind of ammunition. As with Remington's typewriter and the English graphite pencil, here too a military motive was in at the birth of the new medium. Bíró's ballpoint pen had its 'baptism of fire' in the fighter planes of the Royal Air Force whose aircrew no longer wrote up their notes on enemy action and hits with a pencil or fountain pen.[75] Once again the stylus turns out to be a stiletto. The ballpoint pen finds an incredible parallel to its military use in space technology – something not unusual for (media-) technological innovation. While the Soviet cosmonauts used a pencil for their notes due to weightlessness, in the manned space missions of NASA since 1968 the 'Fisher Space Pen' has been in use, a special ballpoint pen developed by the American Paul Fisher that can withstand temperatures up to 200°C without any problem and functions irrespective of weightlessness as the writing paste is pressurized in a sealed container.[76] In writing of course, this calibrated physical writing pressure blends together with the physical writing pressure of the astronaut's hand.

## Amnes/t/ia of the text processor

If writing means blazing a trail for thoughts and putting them in a linear order, then one aspect of writing obstructs this that does not show in the finished, edited text: the backwards movement, the return to a formulation that seems incomplete or inappropriate from the hindsight of the later development of the text. Every writing technique requires the possibility to correct forgotten or incorrectly realised text segments, and creative, inventive writing in the sense of Flusser's *docere* does so even more than hard-and-fast, monolinear copying. But even when copying, mistakes can occur. In the Middle Ages the copyists in the scriptoria told each other the tale of the pedantic quibbler Tutivillus, the little demon sitting on the monks' shoulders watching them writing so as every morning to gather up all the forgotten words in a sack and cart them off to hell.[77] The mistakes were thus stored up irreversibly and for ever in an infinitely expandable archive with no way back to the world of living letters. Thus a demonic monument was set up to oblivion.

That forgetting and remembering, writing and erasing are two aspects of the same operation that is more dynamic than fixed is discussed from the neuro-psychological point of view by Sigmund Freud, in his reflections on the functioning of the mechanism of human memory. And here he takes the writing instrument as an illustration: the mystic writing pad. In his famous 'Note upon the Mystic Writing Pad' ('Notiz über den Wunderblock'), Freud first examines the potential of various storage media. A sheet of paper written on with ink is admittedly excellent for giving a lasting trace of a memory as it retains the notes entrusted to it in sound condition and for an indefinitely long period. According to Freud, a disadvantage, however, is that the area of reception is limited and in addition the notes cannot be erased; the sheet of paper thus cannot be written on again. If, on the other hand, I write with a piece of chalk on a slate, I have a receptive surface which retains its receptive capacity for an unlimited time, and the notes upon which can easily be rubbed out without damaging the medium of storage itself. Here the disadvantage is that I cannot preserve a permanent trace. If I want to put some fresh notes on the slate, I must first wipe out the ones that cover it. The ideal medium for storage is therefore for Freud one with 'an unlimited receptive capacity and a retention of permanent traces' and this is exactly what the 'Wunderblock' does:

> Thus the Pad provides not only a receptive surface that can be used over and over again, like a slate, but also permanent traces of what has been written, like an ordinary paper pad: it solves the problem of combining the two functions *by dividing them between two separate but interrelated component parts or systems.*[78]

This dual function of being able to store and receive – the central business of the archive: selecting, receiving, filing, retrieving and erasing – this dual function can be carried out otherwise only by an electronic writing instrument, and it does this then automatically with the greatest precision. In addition there is no limit to the dissemination of the flow of writing caused by the flexibility of the cursor (the 'running' cursor), always ready to start anew, erase or overwrite in the middle of a line. Some stages of this process can be reversed using the 'cancel' function and then recalled using the 'undo' function in an, in theory, infinitely repeatable process of writing, correcting, erasing and reactivating. In this procedure, as Lorenz Engell tellingly writes, the computer 'extends' the present; its history 'is one of a (completed) present in which the past . . . is in no way past'.[79] This, however, functions only until such time as the text file is saved and the traces of writing are wiped from the memory. The interim versions of the text are captured and will thus be retrievable, even after a reload of the system. The changes made within an interim version, however, are lost. The process of storage is always accompanied by a process of erasure; from this moment on there is a selection taking place of which operations of the archive are preserved and which are to vanish for ever along with their function of constituting the archive even before it is there. For the computer this 'archiviolitic' mode is highly dramatic as the erased stages of use are not only no longer capable of being reactivated but, as Engell writes, they are this in a particularly lasting manner. This is important not only on the microscopic but on the macroscopic level: e.g. disposed, rejected web pages, old versions of programs and out-of-date systems largely disappear or are even completely lost without trace, this can happen even to older machines and types of equipment, whole branches of technology.[80]

Once stored the computer only saves the edited files. And just as the world wide web 'forgets' all the data available on a particular day if they are not considered to be media events worthy of being permanently accessed again, so the PC as a personal storage facility erases any stages of use that are no longer needed. Any infringements against correct spelling – literally: 'orthography' – all backspacing and rejected signs are erased from the random access memory; they do not go to hell but to a final erasure: what is forgotten is forgotten, oblivion forgets itself, its own mode, or to put like Heidegger: it conceals its concealment like a 'signless cloud':

> In the fact that the cloud of forgetting concealment conceals itself as such, the uncanny character of forgetting comes to the fore. Forgetting itself occurs already in an oblivion. If we forget something, we are no longer with it, but instead we are already 'away,' 'drawn aside.' If, in forgetting, we are still with the thing, then we could always retain what is forgotten, and the forgetting would never occur at all.[81]

This illustrates the uncanny 'magic' of the electronic writing instrument: for every mistake, for every infringement of the rules of the art of writing, it grants a final absolution by its RAM not recording what is forgotten or written by mistake. On the surface only a snapshot of the last version saved remains retrievable; the stages inbetween are forgotten – and forgiven. 'As if written in water.'[82]

## Ink Eraser Pen (*Tintenkiller*)

Writing by hand is, on the other hand, totally different to writing on a word processor. Every mistake is noted and recorded. Erasures take the form of scratches, rubbings-out or crossings-out and indiscreetly advertise what is rejected as not up to scratch, as being suppressed variations of the text; later changes remain appendices and excesses of the text because, being second thoughts, they will literally never fit in the line. Since the 1970s, in technologically inadequate anticipation of the 'delete' key on the word processor, the ink eraser pen has come to the aid of the pen. Commerce has made available a bi-polar felt-tip pen with two points, one of them white, the other blue. With the white end one can make the ink invisible, with the other one can then fill in the space anew with a special ink. This correction ink is resistant to the erasing fluid from the white end. The erasure process is a chemical reaction, in which bleaching agents, mostly sulphites or carbonates of the erasing fluid adhere to the central carbon atom of the colours in the organic ink and thus disturb the geometry of the molecules of colour so that the reflected light loses its colour.[83]

As early as 1912 the American May F. Gardner had applied for a patent for an invention for the chemical erasing of ink: a 'pen holder with a compartment for an eradicator . . . whereby a controllable quantity of the eradicator can be removed from the holder for erasure purposes'.[84] Gardner provided his special pen with a small glass container at the top end containing erasing fluid. With a detachable pipette this could be sucked up and then dripped onto the paper.[85]

At the same time during the Imperial period in Germany, Heinrich Louis Steincke from Harburg on the Elbe developed quite a similar 'pen holder with an arrangement for deleting mistakes in writing'. According to the patent this is characterized by

> the detachable hollow pen nib (b) containing a special hollow space (d) to accommodate a chlorine solution, the bottom opening of which is closed off by a conic valve (e) which can be opened by pressure on the end (g) of an angle lever (f) allowing a chlorine solution to run down a channel (h) and come out of the pen-nib.[86]

The remarkable thing about the technology of erasure and correction on the part of the ink eraser pen – the earlier ones and the present-day one – is that the ink is not destroyed by the process of erasure; it is only made invisible. It is possible to change the 'erased' ink

Heinrich Louis Steincke's 'Pen holder with an arrangement for deleting mistakes in writing' of 1914.

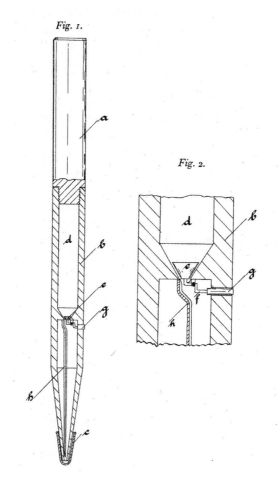

Fig. *1.*

Fig. 2.

back again and return it to a visible form by the use of aldehydes and hydrogen peroxide. Likewise, time can bring back erased writing as the result of an entropic photo-chemical process. A look at old school exercise books brings to light the faded corrections of childhood; all those mistakes and infringements against the rules of the symbolic order, of spelling and grammar, all the inadequacies of childish motor activity in the shape of ink blots and the calligraphic failures of the *ductus* of writing, which with the help of the ink eraser pen were meant to be kept from the corrective eye of the teacher.

In this respect, the technique of erasure of the ink eraser pen also proves to be an inscription technology. That writing and erasure, erasure and writing always precede one another is illustrated in the most fundamental way by the ink eraser pen with its dual points. Schoolchildren are very familiar with this characteristic: you write invisible secret writing with the ink eraser pen which is then – subsequently – made visible by ink as a means of contrast. With this trick they are tapping in to a centuries-old tradition of sympathetic inks: inks promoting 'sympathetic' relations which stay invisible while writing and only by the application of a special process do they become visible: by being moistened using a contrast fluid, dipping in water or by cooling or heating them.

In his *Oekonomische Encyclopädie* (1773–1858), Johann Georg Krünitz divides sympathetic inks into seven different kinds:

> The first kind appears when one spreads another fluid over the invisible writing or exposes it to a vapour of the same. The second kind is one that stays hidden as long as it is enclosed, but it soon becomes visible when one exposes it to the open air. The

A page from one of the author's exercise books from her time at primary school Albert I in Cologne-Ossendorf, with corrections by the class teacher, Miss Soete.

third kind becomes visible when one sprinkles a colouring material in a fine powder on it. The fourth kind does not become legible until it is held up to the fire. The fifth kind cannot be read until one puts the paper with the writing into water. The sixth kind, like the fourth kind, can be induced to appear by approaching a source of heat but this one disappears as soon as the paper grows cold. The seventh kind has the characteristic that the writing is lost, or becomes visible, if one puts it into an artificial kind of air or other vapours.[87]

The tinctures and liquors are prepared from distilled wine vinegar, quicklime, heated, stirred and filtered in clay pots and mixed with litharge, gold powder, gall-nuts, vitriol, alum or sal ammoniac. What most of these secret inks have in common is that the invisible precedes the visible, the erasure the writing: writing only arises *ex negativo* as the unwritten white of the chemically prepared paper. But there are also inks that are visible at first and disappear again after 24 hours. And Krünitz goes on to describe tinctures that make one ink disappear and in the same way make another one appear.

Take a clear solution of common or iron vitriol in water, and with it write onto paper something that one wants to impart to somebody in secret, so that after it has dried one will not be able to make out anything on the paper. However, in order to avoid suspicion, that some writing appears on the paper, then pulverize some tinder very finely together with some quite weak gum solution, in such a way that it resembles a fairly thick ink, and with it write about quite unimportant matters between the lines of the hidden writing which one must have written quite far apart from one another. Now if the other person wants to read the hidden writing, they can only do it, as agreed, by taking a strong decoction of gall-nuts, into which is added approximately ½ quart or a quart of water, one 'lot' [Trans. between 15.5 and 16.6 g.] of finely pulverized gall-nut, and which, after standing for twenty-four hours at a moderate temperature, is sieved through a cloth into another dish. They must dip a clean sponge into this water and with it wipe the black writing off the paper at which the writing that was at first hidden straightaway appears.[88]

In all these processes writing and erasing prove to be two operations that in the end cancel each other out and at the same time radically condition one another. The technical curiosities of the in/visible writing fluids involved in this dual function illustrate once more how imprint and trace, being closely interlinked, mutually attract and repel one another: since if the erased ink script reappears after time, it does not arise from the 'stroke' of a hand movement drawing a meandering line. Already at the time of erasing, the *ductus* of the eraser pen was not the stroke, the trace or the line, but the rapid up and down of the painting-in, the filling-in – or more precisely, the clearing – of a space. The new writing now appears in this other *ductus* that is committed to the hatching of spaces rather than the graphic line or contour, and it becomes glaringly visible rather in a photo-chemical process than in the mechanical-kinetic programme of the trace. As with a photographic print in a developing tank, the faded imprint of the writing becomes visible as the inversion of its erasure. No longer just as a trace but also as an imprint, or more precisely: as the imprint of a trace.

The 'irritation' of the ink eraser pen – for teachers of writing as for handwriting fetishists of any sort – is an effect of precisely this shocking double structure of imprint and trace. Traditionally it is seen as the quintessence of the trace: documentary writing indicating, as with the trace of a foot (or of a hand), that someone has been there: an unmistakeable, physical, authentic writer, the author of a piece of writing. The epitome of such documentary writing is the last will and testament that, being handwritten and signed by hand, testifies to the presence of the undersigned, to their individual hand, their unique and authentic body as the ultimate statement of an irreducible presence here-and-now. It is just this unique, handwritten, auratic trace that Walter Benjamin means when he says that it is mechanically non-reproducible, it is just this trace that is reproduced in the photo-chemical process like a photographic print: as a copy or imprint of a trace.

The moment of erasure was of course already there before the erasing fluid faded the ink colour. Because writing – and the example of the handwritten testament illustrates this very clearly – presupposes

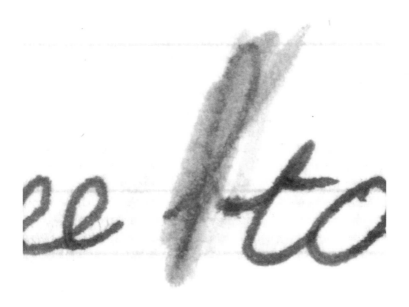

Detail from the author's exercise book, showing the effect of an ink-eraser pen on her handwriting on 17 April 1975.

precisely this possibility of the absence of the writer. Its legal effect is declared by the testament *per definitionem post mortem*. At the moment of writing itself, in the lively *ductus* of the hand, the writing anticipates death. And what is taken to be a unique, unrepeatable singular event: handwriting, the hand, the presence in the present, is *déjà*, always already, deferred.

## Writing Technology

This dual characteristic incarnated in such an exemplary way in the ink eraser pen applies to every writing instrument and every writing practice, and at this point it becomes clear the extent to which a consideration of the 'exceptional case' of handwriting can contribute to a theory of cultural technologies *as* media technologies. The case of the ink eraser pen demonstrates that even though writing functions as however reliable a storage system, it still also carries within it the tendency to erasure. The ancient stylus has a point like a stiletto with which one can score in clay or wax and thus set up writing as a blank space. If one turns the stylus round – *stilus vertere* – the scribe can smooth the wax with the wide end and thus re-write it. It is precisely the stream of ink too that feeds the writing and connects it to its source, still carrying within it the tendency to erasure or to failure. And even the most resistant permanent traces – epigraphic monumental writing on graves and monuments – still nevertheless point towards the tendency to erasure, to the fall of the emperor, to the grave of the pharaoh, the pyramids, which – as Hegel writes – adopt the shape of the great archival letter: **A** – as in archive/ ark/origin.

At the same time the erasure draws the trace of writing anew. And it does this also precisely in a technological way. Because, all together, the technological innovations of the steel pen, the fountain pen, the pencil and the ballpoint pen create a media landscape in which not only the development of handwriting tools keeps pace with tech- nological and mechanical developments but, with the global increase in literacy, writing by hand like mechanized writing is raised to the peak of its form. In this process there arises a broad spectrum of hand- writing techniques, from artistic calligraphy via precious (or fetishistic) writing with a fountain pen right up to shorthand paid as piecework or the mass production of the ballpoint pen. In this sense there is no such thing as pre-technological writing. No technological writing with a typewriter or the keyboard and with an imprint as opposed to pre-mechanical or pre-electronic writing in the sense of a trace, rather writing has always been technology – *hand*work and action (*Hand*lung), skill and know-how.

In this respect, also the competition between typewriter and handwriting is determined less in their relative function as *either* imprint *or* trace. Both of them are related to one another – but in their own areas of being. They are not therefore necessarily mutually exclu- sive but form precisely a media symbiosis in the sense of a specialized division of labour, whereby writing on keys belongs to the official and public sphere and handwriting to the private, and to a certain extent to the subversive, style of writing. It is subversive to the extent that, since the regulation standardization of handwriting at school, the writer's hand is only disciplined once in a lifetime. Once one has been introduced to the symbolic order as a child, in puberty we go in search of our own styl/us and accordingly play out the trace of our 'characters' against the boundaries of writability and legibility, because our personal hieroglyphs are backed by that other way of writing that assigns the formation of letters to the keyboard.

Victor Hugo photographed in 1853 when in exile on the island of Jersey.

## Before a Photograph

Victor Hugo was in the habit of sending photographs along with his poems for publication back to France from his exile in the Channel Islands. They were processed by his son Charles. He surrenders himself to the photographer, presents himself to him and poses for him, but this is not an unconditional surrender. He poses for the treacherous and forgetful French people not just as the poet Victor Hugo, but as Victor-Hugo-in-exile. At least this is what his body language seems to be saying: his left hand placed protectively against the temple of his thinking apparatus, he is holding in his right hand turned away from his writing desk a stick-like object like a baton towards the observer as if about to attack the latter (the forgetful Frenchman). He surrenders to the observer by withholding himself.

Before the photograph, however, the observer is his son, the photographer, Charles Hugo. It was also to him that at spiritualist séances the father gave the task of setting the table in motion to make contact with his deceased daughter Leopoldine.[1] After the photograph, then, the father takes pen to paper. And by signing the dead photo portrait by hand on the salt print, he traces the self-portrait that has been appropriated by his son back to his genealogical roots. With this signature he at the same time proclaims the resurrection of the exile in his struggle against his enemy Napoleon III: '*S'ils ne sont plus que mille, eh bien, j'en suis! Si même ils ne sont plus que cent, je brave créer Sylla; s'il en demeure dix; je serai le dixième ; et s'il n'en reste qu'un, je serai celui-là.*' In this dramatization of the self, even if nobody and nothing is remaining, then Hugo is at the same time deriving his self-portrait from a continual loss of being.

The composition of photograph and handwriting effectively doubles the absence of the pictured 'revenant'. And at the same time it twice summons him to life. The already belated photograph is still signed belatedly, in the process of which the handwritten signature as much as the photograph itself captures the here and now of a physical presence for a future present. At the same time it transmits it directly to the chain of deferral. It is precisely this that gives the composition of photograph and handwriting its wondrous, almost even 'uncanny' aesthetic power: the interrelation of imprint and trace.

# 4 Fore-Word: A Distance, However Close

In principle a work of art has always been reproducible. Man-made
artefacts could always be imitated by men.

Walter Benjamin, '*The Work of Art in the Age of Mechanical Reproduction*'[1]

Aura is neither the mystic idea that its detractors avoid, nor is it the
nostalgic catchword that its defenders refer to from time to time . . .
[O]ne fails to understand the effect of images, including their cultic
effect, as long as one is not willing to secularize one's own categories
of interpretation: the concept of the aura must then be secularized.

Didi-Hubermann, *Ähnlichkeit und Berührung*[2]

Schematic representation of James Watt's press.

## Printed Hands and Electric Pens

The age of industrialization affected the cultural practice of handwriting in yet another respect. Not only did it accelerate the *ductus* of the hand by means of efficient writing technologies and modern mass writing instruments but with it, the uniqueness of handwriting as autography also entered the age of mechanical reproduction. In 1790 a peculiar 'writing instrument' started to be used in the state bureaucracy of the USA. Like other chancelleries, the US State Department had also long been on the lookout for technical processes that would make it easier to carry out the copious correspondence. An unusual way of relieving the secretaries was discovered by James Watt by his making use of the external, material conditions of handwriting: the moisture of the ink and the qualities of absorption of the writing surface. He developed an apparatus using the same principle as that of the copy books made of sheets of tissue paper: the so-called Watt's press. With it, handwritten originals, written on with a special ink developed by Watt, could be copied by placing the side with the writing onto moistened tissue paper and then printing it in the press. George Washington and Benjamin Franklin acquired such handwriting presses for their personal use.[3] With Watt's press the trace of the writing no longer needed to be copied by the continual drawing and looping of a line. Instead, the apparatus put the handwritten page as a whole onto the paper – as in printing the type did to the letter – but, unlike the process of printing type, without thereby losing the trace for good in the imprint. In this respect Watt's press was less a typewriter than a copying machine *avant la lettre*.

These copying processes were accompanied in the nineteenth century by a series of reproductive processes on wax or copying paper similar to the copying processes of typewriter and carbon paper. The writing was done with special copying pens, glass and steel pens, as in lithography for example resistant to corrosive writing fluids, or with an agate pen in the case of which a transparent paper and a double-sided colour sheet were used.[4] In this respect as well writing by hand proved to be a highly technical practice, for example the case of the so-called 'papyrograph' that was patented in London in 1874 by the Italian Eugenio de Zuccato. The way this copying machine worked was based on the principle of a *stencil*: with the steel pen and a corrosive solution of soda as the writing fluid one wrote on thin paper covered with lacquer that allowed ink to permeate it. The lacquer was removed by the written sheet being pressed between moistened blotting paper, and a stencil was produced to print copies off with. Soon after Zuccato developed a follow-up version, the 'trypograph' which he patented in 1878. A thin sheet of paper covered on one side with paraffin was placed with the wax side on a plate with fine grooves on a wooden tablet. When a writer wrote on the wax paper with a blunt pen, the pressure of his handwriting caused tiny perforations along the grooves that later came to serve as a mould for printing by absorbing the ink.[5]

Thomas Alva Edison also followed this perforation principle, however he effected it by the use of an 'electric pen': an electrically driven needle which through the repetition of mini-movements poked tiny little holes in the writing paper, truly 'tattooing' it.[6] There followed a series of similarly functioning printing machines, the 'cyclostyle' in the case of which a writing wheel made perforations in wax; the 'mimeograph' which then turned this idea to commercial use, and also the 'stylograph'.[7] All together, we are dealing with contraptions that transmitted the action of the hand to the precision mechanics of the writing instrument and thus multiplied by mechanical, chemical or electrical processes what had up until then been considered to be 'empirically unique', and admittedly without thereby losing the idiosyncrasy of the trace.

By drawing a sharp division between original and imprint, the processes of copying made a distinction that had never before occurred so radically in the history of handwriting. Because for a millennium handwriting had functioned primarily as scriptography, that is, as an essentially 'allographic' practice in the sense of Nelson Goodman's *Languages of Art*, in other words as a practice whose first principle is its iterability or '*sameness of spelling*';[8] again and again the copyists had formed the letters according to the pattern of an uncial, a Carolingian miniscule or a textura in the tradition of a particular school of writing, without thereby ever giving any recognition of an individual, 'autographic' styl/us.

In this respect, from the beginning the reproduction of handwriting was not such a strange thing. If in the age of the folios it took the form of the craft of scriptography and penmanship, since the introduction of the woodcut, copperplate engraving, etching and since the beginning of the nineteenth century lithography, that could for the first time reproduce writing 'on a mass scale', handwriting and printing have been *joined technologies*. It was precisely the copy books of penmanship, which in the Renaissance served to teach a beautiful hand, that used the possibilities of standardization by means of printing. And it is not by chance that the matrix of writing, after the normalization of school handwriting (in 1741 in Prussia) in the printed writing patterns established the cursive script for official use in bureaucracy and the *Kurrent* for use in schools, is also known as 'copperplate'.[9]

With Watt's press, however, the relation of trace and imprint acquired a new quality, because it was not necessarily an accurate or calligraphic handwriting that was being copied here but also and even more so the individual stroke of a personal image of writing. Perhaps it was a jotting or a scribble, a private note or a letter from the hand of George Washington or Benjamin Franklin: a trace that its writer did not want to pass on to the addressee without keeping a copy for his private archive.

## Original Copy

The imprints from Watt's press are in Goodman's sense allographs: 'correctly spelled' copies of an original model. They spell, repeat – or 'quote' thereby, however, not just the 'spellable' dimension of the handwriting as a symbolic system of notation, but they also repeat its unique visual performance purloined by the mechanical and technical means of writing: what one might following Goodman call 'autography'. This autographic dimension relates handwriting to painting, the art that Goodman sees as the prototype of the autographic arts:

> Let us speak of a work of art as *autographic* if and only if the distinction between original and forgery of it is significant; or better, if and only if even the most exact duplication of it does thereby not count as genuine. If a work of art is autographic, we may also call that art autographic. Thus painting is autographic; music nonautographic, or *allographic*.[10]

According to this, 'autographic' means that which in the work of art is not able to be forged, that which is beyond the technology of copying, however perfect this technology might be, because it can not be encompassed by it. The idea of a non-copyable remainder lies precisely at the heart of Benjamin's concept of the aura of the work of art which is lacking in 'even the most perfect reproduction of a work of art', for the reason that 'its presence in time and space, its unique existence at the place where it happens to be', resists all processes of reproduction.[11] And like Goodman, Benjamin develops his concept of the original as the visual appearance of a *hic et nunc* following the example of painting.

The advantage of Watt's press, but also its monstrousness, consists in its avoidance of the strict distinction argued by Goodman between autography and allography, because it reproduces not only the spellable, alphanumerical dimension of handwriting as writing, but it also captures its visual performance as an autographic *image* of writing. Goodman very well recognizes the necessity for a further differentiation of the concepts and introduces a second binary schema for this which does not cover exactly the same ground as the first, i.e. the distinction between single- and two-stage works of art: painting and literature are single-staged (although painting is autographic and literature is allographic), because their production – even if this takes place in differing stages of work – brings about a finished state. Music, on the other hand, is two-stage because it is divided into the stage of the score and the stage of the performance. Goodman gives etching as a model for autographic, two-stage art.

It is then remarkable that Goodman does not identify the authenticity and the originality of the art work with the first stage, i.e. with the actual physical *manu*-facture of the *radere* (etching): scoring, scratching, when in other words a sharp stylus, with an absolutely unique and physical hand movement, engraves the etching surface made of wax or resin, but for him precisely the products of the second stage only count as 'genuine' if they are correctly copied or 'spelled':

> The etcher . . . makes a plate from which impressions are then taken on paper. These prints are the end-products; and although they may differ appreciably from one another, all are instances of

the original work. But even the most exact copy produced otherwise than by printing from that plate counts not as an original
but as an imitation or forgery.[12]

Goodman therefore locates the difference between original and copy,
not in the difference between engraved plate and etching, but rather
he sees the etchings themselves to a certain extent all as 'original
copies'.

## The Right Copy

For Benjamin it is just these two-stage arts and, outstanding amongst
them, film which, even if they produce 'genuine copies' make the aura
of the work of art problematic by reason of their appearance in the
mass. Unlike Goodman, who takes all of the products of the second
stage to be 'genuine instances' of the work, the two-stage arts can never
count as having aura for Benjamin; on account of their basic structure they are lacking in aura as the uniqueness of the genuine article
can never be attached to them: 'From a photographic negative, for
example, one can make any number of prints; to ask for the "authentic"
print makes no sense.'[13] For Benjamin, a copy can never be genuine
and never have aura. He distinguishes between original and copy, not
just in the relation of the copies to one another, but only the unique-
ly arising work of art – the painting, the statue, the cathedral – has
aura.

    For handwriting – in the sense of its claim to uniqueness, origi-
nality and authenticity –Benjamin's interpretive categories, from the
point of view of media technology, hold another kind of charge.
Because in the case of handwriting, mechanical reproduction *makes a
difference* between original model or matrix and copy, i.e. the casting
moulds of the first stage, and the copy, the imprint, the cliché or the
etching of the second stage. All of the printing processes, whether with
the lines as in the case of a wood press cut deeply into the form or, as
in the cases of copperplate engraving, etching or lithography, etched
into the plate, in the end presuppose that the original serves as a model
for printing and therefore needs to be produced in *mirror image*; not
until it is printed does one get the legible, 'right' writing. The first stage

must technically anticipate the second, just as in the case of photography the negative records the light conditions in reverse, so as to reproduce them positively in the print. The inscription technologies of these processes of reproduction are geared to this *telos*, that is, by means of its temporal progression, to delivering a usable artefact as the end product. Without this end product the in-between products have no value in their own right: they all function as derivatives or special cases of this final, ultimate form. It is precisely this teleological structure that qualifies these technologies as (potentially) 'reproducible' (*reproduzierbar*) in Benjamin's sense (referring to *reproducibility*, not just *reproduction*, as in the English translation of his essay 'Das Kunstwerk im Zeitalter seiner technischen Reproduzierbarkeit'[14]).

In the case of Watt's press, the difference between (handwritten) casting mould and (mechanical) casting, or between manuscript and copy is no less distinctive than in the case of lithography and photography, and yet on the level of its technical process it differs considerably. Because the writing of the first stage is originally positive or in the 'right' aspect and it only gets turned into a mirror image subsequently, or belatedly, in the imprint. To become legible the tissue paper must then still be turned over and thus observed from 'underneath'. The material depth of the bearer of writing has to be concealed in the *trompe l'œil* of its transparency and the 'underneath' of the paper perceived 'as if' it were the top side before the writing itself appears 'as' rightly legible.[15] Unlike in lithography and photography, the product of the first stage does not appear in the process, only its negative copy becomes visible, but it does so only as an intricate special case of the actual handwriting. The legibility of handwriting can not be separated from its originality without thereby being reduced to a problematic case because the line of writing in the imprint running towards the left and with a left-vectoral orientation resists the rightward tendency of writing that has been predominant for millennia and, in line with this right-hand régime of writing, is felt to be lacking.

## Inversion of the Remainder or: The Left-Handed Snail[16]

For handwriting, the use of the mirror-image represents an enormous intervention. In this respect its autographic dimension fundamentally

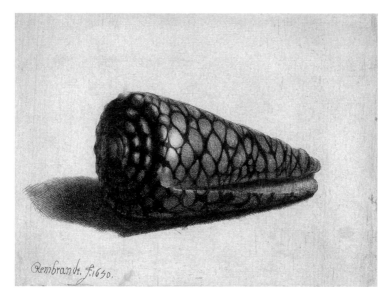

Rembrandt, *The Little Shell*, 1650, etching.

differs from that of the image, which is as a rule reversible without thereby producing a significant difference, except in those cases in which a carefully scrutinizing gaze explicitly studies the direction of the course of the reversal. Such a gaze emerges in the Baroque period when focusing on graphic representations of snails and the spiralling of shells: since 1600 in scientific publications, spirals, coils and windings of variable provenance – Kant in this context referred on the basis of the curly lock of hair to a 'right-hand tendency of nature' – have been represented according to their biological origins as dextral.[17]

A notable exception to this is Rembrandt's famous etching that shows an object from his cabinet of curiosities, the '*schelpje*', an exotic, marbled conic snail (*conus marmoreus*), whose front aspect displays a spiral with a sinistral thread. The direction the spiral is turning in had admittedly been engraved on the etching plate by Rembrandt the 'right' way round, but in the printing process it was then reversed. Once again the Baroque shows itself to be preposterous. However, the artist signed and dated the work – as the shaky, 'gauche' *ductus* of the handwriting reveals, looking as if it were written 'by the left' – foresightedly in mirror writing.

This is precisely the source of the 'irritation' – of mechanical reproduction, thus I should like to appropriate Benjamin's theory of art for the case of handwriting: this infringement against the norm of the right-hand *ductus*, that is 'inverted' by means of the engraving plate or the printing press or – as one could also say – 'subverted'. In this sense the trace of handwriting proves to be beyond reproduction (or beyond the imprint); it simply can *not* be mechanically reproduced, or at least not without thereby generating the 'remainder' that, in the face of all the perfection of modern techniques of reproduction, Benjamin reserves for the aura of the artwork, in this case the painting. Aura comes into being in precisely this dimension of the spiral that takes account of the orientation of the line running either towards the left or the right; it literally takes the shape of a 'winding' in referring to what 'aura' means etymologically: 'breath' (*Hauch*), *spiritus*, or anything winding, blowing or waving.

The aura of the image for Benjamin definitely does not just depend on its correct spelling though, like Goodman's copies of an etching. Rather, Benjamin separates the concept of aura from that of authenticity by drawing attention to a shift of accent brought about by the mass (re-)production of images:

> To the extent to which the cult value of a painting is secularized the ideas of its fundamental uniqueness lose distinctness. In the imagination of the beholder the uniqueness of the phenomena which hold sway in the cult image is more and more displaced by the empirical uniqueness of the creator or of his creative achievement. To be sure, *never completely so* [*niemals ganz ohne Rest*, i.e. 'never completely without a remainder']; the concept of authenticity always transcends mere genuineness. (This is particularly apparent in the collector who always retains some traces of the fetishist and who, by owning the work of art, shares in its ritual power.) Nevertheless, the function of the concept of authenticity remains determinate in the evaluation of art; *with the secularization of art, authenticity displaces the cult value of the work.*[18]

While, for painting in the age of mechanical reproduction, a general flood of images is let loose and with this – following Benjamin

– a secularization of the cult value of the image, the cultural practice of handwriting has seen a contrary development. In the case of handwriting, its characterization as 'autography' – a unique, unmistakable and charismatic 'trace', something that along with its allographic properties it has always been – only becomes troublesome when the 'empirically unique' *ductus* of a physical hand finds an exact correspondence as an imprint. The invention of the copy was the moment of birth of the original. The 'remainder' of the handwriting, the non-copyable 'aura' of its trace, its 'winding', only appeared when the mechanical methods of writing, and of these above all the typewriter, took over the task of mass writing.[19]

## The Polygraph

On the other hand, the so-called polygraph seems in the end to write completely without any remainder, because only irrevocably genuine originals can be written with it. An early advertisement lauds the polygraph as a 'curious and useful machine for writing with two pens, so that two originals are made with great facility at the same instant of time'.[20] In 1803 the American John Isaac Hawkins patented the machine in the USA and in England. What he at first called the 'pentagraph' was an improvement of early European models of drawing machines that combined a non-writing pen with a writing pen by means of a hinged construction shaped like a parallelogram so that graphic artefacts such as drawings and reduced maps could be duplicated faithful to the original. In his application to the British Patent Office of 24 September 1803 Hawkins described the way his 'new Machinery . . . for Writing, Painting, Drawing, Ruling Lines and Other Things' worked as a machine 'by which means I make as many letters or figures at the same time as there are pens, each letter resembling the other'.[21]

Only one year later the multiple handwriting machine was installed in the private office of Thomas Jefferson. It is remarkable here that after studying it for a long time Jefferson did not supply his polygraph just with steel pens, even though it was argued that with them one could write more cleanly, more quickly and more evenly than with a quill. Instead he preferred a steel pen for the writing hand and a quill for the hinged arm, as Jefferson thought that the latter could

Thomas Jefferson's polygraph.

contain more ink and this flowed off more evenly[22] – as if while writing by hand at least one warm-blooded creature had to have his hand involved.

With the polygraph the differentiation between original and copy, which had hardly been recognized with the invention of Watt's press, again straightaway ran into new difficulties, because it now happened that a writer in a singular act of writing produced several original copies at once. The myth of the unity, the uniqueness and the authenticity of autographic handwriting, which still bestows its aura on the handwritten 'original' today, goes back to this period when the polygraph rendered the differentiation between the before and after of writing and copying obsolete. The plural writing strokes written in this way originate irrevocably from one and the same hand; they are thus absolutely the same and of equal value. Like photographic prints from the same negative or etchings from the same plate, copies made by the polygraph differ in – almost – no respect from one another.

## *Infra-mince*

This 'almost is not nothing', writes Georges Didi-Huberman and he argues that: 'it is technology itself that interferes'.[23] Here he is insisting on the imprint being technically conditioned, something that Goodman, in his reflections on the aesthetics of art in relation to the genuineness of the imprint, claims is insignificant. For Goodman the 'minute discrepancies' and even 'however much they differ in colour and amount of ink, quality of impression, kind of paper etc.' *between* two copies of the same etching made at the most an aesthetic, but in no case a *technical* difference,[24] because the technical process that produced them was always the *same*. Also, just like signatures, however different they might be in the way they are carried out, according to Goodman they should all be classed as authentic if they only originate from one and the same hand. The difference *between* the actual individual cases does not make any difference for him. A copy is A copy is A . . .

. . . and yet it can occasionally appear with an un-heard of difference as E as well, as Jacques Derrida has remarked.

The idea of such an imperceptible *différance* was once made by Marcel Duchamp into the basis of his devilish game with the concept of the original. A urinal is a urinal is a u . . . As a serially produced Readymade, it presents itself – this is the essence of Duchamp's first provocation of the classical concept of art – as an object in possession of no original uniqueness. The second provocation is essentially that it not only *looks like* that which it represents, in the same way as a work of art has to resemble the object that it *re-presents*, the urinal like the bottle-rack or the bicycle wheel is not a successful copy but, as Didi-Huberman writes in his masterly analysis of Duchamp, it is '*totally of the same kind*, as it is an exemplar taken directly from the serial production of the represented object *itself*.[25] It is even, I should like to emphasize, not just 'of the same – kind' in the sense of 'such as', because that could also be a successful copy, but is the 'same', that is, identical. Michael Wetzel leaves no doubt about this when he writes about Duchamp's Readymades: '. . . individual examples depart from a context which determines them as a whole unit, so that they become *totally in themselves*, without any reference to what they represent, like an object identical to its image'.[26] The Readymades therefore maintain totality in unity, and that is not a small thing, because according to a classical semiotic model this implies the impossibility of representation as such.

The more essential and relatively more shocking provocation of the Readymade, however, consists in the fact that it does not stop even at this final point of representation but as a serial object it is nevertheless at the same time still also an individual piece. This is shocking in so far as it claims for itself a paradoxical logic: a Readymade is serial *and* unique, identical and different, repeatable (in the sense of iterable and quotable) *and* at the same time absolutely singular. The signature at the bottom of the urinal only helps a little to free the object from its dilemma and authenticate it as a classical work of art, because it is, like the object itself that it signs, singular and at the same time iterable. The signed urinal is no more and no less unique than the unsigned one, and likewise no more and no less a fake. Marcel Duchamp is . . . Marcel Duchamp is . . . Marcel Duchamp . . . Richard Mutt is . . .

That the signature, as with handwriting in general, is accorded the great authority of uniqueness and that it is nevertheless at the same time repeatable in its uniqueness, is an idea Duchamp employs over and over again in his work: to settle the bill for treatment by his dentist Daniel Tzanck he painted carefully and by hand the *Tzanck Cheque* (1919), and in fact so accurately that the trace of his handwriting looks pin sharp, point for point, like a stipple engraving. He exhibits the opposite procedure in his various *Boxes*, for example in his *Green Box* (*The Bride Stripped Bare by Her Bachelors, Even*, 1934). For this he used handwritten notes on loose pieces of paper he had made for *The Large Glass*, all of varying shapes and partly torn up. He reproduced the irregular shapes of the unique pieces precisely to a T, every one in its original form. Then he collected the facsimiles in a box that he produced in several editions in altogether 300 'individual works'.[27] Whereas the *Tzanck Cheque* reproduced the printed original as a trace, *The Green Box* made the unique trace into a serial copy. Two very similar manipulations, but nevertheless very different from one another.

The particular type of difference we are dealing with here can not be located in a comparison between original and reproduction, but it is the mutual relationship between the serial reproductions that is key, i.e. the relation of the urinal to the other urinal of the same rank, or the relation of the cast to another cast from the same casting mould, or of the etching to another etching from the same plate, or of the photographic print to another print from the same negative, in other words the difference that Nelson Goodman describes as being without significance 'however much they differ in color and amount of ink, quality of impression, kind of paper, etc.'[28]

This 'indifference' towards the individual piece and the uniqueness of art has often caused Duchamp to be accused of lacking interest. Although Duchamp was extremely interested precisely in the 'peculiarity of reproduction', as Didi-Huberman emphasizes, i.e., in 'the mutually transformative relation between the *series* (the family) and *singularity* (the subject)'. This relation can not be covered by the dual concepts genuine/false, original/copy, individual piece/series, but integrates these oppositions into a dialectic third term, 'which connects the same kind with the different and the different with the same kind.'[29]

The 'minute discrepancies', that Goodman attempts to remove by magic from his theory on the relation of autography and allography, this difference, particularly if it is in no way visible, tangible or otherwise perceptible any more, is given by Duchamp a technical term dialectically implicating imprint and trace with one another, as it 'in the play of imprint, makes of the reproductive operation, a differential operation, an operation of divergence'. This divergence, or difference, Duchamp calls: '*infra-mince*': 'gossamer', 'infra-thin':

*Séparation infra-mince / 2 formes embouties dans / le même moule ( ?) diffèrent / entre elles / d'une valeur séparative infra / mince – / Tous les 'identiques' aussi / identiques qu'ils soient, (et / plus ils sont identiques) se / rapprochent de cette / différence séparative infra / mince.*

Infra-thin separation / 2 forms cast in / the same mould (?) differ / from each another / by an infra thin separative / value – / All 'identicals' as / identical as they may be (and / the more identical they are) / move towards this / infra-thin, separative / difference.

Séparation; infra - mince.

2 formes emboutties dans
le même Émoulez (?) différent
~~fixe def mutte~~ entre elle
d'une valeur séparative infra
mince —
Toutes les "identiques" aussi
identiques qu'ils soient, (et
plus ils sont identiques) se
rapprochent de cette
différence de séparative infra
mince.
Deux hommes ne sont
pas un exemple d'identité
et s'éloignent au contraire
d'une différence évaluable
infra mince — mais

A note written on 29 July 1937 by Marcel Duchamp.

Such a difference that makes no perceptible difference, Jacques Derrida calls *différant*, as it 'does not depend on any sensible plenitude, audible or visible, phonic or graphic; it is (pure) trace'.[30] Duchamp's infra-thin divergence is such a *différant*, but one which is conditioned in its basic technical and material properties, since the tangible precision in the meeting of form and imprint is produced *by touch*, by the (as in the *Female Fig leaf*) 'gossamer clasping, even penetrating the body' in the meeting of *moule* (in the feminine: female genitals) and *moule* (in the masculine: mould).[31] The infra-thin difference between two imprints of the same trace is conditioned by its material production to be as thin as, if you like, the difference between the very thin hairline *ce* in Mercator's letter square, which is the thinnest line, the *linea tenuissima*, and the fabulous diagonal *cb*, which is thinner than the thinnest line: the *linea definite tenuissima*. This difference is in the realm of the barely measurable, nevertheless it is of a – literally – 'unheard-of' effectiveness.

## A Nearness, however distant

The magic of such a 'gossamer touch' did not go unnoticed by Benjamin. Although in his essay on the work of art he regrets the disappearance of aura by reason of the mechanical processes of reproduction, one notices again and again in his writing something like a 'remainder' of aura that can not be appropriated, something actual in the sense of a becoming visible of something invisible.[32] For example in the third chapter of his essay on the work of art, he composes an image with which he develops the concept of the 'aura of natural objects': 'If, while resting on a summer afternoon, you follow with your eyes a mountain range on the horizon or a branch which casts its shadow over you, you experience [*breathe*] the aura of those mountains, of that branch.' ['das heisst, die Aura dieser Berge, dieses Zweiges *atmen*.'] It is just this 'natural' – or as one might say in Greek, 'physical' – aura that presupposes a final and totally irreducible deictic here and now, this aura related to a positive presence, that Benjamin then defines expressing himself in a paradoxical fashion 'as the unique phenomenon *of a distance, however close it may be*'.[33]

This idiosyncratic way of putting it turns up once more word for word in Benjamin's 'A Small History of Photography', this time while looking at Atget's Paris photographs in the passage where Benjamin asks: 'What is aura, actually? *A strange weave of space and time*: the unique appearance or semblance of distance, no matter how close the object may be'. ['*Ein sonderbares Gespinst von Raum und Zeit: einmalige Erscheinung einer Ferne, so nah sie sein mag*'] There follows the same impression of a summer afternoon: 'While resting on a summer's noon, to trace a range of mountains on the horizon, or a branch that throws its shadow on the observer', and this time Benjamin adds: 'until the moment or the hour became part of their appearance', only to extend the coda of the sentence: ' – that is what it means to *breathe* the aura of those mountains, that branch'.[34] Here Benjamin conceives of the aura as a temporal paradox: the words 'until the moment or the hour became part of their appearance' after all presuppose that this phenomenon in a temporal Before 'was not quite present', that a deferral has taken place, or had to take place in order for the moment to acquire aura.

Such an anachronistic structure is also attributed by Duchamp to the work of art when he proclaims: 'Appearance / Similarity // The same (serial product) // practical approximation to similarity. Within time the same object after an interval of 1 second is not the same.'[35] And also in the domain of the spatial or the tangible, aura is caught by deferral, because, like the shadow of Dibutadis's beloved, 'by the skin of touch'[36] it blazes its trace [*Spur*] as feeling [*Gespür*]. It cannot be emphasized enough that in Greek αὐρα means 'breath', and in occult contexts it also refers to 'fluidum', the 'effect', emanating from a person or a thing and creating a certain atmosphere. To 'breathe' this 'fluidum' remains for Benjamin within the realm of supernatural (or mystical) possibilities. The aura is forever captured by the idea of deferral and in the process of approximation, touch always remains *infra-thin*: a hair's breadth, perhaps a hairline between its existence and its appearance. This 'almost-touching' can, if you like, be called *infra-mince* in Duchamp's sense, since: 'The possible is an infra-mince.'[37]

Just as the imprint needs the nearness of touch, a skin-tight wrapping or clasping that must be an infra-thin distance between mould and imprint in order that the imprint resembles the mould, it also presupposes the absence, as Didi-Huberman illustrates:

In order that a footprint arises, that the process takes place, the foot must sink into the sand, the walker must be *there*, in the exact spot where he leaves his trace. Yet in order that the imprint *appears* as a result, the foot must be lifted, separate itself from the sand and move away, in order to produce other imprints elsewhere; the walker is then obviously *no longer there*.

The imprint is an indexical sign in Peirce's sense but it reserves the touch itself for the observer for whom only the imprint becomes a sign. It only becomes visible and a *trace*able aura by reason of the absence of the walker, or in response to Benjamin's formulation: only when its *nearness is so distant*.[38]

In *The Arcades Project* Benjamin once more plays with the concepts of trace and aura, pushing them to the extreme:

Trace and aura. The trace is appearance of a nearness, however far removed the thing left behind it may be. The aura is appearance of a distance, however close the thing that calls it forth. In the trace, we gain possession of the thing; in the aura, it takes possession of us.[39]

In this note, Benjamin is in fact claiming, as Didi-Huberman remarks, an 'opposition between trace and aura', an opposition that nothing can resolve. This opposition is, however, neither final nor positively logical (and it is disappointing that Didi-Huberman, who is otherwise highly sensitive to the dialectical structure of the concept of aura, has missed it here), because Benjamin embeds the dual concept by means of chiastically entangled parataxes within a grammatical embracement in which the two oppositions struggling to escape one another 'almost' touch. The touch of the auratic moment is for ever conceivable in this 'almost', just as Dibutadis's wand *almost* touches the loved-one – his shadow; at the moment in which she paints the line of the contours of the shadow with the wand on the wall, she anticipates his absence, his future, his death. In this movement of deferral the trace *with*draws from handwriting and at the same time draws *onward*.[40]

With the polygraph we reach the interface from which the *tour d'horizon* of the history of handwriting in the *Exergue* of this book took off. Here we encounter anew the prehistoric handprint and meet up with it in the age of electronic media as a quotation in the form of contact with a touch screen, 'almost' touching the first work of the hand in the Gargas caves. Once again: 'this almost [of touch] is not nothing: it is technology itself that interferes', writes Didi-Huberman. For Benjamin too, the 'appearance of aura' depends on 'technical considerations'.[41] In technology itself, writing slate, mystic writing pad and tablet-PC all relate one with another. Thus it becomes manifest: the individual line that draws *onward* and *with*draws, the *trace* of handwriting forms a preposterously winding line, a *flowing* 'stroke' – following Benjamin – whose 'tiny spark of contingency, of the Here and Now'[42] is im*printed* thousandfold in the medial prisma as a duplication of that which counts as unified and inseparable. Jefferson's polygraph illustrates this double take forcefully. And at the same time it shows that the structure of all writing is always already polygraphematic.

The *mise-en-abîme* of this interface where the past can appear near, the present far, is the ground, or the abyss of media technology, into which I shall be 'drilling down deep' in the second part of the book: through the screen saver, the diaries of Anne Frank and the forged Hitler diaries in the archive and in the museum, continuing through the perhaps most somatic form of handwriting there is – tattooing – and finally graffiti. All of them are detailed individual case studies in which I shall throw light on the way institutional, technological and digital environments 'remediate' handwriting and the way handwriting for its part affects the central inscription technologies of the new media.

Paradoxically, precisely what looks like the greatest threat to handwriting – electricity – turns out then to be the main vehicle of remediation. Thus the new media do not 'erase' handwriting, or rob it of its aura, but these 'erasures' – such as etching, photography, film, xerography and the digital media – serve to restore handwriting, as a repetition. The motor driving the process of remediation is the echo – in the sense of duplication, copying, imitation and quotation – of the respective methods of articulation of the specific media through other media. They provide us with the trace of handwriting which they present also and precisely as imprint and offer us Benjamin's aura as that 'strange weave of space and time: the unique appearance or semblance of distance, no matter how close the object may be'.[43]

INCIPIT LIBER

## Before a Hand

According to the *Didascalocophus* (1680) by Georges Dalgarno
(1626–1687), the *hand*book for the 'the deaf and dumb mans tutor' –
today we would indeed object immediately that people with hearing
difficulties are neither 'dumb' nor 'speechless', but this is literally
what Dalgarno calls them – according to this *hand*book 'handwriting' means writing *with one's hands*. And that is with both hands.
With the index finger of the right hand the 'speaker' touches a particular place on the left hand that is dedicated to a letter. The finger
tips of the left hand are reserved for the vowels; these are indicated
with the right index finger. The consonant letters meanwhile are
located on the palm of the left hand and are indicated by the right
thumb.[1] For practice, the speaker at first wears for some time a glove
on which the letters are written until he is finally able to find them
invisibly on the bare skin. The left hand functions for him as a typewriter; with the right hand he types out pre-defined keys.

   In the course of this 'writing technique' the body is its own
writing instrument. Accordingly, writing is wherever the body is.
Handwriting here appears as a practice that remains for ever inseparable from the writer's hands. It remains a gesture or performance
without ever remaining so. Constantly in the process of being written
and yet forever unwritten. Like speech, Dalgarno's handwriting only
resounds in the moment of its performance; once articulated, it has
already ceased. And even though the principle of this writing for the
deaf is phonetic, it itself remains unheard. It does not hear itself speak
and does not need to observe itself in the act of writing. Its sense is
touch. This handwriting is based on a self-affection, since writing
it presupposes that the writer *feels herself* and by *touching herself*,
she merges sense and presence into an inseparable unity.

   In order to be able to write like this, Dalgarno's handwriting
divides the body into two hands with their own specific remit:
respectively a left hand and a right hand, a writing instrument that
writes and a writing surface that 'reads' by registering the letters
without ever registering them – like an 'archiviolitic' memory: every
act of writing is at once an act of erasure.

   What was there *before* Dalgarno's hand, what was there before
its gesture? *Before* the hand, there must have been writing – the

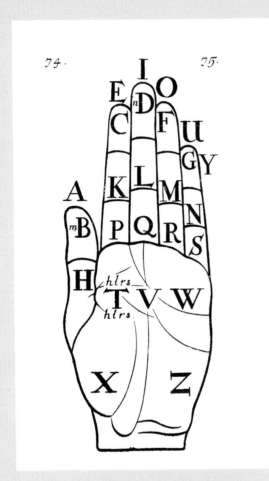

A 'speech glove', from
*Didascalocophus, or
The Deaf and Dumb
Man's Tutor* (1680) by
the Scottish academic
George Dalgarno.

alphabet – the letters of which the hand indicates in the gesture of demonstrating. Before writing, however, was the hand which formed the letters in the movement of its kinetic system, those first letters that first heralded the birth of the hand.

# 5 The Screen Saver: Screen-Writing and Hand-Saving

In this way 'tying-to-celestial bodies' became a permanent institution continuing to the present day and led to further consequences, particularly the 'writing-down-system' . . .

Daniel Paul Schreber, *Memoirs of my Nervous Illness*[1]

I have found a method for an ideal fountain pen, and therefore I will earn a lot of money, only I will ask for a patent because I want to have a lot of money. I know the defects of pens, and therefore when I go to America, I will take out a patent . . .

I want to write and think of other things. I write one thing and think of another. I am God in man. I am what Christ felt. I am Buddha.

. . . I have told my wife that I have invented a pen that will bring me a lot of money,

. . . I showed her a pen and a pencil in order to explain to her the pen I have just invented

. . . The pen will be called God. I want to be called God, and not Nijinsky, and will therefore ask for this pen to be called God.

Vaslav Nijinsky, *The Diary of Vaslav Nijinsky*[2]

## 'Sports'

It is a peculiar writing instrument, the 'Sports' screen saver on the Microsoft operating system Windows '98. A screen acts as a writing surface, as is normal in the age of zeros and ones, and the writing instrument is a keyboard. However, *no hand* is used to write with: neither the left nor the right nor both together, but writing appears only when for a time *no mani*pulation of the interfaces has taken place: neither by pressing a key nor by moving the mouse. Absolutely no movement. Then suddenly the magic takes off:

The monitor screen is transformed into a marbled surface: a slate. *Ping* – an invisible piece of chalk pops up on the slate, a line is drawn – *whoosh*: a curve appears, finally becoming a complete circle. A moment's silence and then again: *ping – whoosh*. A second circle appears on the right next to the first one. Followed by a third. Then in the second line above the first, short straight lines are drawn forming x's: *whoosh-whoosh*, then once again following the same rhythm: *whoosh-whoosh*. Then, more slowly, arrows are drawn. Gradually the arrows push the circles of the lower lines upwards; following the order of their appearance the lower circles disappear and are replaced in the top line by new circles. In this, the arrows seem to act as vehicles for them, while the x's give them the substance. Then suddenly all the signs disappear from the screen apart from one last arrow pulling two more x's after it, before the writing vanishes completely. Finally, a ball bounces along from the left side of the screen; it must have been drawn beyond the edge of the slate and is now dribbled across the screen from left to right.

Now the slate is empty. Nothing happens for a short while. Then the magical operation of writing and erasure begins all over again. The loop only comes to an end when the visible, embodied writer *outside* the screen makes herself known via the interface by communicating a command to the computer.

## Dust-free, not leaving any remainder behind

It has often been claimed that writing at the beginning of the twenty-first century is a disembodied activity, dividing paper off from the hand, writing from the body. The main inscription technologies of writing on-screen – this has been widely discussed in the literature on hyper-text of the first and the second generation – highlight, along with simultaneity, discontinuity, rhizomatic structure, multilinearity and multivocality in the sense of a 'dividualized' authorship and reader-ship in general, liberation from the bother of all physical writing.[3] Still more radical than any electronic hypertext, the screen saver proclaims the disembodiment of writing: its writing subject is a processor which emphatically turns the non-presence of the body into the basic precon-dition of its operation.

Paradoxically, in this process disembodiment is produced by a decidedly physical scenario of handwriting. Writing on screen is *like* writing on a slate: in real time, stroke by stroke in a temporal contin-uum corresponding to the drawing of the line *as if by hand*. As with genuine handwriting, there arise small irregularities in the thickness of the line and the shape of the signs. In addition, the writing surface is covered with small white spots resembling chalk-dust, arising as a material remainder of the application and rubbing-out of the chalk on the slate. The similarity to physical handwriting is enacted in a decid-edly tactile manner as the contact of chalk and writing surface, pro-ducing sounds that the listener fears might at any moment turn into a high-pitched screech. In addition, fingerprints are regularly distributed over the writing surface: signs left by a mysterious presence traceable only by dactyloscopic evidence.

What is remarkable about the inscription technologies of 'Sports', then, is the fact that the act of writing does not share in the technical euphoria of its digital matrix, like the perfectly animated 3-D screen savers capable of utilizing the possibilities of the medium as true *hyper-media* in such a way that the medium itself behind them becomes invis-ible.[4] 'Sports' meanwhile presents itself as being rather atavistic from the technological point of view: instead of spectacular sci-fi worlds it enacts the old-fashioned technologies of handwriting. And it does this even in one of its '*urforms*' as in the earliest stages of learning the abc at infants' school. Its writing materials are chalk and slate: too slow, too exception-al, too temporary and ephemeral and thus too expensive compared with modern and efficient methods of writing on-screen.

The 'real' of this handwriting is, however, purely symbolical, pure simulation, and this is true of the way that the hypermediality of the

computer becomes visible with every stroke of writing. The small irregularities of the *ductus* of writing, of what Benjamin calls this 'tiny
spark of contingency', that is, accidental (*Winziges Fünkchen Zufall*),
turn out to be totally non-accidental as they are carried out over and
over again in an infinite loop in the form of precisely that irregularity.
The writing dissolves just as it came: it is not erased by any hand; it
vanishes without leaving any clouds of chalk or marks on the slate
and without the slightest trace at all. This is not handwriting, but
remediated handwriting. It is written as what N. Katherine Hayles calls
a technotext, as a commentary or a reflection on encapsulation or the
'quotation' of the real in the symbolical. Because a 'technotext' in
Hayles's sense 'interrogates the inscription technology that produces it,
it mobilizes reflexive loops between its imaginative world and the
material apparatus embodying that creation as a physical presence'.[5]

These 'reflexive loops' between the inside of the computer and the
surface of the screen function as it were as quotation marks; they mark
the threshold of the *mise-en-abîme*, and in so doing they allow one to
stare into the abyss of the system, dividing the physical user outside of
the computer from the disembodied writer of the digital handwriting.
They hold out the promise of possible contact between the world of
simulated handwriting and the world of real handwriting: connections
that can not be set up. Even if the writing in the screen saver causes dust
and screeches as on the blackboard in a classroom, nevertheless it is free
of dust and screeches, not leaving any remainder behind.

## Technotext

If the screen saver encapsulates (or even: quotes and remediates) handwriting as a medium within the medium, it does not simply present
itself as a medium but as a medium 'on a higher level': as a 'hypermedium' in the sense described by Bolter and Grusin. As a medium,
however, the screen saver paradoxically enough neither communicates
anything nor stores anything, nor does it transmit or process data. A
signing apparatus is at work here producing signs that neither designate anything nor communicate anything; they do not originate with
any sender and are not addressed to any receiver. The signs of circles
and crosses neither represent nor express anything; except that they

reflect in all cases their operativity as empty signifiers. The programming of this strange writing machine has no aim and does nothing; the screen saver does not even 'save' the screen any more in the sense that earlier CRT-screens were protected from phosphor burning by screen savers during ongoing frozen images on the screen.[6] If screen savers save anything at all, then it is not the screen but the writer's hand, allowing it rest and recreation in the breaks from work. The best case scenario is to see 'Sports' in the same light as one watches sports on television in the worst case scenario: motionless, dumbstruck as if paralysed, hypnotised. Only when the game is over does the observer's body bestir itself once more. Like no other medium, screen savers mark gaps without content. They find their writing surfaces in the interstices, in passivity and lethargy, in which they establish their independence as a medium of self-inscription.

And yet the screen saver does not do nothing. Even if it neither stores nor transmits nor processes data, nevertheless at the same time it persistently communicates its own technical conditioning as a technotext. Because what it does is nothing less than alternating the evocation and erasure of signs and sign-users. And by doing this, it 'produces' the user; it creates, even 'performs' her or him. In terms of our concept of the relation of handwriting and writer, this act of creation is naturally not without its problems, as I shall show more precisely later on in comparing it with other, no less mysterious or even mystic acts of writing.

## Writing at the start of the twenty-first century

Handwriting and computer screen, one seen as a somatic, the other as a technical way of writing, seem not to tolerate one another at all. This is the line also argued for example by Claus Pias in his article 'Digital Secretaries: 1968, 1978, 1998', in which he reviews three milestones in the history of digital apparatuses. 1998 is just such a date. In that year not only did Microsoft introduce the 'Sports' screen saver along with the update of their Windows operating system, but, and this is what Pias is concerned with, in the same year the competitor organization Apple suspended the development of its digital handwriting technology which was almost equally as futile as the Microsoft screen saver, i.e. the so-called Newton. Newton was a Personal Digital Assistant (PDA): as Pias describes it, a 'pen computer in a pocket calendar format', the key feature of which is handwriting recognition. And this is where Pias sees the conceptual impossibility for the success of Newton:

> An entry in *Newton* is recognized by a space, the last surface to be touched is then framed as an image and matched in a statistical 'comparative survey' with stored proto-images. An 'E' thus consists of three strokes that are recognized by the software as more than just three strokes and are combined into an actual 'shape', then to be juxtaposed in the computer with other, virtual shapes. The interrogation of the user by the software thus throws up 'shapes' and sometimes negative returns. The recognition of letters is based then on a kind of 'identikit' or composite Photo-Fit picture forming the search criteria for a data bank of images of the usual suspects.[7]

In other words, the principle of digital handwriting recognition is based, as in the case of human reading, on the recognition of shapes which *look like* the samples of handwriting stored in the data bank of the computer. Handwriting is thus scanned as an image and recognized on the basis of iconic *similarity*, as the same or at least similar copies of the same shape. However, because the individual *ductus* of someone's handwriting (at least in the sense of the handwriting of an 'author' with characteristic subject possibilities that Pias rightly distinguishes from the subject-less handwriting of a secretary) proves to be too irregular, Newton's recognition of handwriting can not work. According to Pias, Newton belongs to the realm of the secretarial and is geared to normalization instead of individualization.[8]

On the other hand, Pias claims, Palm works according to a completely different principle, in which one likewise writes with a pen on a touch-sensitive panel. Unlike Newton, Palm does not work with images, but rather with movements, and this according to Pias is its key to success:

> Every letter is drawn with one stroke, produced as one continuous flow of movement and ending with the lifting of the pen.

It is not the totality of a sum of the parts that is observed from a temporal distance but an ongoing movement is recognized by tracking. One is not dealing with the statistics of pixel distribution but with the recognition of movements in the very act of their completion. In so doing, it is necessary to transcribe from the relevant pixels onto Bézier curves, or to put it more mathematically: from a number of points in a grid . . . onto a continuous function . . .[9]

With this comparison between Apple and Palm, Pias identifies in the scope of the recognition of writing two basic operations of handwriting. If the recognition of handwriting is solely concentrated on the principle of similarity (as in the case of Newton), handwriting therefore being conceived of as the representation of a *similarity*, the program threatens to be derailed by the abnormalities of an individual *ductus* of writing. Consequently, the writing recognition program that will win out is the one which does not conceive of handwriting as a (visual) image (or representation) but as a *tactile* (or as Pias emphasizes: *cybernetic*) *movement*, i.e. that which I referred to in dealing with Didi-Huberman as an action (*Hand*lung), in the sense of a gesture of touching: a *ductus* which, as Pias himself writes, blazes a trail for its trace 'in the very act of completion', in other words, handwriting conceived of as an event. In this, imprint and trace would be mutually separated for good.

When one looks closely at the 'manual of penmanship' of Palm, however, Pias' analysis proves to be questionable even if it refers to no less an authority than to the truth of mathematical formulae. The software that Palm calls 'Graffiti' (although it does not either scrape or gouge but instead produces rapid 'onscriptions' – I shall go into this in more detail at the end of the book) operates with reduced neographs, derivatives of letters drawn from the 'genuine' full forms of the letters just as the hieratic cursive script was derived from hieroglyphics. The simplification of the forms, however, does not primarily act as an improvement to writing capability but instead is intended to prevent predictable lacks of distinctiveness and possibilities of confusion with other letters. Unlike typewriting, the writing recognition program prefers minuscules to majuscules, since the latter can be done in one

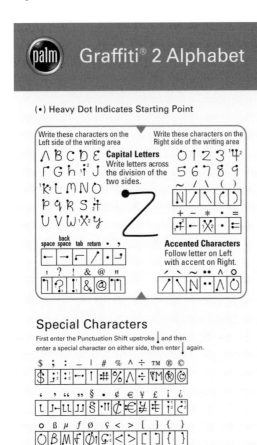

Writing characters of the 'Graffiti' Palm OS writing recognition program.

'Tips & Tricks' on the 'Graffiti' Palm OS program.

stroke. Following the principle of one-stroke motion, the A lacks a cross stroke, the F a second coda stroke, and the E is done like an epsilon minuscule. The only ones combined are I (to be done with a precise dot!), K, T (the cross stroke is not to be placed on the hasta but crosses it) and X.

As with the typewriter one can shift between majuscules and minuscules. In this, the topography of the writing pad acts as a shift key: signs written on the left are registered by the system as minuscules, those written in the middle as majuscules. The 'Tips & Tricks' supplied with Palm recommend one to write carefully with large, straight characters, with long ascenders and descenders: if the downstroke of the

## TIPS & TRICKS

(1) $\boxed{C}$ $\boxed{C}$   Larger characters are more easily recognized than small characters.

(2) $\boxed{N}$ $\boxed{N}$   Write parallel to the sides of the screen, not on a slant.

(3) $U = u$   $V = v$   Write the letter "u" with a tail at the end of upstroke to avoid writing a "v".

(4) $h = h$   $h = n$   Write the letter "h" with a long vertical stroke to avoid making an "n".

(5) $I + \langle = k$   Multi-stroke characters ("i", "k", "t" and "x") are not complete until both strokes are entered. The character will be converted to the multi-stroke character after the second stroke.

(6) $I \leftarrow = I$ (space)   $\not{t} = t$   When writing a "space" after an "L" do not cross the space stroke with the "L" stroke to avoid writing a "t".

(7) Capitalization
Some fields automatically begin with a capital letter. Capitals are also automatic at the start of a new sentence. To cancel automatic capitalization, enter the Punctuation Shift twice.

'U' is missing, it is recognized as a 'V', if the coda of the T does not cross the hasta, it results in a space.

Altogether these writing instructions already display a high degree of attention to the kinetic interplay of hasta and coda elements; they concentrate, as Pias argues, on the pathways of movement in writing. The essential difference between Newton and Palm is, however, not to be found in the distinction between the principle of similarity (imprint) and movement (trace), as Pias claims when he writes that

> the tracking (of *Palm*) with a view to a result does not distinguish between original image [*Urbild*], copy [*Nachbild*] and similarity, but it tracks whether the user's hand still moves within the lower and upper normal borders of a specific way of proceeding.[10]

Instead, both technologies are equally based on the *similarity of processes of movement* and make the interweaving of pairs of opposites the basis of their recognition of writing. The true difference is to be found in the fact that Newton ambitiously collects the already 'abnormal' ways of writing of its user in their whole variety and complexity as a model [*Vorbild*] and a copy [*Nachbild*], whereas Palm takes the definition of ideal types into its own *hands*, by creating a repertoire of forms that are certain not to be confused.[11] Palm operates *pre*scriptively; Newton, on the other hand, *de*scriptively as it takes the principle of iteration into consideration (in its double meaning of *repetition* and of *otherness*). It is precisely this that creates difficulties for the machine.[12]

## Writing at the start of the twentieth century

Handwriting did not start to be measured and quantified only with the arrival of digital media. Just as Gerardus Mercator carried out his calculations of the angles of inclination and the corresponding thickness of strokes using his geometric letter square, which was precise but nevertheless remained static, thus seeing handwriting as the 'end product' of a kinetic program, in the same way, after the technical innovations of electricity and photography, scientists and anthropologists became interested in methods of measurement in the observation of movement itself. The exact calculation of ephemeral movement, nowadays achieving extreme precision in digital technology, took a long time to develop. In the nineteenth century it was mainly studied by medical scientists of nervous diseases and psychiatrists: for example the university professor, military doctor and the founder of the theory of criminal traits Cesare Lombroso (1836–1909) in Turin, the cognitive psychologist Alfred Binet (1857–1911) in the Hospital of la Salpêtrière in Paris, in Germany the staff doctor Alfred Goldscheider and the psychiatrist Emil Kraepelin. However varied their epistemic approaches and investigations were, they were united in their common interest in handwriting. Lombroso summarizes this in his *Handbook of Graphology*:

> Handwriting offers . . . the highly important advantage that, while other movements vanish as soon as they have been carried out, or can only be captured with sensitive instruments, it remains permanently fixed on the paper from its inception. When a person writes, then they are totally absorbed in their pen, and thus also in their hand, forming the instrument of communication, so that, if the word is the momentary revelation of thought, writing represents just as an immediate if not even faster transmission of the same.[13]

With the 'sensitive measuring instruments' addressed by Lombroso here we are talking about mechanical and electric apparatuses that engineers and instrument builders invented as an aid in neurology and psychophysiology making the dynamics of the sequence of movement in writing precisely measurable. Amongst these are such curiosities as Burckhardt's miograph that translated the activity of tension in groups of muscles into graphic lines, admittedly not representing letters but nevertheless to a certain extent something like handwriting.[14] The psychiatrist Emil Kraepelin meanwhile worked with so-called writing scales, an instrument that registers and records the pressure applied by the pen in writing on the writing surface.[15]

Alfred Binet and Jules Courtier specialized in looking more closely at the kinetic program of handwriting in relation to the rate of writing. Like Eadweard Muybridge, who in the 1870s arrested the sequences of movement of galloping horses and dancers by the use of serial chrono-photography, in a similar manner Binet and Courtier sought for a technical process for capturing the movement of handwriting. And they found it in Edison's electric pen which, as I described in the chapter on 'Writing and Technology', was actually conceived as a technology of reproduction: fitted with an electrically driven needle moving up and down approximately one millimetre about eleven thousand times a minute, the electric pen pricks tiny perforations in a sheet of paper coated with wax. The holes are designed to be filled with ink in the gravure process and to release this later in printing. Binet and Courtier used the perforations to read off the rate of writing from the distance between the holes; they thus decomposed the drawn trace of the line into individual dotted holes or needle prints. Their observations are hardly surprising; every car driver will know from experience that 1. the longer the line, the more rapid the *ductus*, 2. at the start and the end of a move-ment the rate of writing is subject to delay, 3. one moves from left to right more rapidly than from right to left, 4. difficult lines are drawn more slowly and 5. changes of direction lead to delay.[16]

Binet and Courtier carried out their experiments (like their German colleagues) at the start of the 1890s, however, not just on 'normal writing', but by preference also on '*écriture pathologique*' in cases of hysteria, Graves' disease, Huntington's disease (chorea), shaking palsy (*paralysie agitante*), amongst other reasons for the benefit of the legend-ary Jean-Martin Charcot in the neurological department of the women's hospital of la Salpêtrière in Paris.[17]

Like Binet and Courtier, Lombroso was also interested in the anomalies of handwriting but he attempted as early as in *L'uomo delinquente* to make use of them for a biometrical definition of the so-called criminal type. In his graphology he concentrated on '[p]articular signs in writing', in order to work out the 'qualities of individuals and their characteristics'. In so doing, he devotes the first part of his study to the 'writing of normal people', the second by contrast to the 'writing of abnormal people', categorized by him into the 'sick', the 'mad', the 'geniuses', the 'criminals' (with several facsimiles of criminals' handwriting), and – how could it be otherwise – the 'hypnotized', amongst whom female hysterics, as is well known, proved themselves to be particularly gifted.[18]

Generally in the discourses of philosophy, medicine and anthropology at the start of the twentieth century, handwriting is treated as a source of highly significant symptoms. Charged with the category of the subject as a unique individual that is revealed in the deviation of their writing from the standardizations of mechanical writing and the collectivism of writing instruction at school, in the scriptorium and in official use, handwriting is stylized into a sure and measurable indicator of anomaly and individuality as such. A precursor of graphology was (after Camillo Baldo, Bologna 1622) Johann Kaspar Lavater (1741–1801), who exchanged silhouettes with Goethe, in order to draw conclusions on the basis of the shapes of the heads portrayed on their character that he then also sought to identify in his 'Physiognomic Fragments towards the Promotion of the Knowledge of Human Nature and Philanthropy' through the interpretation of handwriting. It is not accidental that graphology, arising in parallel with the typewriter in the second half of the nineteenth century, becomes very popular with a real flood of foundations of institutes, scientific journals and studies on handwriting, such as the 'Chirogrammatomantie' (1862) by Adolf Henze, the 'System of Graphology' (1875) by Jean-Hippolyte Michon, the works of Jules Crépieux-Jamin, Laura von Albertini (alias L. Meyer), Hans Hinrich Busse and others, culminating in the relevant handbook by Ludwig Klages, *Handschrift und Charakter* (1917) in which the 'movement of expression' of handwriting becomes the basis of graphological diagnostics.[19]

If 'stylus' etymologically indicates a pen, then the metonymic shift from writing instrument to individual writing style and in its extension

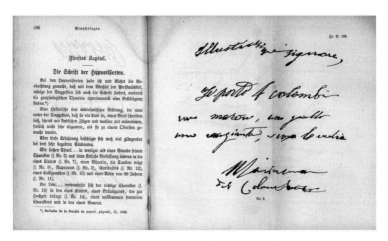

Handwriting by hypnotized hysterics examined by Cesare Lombroso.

to a generalized personal 'style' results from the idea that handwriting, at least when writing freely and without constraint, is the expression of one's character. Making these invisible, psychic characteristics visible and readable through their physical traces was and is the central concern of graphology; beyond that, measuring them scientifically by means of mechanical, electric or electronic apparatuses resembles the Faustian wager of making thought itself capable of being observed, archived and administered and thus of being manipulated.

It is no accident that graphology was always in addition a 'joined discourse' with criminology, that new discipline that at the end of the nineteenth century made use of the anthropometric methods of Francis Galton, the 'discoverer' of the fingerprint, for the purposes of forensic investigation.[20] In this specialism, one does not profile the personality of the writer on the basis of their handwriting but attributes the handwritten 'characters', on the basis of the statistical correspondence of so-called micro-characteristics, to comparative specimens of handwriting from the hand of an identifiable originator. 'Character' means literally 'engraving' (from χαράσσειν, kharassein: scrape, dig) and thus combines the archaic gesture of writing by scoring with a stylus with the idea of the relief and the imprint capable of continually producing new casts from the same mould of a 'character' which as serial products are as it were identical yet infra-thinly different. Today, biometric scans of handwriting, fingerprints, iris, voice, facial physiognomy and DNA evidence are admissible in court because they are considered to be unmistakable and unfalsifiable indicators of identity, reliable clues, or indices on the basis of which criminal subjects can be identified. They gain their force as evidence from the fact that the variations in the correspondence between the specimens for comparison are so wafer-thin, or infra-thin, that they are statistically negligible.

What the experiments with miograph and writing scales showed at the time – as Armin Schäfer argues in his discourse analysis – is that handwriting does not depend exclusively on the organ producing it: the hand. Nor is handwriting a pure product of the brain, as the graphologists had concluded from the fact that the writing of character still retains its basic features when writing with the foot or the mouth. And thirdly, the movements of writing are also not controlled by the eye alone – as the research by Alfred Goldscheider established beyond all doubt – since a practised writer can still go through the motoric process of writing blindfold. Instead, hand and brain prove to be parts of a complex writing system whose basic movement Schäfer translates into the terminology of media studies as 'feedback and systemic control',[21] so disproving the historic Aristotelian theory of a monocausal relation of hand and thought.

## On Ballgames

Feedback and systemic control are to a certain extent also the basic principles of ballgames. Extremely complex sequences of movement take place through the interaction of ball and player. They are controlled by means of highly sensitive sensors that are simultaneously a condition for the game and also at the same time carry it into effect, thus closely associating perception and action. In this context and particularly in relation to the 'Sports' screen saver, a late medieval theological treatise using the example of a ballgame which exemplifies the connection of hand and brain, or hand and thought – or in the language of fifteenth-century theologians, hand and 'will' in the sense of a 'free', human will derived from the will of God – appears interesting: the *Dialogus de ludo globi/Dialogue on the Globe Game* (1463) by Nicholas of Cusa (1401–1464).[22]

In this dialogue – in the interplay between several interlocutors, all young Bavarian princes – Cardinal Nicholas of Cusa uses the drama of the ballgame as a conceptual metaphor, by means of which he approaches difficult philosophical problems. In his first dialogue with Johannes, the young Duke of Bavaria, he describes the toy of the globe game as a wooden ball which 'through the art of the wood turner acquired a more or less concave, hemispherical shape', owing to which it does not roll straight ahead but makes a movement that is 'snail-shaped or spiralling or tightly curving'. The line that the wooden ball describes in rolling will thus be neither 'quite straight' nor 'quite curved . . . having, like the circumference in a circle, equal distance from its centre'. The *ductus* of the line will always be variable even if it is described by one and the same globe and in fact even when the globe is propelled by the same player, the reason being, the cardinal argues: 'that it is always propelled in a different way':

> If someone throws the globe, he does not hold it one time exactly as he holds it another time, as much as he does not dispatch it or place it on a level plane in the same way or drive it with the same force. Since it is not possible for something to happen twice in the same way.[23]

As in the case of Nicholas of Cusa's globe game, the sequence of movement in writing does not occur twice in the same way. As in the ballgame, the manoeuvres in writing are carried out according to rules that are discrete and unchangeable, and yet the writing game can be played in a variety of ways and these can vary infinitely within pre-defined limits – defined by the writing recognition programs as more or less tightly drawn areas of tolerance. At best, printers and typewriters can carry out one and the same preposterous 'arc' over and over again in the same way. In the case of handwriting by contrast, it can not happen that a stroke of the pen, a signature, occurs identically twice.[24]

To make Nicholas' ball nevertheless move twice in the same, unique, snail-like, spiralling or tightly curving trajectory, thus to repeat the singular curved movement *identically* as to its arc, it would have to be propelled by an extraordinary *ductus*, one which would be able to repeat serially, not the standard form, but the deviation from the same. This is exactly the *ductus* generated by the 'Sports' screen saver.

## Italicizing the dot

The *ductus* of writing in the screen saver is a little 'buckled' or uneven; like 'real' handwriting it does not run quite straight. The signs display the somatic traces that lead to the roundness of the circle not being quite round, the vertical strokes of the arrows not being completely vertical, the diagonal strokes of the crosses not being perfectly angled; even the application of the chalk and its adhesion on the writing surface have positively physical material qualities. When one looks closely it is revealed that the *ductus* of writing is made up of two movements: first the initial moment, in which the chalk hits the board and, by touching it, produces a dot; this movement is audibly accompanied by a *ping*. Then there follows the drawing of the line describing an arc and completed as a circle: *whoosh*. In the Palm writing program 'Graffiti', this two-stage movement of writing is unambiguously marked: 'heavy dot indicates starting point'.

It is not just in the case of electronic writing instruments that the composition of the *ductus* of writing out of a point and a stroke is decisive, but it is to a certain extent the basic gesture of any writing: whether one is writing 'by incision' as in cuneiform script where the stylus first scores a triangular point resembling the head of a nail in the soft clay and then draws the shaft of the nail forming a stroke, or one is writing 'cursorily' as with a calamus on papyrus or with a quill on parchment, the writing pen is always brought from a distance into proximity with the writing surface until it finally touches. In so doing, the point has been the opponent of the line from the start. In the seventh and eighth centuries Irish monks scored the *Interpunctum* (from *interpungere*, score inbetween) into the parchment *between* the linguistic segments and thereby interrupted the *scriptura continua* that had fluidized writing into a continual flow since late antiquity.[25]

Whether as a stop sign or an initial sign, the point or the dot nevertheless can – Kraepelin's experiments have measured this exactly on the writing scales – be carried out with more or less pressure; the gesture of the point offers no other kinetic possibilities. A truly comprehensive spectrum of forms is only provided by the drawing of the line that can not only be carried out with more or less pressure but can besides be drawn in any direction whatever and in addition can be reversed at any moment. Circles can at any time begin between the invisible upper and lower reference line and be drawn either running to the left or to the right. And crosses can – as in the screen saver – be drawn from top left to bottom right and then from top right to bottom left or the other way round as well. This is not yet the movement where Nicholas of Cusa's category of 'free will' comes *into play*, as such sequences of movement are largely culturally encoded; they imitate a standard model, as in Mercator's detailed instruction for the writing of the letter X: 'X consists of *N* (not made with the broad diagonal, but more upright than the diagonal'.[26] Individuality – or as Nicholas of Cusa would say: 'free will', is manifested only in forming the possibilities of the line, curves and bends that diverge from the ideal form. Like the teratological measurements of bodily anomalies they distinguish the deviation from the norm.

Unlike the line, the 'pointed' gesture of touch has hardly any subjective possibilities. It corresponds to the keystroke which allows for no significant possibilities of deviation: when the typing arm meets the drum, a letter is produced, in one hit: *ping*, as an always identical imprint.[27] This is the reason why Martin Heidegger accuses typewriting of concealing the subject: 'The typewriter makes everyone look the same.'[28] Individuality counts as what is simply not copyable because it is superior to mechanical reproduction. The only thing that is individual in the sense of stylistically unique (or auratic) is a line that extends in the spiral or curve-shaped deviation from the straight path as *scriptura cursiva*. A point by contrast has hardly any bend or angle of slant, and as it neither flows nor draws, it can not be identified as *cursive* (from *currere*).

Except of course in digital writing. And it is precisely from there, this is the central thesis of this book, that handwriting derives its power, allowing it to persist even and particularly in the age of mechanical reproduction. It is not block writing or typewriting that is the real challenge to digital writing technologies; instead, digitalization only reaches its peak of perfection at the moment when it conceives of the preposterous remainder of writing not as nothing, in other words when it comprehends writing not only seen as block writing, but captures its irregular twists in the shape of the anthropomorphic trace and exploits the cursiveness of writing – *without any remainder*. A case in point: identifying italics not just in a cursive line, but even in a dot.

## Indifference

One October day in London in the late 1880s the master detective Sherlock Holmes in his flat in Baker Street was taken up with quite an involved 'case of identity'. The allegedly missing fiancé of the distraught Miss Sutherland has been revealed by Holmes to be her stepfather, James Windibank, who has set his mind on his stepdaughter's fortune and tricked her by pretending a false identity. Holmes discovers the fraud on the basis of letters. He subjects these to an analysis of the writing, and although the letters were written on a typewriter and even signed mechanically, they provide Holmes with unambiguous proof of the fraudulent identity. 'It is a curious thing', the detective remarks,

> that a typewriter has really quite as much individuality as a man's handwriting. Unless they are quite new, no two of them write exactly alike. Some letters get more worn than others, and some wear only on one side. Now you remark in this note of yours, Mr Windibank, that in every case there is some little slurring over the 'e', and a slight defect in the tail of the 'r'. There are fourteen other characteristics, but those are the more obvious.[29]

In the screen saver the typed characters likewise have small irregularities in the thickness of the line or in the rounding of a curve; like pathological symptoms the swellings and dents, literally oozing out of the standard norm, make the writing look like handwriting. It is, however, unusual in the case of handwriting for the same deviation to be repeated over and over again, such as the little slurring over the 'e' and the slight defect on the tail of the 'r' written on the typewriter by the shady Mr Windibank. In the screen saver, *ductus* of writing and writing pressure are always applied absolutely identically in the repetitions. Even the rate of writing is always the same, they do not speed up at the start of the line and they are not subject to delay at the end, as Binet observed in the case of handwriting. This writing is pure repetition, it does not display the slightest difference between two tokens of the same type. Like the mechanical types on the typewriter in the Sherlock Holmes case, the same system of individuality can be repeated in instant replay. And thus it reduces to a single form the infinite possibilities, described by Nicholas of Cusa, of rolling the globe and drawing the line described by it.

In many digital practices that make handwriting available for the computer, similar stereotyping arises. For example, the Intelligent Font Analysis of Data Becker provides a program that allows the user to produce their personal handwriting on the keyboard. In this, the handwriting is first put on paper letter by letter, then scanned in and stored as a digital letter font. By means of the keyboard, handwritten e-mail messages can finally be written – a nostalgic game that is intended to bring the individual hand back into our correspondence, at the same time, however, ignoring precisely that 'tiny spark of contingency' that sees to it that in physical handwriting no two letters are exactly identical. Or one downloads from the net handwriting by geniuses; in particular Leonardo da Vinci's left-handed mirror-writing operates as a favourite motif for idiosyncrasy in the otherwise monotone digital environments.[30]

Like the signs in the screen saver, these digital kinds of handwriting respond more to the logic of typewriting, being standardized for the purpose of repetition. Following Saussure's idea of writing as a system of differences, they mark the difference between linguistic units by means of the graphic difference between the letters. The principle of difference between the differing signs in a discrete repertoire of signs presupposes another principle, however: the sameness of the same letters. This dual principle is the central problem of writing recognition software which, like human readers, also gets into difficulties when the difference between for example n and u is levelled in a line continually pacing up and down, because in so doing the basic principle of writing as difference is violated.

In this respect, the screen saver remediates handwriting by way of a paradoxical aesthetics; on the one hand, it simulates the specific inscription technologies of handwriting as it copies the accidental anomalies, bumps and dents. As a technotext it then, however, repeats this difference over and over again in exactly the same way so that handwriting is written like the typewriting in the case of Sherlock Holmes. The 'reiteration of differences', writes John R. Searle in his polemical reply to Derrida's 'Signature Event Context', characterizes all meaning-producing systems: 'indeed any rule-governed element in any system of representation at all must be repeatable'.[31] As iteration in this respect does not produce any particular difference, it consequently amounts to an equalization, since the difference is neutralized by the repetition. Here Searle's argument displays a rhetoric that in its day characterized the art-critical debates on Duchamp's Readymades. Just as art criticism accused the Readymades of being *indifferent* – also in the sense of uninvolved or bored – towards the unique work of art, the 'original', in the same way Searle accuses Derrida of harbouring 'no relation to the original'.[32]

The 'Sports' screen saver repeats the exception to the warpage of the zero as a teratological sign for individuality until such time as it no longer appears abnormal, and thereby absorbs the difference which individuality would produce in a unique and singular event like that of speaking or writing by hand. The x-th repetition of the zero results in an iteration without recognizable 'itera', without ever becoming noticeably different, and thus the possibilities of the sign to produce new contexts, as Jacques Derrida describes the basic structure of the semiotic process, appear to be null.

And yet, I should like to claim, this 'null-difference' is not in the end nothing. As an, as it were, 'zero-difference' in other words it emphatically enacts the arithmetic operating mode of zero. 'Zero-difference' conceives of 'indifference' as precisely the difference that Duchamp called '*infra-mince*': casts that are always the same from one and the same mould are admittedly identical, but nevertheless they are always also characterized by difference, even if this concerns only the temporal deferral of a few seconds differentiating them in their appearance. In this respect, 'zero-difference' follows the paradoxical logic of the arithmetical zero, that 'meta-numeral', as Brian Rotman argues, as a 'sign over names' 'indicating the absence of the numerals 1, 2, 3, 4, 5, 6, 7, 8, 9' and, in so doing, 'declaring itself to be the origin of counting, the trace of the one-who-counts and produces the number sequence'.[33]

Like zero, 'zero-difference' has the ability to be everything and nothing at the same time, to multiply the absent and nullify the present. 'Zero-difference' absorbs difference and multiplies it at the same time. And, one could add, it destabilizes the phonetic binary pair Zero/Xerox, that is enacted in the screen saver in the sequence O-X-O…, i.e. as the marking that indicates to the ballplayer his tactical position on the field, even and particularly when he is not in place.

## 0-X/X-0

> A line – any line inscribed on a sheet of paper – is a denial of the importance of the body, the body and its flesh, the body and its humours. The line gives access neither to skin nor to membranes laden with mucous. It speaks of the body only insofar as it scratches and grates (one might go so far as to speak of tickling) . . . Line, no matter how supple, light or uncertain, always implies force, a direction. It is energon work, and it displaces the traces of its pulsation and self-consumption.
> Roland Barthes, '*Non Multa Sed Multum*'[34]

The emptiness of an unoccupied playing position is the central concern of the screen saver. Its provocation consists in the fact that writing is not connected to a body via any interface, either by cable, pens or sensors. Not written by any hand, the signs seem to be pure Becoming, without any origin; without any start and finish, the writing moves forward in an infinite loop of writing and erasure. The idea of such a magic act of writing, coming from nowhere and apparently revealing nothing but the inscrutability of any process of meaning production, is as old as the mystery of writing in general. It therefore also finds its 'spirit' in the realm of the sacred. The theological '*urtext*' of the screen saver is provided by the famous passage in the Old Testament in the fifth chapter of the prophet Daniel, which tells the story of Belshazzar, King of BAbylon, to whom a mysterious script, the Writing on the Wall, appears at a feast in the palace:

> Immediately the fingers of a man's hand appeared and wrote on the plaster of the wall of the king's palace, opposite the lamp-stand; and the king saw the hand as it wrote. Then the king's color

changed, and his thoughts alarmed him; his limbs gave way, and his knees knocked together. (Daniel 5: 5–6)

Like the trace of chalk in the screen saver, the Writing on the Wall is without origin, but at the same time indexical; like the pointing of an *index finger* towards an originator whose physical presence at the precise time of writing it presupposes and simultaneously withholds. In addition writing, although 'over against the candlestick upon the plaister of the wall' it is therefore decidedly *visible*, is nevertheless not *readable*. It is directed emphatically at the king, as if to say: 'Look here! The sign on the wall!' And yet the writing can not be *read*. It does not first and foremost serve the purposes of information but as it were *ex negativo* sets in motion a semiotic process that makes precisely the absence of the signified its main point. The Writing on the Wall speaks – at least initially – without speaking. And thus it ties in with a rhetorical process using negation which negative theology has made its main means of articulation as it found itself faced with the problem that the 'unsayable' can not be said in a positive, affirmative manner. The particular form of language used in negative theology, writes Jacques Derrida, results from the assumption

that every predicative language is inadequate to the essence, in truth to the hyperessentiality (the being beyond Being) of God; consequently, only a negative ('apophatic') attribution can claim to approach God, and to prepare us for a silent intuition of God.[35]

The negative particles following on one after another serve to say *in via negativa* what is *not* X, or to put the unsayable into paradoxical formulations, as something that is itself and yet at the same time something quite different.[36]

The recipient for whom this drama is being staged, in this case the user of a screen saver *avant la lettre*, King Belshazzar, must have his consciousness go into overdrive as he finds himself summoned to give meaning to an event that negates the condition of its own possibility by being completed. The infinite driving force for such a paradoxical structure is dazzlingly explained by Peter Fuchs when he points to the effects of mystical modes of speech, in which 'the user of the schema is trapped in the schema and propelled constantly back and forth between the opposite sides of the schema because every position implies its negation and every negation implies its position'.[37]

It is not surprising then as well that the Writing on the Wall sets off truly dramatic – in the sense of theatrical or somatic – effects: it literally *touches* the addressee and affects him physically. It is written that the king's countenance was changed, the joints of his loins were loosed and his knees smote one against another. Unlike 'normal' writing serving purposes of communication, that is, purely the economy of reading, with this writing one is dealing less with the process of meaning production than with an act of addressing that emphatically directs its empty signifiers at a second person, away from the 'I' and towards the 'you'. The body of the author retreats before the body of the reader.

In Daniel 5 the riddle of the Writing on the Wall is resolved by a record achievement of interpretation on the part of the prophet who as God's messenger is able to decipher the writing definitively:

> This is the interpretation of the matter: MENE, God has numbered the days of your kingdom and brought it to an end; TEKEL, you have been weighed in the balances and found wanting; PERES, your kingdom is divided and given to the Medes and Persians. (Daniel 5: 26–8)

With this Daniel links the Writing on the Wall to a divine teleology, in which the bodily *ab*sence of the writing subject becomes a sign for the *pre*sence of God.[38] It is just this logic of an original origin, whose presence is located in the absent and whose readability is located in the unreadable, that also characterizes the screen saver. Like the divine Writing on the Wall, the writing of the screen saver is written as if by magic. And like King Belshazzar, the reader of the screen saver does not experience the writing in its complete and finished form as the sign of a past act of writing, in which the writer has left her or his trace for future readers, but instead the path of the trace reveals itself in the processing of the movement of writing as an event in real time.

Like the guests at the King's feast, those addressed by the screen become witnesses to whom something will be 'shown'. They testify to the Becoming of zero, the mysterious number, representing everything and nothing at the same time, and by on-looking, they discover that this infinite circle arises not as a unified figure of infinity – like the perfect completeness of a zero produced by typing a key – but is drawn as a line. By on-looking they testify to the beginning and end of this mathematical figure of infinity, from now on located at a defined point in the line in the form of the smallest geometric unit. At least until the circle of the zero is closed and the point in the line vanishes. But still belatedly does the point mark the former moment of touch, or of contact or imprint. And even before it begins to draw the line, it is already defined as *cursive*.

The point in the circle of the zero is situated on either side of the abyss. On the one side, it provides the basic condition for the *currere* of the trace. On the other side, it is the effect of a touch – like making a fingerprint, a foot or handprint or even a letter-type, i.e. all those gestures that cancel the performance of the line in which the difference between cultural norm and individual deviation is revealed. In this respect, the 'cursive point' is the site where subjectivity 'is initiated': here, the subject is extinguished, but not without the promise to be created continually anew. The point plays host to the principle of undecidability, it oscillates between imprint and trace, between the original writing of the hand as the sign of a unique psychosomatic presence and the inscription technologies of typewriting in which it stands for disembodiment, iterability, normalization and indifference. The poetics of the point as a tipping point, a multi-perceptible image (*Kippfigur*), deriving the present from the absent and vice versa, is quite literally demonstrated by the *typographic* point, meaning according to its Latin sense (*punctum*) 'erasure' and thus, as 'omission marks' in the vacuum of the text, it always already communicates in addition the – indeed past – presence of the signs.[39]

King Belshazzar, in the unhappy ending of the story, succeeds in deciphering the writing and thus in 'saving' the hand by inverting the absence of the writing subject into a sign for the presence of God. For the witnesses of the screen saver, by contrast, the hand seems to be lost for ever whenever they find themselves as supermodern paranoiacs insisting on asking the question 'Who is writing?', 'Who has left his fingerprints on the monitor?' As long as no prophet gives an answer, they will in the end perhaps, like so many users of the media before them, presume a divine hand at work or some 'ghost in the machine'. Certainly we are dealing here with something like W's or Flechsig's soul 'produced by miracle' or 'fleetingly improvised' which, as Daniel Paul Schreber, the archetype of a media paranoiac, puts it in his *Memoirs*, is 'tying-to-celestial bodies'.[40] Or, asking in the context of supermodern paranoia: 'Is there an artificial intelligence with a virtual body encapsulated within the computer, perhaps a lonely cyborg who is sending cryptic messages to the user of the monitor?' Are we dealing with one of the creatures that N. Katherine Hayles writes of as having resigned themselves to living on the inside of the computer, producing 'INTERFACES that allow them to preserve the illusion of ordinary human existence'?[41]

But the question then follows: how are we to understand these 'interfaces'? How can we as users with our 'ordinary human existence' interact with this disembodied subject, if this is programmed in such a way that any intervention immediately removes it from the monitor, *defers* it once more, thus even defers it in its absence – as if a null could be nullified? Like Heidegger's cloud which veils concealment and thus conceals concealment or forgets oblivion itself.[42]

The principle of the user of the media, which is surely at the same time the principle of the paranoiac – 'I write, therefore I am', or in the case of electronic writing: 'I compute, therefore I am', or to echo Schreber in his native language: 'Ich bin Schre(i)ber',[43] is here reversed: in writing I do not duplicate myself, but divide myself into one who writes and – in the grammatical middle voice – into one who is the site on which writing is completed. In writing I do not (any more) constitute myself as a subject, but any production of subjectivity in the sense of authorship always proves also to be a parasitical act of 'othering'. Because the writing hand within the computer, the quasi-physical act of writing with its dust and screeching, becomes a complement to my writing activity; it is to a certain extent an effect of my absence as a writer (*Schreiber*). And vice versa, but to no less a degree, the virtual writer creates me as an effect of his absence, performs me as it were as a somatic 'remainder', which is always present when the machine is turned off: as a complement to a marked absence: $X - O - X$ ... here presence becomes a problematic case, and the body an intricate derivative of its *ex-negativo* equivalence, dysembodied so to speak.

## 0/1 or the Great Attack

This mutual conditioning, this back and forth between existence and erasure of the subject, in which any affirmation constantly depends on the negation of the complementary partner and vice versa, is neither an arbitrary nor an accidental process. It is part of a contract; one that arranges the division of sense and presence according to an exactly regulated programme. The course of this programme is configured within a system; it follows an agreement that the parties to the contract have made more or less tacitly. There have always been contractual regulations in the theatrical performance of states of consciousness, in their *mise-en-scène*. The ecstasies of the medieval female mystics were pre-programmed in their *unificatio christi*, and they are not far removed from the hysterical attacks of Charcot's hysterics.

The unexpressed intimacy between Charcot and his female patients has been sensitively described by Per Olov Enquist in his *Book of Blanche and Marie*. Georges Didi-Huberman also underlines the tacit agreement in *The Invention of Hysteria* when he emphasizes that the female hysterics in Charcot's hypnotic séances at the Salpêtrière had their hysterical attacks with calculable 'regularity' and 'punctually' at the Tuesday public lectures.[44] In their hallucinations they writhed about, performing such contortions of 'great hysterical attacks' that in all details at each stage were in conformity with the 'regularities' described by Charcot: starting with twitching of the muscles they passed through the phase of 'substantial movements', of which the most typical is the hysterical arc ('*arc de cercle*'), into the phase of 'passionate postures and gestures', until their state of excitement finally exhausted itself in 'delirium'. Didi-Huberman writes:

> Charming Augustine – the charmed and the charmer; this charm took the form of a contract. In a single movement, it encompassed the *exercise of a law* – depending not on the body but on the states of its *appearance*, poses, *attitudes passionnelles*. – and also something that was always *destined to be repeated*.[45]

The hysterical body *is* not, and Charcot was often accused of this as an inadequacy of his methodology, but it *appears*, in fact whenever the doctors exhibit it. Set off by giving amyl nitrite, as much as by the specific order of medical discourse, the great attack is exposed to the public, in fact specifically to the photographer and stenographer Bourneville who in his handwritten and his photographic notes sought to note it down, even to 'capture' it.[46]

The stages of hypnosis – i.e. 1. lethargy (or limpness), 2. catalepsy (or rigidity of the limbs), 3. somnambulism (dormancy), were recognized by Charcot as 'rule-governed', as 'the exercise of a law'. For him they were physiological symptoms that led to the unquestionable diagnosis of hysterical illness. If the screen saver produces quite particular handwriting, then it generates along with it a quite particular writing subject. As in the mystical act of writing in King Belshazzar's palace and in the séances of Charcot, Binet or Lombroso, the subject of the screen saver is a 'hysterical' subject: the implementation of a system producing subjects according to the technical and discursive conditions of its order. It 'appears' and 'vanishes' in the act of its mediation and in the process strictly employs the discursive demands of the medium. By switching between a state of lethargy, catalepsy or somnambulism and switching itself on and off 'punctually' and reliably at the pre-programmed time, it fulfils the contract in which handwriting as a feature of presence (or of the trace) and screen as a feature of (re-)presentation (in the form of an imprint) are interwoven.

Thus then we sit before our screens and await the right point in time fixed by contract, when we suddenly boldly go off to break out into contortions of our bodies. Only until such time, however, as the machine switches on again and in writing itself draws the trace of our writing. The drawing onwards of the line is, of course, always also a drawing *away*, *with*drawing.

A birthday card sent to the author by Ilse L—— on 26 January 2004.

## Before a Postcard

Dear Sonja,

Greetings on your birthday and best wishes for the coming year,
may it bring you health and success! I hope you are still enjoying it
in Weimar! I was pleased to see all my children again on the 24th.
When like me you are confined to one room, you are happy and
grateful to see anyone [*Wiedersehen*]. All the best for the future,
Vera get well soon
Grandmother
I …rite …o… only by fee… my eyes are failin…

She had almost reached one hundred, when the 'grandmother' – blinded
with age – composed these lines by touch. She writes by 'fee[ling]',
*tracking* [*erspüren*] the trace of the writing. She relies on the motoric
memory that she, a former librarian from Breslau (Wroclaw), started to
practise early on so that the cultural heritage of the German nation was
safe in her capable hands; for the card indexes to be entrusted to her in
keeping with Prussian order, from A to Z. 'The ancestress' ['*Die Ahne*']
as her six children called her reverentially – to them she was alpha
and omega. Only five of them managed to be on board the lorry
that brought the wife of the Oberbürgermeister from Marienburg
(Malbork) to the West in January 1945; the oldest, just fourteen, got
through on his own. She watched over them with astuteness and
a good deal of attention to cleaning, through the years when grand-
father, the holder of a Doctorate in Law, was denazified.

Now blinded by age, she is writing in the dark. She touches the
surface of the card with her fingertips that are not yet as deaf as her
hearing. With a seeing hand she clears a track for memories: the family
got together, and 'all the children' sat down at one table for one (for the
time being) last '*Wiedersehen*'. She has not noticed that her writing goes
over the edge of the card and onto where she is resting it, nor either
that her pen is running out of ink while she is writing. Despite this,
the ballpoint pen scratches its trace in the paper; guided by her tactile
memory, it proceeds by touch digging into the paper, returning to the
old familiar things, the letters so often seen before. And yet it produces

nothing but a blind spot that for a long time *before this postcard* had not been willing to reveal a certain memory.

What was it that she saw once again when her 'eyes were failing'? And what was it that she could not see?

# 6 The Diary: Anne Frank versus Kujau-Hitler[1]

As the subtitle ('A Freudian Impression' indicates, psychoanalysis *would have* to bring about an at least potential revolution in discussion of the problem of the archive. It is not accidental that it emphasizes the concepts of the imprint and printing technology. Frequently taking the site of an archaeological excavation as its basis, its discourse deals above all else with the storing of 'impressions' and the encoding of inscriptions [. . .] Is he [Freud] not in the process of mobilizing a ponderous archiving machine (press, printing, ink, paper) to record something which in the end does not merit such expense? . . . The Freudian lexicon here indeed stresses a certain 'technology of archivization' (*Eindruck, Druck, drücken*), but only so as to feign the faulty economic calculation. Freud also entrusts to us the 'impression' (*Empfindung*), the feeling [and one could also say: '*Gespür*'] inspired by this excessive and ultimately gratuitous investment in a perhaps useless archive: 'In none of my previous writings have I had so strong a feeling [*Empfindung*] as now that what I am describing is common knowledge . . . and that I am using up paper and ink . . . and, in due course, the compositor's and printer's work and material . . . in order to expound things which are, in fact, self-evident' [*SE* 21:117] In sum, this is a lot of ink and paper for nothing, an entire typographical volume, in short, a material substrate which is out of all proportion, in the last analysis, to "recount" (*erzählen*) stories that everyone knows. But the movement of this rhetoric leads elsewhere. Because Freud draws another inference, in the retrospective [or: preposterous] logic of a future perfect: *he will have to have invented* an original proposition which will make the investment profitable . . . And he will not just have to have announced some news, but also to have archived it: to have put it, as it were, *to the press*.

Jacques Derrida, *Archive Fever: A Freudian Impression*[2]

## Traces of Memory and Imprints of Remembering

'If I distrust my memory', Sigmund Freud begins his famous *Note on the Mystic Writing-Pad*, 'I am able to supplement and guarantee its working by making a note in writing'.[3] Here the technique of writing is not *immediate* but it essentially determines what is written down, as it depends on the technique of writing which and how much data can be written down; whether the notations will be permanent and retrievable; whether in addition they will be replaceable by new data or can even be erased; and whether the destruction of the data requires the destruction of the writing apparatus. According to Freud, the human apparatus of remembering works just like the notations in an external storage medium. How this operates from the point of view of writing technology he explains by taking the Mystic Writing Pad as a model, the writing tablet which contains in its deepest layer a layer of wax covered on top by a sheet of celluloid. For writing on the Mystic Writing Pad (or respectively for 'remembering'):

> no pencil or chalk is necessary, since the *writing does not depend on material being deposited on the receptive surface*. It is a return to the ancient method of writing on tablets of clay or wax: a *pointed stylus scratches the surface, the depressions upon which constitute the 'writing'*. In the case of the Mystic Pad this scratching is not effected directly, but through the medium of the covering-sheet. At the points which the stylus *touches*, it *presses* the lower surface of the waxed paper on to the waxed slab, and the *grooves* are visible as dark writing upon the otherwise smooth whitish-grey surface of the celluloid. If one wishes to destroy what has been written, all that is necessary is to raise the double covering-sheet from the wax slab by a light pull, starting from the lower end. The *close contact* between the waxed paper and the wax slab at the places which have been scratched (upon which the *visibility* of the *writing* depended) is thus brought to an end and it does not recur when the two surfaces *come together* once more.[4]

This notion of an impression or an imprint in soft wax as a basic principle of mnemonics is not peculiar to Freud alone. We produce memories by *imprinting* or *engraving* something into our minds; occasionally we even need to *hammer* or *drum* something in. The basic gesture of memory is accordingly writing in the sense of *scribere*: writing by scoring or the engraving of *in*scriptions. The metaphor of the wax tablet has been standard ever since the ancient *ars memoria*, in Plato for example who describes the functioning of memory and knowledge in the Socrates' dialogue with Theaetetus using the image of the 'cast of wax' which can take imprints:

> Socrates: We may look upon it [this cast], then, as a gift of Mnemosyne, the mother of the Muses. We make impressions upon this of everything we wish to remember among the things we have seen or heard or simply thought of; we hold the wax under our perceptions and thoughts and take a stamp of them, in the way in which we *take the imprints of signet rings.*[5]

Sealing, impressing, stamping – Aristotle too places at the centre of his thinking this gesture and along with it the accentuation of a decidedly bodily-material quality of memory as a site of reception and storage. In his observations on memory in *De memoria et Reminiscentia* he discusses the question of the functioning of the mnemonic apparatus as follows:

> One might ask how it is possible that though the affection alone is present, and the fact absent, the latter – that which is not present – is remembered. Because it is clear that we must conceive that which is generated through sense-perception in the sentient soul, and in the part of the body which is its seat – viz. that affection the state whereof we call memory – to be some such thing as a picture. The process of movement involved in the act of perception stamps in, as it were, a sort of *impression* of the *precept*, just as persons do who *make an impression with a seal.*[6]

For Aristotle, memory is the affection (or literally: πάθος, pathos: 'suffering') of the absent or by the absent, whose image has been impressed in the memory as if it had been stamped with a signet ring, that is, impressed or imprinted. The soft wax receives the stamp, it 'suffers' (passively), and still does this long after the signet ring has been taken away; the imprint *remains* afterwards as an 'affect' – *afficere*: 'to do to' comes from *facere*: 'to do' – as that which remains (actively) without remaining. The continuity of remaining described in all these scenarios of sealing in wax is here following one and the same principle as they all identify the work of memory as the recognition of a previously impressed type by means of *similarity*, that is, as iconic.

The idea that iconicity is the prime motor of any successful act of memory is for example paralleled in digital data processing, for example in the field of data verification, when the loops, waves and curls of the papillary lines of a fingerprint, the physiognomic line of a face or an iris are compared with or recognized in the entries of a databank, or when in *Optical Character Reading* a (hand-)written sign is identified as a tolerable deviation of its 'prototype'. Moreover, cognitive science has also emphasized the significance of the imprint for the human reading apparatus. Reading means moving the eyes along a series of written signs, not in a continually smooth movement but bringing more complex units of writing into vision as a whole and jumping with jerky movements, called saccades, from one fixation to another.[7] In this respect, reading is a recognition of patterns in which the reader remembers a pre-fabricated impression. The 'more purely' the letter corresponds to the prototypical 'character' (impression), the easier and more efficiently can patterns be recognized.

On closer inspection, however, it becomes clear that there is an indexical dimension mixed in with the iconic dimension of recognition in the discourses of mnemonics, because the Aristotelian *eikôn*, the 'internal image', can not be exclusively or absolutely recognized visually but must also be *grasped* in a downright tactile fashion. In the case of Freud's writing-pad, the writing becomes readable after the 'close contact' between celluloid layer and wax layer is removed by the grooves of the absent material, and both Aristotle and Plato likewise emphasize this gesture of stamping or impressing into a soft and malleable material (the sealing wax).

Reading is work for the memory. But as working or processing takes place in time, it always also involves a trace. Reading Aristotle *à la lettre*, it is precisely this double structure that is revealed because for him remembering is not just produced by the rigid impression of a matrix or of an 'image of perception', but he characterizes memory literally as a processual 'experience', requiring an 'ongoing movement' for the imprint to be produced and which is therefore also always located within the continuity of a trace. The double structure of icon and index, or imprint and trace in Aristotle's mnemonic theory has also not gone unnoticed by Bettine Menke:

> The trace, that has been impressed [according to Aristotle] as perceptions from and into the soul just as the signet ring imprints and leaves behind its trace in the wax, is an *indexical* sign – with an *iconic* connotation.[8]

For this reason, handwriting as traces of memory can cause problems, particularly those with a distinctive individual *ductus*, because they *mani*pulate the balance between imprint and trace. From the point of view of cognitive science, reading does not proceed by our following the trace of the written line with our eyes. The trace is precisely what in the writing resists being made readable. However, to – literally – *grasp* the readable *imprint* in an illegible piece of handwriting, we have need of a special *process* of reading: By following the *ductus* of the line with our finger on the table-top and writing it anew *as a gesture*, we can track the legible imprint in the *processual experience of the trace*. In the tactile sensation of this act (*Hand*lung), the writing can become recognizable once again through touch and thus iconically readable.

## Authentic Spectres

Pretzien, Saxony-Anhalt, 24 June 2006. Once again the *Diary* of Anne Frank is burning. At the celebration of the summer solstice organized by the Heimatbund Ostelbien, a paperback edition of probably the most famous diary of the Holocaust was consigned to the flames by right-wing extremists – with the words: 'I consign Anne Frank to the fire'.[9] They consigned the book to the fire so that it should turn to ashes; so that the paperback print or imprint of that most fragile eyewitness account should be exterminated and the belated offering to the flames might erase the memory of the great conflagration.

*The Diary* of Anne Frank had provided 'fuel' right from its inception. Diaries in general carry a special historiographical charge as they transmit to us individual lived experience that is remote in time and space; they bring back to us an intimate nearness, however distant. Especially when handwritten, diaries are special memory machines. As a pocket-size jotter, journal or notebook, the diary is also the receptacle of passing thoughts, promising to order them chronologically, to conserve them permanently, to control time, to make what is past accessible for a future present. Like almost no other writing practice, the diary ritualizes the intermingling of past and future. And even though a diary is a private affair, it is nevertheless often such personal accounts that as printed micro-narratives constitute our cultural memory.

Countless diaries write the narrative of the Shoah: in the Archive of Oneg Schabbat in Warsaw there is a collection of them, including the famous one by Emanuel Ringelblum; one would need to know Polish to read them. Viktor Klemperer's *Lingua Tertii Imperii* originated in his diary. Published only recently is a last fragment from Sebastian Haffner's book of memories that half a century after the end of the war problematizes over again the expediency of the villain-victim dichotomy.[10] The list of Holocaust documents left to us in handwritten form is considerable; to mention a few out of several million in alphabetical order: Tova Draenger (Krakov), David Flinker (a boy from Brussels), Éva Heyman (a Hungarian girl), Dawid Rubinowicz (a Polish boy), David Shrakovik (Lodz), Mordechai Tenenbaum (Vilnius), Zalman Gradowski, Zalman Lewental and Leib Langfuss wrote in secret in Birkenau.[11]

In these and other accounts they pass on their stories to us. In the mysterious, auratic handstrokes of their writing the past is brought back to us; in the faded ink of the yellowing paper we hear their testaments like the murmur of a ghostly voice: resurrected spectres, making past experiences in the incisions of their memory imprints accessible to the *touch*, bringing history within our *grasp* in the present. From a historiographical point of view, diaries are so powerful for precisely the reason that in their materiality as autographs they provide documents that promise to give answers once and for all to questions of historical authenticity, and to do that in an absolutely *objective* way, if necessary even with chemical-physical proof. Anne Frank's diary has been doomed repeatedly to precisely this fate.

In similar territory to the 'case' of Anne Frank and yet at the same time a million miles away, there is another 'monument' in the shape of a historical diary, another private account pretending to put its stamp for ever on our historical consciousness: the case of Adolf Hitler, alias Konrad Kujau. Both diaries, as different as they may be in their historical provenance, have one thing in common that is going to be at issue in what follows, as both of them have provided fuel for extensive and heated debate on historiographical authenticity. At first glance this bracketing of Anne Frank and Hitler equally in relation to the question of a certain rhetoric of authenticity may seem illegitimate, if not downright blasphemous, not the least for the reason that the diaries of Anne Frank have been authenticated as genuine while Adolf Hitler's have been unmasked as forgeries. The aim here is by no means to doubt or to detract from this final classification; instead I should like to take a closer look at the discourses about a legal authentication or falsification of these diaries and question how the debate about authenticity has advanced the practice of collective memory and to a certain extent has also affected it.

Both diaries were the subject of a series of examinations for authenticity. In the case of Anne Frank, objections from ex- and neo-Nazis have repeatedly given rise to these expert reports. Since the 1970s the debate about authenticity has resulted in the theses of historical revisionism; at stake was not only the authenticity of the diaries but nothing less than the authenticity of the Holocaust itself. While in the case of Anne Frank considerable efforts were made to unmask the diaries as being forgeries, in the case of the Hitler diaries it was a matter of proving their authenticity. After all, the private notes held out the prospect of a long sought-for answer to the riddle of the Führer's personality whose 'one-dimensionality' as a public figure could now at last be fleshed out with the full depth of his character. However extreme the difference between the narratives of these diaries may be, they both display a rhetorical stance that presupposes a positive concept of authenticity. And, according to my argument, this rhetoric of the material, historical authenticity of their manuscripts also influences not least our concept of the past: the way we locate what is past within our contemporary culture somewhere between memory and amnesia.

## Archive and Museum

In both the case of Anne Frank's diaries and the case of the forged Hitler diaries the debates about authenticity have referred to the work of archives. In this, the archive functions not just as the physical place where documents are stored as witnesses to the past, but *archeīon* literally refers also as a *nomen loci* to the administrative building, the building from which one is governed and ruled over (*árchein*). By the power of this instititutionalized architecture, the archive is authorized to certify authenticity. By authenticating a document (the allusion to John L. Austin's celebrated words springs to mind: 'I hereby declare – by virtue of my office . . .'), it does not so much confirm this as it produces it in the first place.

To certify a document as genuine or fake is not just the business of archives. A museum too functions as a powerful institution awarding certificates of authenticity. Even if less authority as a legal institution is generally accorded to it than to the archive,[12] nevertheless its power of effect from the point of view of cultural technology is highly efficient, relating as it does to nothing less than what Mieke Bal in her cultural theory has identified as the basic gesture of any cultural activity: the gesture of showing.[13] The museum literally 'exposes' authenticity, in the public rooms of its exhibition spaces. In the archive it is the institutional framework – the architecture of the building, the public support, the expert knowledge of the archivists and curators – that 'exposes' the authenticity of a document; this is then reinforced by the media of showing: the display case, the expert's explanation on the caption, the officially published brochures and catalogues.

Etymologically, *mouseīon* comes from Muse and refers – again as a *nomen loci* – to the study or the 'place for learned activity'. Whether now cultural-historically this place appears in the form of a grave with grave goods, a temple with offerings, a basilica with relics and other sacred objects, or as the treasury of princes with their war booty, there is one thing that these 'places' have in common, and it is precisely this that makes them, according to Krystzof Pomian, into a 'museum': they all promote the same thing: 'Bringing objects together so as to exhibit them to the eye'.[14] In this chapter we shall be investigating both *loci*, archive and museum, as to how with their specific cultural techniques they exhibit and produce authenticity.

## Genuinely fake

What is now referred to as *The Diary of Anne Frank* is usually the printed book that was first published in 1947 by Anne's father, Otto Frank, under the title *Het Achterhuis* (*The Secret Annexe*) and has since then been published in millions of editions throughout the world. Translated into more than 60 languages, it has become one of the most widely read books in the world – from being an object in the archive or museum it has become a library object. But both before and after, its effectiveness lay in its being written by hand.

However, from the 1950s on, in a flood of pamphlets, brochures, and other publications that received extensive media coverage, the claim was made again and again that – to quote from a pamphlet distributed by E. Schönborn – the *Diary* was a 'forgery and the product of Jewish anti-German atrocity propaganda to support the lie of six million gassed Jews and to finance the state of Israel'.[15] Between 1960 and 1993, these allegations became the subject of five lawsuits in Germany, mostly filed by Otto Frank, sometimes with the Anne Frank House as co-plaintiff.[16] The charges were of slandering the memory of the dead and publicly inciting racial hatred. Here the focus of the evidence became the technical and graphological examination of the manuscripts undertaken first of all in 1960 by experts appointed by the court in Lübeck, at the end of the 1970s by the *Bundeskriminalamt* (German Federal Criminal Investigation Department) and finally in great detail by the *Dutch Rijksinstituut voor Oorlogsdocumentatie* (*RIOD*, now *NIOD: Nederlands Instituut voor Oorlogsdocumentatie*, the Netherlands Institute of War Documentation). On the basis of this final examination of its authenticity, the court in Amsterdam issued a general ban on public questioning of the authenticity of Anne Frank's diaries; any infringements were to be punished by a fine.[17]

As with the *Diary* of Anne Frank, the debate around the alleged diaries of Adolf Hitler was similarly heated. Their 'discovery' created a major stir in the media. On 28 April 1983, Germany's best-selling weekly magazine *Stern* headlined the sensational find of secret diaries written by Adolf Hitler.[18] The discovery of these documents was presented to the readers by *Stern* reporter Gerd Heidemann as a cloak and dagger story about an heroic pilot named Friedrich Gundlfinger who had managed

The discovery of Hitler's diaries announced on the front cover of *Der Stern* on 28 April 1983.

to escape Berlin at the moment of Russian liberation in May 1945. In the escape he had rescued a burnt suitcase that contained secret documents belonging to the Führer, among which were his personal notebooks. After being lost for 40 years, Heidemann claimed that this testament left by the Führer had now turned up again. He explained that he had received the notebooks from an intermediary who had smuggled them into the country from the GDR with the help of the *Institut für Staatssicherheit* (the *Stasi* or East German Secret Service) and some dubious generals in the *Nationale Volksarmee* (East German Army).[19]

This was all rubbish. What Heidemann was journalistically peddling as a piece of German history soon turned out to be fake, and a very crude one. In fact, Hitler's notebooks, along with other Nazi memorabilia, had been manufactured by Heidemann's mysterious intermediary himself: Konrad Kujau, alias Dr Fischer, a forger and wheeler-dealer in Nazi relics who found his business partners in collectors obsessed with the Third Reich. He had also faked, for example, several handwritten manuscripts of *Mein Kampf* and a comprehensive collection of paintings 'by Hitler'. Almost a quarter of the more than 700 artworks represented in Billy Price's *Adolf Hitler: The Unknown Artist* (1983) were actually forgeries by Kujau.[20]

Both the diaries of Anne Frank and the alleged diaries of Adolf Hitler have been investigated by a battery of internationally acknowledged handwriting experts. The following is not a complete overview of the maze of certifications and reports archived, but rather follows another logic, one that is equally systematic: an investigation of how authenticity is conceived of in some of these assessments. In this, I should like to look more closely at a selection of snapshots in the album of historiography, each capturing a brief moment of an episode from a long and arduous quest for 'historical truth'. These snapshots are taken at the two locations central to this chapter: first, the archive, and later, the museum.

## Archival Authenticity

Whenever the archival question arises as to the authenticity of a document the archive is faced – roughly speaking – with three types of approach. First, the *content* of a document can be subjected to a text-critical analysis for its grammatical, logical and historical consistency and placed in a context. Second, the *material* authenticity of a document can be investigated on the basis of scientific tests. And third, handwriting experts can analyse the visual performance of the handwriting. It was the first procedure – the historical investigation of the content – that, in the case of Hitler's notebooks, led to the diaries initially being considered authentic.[21] Apparently Kujau had collected and read an extensive personal library about Hitler, so that historians who specialized in the history of the Third Reich did not immediately come across any contradictions. Only upon closer inspection did a team of archivists from the German Bundesarchiv identify Kujau's sources: Max Domarus' well-known publication of Hitler's speeches and proclamations, Gerd Rühle's *Das Dritte Reich,* and the Nazi daily *Der Völkische Beobachter.* They recognized a series of mistakes and inaccuracies concerning dates, names of institutions, and historical facts made both by Kujau and one of his sources.[22]

The initial certification of authenticity was also based on the immense amount of autographical material, which included a collection of 62 (!) volumes of diaries, accompanied by a massive archive of 300 watercolour paintings, drafts for speeches and letters, all 'by *Der Führer*', and last but not least, his World War I uniform and helmet.[23] Hugh Trevor-Roper evaluated the find in the London *Times* as follows: 'whereas signatures, single documents, or even groups of documents can be skillfully forged, a whole coherent archive covering 35 years is far less easily manufactured . . . The archive coheres as a whole and the diaries are an integral part of it'.[24]

But some of the assessors, among them the historian David Irving and the German Bundeskriminalamt, remained sceptical despite the large quantity of material relating to Hitler. Their critique introduced a second phase of investigation in which the Bundesanstalt für Materialforschung und -prüfung (German Criminal Court Laboratory), identified by chemical analysis synthetic fibres in the binding as well as paper-bleaching agents in the paper of some volumes, neither of which were used before 1945.[25] Whereas the historical investigation of the alleged Hitler diaries had initially failed, this chemical investigation provided positive evidence that the diaries were fake.

No doubt a (badly) faked document can be conclusively unmasked by such historical and technical investigations. But they can only do this if the questionable document displays anachronisms as regards the content or subject matter; a good forgery can withstand such methodological processes. Nor can they any more prove the Authenticity of an Authentic mAnuscript. This was the problem in the assessment of the diaries of Anne Frank as the analysis could find no clues pointing to a forgery – neither historical nor chemical. To achieve positive evidence of authenticity, the *Gerechtelijk Laboratorium* (Dutch Forensic Laboratory) carried out a thorough investigation of the handwriting. In this a team of writing experts investigated the particularities of the movement and the pressure in the production of the handwriting and categorized them in an extensive list of so-called 'micro-characteristics' ('*microkenmerken*') similar to the minutiae and points of comparison in forensic fingerprinting. These micro-characteristics were noted as visual 'points of identification' ('*identificatiepunten*'), for example appearing in the upper and lower extensions of a letter. They were then subjected to comparison with certified materials, for example with Anne Frank's letters and poetry albums from her schooldays and the systematic scheme of the micro-characteristics was compared with these reference materials.

This comparative method is based on the idea of the mathematical repetition of differences and resemblances. The result of such an investigation is statistical in nature, allowing for a statement on the degree of probability. The origin of Anne Frank's diaries was therefore given in the investigation report in terms of such a degree of

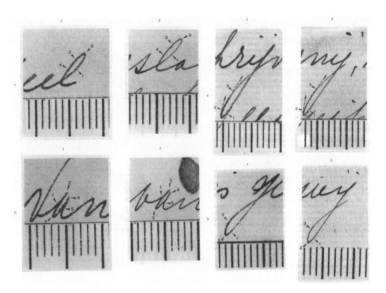

Extract from Hardy's summary of the report of the *Gerechtelijk Laboratorium* in Rijkswijk, showing 'micro-characteristics' noted as visual 'points of identification' in the handwriting of Anne Frank.

probability: the diary was 'probably to a degree bordering on certainty originating from the producer of the reference writing, Anne Frank'.[26] There was of course an infra-thin remainder separating high probability from the absolute certainty aimed at by the rhetoric of those doing the questioning.

These reports offer ample material for a critical discussion of the concepts of authenticity and copy, and their relation to the ideas of originality and uniqueness. First, they demonstrate that the chemical or technical analysis can only be performed on an original document. This presupposes that a unique 'original' cannot be replaced by a copy without compromising the manuscript's authenticity.

By contrast, both historical analysis and handwriting assessments can be performed on a high quality 'certificated' Xerox copy. These methods rely on the idea of writing as iteration, the idea that a written text is repeatable or spellable, like a musical symphony, to repeat Nelson Goodman's example by which he explains the concept of 'allographic' artefacts.[27] Historical assessment, which concentrates on a document's content and on the coherence of an archival collection, relies precisely on this idea of writing as allography: that is, it recognizes writing as authentic even when the text is copied, printed or re-printed. A manuscript's physical materiality, in this view, appears as a nearly invisible medium. Strictly speaking, the document does not even have to be seen; having the written text read aloud is enough.

This 'blindness', in a way, pertains also to the chemist, who – despite his interest in the originality of the material – at the same time ignores the face of the writing along with the content signified by it. Both the technical expert and the text-historical analyst overlook the visual performance of the actual handwriting, or rather, they look through it as their attention is directed either at the originality of a document as a manuscript in its singularity in the world, or – conversely – at the iterability of writing as allography.

## Text-Images

The key point of the manuscript is, however, precisely its dual structure as both autographical and allographical, both singular and iterable. Handwriting opens up a third space *between* original and copy. On the one hand, handwriting emanates from the physical presence of an individual writer who, by the *ductus* of the hand, draws/*traces* a line, the preposterous loops, twists and turns of which produce a similar unmistakable indexical finger profile to that of a unique fingerprint. The visual quality of handwriting is what interests the handwriting expert. The working procedure of a handwriting expert investigating a manuscript always involves turning the page upside-down, so that the text appears *capo volto* and its alphanumeric dimension as 'legible' writing is replaced by its 'perceptible' image. Thus handwriting, like painting, operates as 'autography' in Goodman's sense, since it does not allow for repetition without being considered a forgery.

On the other hand, handwriting is still bound up with the symbolic system of language; even if the trace of the hand causes difficulties for the writing, the central principle of writing nevertheless remains the repetition of the legible imprint. From the start, its ability to be copied has been the basic principle of writing, and in this book I have discussed this in various contexts of cultural history. The pre-mechanical handwriting cultures created entire libraries with their calami or quillpens.

Unlike the library, the archive presents itself as being the place of the originals; only individual documents or rare copies that cannot be found anywhere else are kept there.[28] Whenever a manuscript is preserved or duplicated in the archive, this cannot be done by a typewriter or carbon paper, but only by those technologies that reproduce its image-quality: for a while the image-processing of photocopies or microfiches, now more recently the digital techniques of scanning, imaging and printing. As handwriting is a hybrid medium, both allography and autography, at the same time writing and image, it could be called an 'image-text'. Like a handwritten signature, handwriting is at the same time unique and repeatable, at the same time singular and iterable. Its cultural importance in our contemporary world of print and digital media resides precisely in this paradoxical structure: iterable singularity and singular iterability.

## Deferring Authenticity

The assessments of Anne Frank's diaries and of the alleged notebooks of Adolf Hitler raise yet another question about the relationship between authenticity, singularity and originality. These assessments all show that authenticity cannot be proven on the basis of a single document because each document is always embedded in an encompassing system of documents constituting the archive. In the case of Frank's diaries, their authenticity was established by comparing them with documents of which the authenticity was certified. In this respect, a document's authenticity is thus not a quality in its own right, but is produced by a complex system, a body of sources, whose authenticity is guaranteed by the archive's unity, homogeneity, and consistency. As Derrida puts it: the archive is a locus of *consignation*. By consignation he does not only mean 'in the ordinary sense of the word, the act of assigning residence . . . (to consign, to deposit)', but also and even more that the archive *gathers together signs*: '*Consignation* aims to coordinate a single corpus, in a system or a synchrony in which all the elements articulate the unity of an ideal configuration'.[29] In this process, the ideal configuration thus paradoxically arises by the fact that this system is simultaneously both certifying and certified. Authenticity reveals itself to be always already subject to the movement of deferral, as authenticity does not arise from an original origin: it presupposes claims to authenticity whose authenticity needs in its turn to be checked *previously* so that the idea of an authentic 'origin' and of an original 'authenticity' are deferred in a series of displacements. *Always already.*[30]

In the case of Anne Frank's diaries, the Forensic Laboratory recognized this problem, since the reference material was subjected to the same technical investigations as used on the diary itself: the addressees of Anne's private correspondence were checked, the contents of the letters examined for their historical consistency, and the so-called 'secondary' particularities of the envelopes were also checked: the non-handwritten traces of the serial imprints such as the stamps, postmarks and censure seals. And yet, the 'evidence' that the reference material was authentic was finally based, as with the diary itself, on the fact that no anachronistic elements or document materials could be found.[31] And thus it provided the proof of an authenticity whose relation to the 'genuine' diary was of course *infra-mince* – as authenticity, in the sense of positively original, remains fundamentally phantasmatic.

In the case of the alleged diaries of Hitler, on the other hand, the assessors had to grapple with the fact that apart from the questionable 'discovered archive' there was only very little 'official' material for comparison available in the *Bundesarchiv*. And so it happened – according to *Stern* reporter Bissinger's detailed report – that Gerd Heidemann compiled the so-called 'dossier Heidemann', a file containing autographs and drafts by Hitler to be given to handwriting experts as reference material. This file, Bissinger writes,

> had just one minor flaw: large parts of it originated from the same workshop in which the Hitler diaries were also produced. Thus the experts . . . found that, indeed, these writings stem from the same pen.[32]

Comparing counterfeit with counterfeit here turns out to be the equivalent of comparing original with original. Kujau's diaries were indeed authentic, and they were unquestionably originals, i.e. authentic and original forgeries. In addition, the documents offered to the assessors by the 'dossier Heidemann' were partly authenticated by certificates, which had in turn been manufactured by Kujau. Wherever precisely we stand in relation to the concept of the original in the age of mechanical reproduction, this case illustrates that authenticity can no longer be rooted in a single and conclusive origin, for with any certificate of authenticity there is a doubt that itself needs certification to dispel. The claim of the document – and of the 'documentary' in general – to be a hard and fast origin or source of authenticity proves to be an enterprise aimed at denying the movement of deferral and bringing it to a definite halt. It is precisely in this compulsive search for a Messianic final certainty that there arises the dangerous pressure to produce nothing but more and more forgeries. In the debate about the alleged Hitler diaries, it was precisely this devotion to the idea of originality that led to the denial of the movement of deferral with the result that due to naive enthusiasm the diaries were at first thought to be authentic. The authenticity of handwriting can not be definitively cut off from the concepts of originality and singularity, no more than it can be comfortably disposed of under the heading of an imperturbable originality, the logic of which is based on the phantasm of a handwriting's singular occurrence in the world.

## Fetishism, Nostalgia, Anachronism

And yet we do desire originals. We desire them so profoundly that the Anne Frank Foundation has produced two facsimile replicas of all six notebooks of Anne Frank. These copies serve to protect the original and also to ensure its 'afterlife' – to echo Benjamin's essay on 'The Task of the Translator'. Thanks to these, the original is made accessible to crowds of scholars and film crews, without exposing it to the danger of being damaged. At the same time the copies serve as 'preserving jars' conserving the auratic here-and-now of the physical touch emanating from the 'original' diary in case it is no longer present for future generations. In so doing, the 'similarity of touch', as Didi-Huberman calls the trace of the imprint, is produced precisely by using the digital technologies of scanning, analysing and reproducing documents – techniques of forgery – which make these facsimiles look like 'perfect copies', copies that look like the originals. In effect, each of the replicas is provided with the same tiny details that make the original distinctive and unique.

The famous first diary now appears three times: Anne's handwriting in triplicate, three times the red-and-white cloth binding that, in the Great Archive storing the memory of Humanity, has become an unmistakable memorial icon. Three times the brass clasp is missing on the tiny metal end that fits into the locking mechanism, and even the rust spots on that lock still look the same.[33] And as Anne was a collector and glued photographs, picture cards, pieces of paper, as well as letters and the accompanying envelopes inside her diary, the copies have been painstakingly reconstructed on the model of the original in a complex collage, every piece of which is the result of an extensive production process. In the replicas the stamps and the post and censorship marks on the envelopes are partly retouched or copied, but partly genuine examples from stamp collections, 'original' copies from the same mould. The more we desire the original, the more counterfeits we get.[34]

We desire the original so much that *Stern* at the time was willing to pay the princely sum of 18.5 million German marks to gain possession of Hitler's diaries. And the bill got paid, because even though this sensational story turned out to be a canard, the magazine's profits rose to 190 million German marks that year.[35] Here one can hardly avoid the association of the monetary value of authenticity with the Marxist idea of commodity fetishism, that is, the idea that in capitalist society a commodity is alienated from its specific qualities and deprived of its actual value. Instead, a commodity is perceived only for its exchange value.[36] In the case of the Hitler diaries, the value of the commodity (*Warenwert*) is the validity of its 'truth' (*Wahrenwert*). The higher *Stern*'s investment, the higher the diaries' authenticity rose. The immense *monetary* value was justified by *Stern* claiming that these diaries could be accorded a substantial *historical* value, necessitating a revision of the history of the Nazi era. The archivists carrying out the historical authentication of the material were, on the contrary, astonished by the banality of the diaries' historical content, which was reduced to shallow descriptions of public events lacking any deeper private, political or conceptual reflection.[37]

Consequently, the value of these diaries as objects of economic exchange scarcely resulted from their historical content but above all from their being *autographic,* from the claimed evidence of their physical materiality embodying the original and singular 'here and now' of handwriting. And as handwriting is considered to be inseparable from the origin by the hand, it is at the same time seen as a sure guarantee of the unity of past and present. This nostalgic desire follows the logic of the fetish in still other than economic terms. It not only turns towards the past – *nóstos* means 'return' – but it does this with longing and pain (*álgos*) corresponding, as it were, in the temporal realm to 'homesickness' in the spatial. The driving force for nostalgia is the painful experience of a lack similar to that which in psychoanalytic discourse is the basis of the concept of the fetish, understood as those objects that a subject feels strongly attached to. Freud, in his famous essay on fetishism (1927), describes the fetish as a substitute for the mother's absent penis. The child believes that the mother's penis was once there but that she was deprived of it. The realization that the mother does not in fact possess a penis leads to a metonymic displacement of the absent penis onto some other part of the body or its continuation, such as a piece of jewellery, a particular piece of fabric or – as in the Kujau case – a World War One uniform.

This logic of replacing a desired yet unavailable object with another object also applies to handwriting. For our cultural desire for the 'auratic', authentic original derives from a (childish) belief in an original and physical presence, embodied in a writing movement, a *ductus* or *Hand*lung of which has as an absolutely necessary condition the presence of a subject of writing. Writing originates from the hand of the writer and it is inseparable from it. And yet it has been deprived of it. But not without leaving a trace in the form of a 'line' or a 'track' on whose lines readers seek to catch up with or associate with this absentee belatedly in a future present.

It is not by accident that Hitler's diaries were part of a comprehensive collection of Nazi relics circulating among dealers and collectors, including not only documents and pictures, but also flags and medals, uniforms and helmets, swords, daggers, and pistols, etc. Moreover – and this seems particularly striking for my argument about fetishism – Kujau had identified a certain fascination on the part of his customers: they were, as Hamilton writes, 'always impressed by seals, especially wax seals over silk ribbons'.[38] The historical value of these military kitsch memorabilia seems somewhat doubtful. Rather, they are examples of pure fetish, literally the product of a perversion that can be specified in Freudian terms as a 'collecting drive' or compulsion to collect. The fetishist dimension of collecting is, in psychoanalytical terms, predicated on a separation between subject and object which – and I am following Mieke Bal's summary of Clifford's theory of collecting here:

> makes for an incurable loneliness that, in turn, impels the subject to gather things, in order to surround him- or herself with a subject-domain that is not-other. Small children do this, collecting gravel, sticks, the odd pieces that grown-ups call junk but which, for the child, has no quality other than constituting an extension of the self, called for to remedy the sense of being cut-off.[39]

It is precisely this experience of being separated from a wholeness that sets off a (perverse) compulsion towards the restoration of unity which led to Hitler's alleged diaries being so successful. It is the expression of a nostalgic longing, a homesickness for the lost '*Heimat*' of the *Third Reich* that materialized in the handwriting of the *Führer* and compensated for his absence by the presence of his hand which it promised to 're-present'. In this respect, the Hitler diaries cannot be understood except as a fetish that is the result of an economization of a historical desire that finds its specific expression either 1: in Heidemann's obsession with the *Third Reich*, or 2: in *Stern*'s attachment to a commodity fetish, or 3: in a global public eagerly awaiting the ghostly resurrection of either a monster or a messiah.

## Expositions

For the Frank diaries, the concept of fetishism raises a few uncomfortable, if not shocking questions. The shocking thing about it, the terribly 'awkward' thing or the provocation is that it suggests that one must, ironically enough, assume a similar experience of deep and fundamental lack to be the root of a nostalgic 'homesickness', longing or drive. This drive forms the motive for almost one million people a year to visit the historic site of the Anne Frank House in Amsterdam, to see the authentic place that the diaries were about, where they were written and where now, in Anne's uncompleted future, they can be seen in her place.

The shocking aspect of this idea is that it necessarily requires one to distinguish between the ardent desire of the visitors of the Anne Frank house in their search for authenticity, on the one hand, and the fetishist desire of the recipients of the alleged Hitler diaries, on the other. Is Anne's diary to be considered a fetish, as the Hitler diary is? Given the commercialization of the museum in the way it markets its Anne Frank merchandise in the museum shop and on the website as a sort of Holocaust Disneyland, the comparison, at least in terms of the exchange economy, is not so wide of the mark. There is a subtle difference, however – *there must be one*. But how can we understand this difference? Can or should it be attributed to the ultimate distinction that classifies Anne Frank's diaries as true and the 'Hitler' diaries as false? Or is it enough to point to the fact that Frank's diaries were not written *on demand*, as Hitler's diaries were? Rather, they were 'given' to us by Otto Frank as a 'gift', or a 'pharmakon' (the German word 'Gift' referring to 'poison'), when he came back from Auschwitz extermination camp and handed us his daughter's legacy as a poisoned chalice that we might choke on forever. But if Anne's diary came to us as an uninvited guest, how, then, could it be that we have set it up as a monument in our Archive and in the house of our shared cultural memory, if not by inviting the narrated past to be present as a welcome guest in our present? How is this anachronism to be viewed, this seeping of a past present into the actuality of the here-and-now, driven by the principle of iteration, of repeating – to use a paradoxical expression – the singular original? And how is this dual temporality related to that other 'nostalgic' desire – which must be of a completely different order – the nostalgia for Nazi relics that is rooted in fetishism?

Whereas I have thus far discussed these questions in terms of the archive, with its specific practices of certifying original and singular documents of a past present and preserving them for a future present, I should now like to turn to that other locus of cultural memory: the museum. Like the archive, the museum's capacity for 'certifying' and 'exposing' a document as true or false is based on the authority of the institution.[40] The archive deploys its authority *on the inside* of a building closed to the outside world; originally and etymologically, archive (*arkheion*) means, as Derrida emphasizes, 'initially a house, a domicile, an address', the residence of the superior magistrates, the *archons*, those who had political power in Antiquity. 'On account of their publicly recognized authority, it is *at their home*, in that *place which is their house* (*private house, family house*, or employee's house), that official documents are filed'.[41] This private shield or screening off from the public who have no right of access has always been an integral part of archival power. In this respect, archival documents are 'semiophores', as Krysztof Pomian describes signs pointing like ancient sacred objects in the museum towards the invisible and themselves in addition often locked away out of sight in storeroom cases.[42]

By contrast, the museum's rhetoric is based on this very act of 'making public'. It is not accidental that the modern museum develops just at the moment when it opens its doors to the public.[43] It is precisely this gesture of showing or exposition that Mieke Bal in *Double Exposures* sees as the basis of the museum. And since showing has a discursive form, Mieke Bal analyses it by analogy to the structure of a speech act:

> Exposing an agent, or subject, puts 'things' on display, which creates a subject/object dichotomy. This dichotomy enables the subject to make a statement about the object. The object is there to substantiate the statement. It is put there within a frame that enables the statement to come across. There is an addressee for the statement, the visitor, viewer, or reader. The discourse surrounding the exposition, or, more precisely, the discourse that *is* the exposition, is 'constative': informative and affirmative . . . In expositions, a 'first person', the exposer, tells 'a second person', the visitor, about a 'third person', the object on display, who does not participate in the conversation. But unlike many other constative speech acts, the object, although mute, is present.[44]

In what follows, I would like to continue my examination of the concept of authenticity in the Anne Frank Museum in Amsterdam, and within the theoretical framework offered by Bal, I will be asking if and how the curatorial institution of the museum as an authoritative subject transmits 'speech acts' about an object on display to the museum visitor. To be precise, what is at issue is how the museum, as a cultural agent and as a 'first person' in the discourse on the Holocaust, presents the diary of Anne Frank as an exhibit and thus to a certain extent as a 'third person' and how it makes this available to be looked at as a public object. And as my investigation is located in the Anne Frank House in Amsterdam, I begin right there with a tour round the museum from the perspective of a 'second person' (the visitor) and accompanied by 'you'.

## Fixed Narrative

A Saturday afternoon in December. We have been standing for hours in the cold and rain on the Prinsengracht at the foot of the Westertoren. Nobody complains. Nobody is impatient. Once we are allowed inside the house, we follow the prescribed route through the museum. From the front of the house where Otto Frank had installed his jam-making kitchen and storage area, we climb a staircase on the landing of which there stands a bookcase leading us up a narrow stairway concealed behind it to the back part of the house. There is only this one way. We inevitably have to climb the same steps Anne once climbed. We peer into the same darkness in the blacked-out attic, feel the same lack of space in the rooms where eight people hid for 25 months, we are horrified at the thought of being betrayed and the ensuing deportation to Germany.

Once past the bookcase, it seems silent to you in the canal-side house. This is exactly the situation described by Jessica Durlacher in the opening of her novel *De Dochter* (*The Daughter*), which takes place in the Anne Frank house. 'It is almost like a funeral', as Durlacher describes the silence that comes over the noisy, giggling hordes of tourists as soon as they enter the 'Achterhuis', the annexe. Streams of visitors shuffle through the corridors and rooms silently or quietly whispering, as if they were observing the requirements for surviving once observed by the people in hiding. 'We have to whisper, and tread lightly during the day, otherwise the people downstairs in the warehouse might hear us', reads a quote in English from Anne Frank's diary given in several languages on the museum wall.

On the upper floor, we step into the small room once occupied by Anne Frank and the dentist Fritz Pfeffer. The room is in semi-darkness as it was at the time when the windows were covered with curtains to protect those in hiding from being seen from outside. You notice Anne's wall decorations: posters of Deanna Durbin and Ray Milland, stars of the pre-war cinema. Otherwise, the room is bare, just as it was when the inhabitants were arrested and the entire annexe was cleared out by order of the Nazi occupiers. Since then – one can read in the museum guide – the annexe has remained in this historically authentic state: authentic darkness, authentic silence, authentic emptiness, all are present signs of an absence.

The clearest trace of the former inhabitants is provided by a handwritten letter exhibited in a display case in Anne's room. The darkness prevents you from reading this letter. The only information is given by a transparent accompanying label on the display case. You go nearer and try to read the inscription. However, on approaching the case, your own shadow covers the object. You want to try another angle, but you cannot because you have to share this room with others – just as Anne did with Fritz Pfeffer. Here the muted light of a spotlight reflects off the glass in a way that blinds you. You finally manage to read the sign that describes the manuscript as a 'farewell letter written by Fritz Pfeffer to his fiancée Charlotte Kaletta'. The letter itself remains unreadable as a text, though. The feelings of love expressed in this letter remain unread, for ever undelivered to its beloved addressee Charlotte Kaletta.

Your tour through the museum leads you up to the attic, a large, high and brightly lit room. Coming out of the dark of the secret annexe, you have to blink. Here you are faced with readable matter documenting the Holocaust: the archive material consisting of explicit pictures and writings is well lit; screens show videotapes of Westerbork, Bergen-Belsen, and Auschwitz-Birkenau, the Holocaust appears in stark images. There is no way of avoiding this room; you have to pass through this room to get to the adjacent room where the diaries of Anne Frank are exhibited in brightly-lit display cases.

Whereas Pfeffer's love letter was exhibited vertically on the museum wall – as is normal with an image – Anne's notebooks are laid out horizontally in the display cases like a book, a text inviting the visitor not so much to look at, than to read them. The museum, moreover, instructs you *how* to read them. The museum as your narrator makes use of all the means of exposition at its disposal for its speech act: leaflets, labels to the exhibits, the use of light and darkness as well as the topographical arrangement of the house. The speech act of the museum is, to use Bal's reference to Austin's speech act theory, constative: it portrays true events as true and not faked. For Anne Frank's house this stress on the 'authentic' is not without a reason, for what is after all at stake even today is the need for a statement of the legacy of the Shoah against the slander of right-wing historical revisionism. The museum fulfils this duty by presenting Anne Frank's diaries as authentic documents, or to be more exact, by exposing above all the authenticity of them: they function as imprints that are not fake and with a seal of approval of an original past that they store and rescue in the same way that Noah's Ark archived the original state of life on earth. The expository gesture of the museum is unmistakable: it documents, it authenticates, it makes a constative statement about this one irrefutable truth and allows for no alternative readings. Its topo*graphy* produces a prescribed, stable text, a constative narrative with a mono-linear and fixed structure. This story has its preface in the warehouse of Otto Frank's jam-making business on the ground floor, its beginning is located on a dark landing with a movable bookcase, it continues with inescapable linearity up a stairway to a cramped hiding place, and finally ends upstairs with the brightly-lit attic documenting final destinations of the canal-side inhabitants after they were betrayed. Only then do you proceed to the diaries.

The museum's topography thus metaphorically instructs you how to read Anne Frank's diary: read the diary retrospectively. Accordingly any event recorded in her diaries is framed *belatedly* within a second text located *outside* – or literally *on top of* – the actual annexe, in its attic. You fill in the museum's empty rooms with the anachronistic hindsight of a past future that is not told in the diary: the arrest, the deportation, the camp. You look at Anne's thirteenth birthday party and imagine her joy when she was given the notebook bound in checked material, and you frame this moment within the hermeneutic circle that pushes Anne's future into the past of what was then her present. Thus you create a text presenting a unitary history in which Anne becomes an unequivocal and one-dimensional object that was *always already* a victim of Nazi murder – which she was, indeed. But wasn't she so much more than that?

## Image-Texts

Let us look back at Fritz Pfeffer's farewell letter displayed in the small room on the lower, dark floor of the museum. Whereas Anne Frank's diaries are well lit and the text can be read, Pfeffer's letter does not seem meant to be read. Its presence there is based on a kind of 'cult value' as Benjamin describes, in his essay on the Work of Art, of 'certain Madonnas [that] remain covered nearly all year round'.[45] Their cult value, Benjamin states, 'would seem to demand that the work of art remain hidden'. The value of such a cult work of art resides in their mere *existence*, less in their *visibility*. The exhibition of Pfeffer's letter in the display case is exactly this. Its value as a museum object does not primarily result from its readability as a text that would give voice to the past. Rather, the letter only represents material existence, the physical presence of handwriting as the enactment of absence. Pfeffer's letter does not state anything, it does not articulate any speech act at all and does not display any linguistic signified; it is literally underlit, unreadable, mute. Its value is pure cult. And yet, I should like to argue, this 'cult' character does not necessarily qualify as pure fetishism. Why not?

The key point is that Holocaust reports often deal with the failure of language. How should a text speak appropriately about the Holocaust, or be a 'statement' of it without at the same time becoming unreadable? Conversely, if the Holocaust-text makes its reading all too easy, it risks being considered 'inauthentic'. Since the really authentic

Fritz Pfeffer's farewell letter to Charlotte Kaletta on display in Anne Frank's and Fritz Pfeffer's room.

'proof' against the so-called Auschwitz lie can never be produced, as Jean-François Lyotard says with shocking directness:

> To have 'really seen with his own eyes' a gas chamber would be the condition which gives the authority to say that it exists and to persuade the unbeliever. Yet it is still necessary to prove that the gas chamber was used to kill at the time it was seen. The only acceptable proof that it was used to kill is that one died from it. But if one is dead, one cannot testify that it is on account of the gas chamber. . . . [The plaintiff's] argument is: in order for a place to be identified as a gas chamber, the only eyewitness I will accept would be a victim of this gas chamber; now, according to my opponent, there is no victim that is not dead; otherwise, this gas chamber would not be what he or she claims it to be. There is, therefore, no gas chamber.[46]

The unspeakable experience of the Holocaust can not be 'put into sentences' just like that; it requires, neither the authentication nor the falsification of proof of a case of litigation (*litige*), but it calls for an 'other' kind of discourse and another argument, another *differend* (*différend*):

> The differend is the unstable state and instant of language where-in something which must be able to be put into phrases cannot yet be. This state includes silence, which is a negative phrase, but it also calls upon phrases which are in principle possible.[47]

Traumatic experiences are not just inaccessible to narration, but by definition – and the one follows logically from the other – also not immediately accessible to memory, since memories are in constant danger of failing down due to stress or trauma. And yet they require a mediated form, or a *performance*, to become communicable. Putting memories into narratives requires one to structure events into a textual form using organization of time and an identifiable narrator: a subject who is the 'master' of the story rather than the object 'suffering' the events.[48]

If earlier in this chapter I considered handwriting to be a 'text-image', because its visual performance cooperates in the semiotic process of writing, I should now like to focus on another analytic dimension of the concept of the text-image that is closely related to it and yet it forms a slight shift that I should like to approach with the complementary concept of 'image-text' that W.J.T. Mitchell uses, in *Picture Theory*, for a way of thinking about memory. In relation to the two components of the composite, Mitchell identifies memory as a double structure, i.e. as both textual and pictorial.[49] Memory is, for Mitchell, a text in that it has to do with storytelling 'in the sense of a temporal sequence of events'.[50] 'Image', on the other hand, has to do with 'imagery and imagination', which unfolds in space rather than in time. Whereas an image rather contemplates a private memory located in a realm of the unconscious, narrative seems to be a mode of cognition in the sense of a structured knowing; telling a story that is (de-)scribable, readable and repeatable, and that can be told over and over again and thus can contribute to creating public recollection and cultural memory.

For that reason, according to Mitchell, traumatic experiences often remain within the realm of the visual; they cannot become narratives. At best, they become silent testimonies. Artistic projects on Holocaust experiences are full of such 'differends': 'silent speech acts' in search of a perceptible form of discourse. For example, Armando's 'Holocaust document' *Drawing* can be understood less as a 'drawing' than as a failed attempt to write. As an image-text in Mitchell's sense, the pencil line hints at the movement of writing: going from top left to bottom right it traces its stammering way across the paper, seeking to create a movement of the hand, maybe groping after the symbolic, now and then vaguely managing the start of a recognizable form of a letter without ever giving rise to a readable imprint. As a 'drawing', 'text-image', 'scribbling', 'gauche', 'child-like'; to observe the line, as Roland Barthes writes, 'to scan [it] with our eyes and lips means constantly to disabuse ourselves of *what it would seem to be*'.[51] As if writing blind or *in the dark*, the line leaves an unreadable trace that attempts to remember the past but fails to communicate and master the events using the conventions of an imprint that can be spoken. This line cannot decide between text and image. It never totally abandons the imprint; it alludes to it by *withdrawing* from it.

Pfeffer's handwritten letter is 'silent' in a different way, however. It *would* be readable, highly readable even, as it is written in a formal,

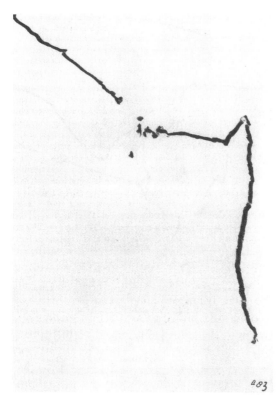

Armando, *Drawing*,
1983, pencil on paper,
18 x 13 cm.

regular hand, in keeping with the importance of the occasion – saying farewell. The museum visitor would be able to read it, were it not for the fact that the museum exhibits the letter in a glass case half-hidden behind a transparent label and in addition projects either too much or too little light onto it.

Whereas Pfeffer's letter is unreadable as an alphanumeric text, Anne's diary is perfectly visible without any visual obstructions. It strikes one as a tourist attraction exhibited as a 're-presentation', literally the 'live performance' of a spectre coming back to us from the past, made available by means of well-lit images and documents. Whereas Pfeffer's love letter is literally 'underexposed', outshone and drowned out by an authoritative, constative speech act on the part of the museum, Anne's diary seems 'overexposed': too quickly, too simply readable. And as such, it is as invisible as a monument.[52]

How much authenticity do we need to rescue us from amnesia? Can there be such a thing as *too much* authenticity?

## 'Dear Kitty'

You are now in the backroom of the attic. You are standing at the glass case with Anne Frank's famous diary like a holy relic before you. The diary is – literally – an object on display. It is lying on a transparent lectern on top of a mirror so that you are free to study the notebook from every angle. From above you look at the entry for 20 October 1942 in the open book. Above the actual diary entry there are notes taped to the diary; one of them contains a series of three portrait photographs of Anne Frank. The various units of text are written in slightly varying styles of childish, school-trained script, and are in some places over-written with pencil corrections in a more mature, individual script. Here the process of writing illustrates her personal development over time. From below through the mirror you can examine the otherwise hidden side of the book, the hardcover already mentioned, bound in orange-yellow checked cloth, as a material object in its three-dimensional depth.

On the left-hand side of one of the text fragments you discover the phrase 'Beste Kitty' ('Dear Kitty') – a vocative in a diary. Who is being

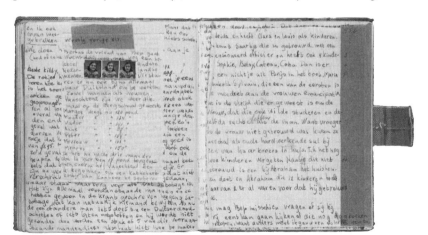

Double-spread of Anne Frank's diary for 20 October 1942.

addressed? Here the practice of diary writing intermingles with that of private correspondence. But who is this Kitty? The museum does not mention her as one of the inhabitants in the secret annexe. And yet she seems to be Anne's second person, the 'you' to whom she directs her discourse. Kitty often turns up in Anne's notes. As a pronoun, she is introduced in the very first lines of the diary: 'I hope I shall be able to entrust everything to you, as I have never been able to do to anyone before, and I hope that you will be a great support and comfort to me. Anne Frank. 12th June 1942'.[53] Later on in the diary, this invented second person is named 'Kitty'. Kitty becomes an integral part of Anne's diary, her fictive reader and at the same time her most intimate friend.[54]

According to José van Dijck, such dedications to an absent audience are more the rule than an exception in the diary genre:

> writing, even as a form of self-expression, signals the need to connect, either to someone . . . else, or to oneself later in life . . . [D]iary writing is, to a large extent, a cultural form firmly rooted in rhetorical conventions: intimacy and privacy are *effects* rather then intrinsic features of the genre.[55]

Such 'public privacy' also characterizes Anne Frank's diary. Anne repeatedly expresses her wish to be a journalist and a famous writer. An appeal, via the 'Oranje' radio channel in London, from the Dutch Minister Bolkestein to the people of Holland on 28 March 1944, to keep diaries as historical documents for the postwar era, inspires Anne to rewrite and edit her diary into a book called *Het Achterhuis*.[56] 'Dear Kitty', writes Anne only one day after this appeal, 'Just imagine how interesting it would be if I were to publish a novel about the "Secret Annexe"'.[57] This is Anne's dream and given her talent, one that seems not unlikely, or at least a possible future for her that we know did not come true. Would we also have been Anne's readers in this other future that never came about?

Even if the name Kitty is readable as text, as a vocative and as a text-image in the museum's display case it is highly ambivalent.[58] The proper name conceals a mystery, referring as it does indexically to an absentee who is summoned from the outside world or from the other pages of the book or who has to be sought in the same way as a footnote refers in the form of a hyperlink to something outside of the text, yet is involved with it. One should be able to read what is under the label stuck on. But the three-dimensionality of the book in the display case retains its mystery. Unlike the allographic print versions available in the museum shop, the autographic original manuscript is not meant to be leafed through. Even though it is exposed on top of a mirror as a three-dimensional object, its readability is reduced to this flat double page on display. This *volume* actually has no *volume*. Thus the proper name of Kitty has neither a referential depth nor a context in which it could become meaningful. The only reduced context it has is the one provided by the institutionalizing frame of the museum: the panopticon of the Holocaust. Thus exposed, the second person addressed by the diary's vocative remains flat, literally two-dimensional and unreadable, deprived of other subject possibilities than that of a silent witness bearing testimony to the unspoken and unspeakable Nazi crimes. Like Anne, 'Kitty' is as much in danger of becoming a flat fetish, no other readings are available to her either. At no point are the two friends allowed to break with the context of the museum's authority.

The logic of an imagined addressee put on display in a museum is so vastly complex because the addressee is simultaneously exposed and withdrawn from view by the visual rhetoric of the display case. The more Kitty is exposed, the more she withdraws. She is exposed by being withdrawn. Both as text and as image. Kitty comes to represent something that is always already absent, an empty signifier with no reference. She indicates nothing but the vacant place of a desired, yet absent, 'you' who is constitutive for the success of the speech act. The moment Anne Frank's private diary becomes a public cultural object constituting our shared history, we all – as readers and as visitors – participate in this second personhood; we become Anne's intimate confidant – at least metonymically.

This metonymic second-person role, if we seriously accept the invitation, is not without its problems, however. What is on display in the display case is, after all, a private diary, and diaries, like love letters, are neither meant to be read aloud, nor to be displayed in public. They belong instead to the intimate private sphere, which deserves protection. The desire of diary writers for a public audience thus appears somewhat exhibitionist. Likewise, the reader or spectator in such an expository situation is in danger of slipping into the role of a voyeur who, herself invisible, gazes unhindered at an immediately available object. We look at Anne's private diary as an object whose readable notes are reduced to a single page. And we look at **Anne**'s flat image of her photo portrait showing her smiling graciously at us from the museum wall with the knowing sadness of a saint to whom the visitor can direct her prayers: 'you who have died for us ... forgive us our sins ...' Are we, as visitors, or voyeurs, implicated in assigning the one in the flat image to her role as a victim in the drama of her future murder? Do we thus murder her once more? Over and over again?[59]

On closer inspection of the display case, however, another aspect comes to the fore. The mirror does not only give a mirror image of the diary but you as an observer are exposed as well on the stage of the visual display: you, your face and your gaze are also reflected back to you in the mirror. This glance disturbs the museum's authoritative first-person speech act, which forces us to gaze freely at an exhibited object, making it well and truly visible with the aid of a mirror and observable

The diary in the display case at Anne Frank House in Amsterdam.

from all imaginable angles. Here you are, Anne's second person, exposed in a display case in a Holocaust museum. Your mono-directional gaze directed at Anne as the *always already* victim of Nazi murder is now returned to you, the sender. Although you can choose to leave this display case at any time, 'you' have nevertheless *always already* been included in it. Like Kitty, you come to stand in for the desired friend; you are the addressee of a speech act directed as a testament towards the future. For it is the basic principle of all writing, including hand-writing: it produces a trace left for a reader of the future.

## Anne Frank live

Jessica Durlacher's novel *The Daughter* is about the (impossible) relation-ship between the protagonist, Max, from a traumatized Jewish family, and Sabine, the mysterious 'daughter' who likewise shares a dark and dominating legacy from the Shoah.[60] Not by chance Durlacher places the first chance meeting of the two characters at the scene of earlier unsuccessful meetings: the Anne Frank House where Sabine works as an administrator. Without any prompting from Max Sabine comments on the place:

> It goes on being the secret annexe here. It will never end. Ever. The house is eternally empty. This is the cruelty of it, the tragedy . . . Actually, it is emptied out every day over and over again, this house. Every day, they are arrested once again. And every day, every morn-ing when I come here, I find the house empty. And they are gone, once again. A horrible repetition, like in hell.
> I find everything horrible that will be no more for ever.[61]

In this passage, Sabine describes the 'horror' of the house in a paradox, calling the secret annexe anachronistically the place where 'everything . . . will be no more for ever'. It is a place of a 'horrible repe-tition' of that which is precisely *un*repeatable and beyond restoration. Here she evokes a repetition of history as the *presence* of a past event in her *present* experience. Miraculously: the past as a 'spectre'.

This spectral recurrence is the rhetorical basis of the memorial, which, unlike most museums, is an authentic place where actual events really happened. The uniqueness of the event cannot be copied and this is precisely the source of the performative power of the memorial for the act of memory. Sabine's words reflect this very singularity. What is repeated is not an event, in the end, but precisely a non-event, a meeting *in absentio*, an intervention involving Anne and the other people living in the annexe which *does not* happen.

'It's so horrible, so tragic', Sabine says. The 'horrible' and 'tragic' force of the abandonment of the secret annexe is paradoxically enough based on the idea of a *possible* presence, of 'speakable words' about a conceivable future that has not come about, it is true, but nevertheless could have been possible – if . . .

The experience of the loss of this other future, along with the knowledge that it has not come about 'for ever', this 'insight' is the basis of any act of mourning constituting our cultural memory of the Holocaust. The desire to participate in this public 'ceremony' is the primary incentive for the many people who make the pilgrimage to visit the authentic location of Anne Frank's place of refuge and to retrace her steps. As a compensation or a metonymic extension of the now absent Anne, the visitors come in search of a 'trace' of her presence: the diaries: unique, unmistakable, physical handwriting produced by her hand. At the Anne Frank House, the visitors are *touched* by Anne's handwriting as by a *belated* handshake, and it is precisely this touching of an absence that makes the handwriting into an event.

The uniqueness of authenticity is always already permeated by the logic of repetition. For the visitor, the museum functions as a theatre, a place of irreducible presence, where a performance is staged as a unique event. And the diary in this play is a prop, in Latin a *requisitus*, which literally means a *required* or 'desired' object. Unlike the innumerable printed editions of *The Secret Annexe*, the definitively readable imprints of Anne's diary, the appearance of this musealized textbook has a *sensational* value, that is, appealing to the senses. Its materiality as a unique manuscript touches us physically. Its individual trace turns the writing into a tender whisper, it breathes Anne's voice into the text. It is as if the note in the diary is speaking to you personally, murmuring her secrets into your ears exclusively to you alone. Handwriting, here, makes a difference, because it not only informs, *stating* meaning in a sober way, but it touches you physically. It functions as a performative.

Paradoxically enough, this touch, although sensational and corporeal, is not the result of material authenticity. Because the diary in the case is, strictly speaking, not identical to the diary of Anne Frank, it is no longer her diary, it has been transformed already by becoming an object in a museum in the same way that documents, for example decrees or acts, even while being the originals, lose their effectiveness by being put in the archive. This transformation is of course *infra-mince*; its auratic effect as a theatrical prop is, however, enormous. This effect has no need of the original, since the two perfect clones allow the viewer to be affected equally by catharsis, a state that seems to have more to do with the theatre than with writing. These theatrical effects result from the phantasm of an irreducible immediacy and presence that distinguish the medial space of the stage or the museum from that of film or photography. This stage, however much it may insist on its unique here-and-now, nevertheless can never be the authentic place for a museum visitor as it once was for Anne.

In this respect, the magic rhetoric of the place is based less on 're-presentation' than on the fact that the memorial operates as a performative, in other words as a speech act, by not so much describing or stating but by *doing* something. In his study on 'Holocaust effects in contemporary art, literature and theory', Ernst Van Alphen describes this concept of memory as a performative practice like this:

> the Holocaust is not re-presented, but rather presented or enacted. In terms of speech act theory I might explain it differently. The Holocaust is not made present by means of a constative speech act–that is, as a mediated account, as the truthful or untruthful content of the speech act; rather, it is made present as performative effect. Those performative acts 'do' the Holocaust.[62]

'Doing' the Holocaust means: putting it into a readable, repeatable form. In such a way, in fact, that there come about new possibilities, for example those that problematize readability by challenging the prevailing codes or opening up subject possibilities for the rigid positions of the first, second and third person in the discourse of the speech act of the museum. No longer condemned to be a Holocaust fetish, an alternative future for Anne is then conceivable, the non-materialization of which remains a call to us. We are then those former future addressees of the Holocaust being called upon and in whose cultural memory it lives on today.

## 'Archivization' and 'Musealization'

However much in the age of mechanical reproduction we desire authenticity and however important this concept may be, threatened as it is by a loss of the unique, auratic here-and-now in the face of contemporary media culture, historical authenticity can never be anything but a product of mediation. In talking about the cultural *loci* of the archive and the museum, one could here go so far as to sum this up using two neologisms: events are either 'archivized' or 'musealized'. I should like to take the technical term 'archivization' used by Derrida in *Archive Fever* [*Mal d'archive*] in which he writes that

> the archive, as printing, writing, prosthesis, or hypomnesic technique in general is not only the place for stocking and for conserving an archivable content *of the past* which would exist in any case, such as, without the archive, one still believes it was or will have been. No, the technical structure of the *archiving* archive also determines the structure of the *archivable* content even in its very coming into existence and in its relationship to the future. The archivization produces as much as it records the event.[63]

The thesis developed here, that the archive not only stores and records events but that the archival process produces the events itself, brings another dimension to the work of the archive. The archive not only 'archivizes', that is, it not only collects, selects, orders, files, conserves, authenticates and certifies, but beyond that it performs an additional task, as its own inscription technologies produce the events in the first place. Derrida describes this addition using in the French version of his text the neologism 'archivation', and the English translator found that this small irregularity brought so much more added value that he in turn added a syllable to the English word 'archiving': 'The *archivization* produces as much as it records the event.'[64]

Eric Ketelaar has drawn attention to this addition and given it his own spin by arguing that the archival production of events depends not only on 'technical structures', as Derrida maintains, but just as much on cultural *values*, and he signals this idea by adding a further syllable: 'achi*val*ization'. 'Archi*val*ization', Ketelaar explains as 'the conscious or unconscious choice (determined by social and cultural factors) to consider something worth archiving.'[65] In illustration of his thesis, Ketelaar points to the examples by Trouillot and Stoler, well-known amongst students of archival practice, according to which the birth of a child that dies on the day of its birth in one culture is considered to be an archivable event – or rather, worth archiving – in another (for example in a colonial context) it is not.[66]

In this respect, one could ask the question by analogy with Derrida's reading of Freud (what would it have been like if Freud had used e-mail rather than handwritten correspondence?): What would our work of remembering the Shoah look like if Anne Frank had been able to write a blog instead of a paper diary?[67] How would we look back today on the events narrated and archived by her, what would this alternative future have looked like? Following Ketelaar, one could push this line of questioning even further since archival activity began as an 'archivalized' event precisely at the time when Anne Frank decided to keep a diary, while in the case of the Hitler diaries, it was the failure to make such a decision, which, in retrospect, set the stage for Kujau's forgeries.

The upshot of these speculations is that the trace of Anne Frank's diary is drawn anew. Not as the trail of someone who has passed by who, if only one sets out determinedly in search of her trace and just follows it doggedly enough, leading the reader of the trail – as Ginzburg describes the basic *ductus* of the researcher – safely to its origin. Instead, the figure of Anne Frank in her house – it is at the same time her archive and her grave and this we visit in the same way, literally as an *archeion*: the original – is complemented by the other, plural Anne Frank figures that did not come about, yet remain possible or imaginable.

Had Anne Frank *blogged* – of this we can be sure – our contemporary remembering would look different. Because the focus of the original, its authenticity and authorship, towards which we are directed by her handwriting and to which we are culturally so attached, would have taken a different form within the ephemeral inscription technologies of the Internet. In our task of remembering we would have been less insistent on authenticity and instead would have considered the possibility of it being a fake. This is something that is always already inherent within the structure of diary writing, not just in fact in the belatedness of remembering an absent writer but as a possibility already arising precisely at the time of writing, this being after all the time in which, a means of expression needing to be found, thinking becomes conscious of itself and has to be grammatically mediated, the time in which, as Heidegger put it, we find ourselves 'on the way to language'. The monument of subjectivity and authorship, created belatedly by the act of remembering, would have been replaced by an anonymous, fragmentary and multiple avatar. The association with a historical-physical place would have been lost in the depths of electronic space, and – this illustrates how far the process of archivization goes – as a blog on the Internet, the inscription would presumably have been erased for good, and this amnesia would not even have been observed or recorded by an archive. This is what Jacques Derrida calls the *Mal d'archive*: the malignity, the evil, but also the suffering, the pain, the illness and at the same time the desire or the 'drive' of the archive is the retreat of the self-observation of amnesia. Print-run following print-run and with every every stroke of the pen, the archive suffers from a thanatomania, or death drive; as Jacques Derrida puts it, it is 'archiviolitic', as the drive 'works *to destroy the archive: on the condition of effacing* but also *with a view to effacing* its own "proper" traces'.[68]

That the museum as a memory machine functions like the archive essentially theatrically (or performatively) I should like to designate by the neologism 'musealization'.[69] By exposing the objects on display as one thing or the other, or as genuine or fake, by making use of the gesture of display in general and by showing objects in display cases, it already destroys the object as an 'original'. The 'musealized' object is not just an *object*, but an *event*. 'To musealize' means, as Austin describes performative speech acts, 'to do': to do, to handle or to negotiate the object. In this sense, musealized handwriting is no *mute* object in the museum exposed by an authoritative first person, the curator, to a second person addressee. Instead, the act of musealization, like the act of archivization, is a performative act that does not so much make a *statement* of an event as it *produces* the event. At the same time, as Bal argues with her concept of 'double exposition', it always also exposes the strategies of exhibiting – the collection, selection and framing of objects – along with its respective inscription technologies and its ideological value systems.

As cultural agents, both the archive and the museum continually express an obligation – as Derrida has described it: 'It is because there has been an archived [or a musealized] event, because the injunction or the law has already presented and *inscribed* itself into historical memory as an injunction of memory.'[70] Both the archive and the museum face the difficulty of intermingling three temporal levels, to be thought of as 'three actual presents, which would be the past present, the present present and the future present.'[71] To *recall* or *re-present* these presents in a preposterous gesture is the task of the archive and the museum; they have 'the injunction of memory' which is for Derrida tied in depth 'with the anticipation of the future to come.'[72] In this process, the cases with their objects to display or the workrooms with their objects undergoing conservation represent the interface betokening the abyss of anachronism; they consign the documents to their places *'en abîme'*, that is – literally – on the 'abyss' opening up between past, present and future.[73]

In the case of the reception of the alleged Hitler diaries, the anachronistic structure of memory was totally denied, disregarding the fact that these diaries were fake. Handwriting served as a fetish to directly and unreflectingly conflate past and present without problematizing the difference. The situation is more complex in the case of Anne Frank's *Diary*, not only because her diaries were legally recognized as genuine, but because it is not enough to base our recall of the past on a positivistic understanding of an authentic origin. Such an understanding likewise risks subsequently erasing past events, just as certain chemical methods deployed to prove a document's authenticity destroy this very document. It is not sufficient to shape the act of memory as an act of certification and classification by exposing documents as either genuine or fake, for this would reduce the work of the archive and the museum to a fetishistic act of re-'collecting' the past, in which remembering means compulsive collecting (as a drive).

Documents pretend to make history present, but they never really do, neither horizontally as documentary text, nor vertically as image. The only effect they can achieve is re-iteration, the basis of all writing, including handwriting that is: iteration with a difference. This difference is of course an assault on the original as the authentic and singular origin of the event, and yet it does not minimize in the least the power of mourning. Because only the theatrical sensation can ever be authentic, *touch* as a performative event.

> If repetition is thus inscribed at the heart of the future to come, one must also import there, *in the same stroke*, the death drive, the violence of forgetting, *superrepression* (suppression and repression), the anarchive, in short, the possibility of putting to death the very thing, whatever its name, what *carries the law in its tradition*.[74]

Documents – even *wrongly* printed [*verdruckte*] (inauthentic) or sup*pressed* [*unter*drückte] (anarchivalized) – are always impressions of past events. In any case, however, in the memory they leave traces to be touched (*Erspürungen*).

## Before a Grave

Walter Benjamin devoted one of his 'Denkbilder' to Weimar.[1] There in the Goethe and Schiller archives he finds the manuscripts bedded 'like patients in hospital beds'; these pages lie there, suffering 'in their repositories':

> The fact that everything which we know today as Goethe's 'Works', and which confronts us consciously and sturdily in countless published volumes, once existed in this unique, fragile handwritten form, and the fact that what emanated from it can only be the austere, purifying atmosphere which surrounds patients who are dying or recovering and which is perceptible to the few who are close to them – this is something we do not care to dwell on.

After here putting 'Goethe's "Works"' in quotation marks as though he wanted to liberate the concept of Work [*Werkbegriff*] from its capital letter and rethink it as 'activity', to question this concept and even discredit it, Benjamin goes on to enquire:

> But didn't these manuscript sheets likewise find themselves in a crisis? Didn't a shudder run through them, and no one knew whether it was the proximity of annihilation or that of post-humous fame? And don't they embody the loneliness of poetry? And the place where it took stock of itself? And don't its pages include many whose unnameable text only rises as a glance or a breath of air from their silent, ravaged features?[2]

In practically no other place than in Weimar can one meet with the afterlife of that founding father of German letters in all its vitality. The 'breath' that Benjamin talks about here, in other words literally the *pneuma* or the aura, this 'breath of air', cannot of course be grasped in the form of the 'Work' but is reserved for the unique manuscript itself. Like patients on their sickbeds, the manuscripts in their archival repositories wait to be called upon to be resurrected like relics by pilgrims worshipping them. The Archive breathes this *pneuma*, or this *spiritus*, and com*poetizes* it into a resounding **A**. Like

The sarcophagi of Goethe and 'Schiller' in the Ducal burial vault in Weimar.

a breeze, the aura of the poet winds its way around the town. In the study in Goethe's house, the bed is still there on which the writer slept and next to which his work awaited, as Benjamin writes, 'to plead nightly for him to be liberated from the dead'.[3]

But who or what is it that the pilgrims meet with on visiting the cultural sites associated with the poets in Weimar? What do they meet in that other repository, the Ducal burial vault? Perhaps they also find a poet besides the Dukes? As the so-called homes of the poets in Weimar have long ceased to be the house of a poet – they are museums, and besides along with Schiller's and Goethe's houses and of course Goethe's famous *Gartenhaus*, they are reconstructions whose scars from the nightly bombing have been carefully airbrushed out. 'Weimar as a whole is therefore', as Lorenz Engell sums up the aesthetic image of the town, 'like every authentic work, already a museum reproduction of its own idea, and even the real, historic *Gartenhaus* is always already a replica for which there is an "original" at best in the imagination of the present-day'.[4] Consequently, the poet's pages are not his pages (but archive documents), and his grave is also not his grave.

Even the skull revealing the poet as a human being to the amazement of visitors in the vault like a relic in a sacred place of pilgrimage, this skull resting for ever alongside Goethe's skeleton and referred to as 'Schiller's' skull, is not just one skull. There are two skulls, alas, lying in this grave.

Before 'Schiller' in 1827 – a good quarter of a century after
his death – was laid to rest *eternally* (for the time being) in an oak
sarcophagus in the *Fürstengruft*, the Ducal burial vault in the historic
cemetery, this skull (or one of the objects that have been described
by the Weimar Foundation of Classics as being Schiller's skull) was
to experience a true odyssey. For a time the noble relic was kept in
another archive, the Grand Duke's Royal Library (in what is now the
famous Rococo Hall of the Anna Amalia Library), on a wooden
pedestal beneath the laurel-wreathed marble bust of 'Schiller'.[5] It had
been moved there on the orders of His Royal Majesty from Goethe's
house on the *Frauenplan*, where his fellow poet had placed him for a
time 'on a blue velvet cushion' under a glass cover edged with silver.[6]

Before this burial place, however, the skull had been kept by
Bürgermeister Schwabe. He had exhumed it in 1826 during a cleaning
of the tomb from a common grave in the vault at the churchyard of
the *Jakobskirche*, in which Schiller along with countless other less
well-off members of the court had been buried. From a 'chaos of
decay and filth', the honest Bürgermeister records, he rescued skulls
by the sack, 23 to be exact.[7] From amongst them he selected, guided
'by a miraculous revelation', the 'true skull of Schiller'.[8] Not surprisingly, in the following years anatomists, anthropologists and dentists
repeatedly raised objections to the authenticity of the poet's skull.
In this context, August von Froriep in 1911 had 63 skulls once more
exhumed from the vault, from which he, on the basis of the death
mask, designated one to be the 'genuine skull of Schiller'. This is how
a second 'Schiller skull' came to be placed in 1914 in the Ducal burial
vault following expert confirmation by the Anatomical Society.[9]

The grave is opened up again and again. In so doing, the poet
is granted an afterlife. The authentic origin that is at issue here and
provides the fuel for the search for the lost source (*arche*) of the poet,
to which one must return, is split in two; Schiller becomes 'Schiller'.
But the quotation marks are neither mocking nor derisive. They mark
'Schiller' as a quotation and ironize the idea of an original, by posing
quite objectively the question whether anyone other than 'Schiller'
has ever existed. Is it not precisely the quotation marks that in*spire*
the 'afterlife' of every poet? The aura, this *pneuma*, or this *spiritus*,
comes *before Aleph* as I mentioned *before*.

(*Remark:* the—written—text of
this—oral—communication was
to have been addressed to the
*Association of French
Speaking Societies of
Philosophy* before the meeting.
Such a missive therefore had
to be signed. Which I did, and
counterfeit here. Where? There.
J.D.)

J. DERRIDA

Jacques Derrida's signature on the printed text of 'Signature Event Context'.

# 7 Tattooing: Performing Perforation

His masterpiece: an extraordinary tattoo with which he is covering the
back of his wife, having understood that such was the condition of his
'ductus'. He is seen pushing in his pin while his wife, who is lying flat
on her belly, turns a suppliant and pained face towards him . . .

She cannot see the masterpiece she is wearing, not directly,
and not without a mirror, but it subsists directly on her, at least for
some time – lodged [*à demeure*] for a limited time, of course.
Jacques Derrida, *Monolingualism of the Other*[1]

Nothing is simpler than . . . giving the inanimate of the imprint the
magic power of the animate which touched it for a moment and to
which the imprint owed its existence.
Georges Didi-Huberman, *Ähnlichkeit und Berührung*[2]

## 'I, the Undersigned'

When Jacques Derrida in the early 1970s sent the written text of his lecture 'Signature Event Context' to the Association des Sociétés de Philosophie de Langue Française, he signed his text and accompanied his signature by remarking: 'That dispatch should thus have been signed. Which I do, and counterfeit, here. Where? There. J.D.' This note, along with the signature in facsimile, is printed in *Limited Inc*.

Reproduced like this, the handwritten signature becomes the instant replay of a unique copy. With this enactment of the signature as *printed trace*, Derrida sums up his critique of an all too positivist view of a metaphysics of presence. Writing as – literally – re*tracing* of the original is, for Derrida, *always already* marked by the movement of deferral, because the movement marked by the sender's hand marks a trace of its presence. Writing, viewed as a trace, means precisely that an absence is *always already*, *déjà* inherent within a presence, that is, both the current absence of the addressee, whose deferred future presence only identifies the remaining writing as readable, and also the absence of the sender,

> from the mark that he abandons, and which *cuts itself off* from him and continues to produce effects independently of his presence and of the present actuality of his intentions [*vouloir-dire*], indeed *even after his death*, his absence, which moreover belongs to the structure *of all writing*.[3]

The sign, according to Derrida, is not only *left behind* by its writer and, thus by the *hand* of the writer who touched it and will still be touching it belatedly, but it actively *cuts itself off* from him, it *breaks* the link with the present – and one could add: the living, psycho-somatic – actuality of the writer. Not until it has cut itself off from this proximity and this touch does it develop the symbolic power allowing it to enter into *relations of similarity* that make it iterable as an individual sign (or trace), i.e. make it into a readable imprint. This power continues to *have effect even after death*, and it constitutes the structure of writing.

All writing in fact?

The implications of this statement are already daringly challenging for the handwritten signature because a signature has always represented a reliable sign for the existence of the writer at the time of writing, for the unity of writing and hand. This unity, after all, provides the legal basis of the signature, the basis for the authentic and unique, indeed the physical presence of the writer *mani*festing itself in the very body in a historical here-and-now: 'presence and present'. A royal proclamation along with a last will and testament or the settling of a bill by a banker's card become in their respective ways legally effective by this act of signing guaranteeing the authenticity of the document and the creditworthiness of the signatory. And yet the somatic actuality of the hand – its presence in the present – is directed towards a future here and now in which it becomes the trace of an earlier physical touch which it *tracks belatedly*. It is true that the signature gains its incontrovertible validity through a singular act – when using a bankcard this is clear – but it is at the same time subject to repetition. Because signing always takes place (at least) twice: first as '*tracing*', a 'specimen signature' on the back of the card itself, and secondly it is countersigned – or '*retraced* ' – on the bill.[4] Repetition proves to be the basic condition for the operation of the signing system in general.

If, on the other hand, not just the act of signing is based on corporeal presence but if in addition the writing surface is a physical body as in the case of a *tattooed* signature, how then can we understand Derrida's theory of signature without falling back on a philosophy of immediacy? How can the writing tattooed *onto the body* cut itself off from the body? How can it *get away* from the proximity of touch, how can it *continue to have effect* even after death?

This chapter sets out once more to closely question the link indicated by the association of hand and writing between the singular, physical presence of the hand producing the trace in the *ductus* of the movement of writing and the symbolic iterability of writing as imprint. I should like to pursue this aim by looking at the practice of handwriting where it appears to be directly opposed to separation from the body: in the tattoo. And as the cultural practice of tattooing is a vast area of considerable diversity with a great variety of historical, cultural and socio-ideological traditions, I will concentrate on tattooing as a postmodern, Western cultural technology, looking at tattooing wherever we meet it nowadays; in other words, anywhere we see the naked body: first and foremost on hot summer days in the parks of our cities, but also particularly through the medium of photographed images in television films, in journals and magazines, online on our computer screens and so on.

## Who is writing?

In a bookshop you can come across a tattoo on the sales assistant's upper arm; likewise on the back cover of a book, for example Margo DeMello's monograph on tattooing entitled *Bodies of Inscription: A Cultural History of the Modern Tattoo Community*. There is a photograph of the author on the back cover. Instead of her face it shows her name tattooed on her back: 'Margo D.'. Like Derrida, Margo DeMello has also signed her text and had her name printed. The name is not, however, done with the usual paper and ink but as a tattoo carried out by the tattoo artist, Joe Vegas.

A tattooed signature such as this claims a lot more than a handwritten signature to function as an undetachable sign of identity. It is not accidental that in nineteenth-century criminology tattoos, along with scars, anomalies of physiognomy and fingerprints, were listed in the records of criminals as reliable signs of identification. Cesare Lombroso paid considerable attention to the practice of tattooing in his anthropological classification of criminal types, dealing with it in *L'uomo delinquente* (Turin, 1897), as does the work by A. Lacassagne, *Les tatouages: étude anthropologique et médico-légale* (Paris, 1881).[5] In this respect, current iris and DNA identification methods were preceded by the interest in tattoos in the processing of criminal records. After all, a tattoo is attached to the body for ever; it identifies it *for a whole lifetime*. This not only conditions the technologies of viewing the other on the part of officialdom but also, the bearer of a tattoo in particular thereby actively determines what he reveals of himself as a visible appearance to that gaze. The tattoo has always been a means of self-enactment.

Tattooing as a practice of emphatic 'self-identification' feeds not only on the other's gaze but it paradoxically demands that an Alien hand is involved in the signature of the self. Because as a rule – except

The back cover of Margo DeMello's *Bodies of Inscription*.

when one tattoos oneself – one goes to a specialist for it, one to whom the undersigned surrenders responsibility for her signature. Who is this 'I, the undersigned'? Who is signing whose proper name?

The professional status of the Western tattooist ranges from an ordinary hairdresser or barber – particularly when the tattooist works from so-called 'flashes', pre-designed motifs displayed in catalogues and transferred to the customer's skin by means of a template – to a tattoo artist who is known for a personal 'style' using the sharp stylus of a tattooing machine. Correspondingly, the activity of tattoo shops may take on quite contrasting forms, resembling either a medieval scriptorium where an anonymous scribe *copies* skillfully pre-fabricated designs, or a postmodern atelier where an artist creates an artwork. In any case, the tattooist refrains from signing their artwork.[6] If there is any signing done it is the name of the tattooed person so that the position of authorship, otherwise usually strictly differentiated as regards signature and handwriting, becomes blurred. Thus the phantasm of an indissoluble unity of writing and body now also gives way to a split as a result of the intervention of another body, a split as a result of the – literally – stiletto-like writing tool with which the tattooist's hand inscribes the body.

DeMello too has commissioned her signature to be performed. Even though this has passed into the hands of another as an autograph, it nevertheless comes back to her. Not just because her name belongs to her alone, but also – and this affection of the self is an extremely dramatic one – because her name is written on her own back. In this alliance of writing and body that cannot be *dissolved*, something is produced that seems to make the highest claim to identity and self-authentication: an inscription of *immediacy*.

Strictly speaking, however, what one is also dealing with here is that 'she cannot see this masterpiece that she is carrying, at least not directly and without a mirror'. It withdraws from her gaze; it is visible and *readable as writing* only *for other people*. Because even if she makes use of a mirror, in the mirror the writing will appear a mirror-image to her. In his film *Memento* (2001), in which he sets tattooing in terms of its potential for authentication and permanence against Polaroids and handwritten notes, the director Christopher Nolan also plays this trick since the protagonist Lennart also occasionally tattoos himself and does this even though he has lost his memory, but with a certain fore-sightedness as he writes his tattoos in mirror-image. Only when viewed in the mirror does the leftward, 'sinister' and 'deceiving' writing – as becomes clear at the end of the film – turn the *right* way round.

DeMello would need two mirrors to be able to read her tattoo. Only when doubly reversed does the nearness of her own name at a distance become readable to her. What she sees then is, however, by no means *her* signature, because carried out like this using calligraphy, the choreography of the execution of the lines with their copious loops and curls suggests more the careful, trained hand of a calligrapher than an impulsive act of signing. This writing resembles more the engraving of one's name on a brass door-plate ('Margo D. is living in this body') than an 'autographic' signature.

The legal logic of a signature, by which the validity of the signature is directed towards the moment of absence (of death) and thus splitting the unity of presence, is sharply paralleled in the case of tattoo-ing by *splitting* the authorship into tattooer and tattooed. Even the present immediacy of the here-and-now requires a mirror (or respec-tively, two mirrors) redirecting the gaze of the viewer for her to catch herself. The tattoo, the ultimate 'technology of the self' is located beyond the reach of one's own, immediate gaze and of one's own, immediate hand. By inscribing the body in the symbolic order, it consigns it to the very split that all symbolism is directed at, i.e. the gap *between* the subjects, precisely in going beyond the spaces and times they are currently situated in. If the trace cuts itself off from touch, it always already does this with a view to the moment of a future reunion, in which one *sees once again* and recognizes *the imprint*.

## The Tattooing Machine

'It's a remarkable piece of apparatus'; with this observation Kafka in his story 'In the Penal Colony' (1919)[7] has the officer begin his long speech to the traveller describing the operation of the tattooing machine. The machine, according to the officer, consists of three parts: 'The lower one is called the "Bed", the upper one the "Designer", and this one here in the middle that moves up and down is called the "Harrow".' The operation of the machine is approximately as follows: After a condemned man is strapped to the bed that is 'completely covered with a layer of cotton wool', the harrow-like needles scan the outline of his body. The bed, powered by an electric battery, is made to vibrate in such a way that the Designer transmits the contours of the writing via the cogwheels to the harrow which for its part 'quivers, its points pierce the skin of the body'. Blood, superfluous ink and water together are then conducted down a waste pipe into a pit into which are thrown the blood-soaked cotton wool and finally the condemned man's body, dead as a result of the procedure. It is true that the machine serves to tattoo onto the condemned man the law that he has broken, but not in order to stigmatize him *for life* as a law-breaker but in order to execute him over the course of twelve hours.

Kafka's 'In the Penal Colony' is like an abyss. Admittedly, no such thing as the tattoo apparatus described exists, even if the corresponding totalitarian state apparatus does, the total control of the body forming part of its integral 'dispositifs' of power.[8] Within this system, tattooing along with branding or mutilation belongs to the techniques of stigmatization, i.e. the legal practices that are inscribed onto the body as *law* using the symbols belonging to the law. The stigmatized body is always a *visible* body exposed to the panoptical gaze of the surveillance state, and within this regime of exposition, 'survey' and 'punish' form an indivisible technology of power. In many – Western and non-Western –

cultures, tattooing was a wide-spread instrument of power for the identification, registration and stigmatization of prisoners: RomAn and EuropeAn colonists tattooed their slaves, condemned prisoners were forcibly tattooed in all periods and in all countries, not the least some of the concentration camps in Nazi Germany, which employed tattooing as writing in the bureaucratic process of their machinery of extermination.⁹ In this respect, Kafka's electrically powered tattooing machine is by no means simply 'kafkaesque'.

Quite apart from that, there is in fact a 'remarkable piece of apparatus' used for tattooing. Remarkable less in the sense of an instrument of torture than for the reason that, as a *writing machine,* it serves to streamline the highly individualistic *hand*work of tattooing into a standardized reproduction process, thus self-authentication to a certain extent into a mass medium of writing. With a consistent movement, the electrically powered needles pierce in a constant, repetitive rhythm. Up to three thousand times a minute they move up and down in the case of a first-class tool and inject ink at standard pressure under the skin. The blood of the person being tattooed issuing in the process is mixed with the superfluous ink, becoming a peculiar serum; the tattooist wipes the mixture off with cotton wool before applying a sterile plaster, enabling the wound to heal.

In 1891 the legendary New York master tattooist Samuel F. O'Reilly took out a patent on the first tattooing machine. He had developed it to keep pace with the demand of his customers in his tattoo shop on Chatham Square in New York's Bowery. The machine, on the one hand made possible a detailed execution of lines and a more accurate colouration and shading than with the manually powered needles, and on the other the process of tattooing could be drastically accelerated and thus the pain associated with it could also be reduced.¹⁰ After all, O'Reilly's tattooing apparatus was no instrument of torture but it was intended to act precisely as a process for the production of post-/modern self-enactments.

O'Reilly's tattooing machine was a further development of Thomas Edison's electric fountain-pen. In other words, he built an instrument that works on the principle of rotation, the mechanism to which both the sewing machine and the mass medium of the newspaper owe their existence. Thus there flourished in the slipstream of the textile and newspaper industry another means of mass production: tattooing.

From the mechanical perspective, this apparatus can be placed somewhere between a typewriter and a sewing machine. Since Kittler's *Gramophone, Film, Typewriter*[11] it has been well known that first sewing machines and later typewriters were built with great success by Remington & Son. 'Not coincidentally', writes Kittler, 'it was William K. Jenne, the head of the sewing-machine division of Remington & Son, who in 1874 developed Scholes's prototype into a mass-producible "Type-Writer"'.[12] However, the company's original activity was in weapons production. Kittler points out the analogy in relation to what, in the case of typewriting, 'not coincidentally consists of strikes and triggers . . . proceeds in automated and discrete steps, as does ammunitions transport in a revolver and a machine-gun'.[13] Here he is referring not just to the accuracy and standardization of the precision engineering essential for the mass production of both weapons and typewriters, but as a by-product of the American Civil War the typewriter also became 'a discursive machine gun'.[14]

For tattooing, all three mechanisms seem vital: firstly, penetration by a mechanically powered needle, which being driven into the skin as into cloth, simultaneously pierces and sews them up, in the course of which – secondly – this penetration repeatedly wounds, as if carried out by a machine gun, and – thirdly – prefabricated symbolic types are stencilled in, as if written by a touch on a typewriter. The oxymoron of an 'electric fountain pen', mentioned twice already before – once in reference to Edison as a technology of reproduction and once in the reference to Binet as a measuring methodology – neatly sums up the binary logic of this enterprise. Because the *ductus* of writing, the properties of the line, the control of movement and the writing pressure, the very characteristics of writing making up the *trace* of writing, also employed by tattooing as a '*track*ing of the self', are shaped on closer inspection according to normalized processes. Tattooing always also represents a standardized, mass–produced process of printing 'in automated and discrete steps'.

## Till Death Do Us Part

On 29 April 2000, the Victoria and Albert Museum (V&A) in London organized a 'Day of Record' in association with a series of exhibitions on the relationship between art and the body. 1,500 tattooed people came to the museum to have their 'body artworks' photographed and the photos documented in the museum's digital archive of tattoos. The photo here replaced the naked body, making it present when it had already been clothed again and left the exhibition space. In the resulting collection of postmodern tattoos a wide variety of body images can be found: fat and thin, tattooed all over the body and those that have tiny images, but mostly they are young people and well-preserved adults who offered themselves up to the public gaze of the website. And there are some very beautiful bodies amongst them, perfect anatomies decorated with piercings and tattoos, putting on show the body as a carefully executed sculpture, for example Patience Agbabi, whose back is covered with a tattoo depicting the Egyptian sun god Ra. In the iconography this motif, depicting Ra carrying the sun on his head through the sky, symbolizes fertility and life. This is a favourite motif for tattoo design in the West, as if the tattooed person hopes to gain eternal youth from it: the tattoo operates as a fountain of youth, transforming the skin into a *charta non nata*, the for ever untainted virgin parchment which at the height of the Middle Ages was obtained from the skin of unborn animals for the production of particularly magnificent manuscripts.

When tattooed onto Ian Day's body, however, the Ra symbolism takes on a slightly bitter aftertaste, the sign of the sun-god on this tired and withered writing surface sagging around the middle, reminding one more of transitoriness and death than of life and fertility. Instead, one

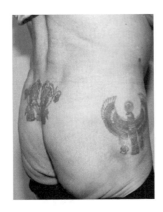

Patience Agbabi.                     Ian Day.

cannot help thinking of Kafka's grotesque presentation of tattooing as a consecration of death that will not even spare Patience Agabi's (still) powerful body in the end. 'The letter killeth', it says not by chance in the second epistle of Paul to the Corinthians (2. Cor. 3,6). In the case of tattooing this statement contains a particular charge. Because the ultimate practice of the authentification of the self, that is, the preempting of one's death by writing, described by Kafka with obscene directness, is the basic rule inherent in all tattoos. As with no other technique of writing, in the case of tattooing the body is implicated in writing. The Derridean concept of writing as a sign which is readable even independently of the presence of the author and 'continues to produce effects *even after his death*', comes over in the *écriture* of tattooing as highly problematic, if not even crude.

In the accompanying text to a photograph of Tim Whitmore from the online database of the V&A Archive, he informs us about his tattoos: the one on his left hand he describes as a version of triangular design inspired by a hand motif of the Maoris of Borneo but which in this case is incomplete. The other half of the design is, according to Whitmore, engraved on the hand of his partner and only in the united *enfolding* of both their hands do they form one complete design. The tattoo was done by Mike from Athens as a gift to the two of them on the anniversary of their first meeting.

Thus the tattoo on the finger, in a way, functions as a wedding ring. However, unlike a wedding ring, a tattoo cannot be removed, or at least

Tim Whitmore.                    Maori hand design.

not without leaving a scar. In this context, the Derridean statement 'even after his death' sounds like the opposite of the other saying 'until death do us part', a vow intended to be lifelong and which loses its legitimacy after death as it frees the one making the vow from his promise. Like the holy sacrament of marriage, the tattoo forms an alliance which – as it says literally in the Christian service – let no man put asunder, an alliance between lovers, as indissoluble as that between writing and body. The motif on Whitmore's hand is thus a sacred sign full of ceremonial significance. As a speech act it says 'With this Ring ("hereby"...) I thee wed', and by saying the magic words 'I will', it celebrates – or performs – the ritual of marriage.

## Perforation

Like Whitmore's wedding ring, tattoos on the upper arm or elsewhere with the first name of a lover is a favourite motif in tattoo art; they count as a promise of love that cannot be revoked, *under any circumstances*. For a lifetime, such names say 'I love you – *forever*'. Another alliance, but still an alliance for life is the assurance of the *ménage à trois* of 'Matthew, Adam, Lucy'. Here, to be sure, the 'forever' becomes problematic if one takes into account a photographic detail that is so tiny that it is easy to miss.

Richard Botheras's right upper arm.

This detail concerns less the tattoo itself than the writing surface of the skin with its little spots, some of them looking like pigment, others like pimples, pustules, little bloody wounds revealing the skin's vulnerability.[15] In this photo and in this sharp lighting they strike the viewer with the force that Barthes in his *Camera Lucida* attributes to the *punctum*, the element in a photograph which he describes literally as 'this wound, this prick, this mark made by a pointed instrument ... [and] it also refers to the notion of punctuation'. While the culturally trained gaze of the *studium*, according to Barthes, is occupied in favourably taking the photographer's view in the context of familiar cultural semantics, the *punctum* 'rises from the scene, shoots out of it like an arrow, and pierces me [the viewer]'. Barthes literally describes the *punctum* also as a 'sting, speck, cut, little hole – and also a cast of the dice. A photographer's *punctum* is that accident which pricks me (but also bruises me, is poignant to me).' And by confusing the calculated *studium* ('which is never my delight or my pain'), the surprise of the *punctum* also has the potential to interrupt the reading and to lead the process of meaning production, suddenly and unexpectedly, in another direction.[16]

The *punctum* of the tattoo is never to be found in its symbolic inscription, since this rather challenges the interpretive act of *studium*. The element of the *punctum* with which it makes visible a 'pro-vident' remainder, is to be found instead in the secondary area of writing, that is, in the *bearer* of writing: the skin itself. On the tattooed upper arm, apart from the tattoo there appears the otherwise invisible writing surface. However, it only becomes visible as a result of the 'other', hardly perceptible signs, the tiny points and mini-wounds. If I referred earlier in this book to the point or the dot arising from the gesture of the imprint, I should like to emphasize once more here its tactile movement of *touch*, putting it slightly differently as precisely this *perforation* of a receptive and sensitive skin.[17] As a clinical detail,[18] the *punctum* expresses what a tattoo is in the end: the result of a procedure in which a series of piercings painfully perforate the skin, in the process of which blood escapes and is replaced by subcutaneously injected ink and in which finally, after the wound has healed, writing will be left, the condition of which is the *mixture* of ink and blood. As a trace it always already bears the escape of blood and the erasure of the sign invisibly within itself.

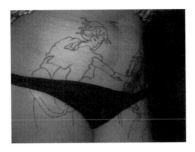

Tattooed 'Natalie'.

'Beautiful strange'

The tattoo on the stomach and abdomen of 'Natalie' consists of a pattern of finely drawn lines in which the 'studious' viewer can make out a Far Eastern scene. Two figures looking at each other come together below her navel. The one at the back, turned away from the viewer and thus not easily recognizable – perhaps a warrior – is done as a shaded area dominating the one on the left, a female figure sketched in outline, in fact as regards both visual presentation and the activity represented, as she is tugging with her left hand at the extended arm of the other figure. It is not clear whether the abduction of a woman or a dance is being shown here, but one suspects that this tattoo has something to do with sexual dominance, having after all chosen her abdomen for a stage, the 'hot spot' between navel and vulva.

This suspicion of a penetration was of course already there before the *studium* of the relation between the two unequal figures revealed a dance or an abduction. This resulted from a second arrangement of lines lying hidden like in a palimpsest beneath the first. This secondary figure does not actually belong to the tattoo and yet interferes with it. Its lines arise from the clothes, perhaps a tight-fitting pair of trousers pulling in Natalie's stomach like a corset and that have left folded creases on her skin after undressing. These fine folds of skin, these barely perceptible imprints, redirect our gaze from the tattoo, as symbolic writing, towards the somatic nature of the bearer of the writing, towards the fact that clothes must have been there protecting the body but now have been taken off, revealing its nakedness.

That the living skin is sensitive to physical stimuli is unmistakable in the case of the initials signed 'at the bottom'. Unlike the 'dead' skin of parchment, linen, paper, celluloid or the monitor screen, in the case of tattoos, the organic liveliness of the material is a technical condition for the optimal success of the writing. What appears at first glance to be pre- or hyper-symbolical, is after all active within the tattoo. These small details – the pustules and spots, the folds of skin and the goose pimples – 'prick' us, remind us of our vulnerability and naked-ness. But in the end they at the same time make it clear to us that we can only *feel* and *touch* ourselves naked.

## The Magic of the Name

> How can we . . . rid ourselves of their names?
> Luce Irigaray, *The Sex That Is Not One*[19]

When between 1768 and 1771 Captain Cook explored the Pacific Islands under the flag of the British Admiralty and on behalf of the Royal Geographical Society, first Tahiti, later Hawaii, he encountered there the widespread custom of tattooing. In his travel journals he described the Polynesian skin engraving as mostly figures made up of lines and other geometric designs; he was especially interested in the 'Moko', the curvilinear face tattoo of the Maori in New Zealand, which serves to indicate genealogical relations, as well as membership of a clan and social status similar to the practice of name-giving in Western society.[20] Apart from Captain Cook, other circumnavigators of the world and pirates also brought 'noble savages' back to Europe as objects of curios-ity for the *salons*, museums and circuses.[21] With this 'cultural transfer' they were importing less the cultural technique of tattooing – this had been known for a long time, though it was now to become more popu-lar than never before – than the word for it: tattooing.[22] Etymologic-ally, the word 'tattoo' is derived from the Polynesian word *ta tatau – ta*: 'to strike' and *tatou*: 'sign', 'skin decoration'. The connection with strik-ing and typing, and therefore the gesture of the imprint, is unmistak-able. Whoever from now on 'tattooed' himself did it in the context that he was 'marking' himself, thus that he was repeating a pre-designed form, marking himself with the seal of the alien that revealed him to be 'a Polynesian', that is to say, wild and exotic.

Herman Melville, who like Captain Cook was a seasoned sea-farer, depicts in *Moby-Dick* the custom of the tattooed proper name widespread in the Pacific. The journey into the marvellous world of the whale hunt passes down the islands belonging to the tattooed, native traditional whale-hunters who thanks to their skill in using the harpoon were to become welcome guests of the Americans hunting the whale. The very first words of the novel make clear the stress on the proper name. 'Call me Ishmael', is how the first person narrator begins the first chapter and thereby presents himself – *nomen est omen* – as being one who has been cast out of God's society. And other, similarly 'christened' characters in the novel also derive their names from a biblical reference – Captain Ahab gets his from one of the kings of Israel, Jonah and Elijah suggest prophets of doom, and the whaler herself, the unfortunate *Pequod*, is like an oracle and called after an exterminated tribe of natives.

The pagan Polynesian Queequeg, who is tattooed all over his body and whose legs look 'as if a parcel of dark green frogs were running up trunks of young palms', the captain, with echoes of the Bible, calls three times by the wrong name: at first he calls him 'Son of Darkness', then he calls 'Quohog there – what's that you call him?' and finally he refers to him as 'Hedgehog there, I mean Quohog'. When the savage then finally has to be recorded by name in the log of the *Pequod*, the problem of the name becomes an official matter. 'Quohog there don't know how to write, does he? I say, Quohog, blast ye! Dost thou sign thy name or make thy mark?', the Captain asks the native. The subsequent description of the ritual of signing is remarkable:[23]

> But at this question, Queequeg, who had twice or thrice before taken part in similar ceremonies, looked no ways abashed; but taking the offered pen, copied upon the paper, in the proper place, an exact counterpart of a queer round figure which was tattooed upon his arm; so that through Captain Peleg's obstinate mistake touching his appellative, it stood something like this:

Queequeg's 'real signature' is engraved into his skin; he now countersigns with the pen. In the alphabetic transcription of his name by Captain Ahab, Queequeg has, however, become 'Quohog'. 'Latinized' in this way, 'quo hoc' can be read – at least in vulgar Latin – as something like 'that which here then', in any case as a purely untranslatable

Queequeg's
signature in Herman
Melville's *Moby-Dick*.

*Quohog*

*his* ∞ *mark*

composite of two pronouns in the neuter (!) with a no more closely
defined antecedent that can be most readily understood as a generic term
for the anonymous worker, unchristened and without papers, who is
signing on – some things have not changed, even now? – on a ship.

Melville's Queequeg with the mysterious hieroglyphs of his skin
engraving represents a myth that had been current in the Western world
since the seventeenth century. Since the days of the great voyages of discovery, tattooing had been popular amongst sailors and seamen as the
expression of adventure and the exotic; then in the nineteenth century
soldiers too demonstrated courage and eagerness for battle in tattoos,
and in the twentieth century bikers and working-class men discovered
tattooing as a badge of social marginalization or exclusion. The *image*
of tattooing has survived into the postmodern period as an import
from an exotic, savage and original culture.

The oxymoron of a 'natural culture' neatly sums up the phantasm
of this alienation from the self. The tattooed subject signs up for a system of classifications, a set of norms that are defined by a community
marked by differences. The logic of this classification is not only based
on the somatic semiotics of the skin as a racial, sexual and social signifier but also the basic symbolic idea of the tattoo is based on it: *ta tau*:
a mark that is struck, coming from outside and inscribing a subject
within a social system. Or – as Kafka would say – erasing it.[24] Because,
after all from the tattoo, there arises the socio-political power to place,
to control or to stigmatize the marked person within the context of
the law.

In this respect, tattooing as an act of christening functions like a
ceremony similar to baptism, the tattooist like a priest, and the statement 'I hereby baptize thee . . .' like a classic performative. The ritual of
name-giving identifies the subject; it does this, however, by no means as
a self-reflexive gesture of the 'self' that itself says 'I' – or her or his

name – since one's proper name is paradoxically not one's 'own'. The giving of one's name is perhaps the first **A**lienation, valid for the rest of one's life, the magic of which can only ever be broken and simultaneously re-established by the use of that other statement 'I will' in the marriage ceremony, as another, no less fateful intercession by the other.[25] The giving of a name is a performative – like baptism, marriage, a promise, a legal judgement, a declaration of war (all favourite examples of Austin's). From this magic moment on, a magic spell becomes effective, by which the subject can be made present even if she is absent. The ambiguous English term for this miraculous quality of the proper name is very apt: *spelling the name*. Queequeg has twice had a spell cast upon him: tattooing by the members of his tribe made him a 'grand old whale-hunter' at the centre of society – the credit accorded to him by this was of course still to be paid by him – and the record in the ship's register of the American whaler rechristened him a heathen, losing his proper name in the process of alphabetization.

## Performance

> The eye of the other calls out the proper names, spells them out,
> and removes the prohibition that covered them.
> Jacques Derrida, *Of Grammatology*[26]

Since the practice of tattooing has the unique, living body as its medium, it counts as 'performance culture' like the theatre, concerts and dance, street processions, rituals, celebrations and fairground attractions, in other words all those practices that require the indivisible unity of the 'presence and present' of the physical body. *Performances* are events that, like a handwritten signature, claim to be singular and non-repeatable. Unlike the repeatable and spellable artefacts of writing culture, performances always have to put up with not being permanent – one reason for UNESCO to protect not only monuments, but now also carnivals as part of world-cultural heritage *for coming generations*.

The cultural role of the tattoo in Europe, from its early beginnings until the present, was always eventful, being directed towards the display of a visibly present body. From the seventeenth century, tattooed 'natives' from the Pacific Islands were displayed in freak shows, dime museums and circuses. In the early twentieth century, such slaves of the entertainment industry were sometimes displaced by tattooed Westerners, who on their advertising pamphlets described themselves as victims of cannibal natives or other savages who had kidnapped and tattooed them by force.

One of the most amazing modern tattoo spectacles in the Western world in the 1930s appeared under the name of the 'Great Omi'. The 'Great Omi', also called 'the Zebra Man' (his 'real' name was Horace Ridler), had tattooed his white skin with bold black zebra-like stripes covering the whole of his body, including his cleanly shaven head, giving him a zebra-like appearance. As the years passed, the Great Omi took to wearing lipstick and nail polish; he had his earlobes stretched and pierced with ivory spikes, all to arouse the curiosity of the paying crowds. He signed his pitch cards 'Barbaric Beauty'.[27]

The 'Great Omi' in his heyday.

Towards the end of his career, the Great Omi, exhausted and demoralized by his life as a showground attraction, complained in a letter dated 1 September 1935 to his tattooist George Burchett that the more outrageous his appearance became, the less respectful he was treated by his employers. A bitter humiliation he had experienced shortly before in a small circus in France, he describes as follows: 'When I was too ill to work they painted up a nigger with white paint and put him in my place.'[28] For the sideshow, apparently it made no difference whether it was a white man exposing black features or a black man exposing white features. Black on white, or white on black, *what's the difference?*[29] For a conceptualization of the tattoo as writing or signature, it makes a difference, even if only an infra-thin one. Black ink on white paper, after all, cannot but be understood as the signifier *par excellence* of a white, literate, Western writing culture, in opposition to a black, oral or ritual culture of events.

The symbols and ornaments on Whitmore's skin appear at first glance to appeal to the same sensationalism as the zebra-mimicry of the Great Omi, since they are both to a certain extent 'imports' from an exotic, 'natural' world. The explanations of his tattoos that Whitmore gives in the online databank of the V&A archive are along the same lines, describing them as a mixture of Japanese, Celtic and Maori- and Thai-inspired designs. It is interesting to note here that these tattoos are traditional in Western tattooing, and indeed not just as citations from traditional iconography but also as authentic and original exhibition objects. The reason for this lies in a macabre chapter in Western history. The Maori custom of tattooing their chiefs and removing and conserving their heads after death became part of a profitable commercial enterprise for the European colonists in New Zealand. In the nineteenth century, museums as well as showground exhibitions and private collectors in Europe and overseas were willing to pay for specimens of the 'barbaric' face-culture.[30] And thus, even now, shrunken heads from the South Seas are on display in Western museums of natural history, anatomy or ethnology – a presence in the present, *even after their death*.

Unlike the case of the 'Great Omi', Whitmore's tattoos, however, strike one as somewhat 'politically correct' after all, admittedly less for the reason that Whitmore makes use of his own body instead of the

Major-General H. G. Robley with his collection of 35 Maori heads displayed in a Japanese teahouse in the garden of an English country house, *c.* 1902.

'original' Maori shrunken heads (this is what the Great Omi was doing too after all) than for the reason that he chooses citation as a means of transmission. And citations are particular speech acts.

Austin firmly excludes citations as 'not serious' utterances from his system of performative speech acts and thereby rejects, along with them, the whole area of poetry and theatre as being metaphorical, that is to say, not actual discourse. In Austin's view, a marriage acted on the stage is null and void because language there is 'not used seriously, but in ways *parasitic* upon its normal use.'[31] In 'Signature Event Context', Derrida argues against this on the grounds that signs can only function as signs when they are readable even in other, particularly non-serious, abnormal or '*parasitic*' contexts:

> For, ultimately, isn't it true that what Austin excludes as anomaly, exception, 'non-serious,' *citation* (on stage, in a poem, or a soliloquy)

is the determined modification of a general citationality – or rather, a general iterability – without which there would not even be a 'successful' performative?[32]

Repeatability, citability and iterability of the singular act accordingly become the *conditio sine qua non* for the possibility of meaning at all. The key thing here is that Derrida sees citation as a repetition or iteration in the sense of the *itera*, otherness.

Whereas Derrida relates citation to the *future*, that is, to future readers, for whom the speech act or the signature must be readable, Judith Butler in her now classic Introduction to *Bodies that Matter* draws attention to the systems of norms within cultural traditions. The context by which to measure the *itera* is for Butler a configuration formed by tradition, the fixity of which is, however, destabilized by the repetition of the citation. 'Performativity', says Judith Butler, echoing Derrida:

> is thus not a singular 'act', for it is always a reiteration of a norm or set of norms, and to the extent that it acquires an act-like status in the present, it conceals or dissimulates the conventions of which it is a repetition.[33]

In this sense, a tattoo is understood to be a citation, i.e. a performative, repeating (or 'citing') the norms and conventions of past contexts, but at the same time definitely exploiting the binary structure of the *itera*: it is a repetition with the possibility of otherness, a break with the context. Even though the practice of tattooing is a singular event, absolutely unique as a live performance, it nevertheless must repeat or cite a cultural context – or a norm-governed tradition – to become meaningful.

Within Butler's theory, the Moko symbols on Whitmore's white skin no longer function incontrovertibly as signs fixed once and forever by convention, as symbols of a (violent) act of imposing a 'proper' name on somebody – as they would do in Moko society. As 'citations', they indeed affirm this socio-cultural context, but they also at the same time break with that context and it is precisely in this break that, according to Derrida, lies the potential for any semiotic process:

> Every sign ... can be *cited*, put between quotation marks; in so doing it can break with every given context, engendering an infinity of new contexts in a manner which is absolutely illimitable.[34]

Just like a signature countersigning, the symbols on Whitmore's skin repeat their cultural pre-text, but not without thereby producing a difference. An autographic signature never looks identically the same twice.

Although in the case of Whitmore's tattoos we are clearly dealing with this provocation exoticizing the Western self and 'iterating' or 'alterating' it by incorporation into an alien context, nevertheless they can not simply be understood as an eye-catching racist stereotyping of a 'savage' other in the way the Great Omi staged his tattoos. The difference between the pre- and postmodern tattoo is manifest in precisely the difference that the postmodern tattoo (in contrast to the pre-modern tattooing practices) has the potential to create 'authenticity'. Susan Benson puts it as follows:

> The identification with the primitive and the exotic is ... no longer abjected, but is reconfigured as *identification with the authentic*, the uncommodified, the pure, in opposition to the corruptions of mainstream society; or, in the case of Japanese tattoo, with the refined aesthetic of an 'ancient civilization'.[35]

Benson's assessment indeed expresses what could be called the 'tattoo dream', as is frequently claimed and sought for: the desire for an 'authentic' and irreducible identity, originality, uniqueness, that handwriting too, especially in the age of mechanical reproduction, can be said to serve. As if such an aura could ever be achieved, an aura bringing an absolute identity, in a self-affective nearness and hence from a perspective beyond that of the other.

Shortly before his death in 1969, the Great Omi confessed that 'underneath it all, I'm just an ordinary man'.[36] 'Ordinary', here, means 'normal' in the sense of white and civilized, and civilization is what is underneath the skin. Skin, thus defined, becomes the opposite of 'mind' or 'soul', a position that has largely shaped Western thinking since Plato. The body has been seen as an external shell or skin; the essentiality and the essence of the human being meanwhile lies within him, hidden deep under the surface. Unlike the Great Omi and in complete contrast to this strict separation of internal and external, Tim Whitmore emphasizes that his tattoos articulate his deepest held *inner* beliefs, his desires, his philosophy, and his partnership intended to be *for life* and making them *externally* visible for the other.

## Enfolding the Other

This idea of skin as a performative that does what it says, comes close to Didier Anzieu's psychoanalytical concept of the 'skin ego'. The ego, for Anzieu, is not a kernel protected by a shell – a basic idea that, according to Anzieu, has dazzled Western thinking since the Renaissance. Rather, it is an effect of cutaneous experiences and fantasies that cause the ego to conceive of itself and to become perceptible or accessible to *feeling* at all. Anzieu observes that the embryo in its early development takes the form of a container consisting of an inner layer (the endoderm) and an outer layer (the ectoderm). Paradoxically, both the skin and the brain grow out of the outer side of the embryo. In this respect they are both essentially surfaces, so that the classical opposites of shell and kernel *enfold one another*: 'the centre is situated at the periphery'.[37]

Hence, for Anzieu, ego and skin are not opposites – as they were for the Great Omi. On the contrary, he attributes three main functions to the skin that are constitutive of the ego and interlock the otherwise opposing positions of inside and outside into one another: the skin is firstly a vessel or an envelope that contains the ego, secondly an interface or a border area that forms a protective barrier against aggressive penetration by the outside world, and thirdly the sensitive (erogenous) zone where information can be exchanged with the outer world. These are processes defined by Anzieu as 'invagination'. He argues that the metaphor of the vagina is apt because 'the vagina . . . is a fold in the skin just like the lips, the anus, the nose and the eyelids'[38] and because as such it is at once on the outside and on the inside; it thus externalizes the inside and internalizes the outside. Palmists base their interpretations on precisely this idea of enfolding when they read folds in the skin of the hand literally like handwriting.

Whitmore's tattoos also work according to the principle of 'invagination'. If Whitmore marks himself out as distinctly non-Western, this 'self-identification' nevertheless does not take place without being inscribed into a social context which it cites by the tattoos. If the Western ego is performing in line with an 'alteration' or 'alienation' in Derrida's sense of *itera*, then his tattooing, which functions distinctly like an ego-technology, must be seen as the effect of an invagination of this type by an (exotic) **O**ther, which comes from outside just like an epidermal stimulus; with the difference that this stimulus does not trigger some short-term reflex of goose pimples or such-like but the 'permanent trace' of a tattoo that works on the basis of a chiastic *enfolding* of the inside and **O**utside, in the 'ectodermal internal' or the 'endodermal external'.

Although this intervention of the **O**ther is indeed constitutive for any production of cultural identity, it is nevertheless an effect of the penetration or perforation of the skin. This 'incision', which is the imprint of the other, if it is meant to be taken seriously and like Barthes's *punctum* is accompanied by a profound interest, always also causes a pain, because it inevitably involves a traumatization of the self by the other, even if (unlike in Kafka's *Penal Colony*) it is by choice. The clinical term, borderline disturbance, clearly states *where* traumatization takes place: on the frontier. This physically violating dimension is even true for the non-pathological 'normal case' of tattooing.

Both a tattoo and the vagina are structurally – admittedly not literally but nevertheless logically – like a scar with which the skin is simultaneously divided and united, pierced and repaired, wounded and healed. Much ink has been spilled in literary tradition over the complex somatic semantics of the scar. Only the latest to be given a scar is that most famous literary character, J. K. Rowling's Harry Potter (as a sign of the attack sustained at the hands of the powers of evil),[39] Captain Ahab's face is also signed by a mark. Since losing his leg in the struggle with the terrible Moby-Dick, 'the moody stricken Ahab' stood on a 'barbaric white leg' that 'had been fashioned from the polished bone of the Sperm Whale's jaw'. Since then, according to Melville, 'the dignity of some mighty woe' was written into his face, and 'his torn body and gashed soul bled into one another; and so interfusing, made him mad'.[40]

The fate of a 'gash . . . bled into one another' Ahab shares literally and without limitation with the female sex. In probably the most remarkable theoretization of the vagina by Luce Irigaray, the female sex is called 'the sex that is not one', simultaneously separated and one, asunder and repaired, a fold of skin divided in two and touching itself by itself, one external and the other internal. Unlike Ahab's mythical scar inscribing the body symbolically into its fate – and many a (freely chosen and postmodern) tattoo claims such a profound woe at this gash – in Irigaray, the 'I/you' divided up within the splitting of the fold of skin refuses to be fixed in any way to a single name. Instead, it appears as

> [t]he birth that is never accomplished, the body never created once and for all, the form never definitely completed, the face always still to be formed. The lips never open or closed on a truth . . . Whereas we are always one and the other, at the same time . . . Arising as a whole: all [*toute(s)*].[41]

This binary logic of being at the same time the one and the other is also the reason why tattooing operates both as a 'perforative' (imprint) and a 'performative' (trace). It is 'perforative' in the sense that it literally perforates the skin by the *piercing* and the *touch* of the needle. As a 'perforative' practice, a tattoo is a singular event of which blood is the fluid: somatic and unique, here and now, authentic and original. A tattoo is performed 'live' and, therefore, definitely can not be repeated. And yet its logic is based on repetition, in Butler's sense, since it is a result, or a citation, of a cultural context, and in Derrida's sense, because as a sign it is only readable if a future reader invokes the conventions of the sign system by repetition. To be readable, tattooing, marking, naming or signing must have 'a repeatable, iterable, imitable form in order to be able to be detached from the present and singular intention of its production'[42] This ability to be cited qualifies tattooing as a performative practice of which ink is the serum of writing with which it makes way for its trace.

Even though a tattoo's performative, 'live' dimension qualifies it as authentic and original, a tattoo must in the end fail in its attempts at fixing the tattooed subject as unitary, and finally identical with himself. This goes for forced tattooing as much as for that done by choice, even for that done by self-tattooing,[43] because in either case, the **O**ther has a hand in the process, be it as a *manus ministra* carrying out the signature, or as the one giving a proper name, or as the one for whom the (imposed or freely chosen) name becomes readable. The unity of such an identity is *always already* split by difference; it will therefore to a certain extent be in the form of a scar, the unity of which is divided as the result of a wound that has healed, produced by the perforation of the skin by a needle injecting the ink as an alien substance (as the writing fluid of the symbolic **O**ther) into the skin. This scar, then, becomes a signifier for the fissure between presence and present, inside and outside, self and other, just as it embodies the somatic sign of the vagina.

This idea of the f**O**ld, the enfolding of the exterior within the interior and of the interior within the exterior does not only apply to the practice of tattooing, but it also holds good for handwriting in general. After all, handwriting is in a similar way produced by a self-reflexive *touch*, the unity of which is divided by the (traumatizing) intervention of the **O**ther. Even the absolutely authentic autographic signature, that touchstone of identity, is split between the one named and the one naming. This **O**ther comes from the outside and yet is active within the signature. It is the one who 'spells' the name in the double meaning of 'casting' the letters of the alphabet and 'dispelling' the one named to the symbolic realm. Its magic wand is in the form of a stylus which, even if I personally write with it, is conducted by a latently ever-present **A**lien hand. This Other provides not only the letters that I sign with, but also the system of signification at all, and every signature goes back to it. 'Even after . . .'

Gable-stone on No. 52 Egelantiersstraat in Amsterdam.

## Before a Wall

In the Jordaan district of Amsterdam in the Egelantiersstraat, not far from the former home of Anne Frank, there stands the house with the number 52.[1] The Amsterdammers call it the 'de schrijvende hand' ('the writing hand'). The house has a stone on the gable illustrating a right hand holding a quill pen, the shaft of which is decorated with a golden crown. The story goes that here in 1630, during the golden age of Holland, the schoolmaster Hendrick Theunis Wient lived who wrote letters to order as a *manus ministra* for the illiterate, but also for booksellers and cartographers. The gable-stone was the sign for the *maîtres de la plume coronée*, the renowned masters of writing who supplied evidence of their art internationally at letter-writing competitions.

But the gable-stone did not only serve as a seal of approval; it also advertised to his customers that this was the address where he plied his trade, even though it did not have a number. In Amsterdam, house-numbers were only introduced in 1795 by Professor Jan Hendrick van Swinden on the orders of Louis Napoleon: they soon replaced gable-stones. But before then, the gable-stones provided the irremovable coordinates directing one safely to an address and they were even made use of in the historic transportation documents: 'waar de Keyser uithangt' ('where the Emperor is displayed'), or: 'daer de wildeman op de stock uitsteekt' ('where the wild man looms out on the stick').

It sometimes happened, however, that the occupier of a house with a gable-stone moved and left his gable-stone to the next occupier. The latter found himself addressed by a stone that did not necessarily correspond to his trade. Thus the story is told in Amsterdam of the woman who opened an apothecary's shop in a former butcher's shop. She had the following sentence added to the calf belonging to the Guild on the gable-stone: 'In het gildekalf, verkoop ik nu wondpleister en zalf.' (At the calf of the Guild, I now sell sticking plaster and ointment.')

Who might have been the later occupier of the 'writing hand' in the Egelantiersstraat? What trade might he have followed? Did he – something that is unlikely but not completely impossible – acquire the pen *from the hand* of his predecessor and continue writing *for him for others*? As it were, a *manus ministra manus ministrae*.

Even if the gable-stone attaches the writing hand irremovably to its location in the Egelantiersstraat with the same authority of materiality with which handwriting points to the physical presence and the body of its originator, then its topographical logic, the safe and *irremovable* pointer: 'here lives . . .' is nevertheless highly ambivalent. And indeed from its very base. Because it is not necessary that a change of location, in the sense of a move or even of a death, happens before it becomes apparent that 'the writing hand' is *not quite in place.* On the contrary, the possibility of the change of location is the first characteristic of the profession of the *maître de la plume.* His writing hand is always already not actually in its place, even before the change of location, since the letters written there, under the seal of approval of the *plume coronée*, derived irrevocably from the other by reason of their being 'dictated handwriting'. The main business of the writing hand has always been marked by the movement of deferral, the basic gesture of which is again the trace.

If the gable-stone indicates any place at all, then it is that of an address, the essence of which is to be a sender. It functions as a mail sorting office, an intermediary space that does not itself receive mail or send any off. In this respect, the writing hand does not belong to any body or any individual; it is without an originator. The illustration on the gable-stone demonstrates this very nicely, since the lower arm appears from the right-hand border of the image as if from a cloud. The writing hand points neither to a clear *addressee* nor does it reveal an identifiable, unified *sender*, since its task consists precisely in serving multiple and changing senders as the medium of writing. Indeed it does this with *always the same hand*, in other words presumably with the current, standardized Humanistic cursive for letter-writing, written expertly and sealed with a crown.

# 8 Graffiti: Passages of Writing

Exhibitions. 'All regions and indeed, retrospectively, all times . . .
Sigfried Giedion: *Bauen in Frankreich*, 1928'
Walter Benjamin, *The Arcades Project*[1]

## Passing by

Autobahn A4, going east. The panorama behind the windscreen consists of scenic views, the gently curving lines of the hills of central Germany, villages nestling against them with church towers reaching skywards. A *typically German* landscape. The moving image of the panorama is cut out of the rimless visual field by the window frame of the car, the sutures of the image continually changing as in film. Power cables range across the field of vision, dividing the hills up geometrically into parallel areas. This is Germany, isn't it? Road signs serve to confirm the names of the possible stopping places where we could rest for a while. As motorway exits, however, they rather indicate places where we don't stop.

Next exit: Eisenach. On a brown road sign the outlines of a castle are sketched in white, geometric lines: 'Wartburg' it says underneath. (Yes, this is Germany!) Soon the famous castle appears in the right-hand window – like magic. For a few minutes drivers can admire in the distance the historic site where Martin Luther once sought refuge from capture by the Catholics. In the meantime, sight-seeing is intercut with other views: staccato white stripes on the road pass by – a sign indicates a speed-limit of 100 km per hour – after a bend Wartburg Castle again appears briefly – graffiti (huge silver pieces) flashes past on a sound-proofing barrier – no overtaking for lorries. Our attention stays focused on the castle even while the road passes through an industrial area with yards and warehouses covered with graffiti. Here simple silver pieces are accompanied by bubble style graffiti blowing up the age-old, noble letters of the Roman alphabet like bubble-gum about to burst. How can we read them, get what they are about? But there is no time to decipher them.

The castle is now in the rear-view mirror. Then, legible even at a glance. 'McDonald's at 500 metres'. And although Wartburg Castle is a distinctly historic site with a unique cultural and religious significance in the world, this place could be anywhere and nowhere. Keep right, you are being overtaken. The castle disappears in a burst of speed. Keep right, you are being overtaken. The castle disappears in a burst of speed. Watch out: speed control! Then it materializes just for a moment as a certain sign, a name on a road sign in literal anticipation of the place.

Sightseeing as a combination of seeing and travelling produces a topographical logic that is determined by a movement rather than by a stable location. As in the theatre or the cinema, it gives a view of the world that is fragmented into partial glimpses and then put back together again in a particular order. The landscape you are passing through is in motion, or, as Marc Augé has described in his 'supermodern' ethnography, it is 'shifted'. It is the very '*track* of the Autobahn' that strikes him as symptomatic. And for two reasons: 'it avoids, for functional reasons, all the principal places to which it takes us, and it makes comments on them.'[2] The road signs act as points of fixation for the traveller, combining the fractured and fictional elements together into an order that can be experienced and navigated. They point towards places on the move as transit zones, 'non-places' that are more ubiquitous than identifiable and authentic.

Marc Augé derives the concept of 'non-place' from de Certeau's 'Spatial Stories'. In this essay de Certeau makes a fundamental distinction between spaces and places. A place, according to de Certeau, is 'an instantaneous configuration of positions. It implies an indication of stability'. A space, by contrast,

> . . . exists when one takes into consideration vectors of direction, velocities and time variables. Thus space is composed of intersections of mobile elements. It is in a sense actuated by the ensemble of movements deployed within it. Space occurs as the effect produced by the operations that orient it, situate it, temporalize it . . . [It] is situated as the act of a present (or of a time), and modified by the transformations caused by successive contexts. In contradistinction to the place, it has thus none of the univocity or stability of a 'proper'.
>
> In short, *space is a practiced place*. Thus the street geometrically defined by urban planning is transformed into a space for walkers.[3]

To sum it up, de Certeau sees 'space' as a place which has become movement, which is moved through and which accordingly is constructed or narrated ontologically in terms of the 'spatial syntax'. A space is a place that is not quite in place, hence its identification as a 'non-place'.

Augé puts this concept of 'non-place' more radically by setting it up as a 'supermodern' topographical utopia, in which already during the period of 'Modernism' (e.g. in the case of Baudelaire or Chateaubriand) the beginning 'solitude' of the traveller exchanged its delightful, melancholy aura for the mood of the supermodern traveller, at one moment a bored and indifferent consumer, at other moments hectically on the move and hyperactive. We come across supermodern non-places in the shape of chain restaurants and hotels, supermarkets and shopping centres, railway stations and petrol stations as well as transit lounges, duty-free shops for airline passengers and motorway service stations. 'Certain places', according to Augé, 'exist only through the words that evoke them, and in this sense they are non-places, or rather, imaginary places: banal utopias, *clichés*.'[4] They are clichés in so far as the main signs one recognizes them by are their mass-production and interchangeability; they are boring because, as *clichés*, i.e. literally: as never-varying copies or imprints, they spirit away any historical or personal identity from their visible surface. In this process it is, as Augé writes in reference to the idea of the trace, the '*track of the Autobahn*' along which non-places are largely ranged, reduced to ubiquitous, carbon-copy or 'clichéd' imprints.

It is not accidental that graffiti tends to occur mostly in those sites of writing identified by Marc Augé as 'non-places': on trains, subways, tunnels, bridge pillars and blind walls, even on the steps of the escalators in underground stations, everywhere where the users of signs are travellers 'between' identifiable, 'authentic' places. Often graffiti can only be seen from the windows of a car, bus or train – in passing or driving by. The speed and acceleration of the moving vehicle congests the writing line in its extension, and along with it, the syntactic flow of the language; in rushing by they blur the image of the writing. Just as the observer catches sight of a piece of graffiti as in a snapshot, it has already gone again, and the symbolic meaning of the graffiti always threatens to collapse in the drawing out and congestion of the trace. In the trace itself moving and being moved, the imprints of the letters are contorted into becoming illegible. At least, so they seem. That is what the concept of the non-place seems to suggest.

## Passages

Once the Wartburg Castle has been passed by, the great excitement about almost having visited gradually wears off: 'I was *nearly* there, I *almost* touched the place'. The travellers are disappointed when they realize that the indexical function of the sign 'Wartburg' has not kept the promise it was proclaiming. The name did not produce the place, but rather the non-place. The 'names create non-place in the places; they turn them into passages', Augé quotes from de Certeau and adds: 'We could say, conversely, that the act of passing gives a particular status to place names . . . and that the movement that "shifts lines" and traverses places is, by definition, creative of itineraries: that is, words and non-places.'[5]

The special status of the Wartburg Castle as at the same time 'word' and 'passing place' or 'passage' conceals within it another quite different charge. In hindsight, the visitor from the West may realize that Eisenach – in the temporalization of the space covered – is 'already' in Thuringia. This means that, a mere five minutes ago, the road must have crossed the former border. Strictly speaking, it did so three times, for at the division of Germany, this section of the historical motorway was severed by a sharp bend of the border. In divided Germany one left the Autobahn in Hessen just before the border, drove along the border via a country road and at the crossing point of Herleshausen, the Autobahn then led into the GDR. Only after reunification were the two linking sections reconnected by means of the old section of Autobahn. They are not of course visible as interconnections between East and West. Today a bridge crosses over the Werra at the section where the river formed the border. East and West seem to blend together seamlessly into one another. Travellers go in and out, leaving the former 'American Sector' without seeing a 'caution' sign, without danger to life and limb, almost effortlessly. Almost unnoticed.[6]

Whereas along French *autoroutes* and *routes nationales* you find signs saying '*la méridienne verte*' indicating the Greenwich meridian – 'When you pass this spot, you are crossing into the Eastern/Western hemisphere' – the historic inner-German border remains unmarked, no sign even on the wide green strip along the edge of a wood.[7] The specific sign system of the Autobahn enacts either places that are not really there and at the same time absorbs existing places by not pointing them out. Places which were once strictly separated are now linked together by the bridges and viaducts of the Autobahn leading one over all obstacles, into a unified space designed for movement, transit and passage and in no way gives the impression of a 'former' border area.

The old border is erased without trace, at least so it seems. Is that not a tell-tale scar there in the landscape, that well-mown edge of the wood left by the former death strip? Is not the death strip without a trace the epitome of a trace?

## Killing Kool

In 1975 Jean Baudrillard published – perhaps the first – in-depth study of graffiti as a post-modern cultural practice in an essay that has become legendary: 'KOOL KILLER or the Insurrection of Signs'. Significantly he introduces the phenomenon of graffiti by using the image of a flood:

> In the spring of 1972 in New York a spate of graffiti broke out which, starting with ghetto walls and fences, finally overcame subways and buses, lorries and elevators, corridors and monuments, completely covering them in graphics ranging from the rudimentary to the sophisticated, whose content was neither political nor pornographic. These graphics consisted *solely of names, surnames* drawn from the underground comics such as DUKE SPIRIT SUPERKOOL KOOLKILLER ACE VIPERE SPIDER EDDIE KOLA and so on, followed by their street number – EDDIE 135 WOODIE 110 SHADOW 137, etc. – or even by a number in Roman numerals, a dynastic or filiatory index – SNAKE I SNAKE II SNAKE III, etc. – up to L (50), depending on which name, which totemic designation is taken up by these new graffitists.[8]

The graffiti wave burst from the 'ghetto', thus Baudrillard continues, 'into the white city' and quickly spread all over the industrialized world.[9] In this process, he writes, they are 'solely names': arbitrary signifiers; any word could replace any other without changing the meaning. Admittedly, the political or pornographic signs are shocking but they totally lack any message. Graffiti only gets its *power* to shock from the semiotic process and not its *meaningful* content, Baudrillard maintains. Because the graffiti signs do not serve any purposes of communication.

In fact, graffiti often distorts the letters so much it is illegible. In so doing, the graffitists accelerate the act of writing into a sort of stenographic battle, often sprayed on in quick sweeps, and frequently their appearance takes on the marks of a 'flood-like' onward striving, menacing invasion. Graffiti is either, to use the terminology of the scene, 'bombed' as a simple calligraphy of coded names from the scene or 'thrown up' as quick pieces, and even the sophisticated painted masterpieces are skillfully sprayed on fast as the wind. In vast numbers – they even seem to be 'a wave' and are mostly seen accordingly as *plurale tantum* – graffiti is (or 'are') 'tagged', that is, sprayed on as a paraph in a single go. They turn up by the hundreds at different places in the city as unvarying signs on electricity boxes and in underground tunnels, on road signs, likewise on the fronts of blocks of flats, restructuring the individual places where they occur according to their own symbolic order.

These graffiti-artists whizz through the city like winged Mercuries. Like postmen, they often make use of the mail-packet forms that the post-office give out and turn them into serial stencils which they subsequently stick onto electricity boxes and drainpipes, themselves emblems of the systems of supply and communication. As an illegal activity this way of writing is safer, the faster it is. Also the technique of '*pochoirs*', sprayed on quickly and with great precision using preprepared stencils and mostly in one colour, give to the autographic act of writing the look of an allographic printing process.[10]

On moonlit nights 'wild style' graffiti is bombed on trains in sidings and the anonymous sprayers celebrate their greatest victories when they manage to do a 'whole train' that on the following morning has their handiwork on display with a *vernissage* at every station in the country. The train is totally covered with their graffiti, their lines flow seamlessly from one carriage to another. As Baudrillard describes, graffiti 'runs from the wall onto the window or the door or windows on subway trains'[11] as the graffiti-artist takes neither window frames nor street corners into account, if necessary his images run right round the corner.[12] In this respect too, graffiti can be seen as writing of passage since the crossing of borders, albeit the edges of its writing surface, counts as one of its main inscription technologies.

For Baudrillard and generally in the relevant, mainly sociological and criminological discourse,[13] graffiti has up until now been seen as writing without writers, produced by anonymous masses, by hordes of writers, who like the armies of nameless copyists and secretaries, reel off their pre-fabricated type as a never varying imprint. In the end it is a form of writing whose style is without style, in so far as it displays no 'officially' identifiable, personal handwriting. Rather, the attribution of the writing to an originator takes place via secret codes that are only known to the community. Unlike almost any other handwriting, graffiti stands as a global way of writing, written by the international community of postmodern, post-industrial, nameless graffiti-artists, shooting up from nowhere out of the shadows just as once upon a time thieves and tramps put their secret marks on the front of houses that were ripe for being burgled, plundered or on the contrary were the ones to be spared.

Precisely on account of its being enciphered, the 'nameless' way of writing of adolescent graffiti-artists is considered to be self-expression, authentification of the self, like tattoos and other acts of signing. The writers use graffiti as a means, as Baudrillard and the relevant contributions to the debate put it, to claim a counter-identity in opposition to bourgeois identity and thus to stand out against the anonymity of the city. They 'tag', 'bomb' or 'throw up' their signatures on every available writing surface of the city, the summit of self-expression being feats of daring successfully carried out on traffic signs at neck-breaking height or on sections of the railway or motorway where they are dicing with death.

This is how Baudrillard describes the KOOL KILLER: He sprays his subversive sign as a protest *against* the 'semiocracy of the city' with their direction signs and warnings, information boards and advertising hoardings, in order 'to regain an identity (which is impossible in any case)'.[14] His sign is 'like a scream, an interjection, an *anti-discourse*, as the waste of all syntactic, poetic and political development, as the smallest radical element that cannot be caught by any organized discourse'. In general, Baudrillard adds, graffiti escapes 'the principle of signification, and as *empty signifiers* erupts into the sphere of the full signs of the city'.[15] As 'indifferent', 'empty signifiers', graffiti has neither content nor a message, 'it alone is savage in that its message is zero'.[16]

## Force or Meaning

At the same time, according to Baudrillard, 'this emptiness gives it its strength'. '"Force" instead of "difference"' is his slogan for graffiti. By the power of this force admittedly graffiti does not say anything any more but it *does* something, i.e. it

> turns the city's walls and corners . . . into a *body*, a body without a beginning or end, made erotogenic in its entirety by writing just as the body may be in the primitive inscription (tattooing) . . . By tattooing walls, SUPERSEX and SUPERKOOL free them from the architecture and turn them once more into living, social matter, into the moving body of the city.[17]

By the power of its force, graffiti sabotages the process of designation that normally makes writing useful for purposes of communication. On this basis, graffiti becomes a special case of writing in so far as it transforms the otherwise dead bearer of writing into a live and sexualized body. This is admittedly unfit for the purpose of communication (or mute), but it is all the more provocative, if not even obscene, and to that extent not at all 'unpornographic', as Baudrillard maintains at the start of his essay.

On the contrary, the graphism of graffiti operates precisely 'porno-graphically', i.e. literally 'as the *porne* (whore) writes'! Writing can then still be 'pornographic' if – in Baudrillard's terminology – it presents itself totally 'anti-discursively': if it excludes the discursive potential of the erogenous body. In my opinion, graffiti is exactly what Judith Butler has termed 'excitable speech': hate-speak: words that do not just wound as performative speech-acts but at the same time always also communicate the function of wounding.[18] Because like pornography, graffiti presents an ideal model for a cultural articulation that sometimes *in*cites but always *ex*cites. So what is interesting is, rather, the discourse *about* graphisms which, whenever it critically exposes the (patriarchal) politics of discrimination, also always brings into the discussion the mechanisms of (feminist) censorship. Just as pornography always functions as a topic and is – in one way or another – constructed around gender, similarly graffiti always stirs up debate about cultural processes of signification as processes of values, even and above all when it presents itself as completely valueless.

Up until now, Baudrillard's ideas have been both prominent and widely accepted in the discourse about graffiti: in summary, graffiti for him counts as 'indifferent' as well as 'anti-discursive', 'a-political' and 'a-pornographic', 'empty signifiers' produced by nameless 'non-subjects' and having 'force' instead of 'meaning'. The recognition his theory has received is justified to the extent that Baudrillard was the first to deal with graffiti; he deserves recognition as the first one to formulate an adequate language to describe graffiti.

And yet, this theory too runs 'as if on wheels'.

And indeed, not just on account of the overlooked pornographic dimension. Rather – and this is the actual Archimedes point, from which I should like to upset Baudrillard's theoretical edifice – because, strictly speaking, graffiti is handwriting. As such it is therefore not just either readable or unreadable, either political or a-political, pornographic or a-pornographic, etc. Rather, handwriting is always also an eventful action (*Hand*lung). Handwriting does not only designate or state a *signified*, but it also *touches* writers and readers, makes a contract between them *by a shake of the hand*, and contracts are distinguished by retaining their validity precisely even in the absence of one of the signatories to the contract.

The thesis of handwriting as action puts a new spin on the debate about graffiti, since it no longer insists on enquiring into the semiotic operations of graffiti as a (non-)sign that is either meaningful or not. It remains undecidable whether writing, and certainly handwriting, is either powerful and bodily, or meaningful and disembodied, as Baudrillard maintains. The question, *what does graffiti mean?*, does not compensate for that other question: *what does it do?* Handwriting as a performative (like all writing and every sign) does not have force *instead of* meaning but it *means* precisely *because* it has force.

## Showing

Graffiti (like handwriting in general) is writing in passing. Not only is it written and read *en passant* and is in addition highly ephemeral but in line with its nomadic structure 'it passes' mostly in the in-between spaces of transit that Marc Augé calls 'non-places'. With the term 'passage', however, it is impossible to ignore another epistemic meaning, i.e. the *passages* of Paris, those peculiar pieces of architecture involving narrow side-streets and arcades whose shop-windows and display cases inspired Walter Benjamin in his project of modern perception. If according to Benjamin, passages stimulate one to reflect on the anticipation of future (modern) times, they use as the medium for the augury the presentation sites of displays, hoardings and world exhibitions attracting the gaze of the passers-by in urban Europe. To put it another way: passages are exhibition spaces.

In her book *Double Exposures* on museums, Mieke Bal devotes an in-depth study to the act of exhibiting that I mentioned before and which I should now like to discuss further. According to Bal, all cultural activity starts with the gesture of 'showing' or 'exposition'. For Bal, the verb 'expose' has three meanings: exposition, exposé and expose (oneself). The Greek verb *apo-deik-nymai*, grammatically in the 'middle voice', very nicely illustrates these self-reflexive and at the same time object-oriented aspects, because it means all these:

1. 'making a public presentation' (i.e. here and now).
2. 'publicly demonstrating' (at or towards an indirect, dative object). 'It can be combined with a noun meaning *opinions* or *judgments*' (of a subject); and
3. it can 'refer to the performing of those deeds that *deserve* to be made public'.
   (It therefore includes the aspect of *value* which Ketelaar has considered in relation to the archive by coining the term '*archivilisation*'. If in the chapter on the diary I used the erm 'musealize', then one should here also add that syllable of Ketelaar's: 'muse*valize*'.)[19]

Common to all three meanings is that they emphasize the distinctly dative focus of address by the museum: the museum is directed *at the public*, and this interest in the other makes showing into a discursive practice. To quote Bal again: 'exposition as display is a particular kind of speech act'.[20]

If Baudrillard describes graffiti as 'anti-discursive', Bal in her programmatic 'Introduction' to the *Practice of Cultural Analysis* puts forward a theory which, taken literally, is diametrically opposed. For Mieke Bal understands graffiti not as a dismantling of the semiotic operations of culture, but as a cultural act – or here I might add *Hand*lung – *par* *excellence*. She takes a piece of graffiti in the Biltstraat of the Dutch city of Utrecht as a prototypical example to demonstrate the *modus operandi* of cultural processes of signification as such.[21] What interests Bal particularly is that the piece of graffiti takes the public city wall as its writing surface and, in so doing, it is 'an exhibit; it is on show; and it shows itself, shows its hand, its presence.'[22] This 'being public' makes graffiti into an exposition, it presents itself, if you like, paradoxically as a highly personal, and at the same time public, sign, one could go so far as to say: as exhibitionist intimacy, or else: as the imprint of a trace.

In the case of the diaries of Anne Frank in the museum in Amsterdam, I gave a detailed analysis of the drama of 'musealized handwriting'. In the case of graffiti, the specific context of the museum takes on a broader meaning, since the museum becomes a conceptual metaphor for the walls of the city and vice versa. On the basis of this museum metaphor, Bal develops her understanding of the cultural processes as processes of 'drawing' and 'showing'.

## The Graffiti Museum

Here one might wonder what gives the museum metaphor added value. Certainly the metaphor of the 'graffiti museum' is not very original; it has been used repeatedly in discourses on graffiti, notably in debates in which graffiti is being defended against the charge of being primitive, 'low', subversive or criminal. From the 1980s onwards, post-modern cultural activists sought to benefit from the 'wild', uncontrolled image of graffiti. After the release of the documentary films, Charlie Ahearn's *Wild Style* and Henri Chalfant's *Style Wars*, several art galleries in New York became interested in 'graffiti-as-art', and so graffiti moved from the 'ghettos' into the museum. Keith Haring's career is emblematic of this shift; he started as an anonymous painter initially scribbling life-size stick men with chalk on black advertisement posters in the New York subway, but soon became the starsprayer in Toni Shafraze's gallery and, from there, an internationally acknowledged pop artist.[23] Baudrillard is critical about such 'recuperation' of 'graffiti as art', claiming that the aesthetic content of graffiti does not contribute to its 'force' but is 'a sign of weakness' because it promotes a process which he labels – intentionally pejoratively – 'museum-culturalization' (*muséification*).[24]

Mieke Bal's concept of the 'Graffiti Museum' has quite a different purpose. When Bal proposes the city wall as a museum, she does not only reject the idea of the absorption of a free and anarchic subcultural underworld by a colonizing takeover bid on the part of the art market but she completely avoids the rhetorical position that Baudrillard implicitly bases his argument upon, of an opposition between 'high' and 'low', official and subversive. Any idea of a popular or subculture, as has been pointed out by many critics as well as Mieke Bal, can thus only be taken as being derived from a high culture of which the lower one is an intricate offshoot and the higher implicitly privileged as a concept.

A long way from such logical dichotomies, the metaphor of the museum in Bal's theory functions as a tool of cultural analysis.[25] According to this, the act of exposing presupposes a complex discursive process in which diverse cultural agents are involved, and these agents cannot be labelled simply 'non-subjects', even if they, like the crowds of museum visitors, are mostly anonymous, nor can the signs produced by them be dismissed as just 'non-signs'. In this respect, Bal's theory does not so much *oppose* Baudrillard's idea that graffiti is 'non-discursive', because it is without content and without meaning, but it redefines and secularizes the terms so that they can be useful as analytical tools. Which is just what they are intended to *do* in the following.

## Aerosol

If such a thing as a graffiti museum exists, an institutionalized transit zone, a passage, in which graffiti as an object on display (direct object, accusative) is exhibited by a curator (subject, nominative) *for* transient or passing visitors (indirect object, dative), then it does so literally on the Internet. The Internet is full of graffiti websites used by sprayers and their sympathizers as showcases, allowing them to put their work before the public under the protection of the anonymity provided by the web. An outstanding graffiti website is on display at www.pipslab.nl. The visitors to this website are like the visitors to a museum, interactive. They are invited to view some lab proofs by PIPS, an Amsterdam-based group of performance artists, working on the interface of photo and video art and multimedia performance.

The homepage opens with a Quicktime trailer showing nothing but a black screen with a yellow dot on it. Suddenly, the dot begins to move independently, as if summoned to life by the viewer. It hops and twitches back and forth, holding on for a fraction of a second, only to move off in the opposite direction, describing lines and loops in flashes of light. Then, the imaginary trace left by the yellow dot of light becomes visible as an accumulation of individual stills now forming one continuous, sweeping line. Finally, individual images flash up in very quick succession, snapshots revealing illuminated captions written in wild handwriting: 'Lumalive', immediately followed by 'by PIPS:lab'.

Underneath this Quicktime trailer, another animated image on the screen presents a strip with other 'light writings'. When the visitor touches this strip with a roll-over, it starts scrolling from right to left, offering an animated menu of lab proofs selectable with a click of the mouse. One of these Quicktime tracks shows from the front-view and as in an American shot a youngster standing in front of a bare brick wall in a dark hall. A cap is hiding his eyes, his sweatshirt with the hood ready to be pulled right over his head, as if to prevent recognition.

His left hand is in his trouser pocket, and in his right hand, contrary to the expectations aroused by this type of scene, he holds an aerosol can rather than a revolver. With his back to the bare wall ripe for writing on, he chooses his writing surface in the open air. With the aerosol he sprays looping lines of light into space. His hand's movements leave no trace of writing, they register no line at all. To become

Screenshot of the PIPS:lab home-page.

Screenshot from the 'OASE' trailer.

visible as a permanent trace and readable as writing, this light performance needs the technical manipulation of what the artists call 'PIPS (matrix) recorded effects': multiple cameras record the act of writing in a real-time multi-angle representation and then combine the individual light images together into a three-dimensional letter sculpture. Thus the graffiti-artist signs with his name: 'OASE'.

This staging of the graffiti tag as a light performance highlights the fact that graffiti – at least this goes for postmodern urban graffiti – is an ephemeral 'live' performance rather than a permanent 'inscription', in Flusser's sense. Spraypaint graffiti is light years away from such historic inscription technologies; in other words, it is definitely not an engraving or an incision on a durable or resistant material indicated by what graffiti literally in line with its etymology means, that is, an inscription engraved, in accordance with the architecture of the Renaissance, into the thin scratch layer of painted rendering. The surface to be written on by light graffiti does not consist of stone or a wall. Rather it takes air as its medium, air in which light waves develop at lightning speed, that then, due to the sluggishness of vision and the technical manipulation of time by means of the 'PIPS matrix', form lines revealing writing.

Strictly speaking, the *passage* that writing goes down here is as follows: from a certain standpoint writing blazes its preposterous trail, and by allying the present delay coordinates of the yellow point of light with the future and past ones and merging them into a ligature, it displaces not just space but at the same time it merges different time-frames together. The gesture of the hand *compresses* movement *in its extension*, and only in the sum of the individual coordinates does a segment of writing arise – belatedly. And indeed, with every act of writing anew, since the topography of handwriting is always and fundamentally caught in this paradoxical structure of space and time; the trace is simultaneously here and there, simultaneously now and coming soon and yet always already past. The space of handwriting is the archetype of the *non-place*.

This *ephemeral* and *passing* dimension, along with its *provisional* or *temporary* quality, is the main business of graffiti. After all, tagging or bombing is scarcely sprayed when it is already tagged over by other, competing graffitists and it vanishes into the depths of the palimpsest. Or when sprayed on the official faces of the city, it is swiftly and professionally removed. Even for the often short period of its existence, graffiti is an illustration of speed, and this is exactly how it is written: as quick pieces, with rapid writing movements, not carefully negotiating the line within the restrictions of the four-line system but rather in passing in one go and often done blind under the cover of darkness. In this respect, the writing *ductus* of the graffiti-writer is not just a visual *sign* (from which a semiotic function is to be expected) but also, and not least, a tactile gesture.

More than in the normal case of handwriting written with a pencil or ink on paper, graffiti is a writing of the body, chiefly not limited to the (right) hand but extending beyond the hand and the wrist to the underarm, all the limbs, even those on the left, and involving the whole body in the act of writing. Drawing the outlines, graffiti-writers at times get up on the tips of their toes, at other times they kneel down; for the prolongations of the lines they bend and stretch in all directions. Shading in the outlined surfaces, they go in for repetitive movements: up and down – up and down, until the surface is covered. The graphism of graffiti is a 'choreography'. The writer does not scratch or gouge with a stylus at all, nor does he apply writing fluid with a quill or a ballpoint pen. He *sprays* his gaseous writing fluid onto the background. He expires aerosol like the pneuma of a breath; a soft, hissing stream of air, aspirate like Heta, before it fell silent, hardly audible and writable only with a diacritic that has been called *spiritus*.

By 'expiring' his signature in this way, he is enacting it as a unique and distinctly physical act that is irrevocably linked to the presence of the body. Just as handwriting also always claims to guarantee the presence of the writer in a historically defined, unique moment of time in a topographically exactly definable 'place', in the same way graffiti also claims to bring together a date with a place and a signature in an indivisible unity. 'I was here' (not just 'almost'), is what graffiti on top of the Eiffel Tower or on the bark of an ancient oak is saying. The originator of the signature is of course not to be found at that address.

More than in the case of graffiti done with aerosol, writing in the case of the PIPS:lab is first and foremost – that is, before treatment with the PIPS:lab matrix – pure *ductus*, pure choreography. The technical term 'choreography' sums up the double structure of the performative as being one of a singular iterability or of an iterable singularity. Because dance is in its actual performance irrevocably related to the actuality of a real and unique body *writing* the 'choros' (the dance) *by performing it*. It is writing, not only in the sense of a pre-*scription* of the dance movements – literally – preceding the actual dance, but also and not least because the dance itself carries the structure of the possibility of repetition within itself. Choreographic patterns are in this sense writing. Vice versa, writing, hand-writing in particular, is in this sense choreography: the unique performance of moves that are in principle repeatable, upstrokes and downstrokes, producing with every iteration the 'itera' that makes a difference.

## 'How can we Know the Dancer from the Dance?'

> From the legal point of view a signing subject did not exist before the text [of the Declaration of Independence of the United States] that is thus itself the producer and guarantor of its own signature. Through this incredible event, this fable, which implies the trace and hence is only possible through the inappropriateness of being one present to oneself, a signature gives itself a name. It lends credit, its own credit, from itself to itself. The self appears here in all its cases (nominative, dative, accusative) just as a signature gives itself credit, with a single act of violence.
>
> Jacques Derrida, *Otobiographies*[26]

For the dancer, as Paul de Man has forcefully argued in his close reading of Yeats's *Among School Children*, it is of course *undecidable* to what extent he is a producer of signs or a sign deriving from this source itself.[27] Like Yeats's dancer, the PIPS:lab light performer throws up the question of the status of the sprayer as 'writer' or 'author'. Dancer or dance? Jean Baudrillard decides the undecidable, leaving no doubt when he unequivocally claims that 'graffiti, composed of nothing but names, effectively avoids every reference and every *origin*'(my emphasis). And as the subject of graffiti is *without origin*, it makes use of 'nicknames drawn from underground comics such as DUKE SPIRIT SUPERKOOL',[28] in which this pseudonym is emblematic for the rhetoric of erasing the subject.

'KOOL KILLER', is not just *killing* the subject *kool*. It is also neither 'without origin' nor is its reference 'equalling zero'. After all, these nicknames refer, if not to a bourgeois person or a bourgeois fictive character, to the heroic figures of comics, as Baudrillard himself explains. In so doing, they have an intertextual reference, and indeed the pretexts are not cited to re-establish a bourgeois identity. Rather, the citations evoke the specific inscription technologies of the comics in the form of eminently integrative text-image compositions. Comics and graffiti have always been joined technologies, and as 'intertexual quotations' they thus have, as Mieke Bal emphasizes, an 'interdiscursive complexity' which is 'transcultural', in so far as they transfer – or translate – a sign from one discursive context ('comic') to another ('city walls').[29]

In the case of visual art works, the signature is normally written *at the bottom* of the picture; in painting, it is added to the picture after completion in a corner of the canvas, and this final sealing confirms *belatedly* that the act of painting is completed. In a similar way, letters, even typed ones, are first written and then signed – at the bottom, as an addition, using another technique of writing: by hand. The signature does not belong to the body of the letter, the message is imparted, the textual communication typed mechanically or electronically, and then, *afterwards*, signed by hand. The signature is an addition, an accessory, or a supplement, as Derrida puts it, that 'is added to a thing that counts as complete for its completion'. And although it counts as external to the thing itself, like a frame to a picture, like an accessory (or *Par-ergon*) to a work of art, it is nevertheless active at its very heart, since it is only by the addition of the signature that a letter, a document, a certificate, a painting, an order and any authoritative communication is authenticated.[30]

The PIPS artist undertakes precisely this tightrope walk. Like a dancer, he performs the art work in the very moment that he carries out the signature, and by so doing, he 'invents' himself as a graffiti-artist who is christened under the name of 'OASE'. His signature is not external to the art work; it *is* the art work. There is no art work and no writing preceding the graffiti-artist's name or following after it; the art work emerges at the very moment that the artist is 'spraying' his signature, and, as soon as a letter flashes up, it has always already disappeared. The name is still, however, valid. It remains safe within the trace of the writing, like 'credit', as Derrida puts it – available on call (if you like, imprintable).[31]

## The Right Side of the Writing

OASE's handwriting, it is clear, is peculiar. Not only because he uses unusual writing materials and thus places the writing just as pointlessly as those madmen who write with water. But there is the additional fact that the particular materiality of light onto/in the air requires the application of a particular technology to become readable: the PIPS-matrix. This involves, on the one hand, video technology to compress the flow of time, on the other, it requires, in order for his writing to become readable for the one he is addressing, i.e. the *one opposite him*, that the graffiti-artist writes in mirror-image. Correspondingly, OASE moves his hand *contrary to the right direction of writing*: from right to left. It is true that he uses the letters of the Roman alphabet, nevertheless at the same time he infringes against its basic convention, that of the rightward *flow* of writing.

It is not just that he writes in mirror image, but his contravention goes even further, as he not only turns the *image* of the writing around (as Leonardo who began with the first coda of the first letter and carried this out in mirror image), but the whole piece of writing. That is, he begins with the last coda of the last letter and draws the trace of the writing in a reverse direction from right to left, thus finishing at the first hasta of the first letter. Unlike Leonardo and other left-handed people he does this, not from the needs of writing ergonomics of the left hand, but he writes sinistrograde and against the flow *with his right hand*.

The reason for this peculiar way of writing can only lie in the economy of writing itself which is after all a sign *for* somebody.

The preposterous nature of this way of writing does not lie in a simple infringement against the inscription technologies of the Roman alphabet, running more or less consistently from left to right for over two millennia, but rather in the fact that the reversal of the trace remains invisible to the reader/observer. Because the sign is so oriented towards purposes of communication that it counterbalances the first infringement against the order of writing (its sinistrograde reversal) by a second one (the drawing backwards of the trace). The provocative element of this way of writing lies in this double take, in the (gauche) simulation of a rightness by the reversal of its reversal.

The responsibility for the *success* of the writing is to a great extent dependent on this technical intervention, that is, the work of cameras that *are placed opposite* the writer at various angles of vision. In this opposition the cameras anticipate the **O**ther, the reader/observer who, even if she is positioned outside of the act of writing, nevertheless always forms an integral part of it.

## 'I baptize myself'

OASE's act of writing is preposterous in another respect. In christening himself by the name OASE, he is implicitly articulating a speech act ('I hereby baptize thee/myself'), by which traditionally a baptist (subject) initiates a person to be baptized (object) into a social system, and indeed by the power of his god-given, priestly or whatever shamanic authority. Self-baptism is in this respect an infringement of the norm, because the baptizing baptized person is carrying out an office to which he is not entitled. The giving of a n**A**me has always been the role of the other. In general, a b**A**ptism can never be self-referential, after all it is inscribing the subject into the **A**rchive of a cultural community (of a register office), so that the baptized person, even in his very absence, can be named *by others* or *for others*.

The Greek word for 'baptize' is 'baptizein' (βαπτίζειν) and means 'dip', 'submerge', 'wash'. As a transitive verb it presupposes a subject-object relation, as in Matthew 28:19, 'Go therefore and make disciples of all nations, baptizing them in the name of the F**A**ther …'. But there is another use of 'baptizein', and no less a text and no less an authoritative one than the Holy Bible itself offers it: (have) (oneself) baptize(d) is a prototypical example of the active-passive mode of the 'middle voice', for example in the speech where Ananias commands Saul: 'Rise and be baptized, and wash away your sins'. (Acts of the Apostles 22:16).[32] Whenever 'baptizein' is also used intransitively outside of religious contexts, i.e. without any object reference, it significantly does not mean 'submerge' but 'sink' – like Narcissus.

Sinking and drowning like Narcissus, this also appears to be the consequence for OASE's contrariness. His baptism is null and void, and – as Baudrillard would say – his sign meaningless. That is how the theory seems to run on wheels.

At least it would run on wheels, if this distinctly peculiar gesture *for the other* were not there. Because if 'OASE' baptizes himself (as a 'graffiti-artist'), at the same time he always includes the other as well. Even if he baptizes himself, he anticipates the **O**ther as an implied addressee, as a dative, indirect object; I baptize myself *for thee*. The mode of his baptism is the middle voice: the subject-function merges into this object-function. Because the ritual that OASE performs is derived by him, like the letters of his name, *from the other*, and *to him* he returns them. He addresses him as an *opposite* in his specific *otherness*, doubly turned in a rightward direction, and in end-effect, writing will be *for him alone*.

## The Right Side of the Wall

With the same authority with which writing dictates where left and right, where the top and the bottom are on the paper, the museum also creates a topographical order. The walls of the *white cube* separate the interior of the museum from its exterior just as the frame separates the exhibition objects from the exhibition space. With the authority of the *connoisseur*, the museum itself as a first person makes the distinction between the right and the wrong, the original and the copy, the valuable and the worthless, etc. In a certain sense, graffiti also restructures the spatial order. Even if it does not claim the authority of an academically or institutionally legitimated curator, nevertheless it in its own way functions as topographical intervention. After all, graffiti is as a rule sprayed on the *exterior* of walls, walls that shield a private *interior* from the public sphere. In cultivating the outside of walls with symbols, graffiti-artists literally 'wallpaper' the streets and occupy the public space as their private domains.[33] In taking over walls, they infringe against spatial order; they 'inhabit' the city, turning its outer fronts into interior walls. The public street becomes a living room for graffitists.

This politics of a fixed distinction between an inner and an outer side, or a left and a right side, or a Western and an Eastern side, were to have highly dramatic repercussions in the case of the Berlin Wall, the concrete wall running for 160 kilometers that became the canvas for the biggest graffiti project ever. On 13 August 1961, overnight the GDR started building what it called its 'antifaschistischer Schutzwall' ('anti-fascist protective wall'), totally walling West Berlin in and turning it into a Capitalist island in the homeland of 'Real socialism'. It initially consisted of provisionally erected barbed wire and wooden barricades that were soon replaced by massive walls and anti-tank obstacles and continuously developed and modernized. The wall of the first generation, initially 30 cm thick, was strengthened; on streets that were ideal

Building of the Wall in Berlin, 21 August 1963.

The third-generation Wall at the Potsdamer Platz, Berlin, in 1974.

for breaking through in heavy vehicles, it could reach 1 metre in width. From 1963 onwards, these predecessors were replaced by a wall of mass-produced concrete slabs, manufactured in 'Volkseigenen Betrieben' (state-owned companies), and held together by steel reinforcements.

The Wall developed in time into a total border-protection system consisting of an inner and an outer wall and a patrol road, a control and security strip inbetween with watchtowers, electric contact fences, and spotlights. The border *line* was really a border *zone*, the death strip an inbetween space at times additionally protected with automatic spring-guns and – as a monstrous combination of the human with the technical – 'orders to shoot and kill'. In 1974 the Wall was finally rebuilt with concrete slabs reinforcing it with a meter-wide base set against the West and with deeply implanted foundations to stabilize it against forces breaking through westwards. A split pipeline covered the top to prevent any attempts to climb on the Wall. In general, it represented a proper work of architecture, looking as if it was following the laws of the classic column with base, pillar and capital.

The fourth generation Wall was the opportunity for the graffiti-artists, all the more so because the panels were now plastered and even whitened, providing an ideal background for painting. These improvements were carried out on both sides of the Wall. To whiten the outer, Western side of the Wall, a cage of steel barriers needed to be built for the painters, standing as a *pars pro toto* for the big cage that was the GDR. During the work the painters were surveyed by armed border

The fourth-generation Wall being whitened on its West side.

guards.[34] Through this aesthetic white-washing, the government aimed at making the Wall – in line with Robert Musil's famous saying – 'as invisible as a monument'[35] – so that people from both sides would get used to, and thus become indifferent, to it.

But the whiteness of the Wall was not invisible. On the contrary, it provided the painting background and writing surface for a symbolic recoding of the topographic order. Because now it happened that graffiti-artists took on this barely visibile remainder and integrated the Wall and its seeming immateriality into their art works, thus exposing them by emphasizing their 'invisibility'. Frequently used motifs included breaks, holes, doors, windows, or zips opening. Such a sprayed split in the Wall bends the rendering outwards like the labia of genitals during childbirth; the blood-red stone wall behind is broken open revealing the view of the border security strip. Behind it is the inner border in which a first escape hole has opened up.

A *trompe l'œil* work of graffiti was made by Iranian painter Yadiga Azizy in Berlin Kreuzberg between Legien- and Leuschnerdamm in 1988, restoring the interrupted view of a church the tower of which had been disconnected from the nave by the Wall. The illusionist logic of the

Yadiga Azizy's graffiti in Berlin Kreuzberg between Legien- and Leuschnerdamm, 1988.

view undermines the border, and, paradoxically enough, it does so by using the Wall as its medium. With no regard to the materiality of the architectural frame, the piece of graffiti transforms the Wall into a space less of separation and division than of seamless movement, transit and passage – at least symbolically.

## Border-Crossings

In his essay 'Spatial Stories', Michel de Certeau interprets all such border activities – their formation, displacement, or crossing – as discursive acts, speech acts performed by a first person authorized to define or control a border. De Certeau discusses the walking on or crossing of the border by reference to the example of a rite that, in ancient Rome, was celebrated by priests called *fetiales* prior to any contact with a foreign people,

> such as a declaration of war, a military expedition, or an alliance. The ritual was a procession with three centrifugal stages, the first within Roman territory but near the frontier, the second on the

frontier, the third in foreign territory. The ritual action was carried out before any civil or military action because it is designed to *create the field* necessary for political or military activities. It is thus also a *repetitio rerum*: both a renewal and a repetition of originary founding acts, a recitation and a citation of genealogies that could legitimate the new enterprise, and a *prediction* and a promise of success at the beginning of battles, contracts, or conquests. As a general repetition before the actual representation, the rite, a narration in acts, precedes the historical realization. The tour or the procession of the *fetiales* opens a space and provides a foundation for the operations of the military men, diplomats, or merchants who dare to cross the frontiers.[36]

Just as the *fetiales* prepared the occupation of the 'foreign land' by first taking possession of it symbolically, one could interpret the graffiti activity on the Wall as a symbolic conquest of the border space.

In 1982 artists around the world were invited to participate in a graffiti competition: 'Overcoming the Wall by Painting the Wall', sponsored by the *Haus am Checkpoint Charlie*. The reaction to this invitation was considerable and lasting: Christophe Bouchet and Thierry Noir painted bright and fanciful 'Red dope on Rabbits' on the Bethaniendamm/Adalberstrasse section of the Wall in 1985; Nora Aurienne created arrows and snakes, all directional lines seemingly bumping up against the Wall; most famously, in October 1986 Keith Haring created a panoramic mural forming a chain with his famous figures over a length of 100m in the Zimmerstrasse right next to Checkpoint Charlie. These graffiti projects had in common that they were all designed to stage the symbolic possibilities for overcoming the Wall, and, in doing so, they turned it from an identifiable, stable and fixed 'place' into what Michel de Certeau has called a 'space' that is marked by narrative movement rather than by rigid topography.

In turning the Wall from an ugly architectural monster into a gigantic global art work, the graffiti-artists gave it considerable economic value. An effect of the art competition – apart from making the Wall visible – was the increase in its monetary value. Flogging off the works of art, so the organizers calculated, would be for the legal owner (the GDR) a lucrative opportunity to improve the disastrous financial

Keith Haring, graffiti, Zimmerstrasse, 1986.

position of the state; selling the art works, however, would involve breaking down the Wall as a border.

And so it happened.

However, the bargain was not struck by the GDR as owner and to a certain extent also art collector, curator and promoter of the gigantic canvas. Because, when the Wall came down, pieces of the Wall were broken out of it by souvenir hunters and other 'Wall peckers' from all over the world, and the best pieces were offered up for sale.[37] Even today, visitors to the *Haus am Checkpoint Charlie* can pick up a 5 g piece of inner German history for 20 euros. A few parts of the former Wall are preserved in all their glory in front of the shopping centre at the Potsdamer Platz where they form a favourite background for souvenir photos taken by tourists to Berlin.

Despite the visual 'strength' of the graffiti – or because of it – the Wall has now become almost invisible in the city. It was torn down without leaving any visible mark. It disappeared without trace – except for a few sections that were preserved to become the official Wall memorial, for example the section in the Bernauer Strasse in Wedding, in which the Wall Museum has conserved and 'musealized' the state of the Wall as a complex border security system.[38]

Looking back at the historical event that was the Fall of the Wall, it seems that it was precisely this economic drive that was the source of the 'force' which brought the Wall down. In this respect, the symbolic taking-over of the border by graffiti among other forces prepared the 'successful' Fall of the Wall, precisely in terms of the economic mechanisms of a free and globalized market economy. If the museum is a 'container' in the sense of a place where objects are collected, selected, stored and 'contained' for conservation and restoration, then such issues of 'containment' belong to the central concerns of the museum that, as an official institution, holds the first-person position of what Mieke Bal calls a true 'value factory'.[39]

At the time when the power legitimizing any civil, military, political or trade action across the border was exclusively reserved for the officials of the GDR, the graffiti symbolically superimposing West onto East undermined the basis of this first-person authority. The official speech acts (Stop! Do not cross! Achtung! You are entering the Soviet Zone! Danger to Life! Mines!) were now answered by their hitherto mute or passive addressees; speakers and addressees changed places in a new grammatical order. In this swapping of roles, the Wall did not just operate as a medium of storage for the graffiti that it received and exposed but by the act of showing it also put on display its specific mode of exposition; to use Mieke Bal's terminology, its 'double exposure' as a subject showing *something* and, in so doing, staging 'an exposure of the self'.[40]

In this respect, the Wall has always been a double exposition in the same sense as a museum. When its owners painted it white to make it mute and invisible, it was, at least from the 'outside' (the Western side), brightly-coloured and glaring, all the more revealing of the strategies of its authoritarian first person. And when this symbolic *pre*paration, that was – as de Certeau describes – a *pre*diction or even a prophecy, was fulfilled or 'was successful', it destroyed its own colourful archive that had been its own memory store. The Wall destroyed itself as an archive following the drive which according to Derrida makes one forget memory and in the end oblivion itself.

But not without leaving a remainder. Because unnoticed and invisibly there is a trace moving around the city. At one moment it takes the shape of a scar in the architecture, at another, of a conversation in the city or a museum. Or it turns up as a document that has lain in the depths of the archive as a permanent trace, ready to flash back into, what Sigmund Freud calls, 'the system Pcpt.-Cs.' (perception system). This Archive is always readable in the order of the Alphabet that everything is endlessly inscribed in.

If graffiti as a 'non-sign', following Baudrillard's claim, leaves its meaning by the wayside – in the overstretched spaces that are created *in passing* by the speed and acceleration of the observer – then this 'wayside' does not mark an end; neither the end of signs or writing, nor the end of a user of signs. The drawing out and stretching of writing in ephemeral graffiti is of course a symptom for the disappearance of writing, but like the trace in general it is precisely this disappearance, the forward movement and the re*trait* of writing as such, that testifies to the persistence of handwriting, blazing its preposterous trail, even and especially where there is nothing but rubble and cinders.

# 9 Paralipomena: This Side of Writing

I have the impression now that the best paradigm for the trace . . .
is not . . . the trail of the hunt, the fraying, the furrow in the sand,
the wake in the sea, the love of the step for its imprint, but the cinder
(what remains without remaining . . . from the all-burning, from the
incineration the incense).

Jacques Derrida, *Cinders*[1]


[The] passage [of the ur-trace] through form is a passage through
the imprint. And the meaning of *différance* in general would be
more accessible to us if the unity of that double passage appeared
more clearly . . . [W]ithout a trace retaining the other as the other
in the same, no difference would do its work and no meaning would
appear . . . *The (pure) trace is différance.* It does not depend on any
sensible plenitude, audible or visible, phonic or graphic. It is, on the
contrary, the condition of such plenitude . . . *Différance* is therefore
the formation of form. But it is on the other hand the being-imprinted
of the imprint.

Jacques Derrida, *Of Grammatology*[2]

There remains in the end the question of writing. Even in the final word on writing, even in this piece of writing, the question comes up again, forces itself upon us and draws attention to a 'paralipomenon', something that was left out or left aside in the foregoing (from 'paraleípein', leave out or aside) and is now to be added as a *belated* footnote or completion. Because writing, even this writing, has come up with no satisfactory answer; it has remained incomplete in relation to itself. No final word, not even a final conclusion to a sentence can be put in this paralipomenon. In this sense the last word of writing belongs to writing itself. And for this reason there is no final word at the end of it, the supposed end, but a plural ending: 'paralipo-*mena*', questioning the idea of ending itself by splitting it into several endings, plural final words, a tangle made up of the loose ends of an incomplete texture.

For 40 years now – since the start (or the outbreak) of the age of digitalization and the global network – the question of writing has often been brought up again and again and by prominent thinkers – and answered positively: in *Die Schrift* (1987), Vilém Flusser asks in line with his apocalyptic view of the media: *Has Writing a Future?* And while he sees the evolution of the media otherwise heading for increasingly reduced dimensions, a dumbing-down towards a 'zero dimension', in which the concrete world of experience is being negated in the abyss of a final abstraction, he concludes this essay on writing with a remarkable postscript in which he formulates a 'petition on behalf of writing standing trial'. He presents his essay as an attempt, 'to write beyond writing'. And if he has 'not even written far enough', he intends nevertheless to keep on writing anew: 'No doubt, oceans of writings will in the future flood out from the printers and technically advanced apparatuses of reproduction.'[3]

Jacques Derrida also raised the question of writing again and again in his work. In *Of Grammatology* (1967) he writes of 'The end of the book and the beginning of writing'. He continually interlinks deferral of the origin and anticipation of the future. The big **A** graphically illustrates the preposterous idea:

> The erection of the pyramid guards life – the dead – in order to give rise [*donner lieu*] to the for-(it)self of adoration. This has the signification of a sacrifice, of an offer by which the all-burning

annuls itself, opens the annulus, contracts the annulus into the anniversary of the solar revolution in sacrificing itself as the all-burning, therefore in guarding itself.[4]

As an epitaph the **A** of the pyramid secures (for the Pharao) a continuation of life which at the same time it withdraws (from him).

Michael Wetzel in his *Die Enden des Buches* (1991), in reply to and as a radical development of Derrida's concept of *écriture*, has spoken of *the return of writing*, even and above all in the age of digital media. For him, the media technological arsenal of photography, film, gramophone, telephone, radio, television, video, walkman, etc. – some of his examples significantly now already count as dated technology in the age of mobile phones, DVD and MP3 players – are a *re*writing, indeed a shift of writing diminishing the trace, but at the same time only serving to continue that which is integral to the trace and which it will continue to do: diminish.

The succession of final words could be extended even further. At this place where the present book on handwriting is coming *to an end*, it is enough to pick up the thought that comes up again and again and in different epistemic contexts, in which the aporia regarding a survival or afterlife of writing has always been addressed by the idea of the trace as a track without end.

For the project of the present book the question of asking '*after*' writing arises once more in a different way, more trickily, since here we are dealing, not with writing as such, but with it as an anthropomorphic, somatic special case: *hand*writing. As a cultural practice, handwriting in the age of mechanical reproduction raises less the question of the symbolic nature of writing than of its being a *Parergon*, an '*hors-d'œuvre*' of the hand, strongly somatizing writing and thus making it receptive for all those cultural attributions – uniqueness, authenticity, distinctiveness – that identify handwriting as having aura. With handwriting in the age of mechanical reproduction, the here and now of the auratic apparition, of the un-spellable remainder of handwriting, comes up against some difficulty.

One could approach the question from a different angle by painting an alternative scenario questioning the premises and the preconditions of the question itself. Then one would have to ask what the questioned '*after*' might look like and whether there can ever be such a state. What kind of *disturbance* could the rewriting of handwriting bring to an end once and for all? Disturbances have always been registered throughout the history of handwriting: every infringement against the norm of the art of writing has been seen as a 'disturbance'; without equal in this role has been the use of the left (sinister, gauche) hand, demonized as a deviation. Likewise, every shift of media has been seen as a disruption: the passage from a prehistoric handprint to the engraving stylus, from the feather-light quill-pen to the scrawling ballpoint, the use of the tablet PC, e-mail and blogging. Every time the library is burned down, the end of handwriting has been prophesied. The most recent case was the memorable night in September 2004 when the historic collection of manuscripts of the Duchess Anna Amalia Library in Weimar went up in flames, amongst them the unique scores belonging to the music collection of Anna Amalia, medieval manuscripts along with the scholarly libraries of Nietzsche, Arnim, Haar and of the first director of the library Schurzfleisch which as a *hand-dictated* collection can never be reconstructed.[5] This seems to be the situation now as regards handwriting, and worse than that, since not only did the fire consume the priceless manuscripts of the library but such a fire has been smouldering barely noticed for a long time, so it is said, slowly and steadily it is consuming handwriting as a cultural practice as such.

But which of these 'disruptions' would ever have been able to produce a homo sapiens without 'manual intelligence' (in Leroi-Gourhan's sense) and therefore a culture without a hand? How would an archive without the technique of writing ever survive and at the same time *draw* up a record of its erasure, how would a museum exhibit anything without bringing the gesture of the index finger into play? Cultural processes are *practices*, and to that extent they are actions (*Hand*lungen).

The *return* of handwriting in the age of the photocopy and the computer marks neither an end nor a radical turning point. The claim has often been made that with the typewriter the great change came that the digital media are about to complete. This thesis has the keyboard as its technical signifier and, following on from that emblematically, the key shift by which one switches from flowing minuscules to printed majuscules. Here one is overlooking the fact that this switching is not mono-directional: rather, it switches back and forth. And generally, handwriting has always been committed to this preposterous switching, since its line continually follows a kinetic program that has the bow, the curve and the loop as its key characteristics, likewise lines crossing over, crossings-out, corrections and improvements. The re*turn* of handwriting is re*writing*, and it takes the shape of a loop. Whenever handwriting goes on writing its trace or writes it anew, the result of the imprint is neither predictable nor foreseeable: literally, it cannot be seen in advance. 'To make an imprint', according to Didi-Huberman means, '*setting up a technical hypothesis to see what results from it*. The result is full of surprises, surpassed expectations and horizons suddenly opening up.'[6]

Examples of this are the chalk scribbles in the 'Sports' screen saver, just as much as the ultra-thinly drawn line in Mercator's *Literarum Latinarum*, the diaries exhibited in the museum and the manuscripts conserved in the repositories of the archive, the lively tattooed stigmata as well as the signs aspirated onto walls with aerosol. The number of examples that can be accommodated within a book on handwriting in the age of mechanical reproduction is endless. We have been supplied with some 'surpassed expectations' and 'surprises' by classical Modernism in the age of that particular era of mechanical reproduction: the *écriture automatique* of the Surrealists as well as the serial and infra-thinly distinguishable imprints of Marcel Duchamp. A 'resounding' rewriting of handwriting was provided by Lászlo Moholy-Nagy in *De Stijl*:

PRODUCTION – REPRODUCTION
. . .
The composition of a man is the synthesis of all his functional mechanisms . . .

Since production (productive creativity) is primarily of service to human development, we must endeavour to expand the apparatus (means) which has so far been used solely for purposes of reproduction for productive ends . . .

The gramophone: until now the gramophone had the task of reproducing existing acoustical phemomena. The sound vibrations to be reproduced were scratched by a needle on a wax plate and were then transposed back into sound with the aid of a microphone.

An expansion of the apparatus for production purposes might make it possible for scratches to be made in the wax by a person and without the aid of mechanical means. The sound when reproduced might result in acoustic effects which, without any new instruments and an orchestra, might signify a fundamental renewal in the production of sound (i.e. new, not yet existing sounds and sound-relationships) for the purposes of composition and the very concept of music itself.

Laboratory experiments are a basis for such work i.e. the thorough investigation of the different kinds of sound vibrations produced by scratches, their different lengths, breadth, depth etc.; the investigation of self-produced scratches; and finally mechanical and technical experiments to perfect this kind of handwriting done by making scratches.[7]

And what comes after that?

## After Omega ...

Whoever finally says, after everything seems to have been written and said – Alpha and Omega – one last . . . omegA . . . is thus starting to speak all over again at the beginning with an . . . Alpha . . . The downstroke of the last coda is always a ligature and the upstroke of a coming hasta. *Between* **A**lpha and **O**mega, **O**mega and **A**lpha, the spiritus is being breathed as a barely perceptible punctuation mark (from inter-*pungere*: both 'to prick inbetween' and 'to erase') indicating the division *between* grammatical units, the spiritus – whether aspirated like *gravis* or glottally-stopped like *lenis* – as the eternal sign of an ineradicable and at the same time archiviolitic *pneuma*.

. . .?. . .

# References

### . . . before Aleph

1 The relationship between numbers and letters has had a detailed study devoted to it by Georges Ifrah in his *Universalgeschichte der Zahlen* (Frankfurt am Main and New York, 1991). On the numerical value of Aleph in the Semitic alphabets see pp. 279–309.

2 Cf. ibid., p. 309.

3 Cf. Josef Tropper, 'Die nordwestsemitischen Schriften', in *Schrift und Schriftlichkeit. Ein interdisziplinäres Handbuch internationaler Forschung*, Band 10.1, eds Hartmut Günther and Otto Ludwig (Berlin, 1994/1996) (Handbücher zur Sprach- and Kommunikationswissenschaft), p. 299, also Marc-Allain Ouaknin, *Mysteries of the Alphabet: The Origins of Writing*, trans. Josephine Bacon (New York, London and Paris, 1999), pp. 117–23, and Alfred Kallir, 'Letter A', in *Sign and Design: The Psychogenetic Source of the Alphabet* (London, 1961), pp. 13–79.

4 For a review of the transcription of vowels in Arabic script from the perspective of the history of writing, see Thomas Bauer 'Arabic Writing', in *The World's Writing Systems*, eds Peter T. Daniels and William Bright (New York and Oxford, 1996), pp. 559–64; in Hebrew script, see Richard L. Goerwitz, 'The Jewish Scripts', in *The World's Writing Systems*, eds Peter T. Daniels and William Bright (New York and Oxford, 1996),pp. 487–98.

5 Alfred Schmitt, *Der Buchstabe H im Griechischen* (Münster, 1952), p. 5. My emphasis.

6 Cf. Annette Glück-Schmitt, 'Spiritus', in *Metzler Lexikon Sprache*, ed. Helmut Glück (Stuttgart and Weimar, 2005); also Kallir, *Sign and Design*, pp. 48–50.

7 Jacques Derrida, 'Différance', in *Speech and Phenomena and Other Essays on Husserl's Theory of Signs*, trans. David. B. Allison (Evanston, IL, 1973), p. 3.

8 Ibid., p. 4.

9 Jacques Derrida, *Archive Fever: A Freudian Impression* [1995], trans. Eric Prenowitz (Chicago, 1998), p. 11.

### Introduction

1 Jacques Derrida, *Cinders*, trans. and ed. Ned Lukacher (Lincoln, NE, and London, 1991), p. 43.

2 Friedrich Kittler, 'Gleichschaltungen. Über Normen und Standards der elektronischen Kommunikation', in *Geschichte der Medien*, ed. Manfred Faßler and Wulf Halbach (München, 1998), p. 261.

3 Friedrich Kittler, *Draculas Vermächtnis. Technische Schriften* (Leipzig, 1993), p. 8.

4 Jacques Derrida, *Of Grammatology* [1967], trans. Gayatri Chakravorty Spivak (Baltimore, MD, and London, 1976), Part One, Chapter 2:

'Linguistics and Grammatology', pp. 27–73. In particular on Saussure's view of writing as a limited and derivative function of language, as the secondary signifier of a first signifier, see Derrida's section 'The Outside and the Inside', pp. 30–44.

5 Sybille Krämer, 'Sprache und Schrift oder: Ist Schrift verschriftete Sprache?', in *Zeitschrift für Sprachwissenschaft*, xv/1 (1997), p. 93.

6 Since 1980 this gap in the research has become a more central concern of linguistics, see for example Peter T. Daniels and William Bright, eds, *The World's Writing Systems* (New York and Oxford, 1996) and Hartmut Günther and Otto Ludwig, eds, *Schrift und Schriftlichkeit. Ein interdisziplinäres Handbuch internationaler Forschung*, Band 10.1 and 10.2 (Berlin, 1994/1996) (Handbücher zur Sprach- and Kommuni-kationswissenschaft), plus Martin Neef/Rüdiger Weingarten (eds) *Schriftlinguistik. WSK Band 5* (=*Wörterbücher zur Sprach- und Kommunikationswissenschaft*, ed. by Stefan J. Schierholz und Herbert Ernst Wiegand).

7 André Leroi-Gourhan, *Gesture and Speech* [1964/65], trans. Anna Bostock Berger (Cambridge, MA, and London, 1993), p. 255.

8 N. Katherine Hayles, *Writing Machines* (Cambridge, 2002), p. 24; emphasis added by Hayles.

9 Ibid., p. 22.

10 Cf. Derrida, *Of Grammatology*, in particular Chapter 1, 'The End of the Book and the Beginning of Writing', pp. 6–26.

11 Michael Wetzel, *Die Enden des Buches oder die Wiederkehr der Schrift* (Weinheim, 1991) (Acta Humaniora), pp. 10–11.

12 Ibid., pp. 3–4.

## Before a Stele

1 My synoptic transcription; diplomatic marking of the beginnings of words, reconstruction of illegible signs and translation by Hermann Wankel, ed., *Inschriften griechischer Städte aus Kleinasien*, xi/1, *Die Inschriften von Ephesos*, no. 40, pp. 256–7, with table 32. I thank Hans Täuber of the Austrian Archaeological Institute, Vienna, for drawing my attention to this publication.

## 1 Exergue

1 Georges Didi-Huberman, *Ähnlichkeit und Berührung: Archäologie, Anachronismus und Modernität des Abdrucks*, trans. Christoph Hollender (Köln, 1999), p. 14.

2 Johann Heinrich Schulze, quoted by Jan Strzyzewski, in *Neue Solidarität*, 47 (2003), p. 2.

3 This essay first appeared in 1719 in Latin in the periodical published in Halle *Bibliothecae novissimae observationum ac recensionum* (Newest

Library of Observations and Discussions). The extended edition with the supplement 'seu experimentum curiosum de effectu radiorum solarium' (or: Remarkable Experiment on the Effect of the Sun's Rays) appeared in 1727 in Latin and German in the periodical of the Kaiserliche Akademie der Naturforscher Leopoldina-Carolina *Acta physico-medica* (physical-medical treatises); see Jan Strzyzewski, 'Lichtgestalt des deutschen Barocks: Johann Heinrich Schulze (1687–1744)', in *Neue Solidarität*, 47 (2003), at www.solidaritaet.com/neuesol/2003/47.htm [accessed 11.07.2006].

4   See Michel Frizot, 'Die Lichtmaschinen. An der Schwelle der Erfindung', in *Neue Geschichte der Fotografie*, ed. Michel Frizot (Köln, 1998), p. 19.

5   Roland Barthes, *Camera Lucida: Reflections on Photography* [1980], trans. Richard Howard (London, 1984), p. 76.

6   Charles Sanders Peirce, 'The Icon, Index and Symbol', in *Collected Papers of Charles Sanders Peirce*, eds Charles Hartshorne and Paul Weiss, vol. II, *Elements of Logic* (Cambridge, MA, 1932), Book II, 'Speculative Grammar', Paragraphs 281–2, p. 159.

7   On the history of the signature as a legal instrument, see Béatrice Fraenkel, *La signature. Genèse d'un signe* (Paris, 1992), particularly p. 10. For the continuation of the writing of the signature as a legal and authenticating instrument in the digital age, see the collection edited by Sonja Neef, José van Dijk and Eric Ketelaar, *Sign Here! Handwriting in the Age of New Media* (Amsterdam, 2006), in particular the contribution by Hannelore Dekeyser on the EU regulations on electronic signature, 'Authenticity in Bits and Bytes', pp. 76–90.

8   Peirce, 'The Icon, Index and Symbol', p. 159.

9   Barthes, *Camera Lucida*, p. 71.

10  Ibid., p. 66.

11  Paul de Man, 'Semiology and Rhetoric', in *Allegories of Reading: Figural Language in Rousseau, Nietzsche, Rilke, and Proust* (New Haven and London, 1979), pp. 9–10.

12  Carlo Ginzburg, *Spurensicherung. Die Wissenschaft auf der Suche nach sich selbst* (Berlin, 2002), p. 18.

13  Ibid., p. 19.

14  Didi-Huberman, *Ähnlichkeit und Berührung*, p. 26.

15  On the practice of the prologue, see for example Jacques Derrida's introduction to the essay by Nicolas Abraham and Maria Torok in *Kryptonymie. Das Verbarium des Wolfsmanns*, ed. Nicolas Abraham and Maria Torok (Frankfurt am Main, 1979), in which Derrida takes the precaution for his foreword of dealing – in this prologue and at the same time preempting it – with the myth of the closure of the text.

16  André Leroi-Gourhan, *Gesture and Speech* [1964/65], trans. Anna Bostock Berger (Cambridge, MA, and London, 1993), p. 21.

17  Ibid., p. 26.

18   See Andrew Carstairs-McCarthy, *The Origins of Complex Language: An Inquiry into the Evolutionary Beginnings of Sentences, Syllables, and Truth* (Oxford, 1999), pp. 125–9. This focus on the moment when *Homo sapiens* evolved into a civilized being, still does not justify any conception of the mouth whereby the natural tool of devouring or eating diverged from the cultural tool of speaking. Linguistics also indicates that the organs of speaking and of eating are closely associated with one another: tongue, lips, gums, lower jaw and teeth form a sound when speaking, as when eating food they serve to chew and taste. The junction that switches between eating and speaking, is formed by the larynx separating the acts of breathing and swallowing from one another: when speaking it releases the flow of air and closes the oesophagus, when taking in food the valve works in reverse.

19   See on this Jochen Hörisch, *Der Sinn and die Sinne. Eine Geschichte der Medien* (Frankfurt am Main, 2001), pp. 28–32.

20   See Wolfgang Krohn, 'Technik als Lebensform – Von der aristotelischen Praxis zur Technisierung der Lebenswelt', at www.cipa4u.net/fileadmin/iwt2003/PDF/tech_leben.pdf [accessed 6.01.2006], pp. 2–5.

21   Aristotle, *Parts of Animals*, trans. A. L. Peck (London, 1937), 687a, 5–15, pp. 371–2.

22   Martin Heidegger, *Parmenides*, trans. André Schuwer and Richard Rojcewicz (Bloomington, IN, 1992), p. 80.

23   Leroi-Gourhan, *Gesture and Speech*, pp. 187–8.

24   Heidegger, *Parmenides*, p. 80.

25   Jürgen Habermas has repeatedly pointed out that Heidegger's sympathy for National Socialism lasted well into the 1950s. A detailed study on this has been presented recently by the French philosopher Emmanuel Faye: *Heidegger – l'introduction du nazisme dans la philosophie* (Paris, 2005) (Bibliothèque des idées).

26   Jacques Derrida, 'Heidegger's Hand (Geschlecht II)', trans. John P. Leavey Jr, in *Psyche: Inventions of the Other, Vol. II*, ed. Peggy Kamuf and Elizabeth Rottenberg (Stanford, CA, 2007–8), pp. 42–3, p. 50.

27   Jacques Derrida, *The Truth in Painting* [1978], trans. Geoff Bennington and Ian McLeod (Chicago, 1987), in which Derrida deals with Immanuel Kant's third critique, the Critique of Judgement, as a theory that runs 'as if on wheels' (p. 78).

28   Didi-Huberman, *Ähnlichkeit und Berührung*, p. 25; Fraenkel, *La signature*, p. 206.

29   André Leroi-Gourhan, *The Art of Prehistoric Man in Western Europe*, trans. Norbert Guterman (London, 1968), p. 148.

30   For a brilliant and wide-ranging cultural semantics of the left/Left, I refer to Adriano Sofri, *Der Knoten und der Nagel. Ein Buch zur linken Hand*, trans. Walter Kögler (Frankfurt am Main, 1998).

31 Leroi-Gourhan, *The Art of Prehistoric Man in Western Europe*, p. 148.

32 See the more detailed discussion in André Leroi-Gourhan, *Le fil du temps* (Paris, 1983), p. 305. Calvet discusses the notion that the 'writing' by the broken-off fingers may also have had a use as a system of communication during the hunt or in battle to coordinate the actions of the group of hunters or warriors without making a noise.

33 Didi-Huberman, *Ähnlichkeit und Berührung*, p. 28.

34 On this see Michael Wetzel, 'Ein Auge zuviel. Derridas Urszenen des Ästhetischen', in Jacques Derrida, *Aufzeichnungen eines Blinden. Das Selbstporträt und andere Ruinen* (München, 1997), pp. 129–55 (Bild und Text), pp. 133–4. The idea in Derrida's writing of the stylus as the instrument of a barely perceptible difference is discussed by Michael Wetzel in 'The Authority of Drawing: Hand Authenticity and Authorship', in *Sign Here!*, particularly pp. 55–6.

35 Derrida, *Of Grammatology* [1967], trans. Gayatri Chakravorty Spivak (Baltimore, MD, and London), p. 234.

36 Eckhardt Schumacher, 'Performativität und Performance', in *Performanz. ZwischenSprachphilosophie und Kulturwisssenschaft*, ed. Uwe Wirth (Frankfurt am Main, 2002), p. 329

37 Michael Wetzel, *Die Enden des Buches oderdie Wiederkehr der Shrift* (Weinheim, 1991) (Acta Humaniora), p. 134.

38 For observations going into historical and systematic detail on the concept of style, see the collection edited by Hans Ulrich Gumbrecht and K. Ludwig Pfeiffer, *Stil. Geschichten und Funktionen eines kulturwissenschaftlichen Diskurselements* (Frankfurt am Main, 1986). In particular on the writing instrument as a stylistic means of violence see: Aleida Assmann, 'Pflug, Schwert, Feder. Kulturwerkzeuge als Herrschaftszeichen', in *Schrift*, eds Hans Ulrich Gumbrecht and K. Ludwig Pfeiffer (München, 1993) (Materialität der Zeichen: Reihe A, Band 12).

39 Wolfgang Schäffner in 'Mechanische Schreiber', in *Europa. Kultur der Sekretäre*, ed. Joseph Vogl (Zürich and Berlin, 2003) is fascinated by the particular form of writing of such 'mechanical writers': 'If in that case the movement of the writing only records nothing but itself, then writing moves into a realm in which it means nothing but its materiality. In other words there is no signified, no meaning presupposed by the writing, nor expressed within it.' (p. 222). One surely cannot argue against this. But one can say, on the other hand: this euphoria for the mechanical tacitly also suggests that writing, in particular handwriting, as a non-technical and pre-mechanical process consists only in operations of the symbolic order. As if writing could ever be definitely non-imaginary and outside of the real. Writing, in the sense of *écriture*, can never be reduced to pure Logos; it can never do without its material performance.

### Before a Line

1   Apparently Mercator is here using *calamus* (reed) as a synonym for
    *penna* (bird quill), something that was not unusual in reflexions about
    writing and writing tools in the Renaissance. I shall be talking about the
    difference in some detail later on.

2   Quoted here and in the following from the facsimile edition by Arthur
    S. Osley, *Mercator: A monograph on the lettering of maps, etc. in the 16th
    century Netherlands with a facsimile and translation of his treatise on the
    italic hand and a translation of Ghim's 'VITA MERCATORIS'* (New York,
    1970); p. 124. The English translation from the Latin is by Arthur S.
    Osley.

3   Ibid., pp. 134–8. My emphasis. I have Heinz Görgner to thank for the
    exact analysis of 'tenuissima' as a superlative/elative; particularly so, since
    here Osley's English translation gives this simply as 'narrow'.

4   Osley, English translation of Mercator, *Literarum latinarum*, in *Mercator*,
    p. 136, fn. 1.

5   Cf. Osley, 'Census of editions of *Literarum latinarum*', in *Mercator*, p. 177;
    Jan Denucé, 'Introduction', in *Mercator, Gerardus, 1512–1594: The Treatise
    of Gerard Mercator: literarum latinarum, quas italicas, cursoriasque vocant,
    scribendarium ratio (Antwerp 1540)*, ed. in facsimile by Jan Denucé
    (Antwerp and Paris, 1930), p. VIII.

### 2 Preamble

1   Immanuel Kant, *Critique of Pure Reason*, trans. and ed. by Paul Guyer
    and Allen W. Wood (Cambridge, 1997), p. 258.

2   Cf. on this Florian Coulmas, *Über Schrift* (Frankfurt am Main, 1981), in
    which writing is differentiated into 'mechanical' and 'manual'. Manual
    writing is further subdivided into 'printed (standardized)' and 'cursive
    (individual)', p. 134.

3   Rüdiger Weingarten in 'Der Computer als Schriftmuseum. Latinisierung
    von Schriften durch computertechnische Zwänge?', in *Materialität and
    Medialität von Schrift*, eds Erika Greber, Konrad Ehlich and Jan-Dirk
    Müller (Bielefeld, 2002) (Schrift and Bild in Bewegung, Band 1), describes
    how industrial initiatives such as ISO 10646 and UNICODE develop
    common standards for the coding of universal writing signs in a binary
    code. Their declared aim '[t]o preserve world cultural heritage' (p. 173) is
    considered by Weingarten to be technically and economically achievable
    in principle thanks to the good memory and transmission capacity
    of the internet, were it not for cultural globalization accompanied by
    Anglicization (of language) and Romanization (of script) and thus at
    the same time the threat of extinction to many kinds of script.

4   Champollion published his discovery of the phonographic principle
    under the title 'Précis du système hiéroglyphique' (1822); Champollion

undertook a systematic and then also complete analysis of hieroglyphic script under the title *Principes Généraux de l'écriture sacrée égyptienne* (MS 1830) which was only published posthumously on 23.12.1835. Cf. Christiane Ziegler, 'Préface de la nouvelle Édition', in Jean-François Champollion, *Grammaire Égyptienne, ou principes généraux de l'écriture sacrée égyptienne (appliqué à la représentation de la langue parlée)* [1835], ed. Michel Sidhom (Paris, 1984), also Carol Andrews, *The Rosetta Stone* (London, 2003); Harold Haarmann, *Universalgeschichte der Schrift* (Frankfurt am Main, 1991), p. 101.

5   Porphyry, *De vita Pythagorae*, p. 41, 10–15, quoted in Jan Assmann, 'Sieben Funktionen der ägyptischen Hieroglyphenschrift', in *Materialität and Medialität von Schrift*, eds Erika Greber, Konrad Ehlich and Jan-Dirk Müller (Bielefeld, 2002) (Schrift and Bild in Bewegung, Band 1), p. 48.

6   Cf. Champollion, *Grammaire Égyptienne*, p. 2. Plato's entry on the hieroglyphs as the capture of the beautiful in iconic images is often quoted in this context. (*Laws*, 656–657). The first principle of the Egyptian writing according to him lies in the standardization and codification of the beautiful in hieroglyphs, that were 'pre-drawn' and then chiselled by the stone-masons as copies. (Jan Assmann, 'Sieben Funktionen', pp. 36–7.) In a detailed philological analysis of 'Plato and the Egyptian Alphabet' ('Platon und das ägyptische Alphabet', in *Archiv für Philosophie*, 34 (1922), pp. 3–13 (Berlin, 1970)), however, Robert Eisler-Feldafing points to a place in Plato's *Philebus* that immediately follows the famous passage about the invention of the letters by Theut (18b) and has itself remained rather unknown. In these lines Plato develops a graphematic perspective on the Egyptian alphabet as a relation of sounds and letters in which he emphasizes that the 'link' between them is a 'numeral link'. With this formulation, as Eisler-Feldafing observes, Plato makes use of a technical term from the Pythagorean teaching of proportions. The structure of Egyptian writing is for him less iconic/representational than mathematically abstract: an 'arithmetic mean between two quantities' (p. 7). In this respect, the process of reading involves, along with 'seeing' in the sense of observation of iconic, curvilinear constructs, also 'reckoning' in the sense of calculating the abstract relations of graphematics. The digital algorithms of computers today provide us with admittedly different evidence for Plato's apodictic observation of reading and writing as a calculation of the numeral link.

7   Champollion, *Grammaire Égyptienne*, pp. 13–17.

8   Ibid., pp. 1–2; Jan Assmann, 'Sieben Funktionen', p. 48.

9   Cf. Andrews, *The Rosetta Stone*, pp. 9–12, also Haarmann, *Universalgeschichte der Schrift*, pp. 101–5. Detail on the di- (or tri-) graphics of hieroglyphs, (hieratic) and demotic: Jan Assmann, 'Die Ägyptische Schriftkultur', in *HSK*, x/1, pp. 472–91.

10   Jozef Vergrote, 'Clément d'Alexandrie et l'écriture égyptienne', in

*Chronique d'Egypte*, 16 (1941), pp. 21–8, also Jan Assmann, 'Sieben Funktionen', pp. 48–50.

11  Michael Wetzel, *Die Enden des Buches oder die Wiederkehr der Schrift* (Weinheim, 1991) (Acta Humaniora), p. 8.

12  Vilém Flusser, *Die Schrift. Hat Schreiben Zukunft?* [1987], ed. Andreas Müller-Pohle, Edition Flusser, Band 5 (Göttingen, 2002), pp. 20–21.

13  Harold Adam Innis, 'The Problem of Space' in *The Bias of Communication*, eds Harold Adam Innis, Paul Heyer, David J. Crowley (Toronto, 1951), pp. 92–131 (p. 92).

14  Ibid., pp. 93–4.

15  Here Paul van Ostaijen's hypnotic and magical river poem 'Melopee' must be quoted, written in untranslatable assonant Dutch with the line-breaks following one another in a relay downstream: *"Melopee // Onder de maan schuift de lange rivier / Over de lange rivier schuift moede de maan / Onder de maan op de lange rivier schuift de kano naar zee // Langs het hoogriet / Langs de laagwei / schuift de kano naar zee / schuift met de schuivende maan de kano naar zee / Zo zijn ze gezellen naar zee de kano de maan en de man / Waarom schuiven de maan en de man getweeën gedwee naar de zee".* (VW2, p. 213) in English (roughly): 'Melopee // Under the moon the long river pushes on / Over the long river the moon pushes on wearily // Under the moon on the long river the canoe pushes on to the sea / Past the reeds / Past the water-meadows / the canoe pushes on to the sea / the canoe pushes on with the moon pushing on to the sea / Thus canoe, moon and man are fellow-travellers to the sea / Why do the moon and man push on together obediently to the sea.'

16  Johann Georg Hamann, 'Aesthetica in nuce' in *Writings on Philosophy and Language*, trans. and ed. by Kenneth Haynes (Cambridge, 2007), pp. 60–95 (pp. 63 and 66), cf. on this Michael Wetzel, 'Unter Sprachen – Unter Kulturen. Walter Benjamins 'Interlinearversion' des Übersetzens als *Inframedialität*' (2002), at www.uni-konstanz.de/paech2002/zdk/beitrg/Wetzel.htm. [accessed 11.10.2006], section I. (Translator's note: 'curiological refers to the stage when objects are represented by pictures and not by symbols; 'characteristic' refers to alphabetic writing. With these three phases, Hamann connects poetry, history, and philosophy, respectively.)

17  In *The Bias of Communication* Innis attempts a categorization of the media in space and time in order to develop the relation between scientific technology and geopolitical organization within them. According to Innis, the ancient Egyptian state was centralized and rigid due to its writing technology based on temporal continuity, whereas the Catholic Church with its culture of paper and parchment was directed towards both temporal and geographical expansion.

18  Derrida in his 'Otobiographies – The Teaching of Nietzsche and the Politics of the Proper Name', in Derrida, *The Ear of the Other*, trans. Peggy Kamuf (Lincoln, NE, and London, 1988), gives the (counter-)example of

the Declaration of Independence of the United States, in which the American people as the 'signatories' are constituted only at the very moment the signature is performed. Both colonization (of Ephesus by Byzantium, of Rosetta by Thebes) and decolonization (of the USA from Europe), however much at first sight they might seem to be opposites, turn out to be both processes of the establishment of a non-a priori power that they 'cite into being' performatively by declaring them.

19   For a writing-historical discussion of the development of ancient Egyptian writing through to the early Semitic alphabets and cuneiform scripts and up to the Phoenician and Greek alphabet I refer to Josef Tropper, 'Die nordwestsemitischen Schriften'. Aleph on its own is considered by Marc-Alain Ouaknin in *Mysteries of the Alphabet: The Origins of Writing*, trans. Josephine Bacon (New York, London and Paris, 1999), pp. 117–23.

20   Herbert Brekle in *Die Antiqualinie von ca. -1500 bis ca. +1500. Untersuchungen zur Morphogenese des westlichen Alphabets auf kognitivistischer Basis* (Münster, 1994) has devoted a detailed study to the development of the letter forms of the Western alphabet from –1500 to +1500.

21   Cf. Herbert Brekle, 'Die Buchstabenformen westlicher Alphabetschriften in ihrer historischen Entwicklung', in *HSK*, x/1, pp. 174–5.

22   Thomas Bauer in his description of Arabic writing discusses 'the effects of defectiveness' ('Arabic Writing', in *The World's Writing Systems*, eds Peter T. Daniels and William Bright (New York and Oxford, 1996), p. 563).

23   In *The Literate Revolution in Greece and Its Cultural Consequences* (Princeton, NJ, 1981), Eric Havelock, philologist of antiquity and scientist of media culture *avant la lettre* demonstrates the exceptional efficiency of the Greek alphabet as the first complete and vocalized alphabet. In his fascination for the Greek script he unreservedly claims its superiority over any other scripts: 'The introduction of the Greek letters into inscription somewhere about 700 BC was to alter the character of human culture, placing a gulf between all alphabetic societies and their precursors.' (p. 82) According to Havelock, the Greek vowel alphabet is the first writing system able, not only to memorize pre-formulated thoughts, but in addition for the first time in human history to make 'possible the production of novel or unexpected statement, previously unfamiliar or even "unthought"'. (p. 88) This essentially culturally chauvinist thesis is not limited by Havelock only to historically older, non-alphabetical and syllable-based writing systems such as the ancient Oriental cuneiform scripts, but also and particularly extends to the non-vocalized writing systems of Persian, Hebrew and Arabic, which lacking vowels force the reader to derive the vowels from the context. In this process these scripts always leave 'room for guessing', thus creating ambiguity and making them 'less efficient instruments for reading'. Against such a Eurocentric privileging of the Greek/Latin alphabet advanced by Havelock, I have (in 'M/Othering Europe') suggested a view of the Western vocalized manner

of writing running left-to-right as a 'translation'. In a re-reading of the classical myth of the abduction of Europa I have argued that the daughter of the King of Phoenicia in her migration from the Orient to the West 'brought over' (meta-ferein), not only the name of the continent, but also the letters. In this respect, our alphabet is revealed as a form of writing that also still derives from the particular way of writing of the 'Other', adapting, transforming and continuing its writing. (Sonja Neef, 'M/Othering Europe. Or: how Europe and Atlas are Balancing Hand in Hand on the Prime Meridian – she Carrying the Alphabet, he Shouldering the Globe they are Walking on', in *Discerning Translations. Special Issue Visual Culture*, 6, eds Mieke Bal and Joanne Morra (2007))

　　Compare also on this critique of Euro- and Logocentrism: Aleida and Jan Assmann, 'Einleitung. Schrift-Kognition-Evolution. Eric A. Havelock und die Technologie kultureller Kommunikation', in Eric Alfred Havelock, *Schriftlichkeit. Das griechische Alphabet und die kulturelle Revolution*, eds Aleida and Jan Assmann, pp. 1–35 (Weinheim, 1990), pp. 7–10; 23–25. In this Assmann and Assmann also present a basic critique of media studies, accusing Havelock's theory of '*making absolute* and *distorting*' the question of media (p. 7, emphasis by Assmann and Assmann). Peter Koch and Sybille Krämer take a similar line in their 'Einleitung', in *Schrift, Medien, Kognition. Über die Exteriorität des Geistes* (Tübingen, 1997): 'With the conviction that the specific efficiency of the alphabetical script consists precisely in the fact that it can transcribe spoken language flexibly and yet completely, medial modes are neglected that do not deal with the setting down and transmission of spoken language, for example genuinely graphic, logical and mathematical notations or forms in which the iconic is in play.' (pp. 17–18)

24　Brekle, *Die Antiqualinie*, pp. 34–40.

25　Ibid., p. 158.

26　For an investigation into eye movement while reading, see Stefan Gfroerer, Hartmut Günther and Michael Bock, 'Augenbewegungen und Substantivgroßschreibung', in *Schriftsystem and Orthographie*, eds Peter Eisenberg and Hartmut Günther (Tübingen, 1989), pp. 111–35.

27　Both scripts are to a certain extent frozen in time as the (pre-ancient) script of the Torah or the (early medieval) script of the Koran. Unlike the Greek and Roman alphabet they were not used primarily for secular purposes and are therefore more sharply characterized by cultural and religious tradition than by the kinemotoric economy of writing. See on this Richard Goerwitz, 'The Jewish Scripts', in *The World's Writing Systems*, eds Peter T. Daniels and William Bright (New York and Oxford, 1996), pp. 487–98, also Bauer, 'Arabic Writing', pp. 559–64.

28　For more detail see the classic introduction to this by Bernhard Bischoff, *Paläographie des römischen Altertums und des abendländischen Mittelalters*, 2. extended edn (Berlin, 1986) (Grundlagen der Germanistik

24), pp. 263–76, also Hans Foerster and Thomas Frenz, *Abriss der lateinischen Paläographie* [1949], extended edition with additional chapter 'Die Schriften der Neuzeit' by Thomas Frenz (Stuttgart: Hiersemann, 2004) (Bibliothek des Buchwesens, Band 15), pp. 201–22.

29  For more detail on the difference between the Carolingian minuscule and Gothic scripts, see Karin Schneider, *Paläographie und Handschriftenkunde für Germanisten. Eine Einführung* (Tübingen, 1999), pp. 19–84, particularly pp. 28–9, also Foerster and Frenz, *Abriss*, pp. 223–56.

30  Quoted in Bernhard Bischoff, *Ein neu entdeckter modus scribendi des 15. Jahrhunderts aus der Abtei Melk* (Berlin, 1939), p. 25). Bischoff, the famous paleontologist who discovered and published the Codex, translates 'littere manuales minus principales' by 'the common ones of secondary size' as there are still the 'handletters' of the first order.

31  Flusser, *Die Schrift*, p. 21.

32  Jacques Derrida, 'Signature Event Context', trans. Samuel Weber and Jeffrey Mehlman, in *Limited Inc.* (Evanston, IL, 1988), p. 7.

33  Ibid., p. 7.

34  Didi-Hubermann, *Ähnlichkeit und Berührung* (Cologne, 1999).

35  Victor Hugo, *Notre-Dame de Paris* [1831], trans. Alban Krailsheimer (Oxford, 1993), pp. 189, 190.

36  Detailed studies have documented this shift in media: Elizabeth Eisenstein in *The Printing Press as an Agent of Change: Communications and Cultural Transformations in Early-Modern Europe* (Cambridge, 1980), vol. I, shows how in Europe of the early modern period the move from handwriting to printing, from the writer to the publisher and from the manuscript to the book is accompanied by profound and lasting cultural, religious and political changes. In reference to Victor Hugo's 'ceci tuera cela', Eisenstein comments that along with the destruction of the cathedral there begins a general iconoclasm affecting the techniques of human memory (pp. 66–7). It remains an open question, however, as to the consequences in particular for the cultural practice of handwriting. Michael Giesecke in *Der Buchdruck in der frühen Neuzeit. Eine historische Fallstudie über die Durchsetzung neuer Informations- and Kommunikationstechnologien* (Frankfurt am Main, 1998) for his part discusses how book printing acts as a catalyst of cultural change and signals the birth of the modern knowledge society. In this Giesecke approaches this on two fronts as he sees in retrospect the historical media revolution of book printing reflected point-for-point in contemporary information and communications media, drawing parallels and setting out to reach a deeper understanding of the systems of a so-called 'ecology of communications'. Walter Ong, Jack Goody and Ian Watt, along with Marshall McLuhan, likewise see in book printing the birth of the writing society as such, set this new medium up in opposition to oral culture and in so doing simply ignore

the culture of manuscripts that is highly significant for human cultural memory. It is true that Giesecke criticizes the dichotomy of 'scriptorial' versus 'oral' and insists on another opposition, i.e. that between hand-writing and book printing, but he then engages in a similar privileging of the new medium so that the examination of handwriting affected by book printing and after remains marginal (*Der Buchdruck*, p. 60). It is symptomatic of these canonized media-historical studies that the attention of the authors is directed to the new medium and to the long shadow it casts on our contemporary media culture. All in all, the history of media appears as a steeply rising curve, either as the invasion of writing technology into an original, primitive and forgotten oral culture (Ong, Goody, McLuhan) or as a correction to the inadequate, slow and inky business of manuscript technology by the improved writing technology of book printing (Eisenstein, *The Printing Press*, Giesecke, *Der Buchdruck*, pp. 29–30). The rear-view perspective of the Janus head towards the precursor media is here rather superficial. In general, the relation between new and old media is seen from a mono-linear perspective as genealogical progress, and the idea that technology means not only 'progress' and 'novelty' but 'points in all temporal directions' is not sufficiently developed. Cf. here also Sybille Krämer, 'Friedrich Kittler – Kulturtechniken der Zeitachsenmanipulation', in *Medientheorien. Eine philosophische Einführung*, ed. Alice Lagaay and David Lauer, pp. 201–24 (Frankfurt am Main and New York, 2004).

37 Eva-Maria Hanebutt-Benz, 'Gutenbergs Erfindungen. Die technischen Aspekte des Druckens mit vielfachen Lettern auf der Buchdruckerpresse', in *Gutenberg. Aventur and Kunst. Vom Geheimunternehmen zur ersten Medienrevolution*, Catalogue to the exhibition of the City of Mainz on the occasion of the 600th anniversary of the birth of Johannes Gutenberg, 14 April–3 October 2000 (Mainz, 2000), pp. 184–8. Giesecke argues in *Der Buchdruck* (pp. 134–46) that Gutenberg was not concerned with a fast and efficient copying machine but with improved handwriting. This is indicated also by the investment in forming, casting and setting the letters with variable ligatures.

38 Marshall McLuhan, *The Gutenberg Galaxy: The Making of Typographic Man* (London, 1962), pp. 24–5.

39 Giesecke, *Der Buchdruck*, p. 134. The individual *manual* stages of book production are described in detail by Hanebutt-Benz in 'Gutenbergs Erfindungen'. Cf. also Giesecke in his chapter on the stages of the printing process ('Ablauf des Druckvorgangs'), pp. 111–18.

40 Giesecke, *Der Buchdruck*, pp. 319, 230–31.

41 On the dispute between Erasmus and Luther, see Erasmus of Rotterdam, 'Hyperaspistis diatribae adversus servum arbitrium Martini Lutheri. Liber primus' ('First book on the Hyperaspistes diatribe against the "unfree will" of Martin Luther'), in *Ausgewählte Schriften*, Latin and German,

vol. IV, trans., intro. and annotated by Winfried Lesowsky, pp. 197–673 (Darmstadt, 1995).

42 Cf. here Isodorus (IV, c 14): 'Calamus arboris est, penna auis, cuius acumen in duo dividitur', quoted in Henrici Ackeri, *Historia Pennarum. Pennae inclitissimi polyhistoris et consumma-tissimi theology. 10. Francisc. Buddei* (Altenburg, 1726), p. 8, which collects sayings and quotations from Antiquity up to modern times and at the same time goes into the advantages and disadvantages of the quill pen versus the reed pen. It contains the famous poem about Erasmus's pen on p. 23.

43 *The Collected Works of Erasmus. Vol. 85: Poems*, trans. Clarence H. Miller, ed. Harry Vredeveld (Toronto and London, 1993), p. 135.

44 Lorenz Engell and Joseph Vogl, 'Editorial', in *Mediale Historiographien*, eds Lorenz Engell and Joseph Vogl (Weimar, 2001), pp. 5–8 (Archiv für Mediengeschichte 1), p. 7.

45 Mieke Bal, *Quoting Caravaggio: Contemporary Art, Preposterous History* (Chicago and London, 1999), pp. 6–7.

46 Albert Kapr, *Fraktur. Form und Geschichte der gebrochenen Schriften* (Mainz, 1993), pp. 49–53.

47 For a historically and analytically interesting study of the writing styles of the Renaissance in the British Isles I refer to Jonathan Goldberg, *Writing Matter. From the Hands of the English Renaissance* (Stanford, CA, 1990).

48 Brekle, *Die Antiqualinie*, pp. 235–238; Foerster and Frenz, *Abriss*, p. 257 et passim.

49 Goldberg, *Writing Matter*, p. 115.

50 Bal, *Quoting Caravaggio*, p. 6.

51 Like the term *preposterous history*, 'remediation' does not refer to a causal genealogy of media but to systematic affiliations of media practices and formal-aesthetic resonances of one medium within another. Cf. Jay Bolter and Richard Grusin, *Remediation: Understanding New Media* (Cambridge, MA, and London, 1999), also – more to the point in relation to hand-writing – José van Dijck and Sonja Neef, 'Introduction', in *Sign Here! Handwriting in the Age of New Media*, eds Sonja Neef, José van Dijck and Eric Ketelaar (Amsterdam, 2006), pp. 12–15.

### 3 Prolegomenon

1 Walter J. Ong, *Orality and Literacy. The Technologizing of the Word* (London and New York, 1987) p. 81; my emphasis.

2 Like Kittler, Frank Hartmann for example also keeps the term 'technical media' for the machines and equipment after 1800: photographic and film apparatus, the cylinder press, the daguerreotype, the telegraph, etc., finally digital calculating machines, the computer and the Internet. In so doing, Hartmann definitely excludes 'anthropomorphic models of technology that put man at the centre and see technology *simply as a tool*

*and prosthesis of the human body*' (my emphasis) from his concept of the technical media. Hartmann would likewise qualify handwriting, hand-prints and line-traces as non- or pre-technical. It is then remarkable that he sees the essence of the technological in an artificial condition of media products because in the case of these technical media

> we are dealing with a reality defined by machines and equipment that is not just reproduced or represented by them . . . mechanisms used for the production of secondary realities or media realities. This characterizes a reality that is permeated by hardware. Like every advanced technology, through this permeation and transformation of reality, media technology also produces systems whose complexity overtaxes the individual. Both as regards production and reception, its subject is therefore in fact not the individual human being but a cultural or societal collective [cf. Schnell 2000, 149]. The technical media thus play their autonomous part in the conception of the reality of our culture.

Frank Hartmann, 'Techniktheorien der Medien', at http://homepage.uni-vie.ac.at/Frank.Hartmann/Vorlesung/new/medientechnik.html; [accessed 13.06.2006], p. 1. In his fascination with the (would-be) autonomous machines and the realities (allegedly) hermetically sealed off by them, Hartmann draws an all-too-sharp distinction between a before and an after of technology. By this particularly rhetorical way of expressing it: 'simply' the human being, '*simply* a tool and a prosthesis of the human body' Hartmann is postulating precisely that beyond-the-human and beyond-writing in his argument, the inversion of which (a 'this side of writing') he himself criticizes in the positivist anthropomorphic epistemes (that surely need to be examined more closely).

3    Friedrich Kittler, *Draculas Vermächtnis. Technische Schriften* (Leipzig, 1993). Cf. on this subject Sybille Krämer, 'Friedrich Kittler, Kulturtechniken der Zeitachsenmanipulation', in *Medientheorien. Eine philosophische Einführung*, ed. Alice Lagaay and David Lauer (Frankfurt am Main and New York, 2004), pp. 202–3, 209.

4    Aristotle differentiated between objects that are formed by nature and carry within themselves the beginning of movement and rest, and those that are formed by man and do not carry their source of production within themselves. In opposition to this Aristotelian concept of techno-logy that persisted for centuries up to the Marxist theory of evolution, Bernhard Stiegler, in *La technique et le temps. 1. La faute d'Épiméthée* (Paris, 1994) (particularly the 'introduction générale'), proposes a new concept of the 'technical object' as a simultaneously inorganic and yet organized object with an autonomous temporality and dynamic. (p. 30–31.)

5 Georges Didi-Huberman, *Ähnlichkeit und Berührung: Archäologie, Anachronismus und Modernität des Abdrucks*, trans. Christoph Hollender (Cologne, 1999), pp. 29–30; my emphasis.

6 Ibid., pp. 14–5; emphasis in the original. Didi-Hubermann is referring to Bernhard Stiegler, *La technique et le temps, 2. La disorientation* (Paris, 1996), p. 9 et passim.

7 'L'avance prométhéenne et le retard épiméthéen (qui est aussi la faute d'Épiméthée comme *oubli*) trament *ensemble* la *prométheia* comme prévoyance et l'*épimétheia* comme distraction insouciante et médiation après coup.' Stiegler, *La technique et le temps. 1. La faute d'Épiméthée*, p. 30; emphasis in the original. Such a conception of inverted temporal orders is also found besides in Kittler where it is termed 'technique of temporal manipulation' (*Draculas Vermächtnis*, p. 58) – one further reason to revise and dialectically interlink the linear sequence and opposition of analogue and digital put forward by Kittler.

8 'La logique du supplément qui est toujours déjà l'*histoire* du supplément est une *techno-logique* par laquelle la matière inorganique *s'organise* et affecte l'organisme vivant dont elle est le supplément originaire.' Stiegler, *La technique et le temps 2. La disorientation*, p. 12, emphasis in the original.

9 Martial, AD 85, quoted in Arthur Mentz and Fritz Haeger, *Geschichte der Kurzschrift* (Wolfenbüttel, 1981), p. 16.

10 On the '(schizo-)script' of the telephone see Avital Ronell, *The Telephone Book: Technology, Schizophrenia, Electric Speech* (Lincoln, NE, 1989); on the history of the telegraph, Helmut Schanze, ed., *Handbuch der Mediengeschichte* (Stuttgart, 2001), pp. 519–54.

11 Thomas van den Bergh, 'Handschrift. Van krul tot hanenpoot', *Elsevier*, 21.10.2006, pp. 120–21; also 'De school, 100 jaar geleden', pp. 8–11.

12 Cf. on this subject Friedrich Kittler, *Discourse Networks 1800/1900*, trans. Michael Metteer (Stanford, CA, 1990), p. 83.

13 *Palmer's Guide to Business Writing*, quoted in Tamara Plakins-Thornton, *Handwriting in America: A Cultural History* (New Haven, CT, 1996), p. 66.

14 Cf. Mentz and Haeger, *Geschichte der Kurzschrift*, p. 13

15 Quoted in ibid.

16 Helmut Jochems, "Stenographie', in *HSK*, 10.2, pp. 1604–8. For more detail on this, Herbert Boge, *Griechische Tachygraphie und Tironische Noten. Ein Handbuch der mittelalterlichen und antiken Schnellschrift* (Berlin, 1973).

17 Franz Xaver Gabelsberger, *Anleitung zur deutschen Redezeichenkunst* (München, 1834); Karl Erbach, *Handbuch der deutschen Einheitkurzschrift* (Darmstadt, 1938). For an overall view see Helmut Jochems, 'Schreiben in Gedankenschnelle. Wegleite durch eine terra incognita der Graphematik', in *New Trends in Graphemics and Orthography*, ed. Gerhard Augst (Berlin and New York, 1986), pp. 105–23.

18 Quoted in Christina Killius, *Die Antiqua-Fraktur-Debatte um 1800 und*

*ihre historische Herleitung* (Wiesbaden, 1999) (Mainzer Studien zur Buchwissenschaft), p. 85.

19   Cf. Albert Kapr, Fraktur. *Form und Geschichte der gebrochenen Schriften* (Mainz, 1993), pp. 49–53.

20   Quoted in ibid., p. 64. For detail on German script see Peter Bain and Paul Shaw, eds, *Blackletter: Type and National Identity* (Princeton, NJ, 1998); Killius, *Die Antiqua-Fraktur-debatte um 1800 und ihre historische Herleitung*, also Hans Foerster and Thomas Frenz, *Abriss der lateinischen Paläographie* [1949], extended edition with additional chapter 'Die Schriften der Neuzeit' by Thomas Frenz (Stuttgart: Hiersemann, 2004) (Bibliothek des Buchwesens, vol. 15), particularly the chapter 'Die Schriften der Neuzeit'.

21   D. Heinrich Stephani, *Ausführliche Beschreibung der genetischen Schreib-methode für Volksschulen* (Erlangen, 1815). Hermann Rudolf Dietlein, *Wegweiser für den Schreibunterricht. Eine theoretisch-praktische Anweisung zur Begründung und Durchführung einer allseitig natur-gemäßen Schreiblehr-Methode, mit besonderer Berücksichtigung der Volksschule, für Lehrer aller Schulanstalten, welche Schreibunterricht zu ertheilen haben* (Leipzig, 1856).

22   Ibid., p. 12.

23   Ibid., p. 30, emphasis in the original.

24   Ibid., pp. 118–120.

25   Stephani, *Ausführliche Beschreibung*, p. 3; my emphasis.

26   Kittler, *Discourse Networks, 1800/1900*, p. 82.

27   Plakins-Thornton, *Handwriting in America*, pp. 42–71.

28   Elisabeth Neuhaus-Siemon, 'Aspekte und Probleme des Schreibunterrichts', in *HSK* 10.2, p. 1243.

29   The attempts to reintroduce *Fraktur* in Germany, promoted since 1945 by diverse associations and groups for its propagation, often therefore take on a similar 'Nazi brown' hue; cf. on this subject the booklet printed in blackletter by Thorwald Poschenrieder and Christian Stang on the proposal 'for the regulation of the special qualities of German scripts', published by the Bund für deutsche Schrift und Sprache. With historical detail and politically neutral, on the other hand: Killius, *Die Antiqua-Fraktur-Debatte um 1800 und ihre historische Herleitung*, also Kapr, *Fraktur*.

30   In 1890 in the Netherlands Willem Kloos coined the famous dictum along the lines of the 'most individual expression of the most individual emotion' ('allerindividueelste expressie van een allerindividueelste emotie') that was to become the basis of the art movement of the 'Tachtigers' (the 'Movement of the Eighteen-Eighties').

31   Walter Benjamin, *One-Way Street and Other Writings*, trans. Edmand Jephcott and Kinsley Shorter (London, 1997), pp. 64–5.

32   Friedrich Kittler, *Gramophone, Film, Typewriter*, trans. Geoffrey Winthrop-Young and Michael Wutz (Stanford, CA, 1999), pp. 187, 206.

Kittler's statement on Nietzsche's typewriter has led to a whole genre
of similarly based researches, e.g. Martin Stingelin, 'Kugeläußerungen.
Nietzsches Spiel auf der Schreibmaschine', in *Materialität der
Kommunikation*, ed. Hans Ulrich Gumbrecht and K. Ludwig Pfeiffer
(Frankfurt am Main, 1988), also under the same Nietzschean motto:
the collection edited by Davide Giuriato, Martin Stingelin and Sandro
Zanetti, '*SCHREIBKUGEL IST EIN DING GLEICH MIR: VON EISEN*':
*Schreibszenen im Zeitalter der Typoskripte* (München, 2005) (Zur
Genealogie des Schreibens 2). Cf. on this subject also Christof Windgätter,
*Medienwechsel. Vom Nutzen und Nachteil der Sprache für die Schrift*
(Berlin, 2006), pp. 235–52.

33   Cf. on this subject also Kittler, *Discourse Networks, 1800/1900*, pp. 359–63,
and *Gramophone*, p. 227; also Rüdiger Campe, 'Schreiben im *Prozess*.
Kafkas ausgesetzte Schreibszene', in '*SCHREIBKUGEL IST EIN DING
GLEICH MIR: VON EISEN*', eds Giuriato, Stingelin and Zanetti.

34   Cf. Sonja Neef, *Kalligramme. Zur Medialität einer Schrift. Anhand van
Paul van Ostaijen's 'De feesten van angst en pijn'* (Amsterdam, 2000), pp.
84–96; also 'Handspiel. Stil/us und rhythmische Typographie bei Paul van
Ostaijen', in '*SCHREIBKUGEL IST EIN DING GLEICH MIR: VON
EISEN*', ed. Giuriato, Stingelin and Zanetti.

35   Otto Burghagen, *Die Schreibmaschine* (1898), p. 20, quoted in Kittler,
*Gramophone*, p. 191.

36   Silvio Bedini, *Thomas Jefferson and His Copying Machines* (Charlottesville,
VA, 1984), p. 193; Wilhelm Eule, *Mit Stift und Feder. Kleine Kulturgeschichte
der Schreib- und Zeichenwerkzeuge* (Leipzig, 1955), pp. 123–4.

37   Bedini, *Thomas Jefferson*, p. 195.

38   Kittler, *Grammophon*, p. 191. It is not only the media that highlight the
change of media from manual to digital ways of writing, but the discourses of communications and media studies are also full of it. Cf. for
example John Mackenzie Owen, 'Authenticity and Objectivity in
Scientific Communication: Implications of Digital Media', in *Sign Here!
Handwriting in the Age of New Media*, eds Sonja Neef, José van Dijck and
Eric Ketelaar (Amsterdam, 2006), pp. 60–75.

39   Timothy Salthouse, 'Die Fertigkeit des Maschineschreibens', in *Spektrum
der Wissenschaft* 4 (1984), pp. 94–6; quoted in Kittler, *Gramophone*, p. 191.

40   Cf. Bedini, *Thomas Jefferson*, p. 63.

41   Eric Le Collen, *Feder, Tinte und Papier. Die Geschichte schönen Schreibgeräts*, trans. Cornelia Panzacchi (Hildesheim, 1999), pp. 53–9; Eule, *Mit
Stift und Feder*, pp. 101–12.

42   Letter from Friedrich Nietzsche during his stay in Tautenburg, KSB 6, Nr.
255, 416; KSB 8, Nr. 862, additions in square brackets by and quoted in
Christof Windgätter, 'Und dabei kann immer noch etwas verloren gehen!
– Eine Typologie feder- und maschinenschriftlicher Störungen bei
Friedrich Nietzsche', in '*SCHREIBKUGEL IST EIN DING GLEICH MIR:*

*VON EISEN*', eds Giuriato, Stingelin and Zanetti, p. 57.

43   Tobias Eisler (1733), *Das aufs neue wohl zubereitete Tinten=faß: oder Anweisung wie man gute schwarze, buntfaerbige, auch andere curioese Tinten auf mancherlei Weise zubereiten, auch wie man Gold, Silber und anderen Metallen aus der Feder auf Pappier, Pergament und andere Dinge schreiben solle; nebst noch andern zur Schreiberei gehoerigen und nuetz-lichen Stuecken*, p. 54–5, quoted in *Werkzeuge des Pegasus. Historische Schreibzeuge im Goethe-Nationalmuseum*, eds Egon Freitag et al., exh. cat., Stiftung Weimarer Klassik, 9 November–5 January 2003, designed and produced by Egon Freitag, Viola Geyersbach, Susanne Schroeder, ed. Reiner Schlichting (Weimar, 2003), p. 105.

44   Le Collen, *Feder, Tinte und Papier*, p. 26.

45   Ibid., p. 23.

46   Ibid., p. 57.

47   Cf. ibid., p. 69.

48   Quoted in ibid., p. 65.

49   Ibid., p. 26.

50   Ibid., p. 68.

51   On the poetics of the nation state as a poetics of penmanship cf. Kittler, *Discourse Networks, 1800/1900*, pp. 77–84, where Kittler discusses peda-gogical efforts around 1815, addressing 'the charge against an empirical standard rather than the general norm of a "national script". Like sounds and sound combinations, letters and their coordinates are henceforth to arise genetically out of the pure ego'. (p. 82)

52   Kittler, *Gramophone*, p. 193.

53   Cf. Le Collen, *Feder, Tinte und Papier*, pp. 59–62. For a hundred years the calligraphic qualities of the steel pen have been central to discussion within the relevant copy books of penmanship, e.g. from S. Freiwirth, *Der Arzt für Hand und Handschrift oder S. Freiwirth's neuestes Lehrsystem, nach welchem sich ein jeder Schlechtschreibende ohne Lehrer in nicht mehr als acht Lektionen eine Fertigkeit im Schön-Schnellschreiben aneignen kann. Erster Theil: die deutsche Handschrift* (Leipzig, 1855), p. 37, up to Ludwig Sütterlin, *Leitfaden für den Schreibunterricht* (Berlin, 1917), pp. 23–6.

54   Goethe, *Dichtung und Wahrheit*, IV. Teil, 16. Buch; WA I 29, pp. 12 and 14–15; quoted in *Werkzeuge des Pegasus*, ed. Freitag et al., p. 13; on Goethe's writing drives and inhibitions cf. ibid, pp. 11–37.

55   At the 43rd Intersteno-Congress in 2001 in Hannover the world's best stenographers managed 250 syllables per minute and after the eighth minute 470 syllables, thus working faster and more accurately for court authorities and parliaments up to now than digital text-recognition software. Cf. Arne Boecker, 'Durchhalten mit Härte 2B', in *Die Zeit*, 30.07.2001, also http://www.intersteno.de/ [accessed 4.11.06]

56   Henry Petroski, *Der Bleistift. Die Geschichte eines Gebrauchsgegenstands. Mit einem Anhang zur Geschichte des Unternehmens Faber-Castell*, trans.

Sabine Rochlitz (Basel, Boston and Berlin, 1995), pp. 37–56.

57  Cf. ibid., pp. 73–95; Jürgen Franzke and Peter Schafhauser, 'Faber-Castell – Die Bleistiftdynastie', in Petroski, *Der Bleistift*, pp. 331–60; Eule, *Mit Stift und Feder*, pp. 73–80.

58  Cf. advertising brochure *Graf von Faber-Castell. Collection 2004/2005*.

59  With the help of pencil scribbles and the paper notes covered with jottings in the book, the reader (or 'secretary' or 'secret writer' or 'archivist') can 'distil' the book, as Connie Palmen describes it in *De Erfenis* (The Inheritance) (Amsterdam, 1999), (p. 23). By applying her own hand the reader gains access and she marks this intrusion with traces which allow her and the other reader who will be her heir to participate in the intimacy of the meeting. 'Morgen moet je even het dagboek van Gombrowicz destilleren' ('Tomorrow you must distil the diary of Gombrowicz'). (p. 25).

60  Roland Barthes, *The Pleasure of the Text* [1973], trans. Richard Miller (London, 1976), pp.16–17 (my emphasis).

61  Cf. Freud's engagement with the male sexual symbols in dreams, including apart from sticks and umbrellas, sabres and guns there also figure writing instruments: 'pen-shafts' and 'extensible pencils'. 'Symbolism in Dreams' [1915]. Part Two: 'Dreams', Chap. 10, in *The Standard Edition of the Complete Psychological Works of Sigmund Freud Vol xv*, trans. John Strachey (London, 1961), pp. 154–5.

62  On the material characteristics of the fountain pen from the point of view of the history of technology see the chapter 'Der Füllfederhalter', in Eule, *Mit Stift und Feder*, pp. 113–22.

63  'Houd je een vulpen in je hand, dan wordt de inkt warm. De inkt komt net zo warm als je bloed op het papier.' Harry Mulisch, quoted in Jan Brokken, 'Schrijven is bijna niet kunnen schrijven' ('Writing is almost not being able to write'), in *Schrijven. Interviews met*, pp. 11–21; digitale bibliotheek voor de nederlandse letteren, 2002 [1980], at www.dbnl.org/tekst/brok002schr01_01/brok002schr01_01_0002.htm [accessed 22.07.2006], p. 13.

64  Derrida in Geoffrey Bennington and Jacques Derrida, *Jacques Derrida* [1991], trans. Geoffrey Bennington (Chicago and London, 1993), pp. 4–8; my emphasis.

65  One could add, less taken into consideration but no less acute, blood of the third category, menstrual blood that cannot be subsumed either by 'cruor' or 'sanguis'; cf. Sonja Neef, *Kalligramme*, pp. 101–6. Murat Aydemir writes in detail and with analytic clarity on menstrual blood: *Images of Bliss: Ejaculation, Masculinity, Meaning* (Minneapolis, MN, 2007), particularly the first chapter on the mixture of sperm and menstrual blood in the photographic studies by the Cuban-American artist Andres Serrano, 'Semen, Blood, Stars, and Ice: Serrano and Aristotle'.

66  Sigmund Freud, 'Fetishism' [1927], in *The Standard Edition of the Complete Psychological Works of Sigmand Freud Vol xxi*, trans. Strachey

(London, 1961), p. 154.

67  Le Collen, *Feder, Tinte und Papier*, p. 104.

68  Ibid.

69  'Jouons ici, bien entendu, sur la resemblance fortuite . . . entre la *sème* et le *semen*, le sens et la semence. Il [ce mot : la dissémination] a le pouvoir économique de condenser . . . la question de la différance sémantique . . . et de la dérive séminale, l'impossible réappropriation (monocentrique, paternelle, familiale) du concept et du sperme.' Jacques Derrida, *The Ear of the Other*, trans. Peggy Kamuf (Lincoln, NE, and London. 1988), p. 309. Western literature is full of this motif. To mention only two prominent examples here: in Proust's *À la recherche* in 'Solitary Pleasure' ejaculation forms a readable trace on the lilac leaves of a tulip, Ariadne's thread similar to the trace of slime left by a snail (cf. Aydemir, 'Gossamer Thread: Textuality, Ejaculation, Proust'); and according to Naomi Schor, in Flaubert's *Madame Bovary* the feminine scriptorial serum of *écriture féminine* supports the somatic metaphor of milk and menstrual blood (*Breaking the Chain: Women, Theory and French Realist Fiction* (New York, 1985), pp. 19; 25f.)

70  Advertising brochure *The Art of Writing. Mont Blanc.*

71  Cf. Jochen Hörisch, *Der Sinn und die Sinne. Eine Geschichte der Medien* (Frankfurt am Main, 2001), pp. 187–8.

72  'Een ballpoint vind ik een minderwaardig instrument. De ballpoint is voor obers die *hfl.* 1,25 en *hfl.* 2,37 moeten optellen, niet voor schrijvers. Met een ballpoint kun je geen enkele nuance in de lijn aanbrengen. Niet dat ik calligrafeer, maar ik wil de ene keer dik an de ander keer dun kunnen schrijven. De ballpoint, dat is altijd dezelfde domme driekwart millimeter dikte.' Harry Mulisch, quoted in Brokken, 'Schrijven is bijna niet kunnen schrijven', p. 14.

73  Cf. Le Collen, *Feder, Tinte und Papier*, pp. 141–55, also Eule, *Mit Stift und Feder*, pp. 123–8.

74  The ballpoint pen has also influenced important artists who – like Dubuffet – did drawings with it or – like Elisabetta Gonzo - used it as a creative element in design objects.

75  Cf. Hörisch, *Der Sinn und die Sinne*, p. 188.

76  Cf. Christoph Drösser, 'Schreiben im All', in *Die Zeit*, 10, 02.03.2006.

77  Cf. Margaret Jennings, 'Tutivillus: The Literary Career of the Recording Demon', in *Studies in Philology*, LXXIV/5 (1977), pp. 13–16.

78  Sigmund Freud, 'Note upon the Mystic Writing Pad', *Standard Edition Vol XIX*, p. 230.

79  Engell, 'Die genetische Funktion des Historischen in der Geschichte der Bildmedien', in *Mediale Historiographien*, eds Lorenz Engell and Joseph Vogl (Weimar, 2001), pp. 33–56 (Archiv für Mediengeschichte 1), p. 56.

80  Ibid., p. 56; my emphasis. Cf. on this subject also the detailed study by Ann van Sevenant on 'traceless' digital ways of writing: *Met water*

*schrijven. De filosofie in het computertijdperk* (Antwerp, 1997).

81  Martin Heidegger, *Parmenides*, trans. André Schuwer and Richard Rojcewicz (Bloomington, IN, 1992), p. 82.

82  The criticism that writing always already carries the erasure of the logos within itself is voiced by Plato in the *Phaedrus* 276c using exactly this image: 'Then when he [the man with real knowledge of right and beauty and good] is in earnest he will take a pen and *write in water* - disseminating the seed with ink through the kalamos [μελάνι σπείρων διά καλαμού], to produce discourses which cannot defend themselves viva voce or give any adequate account of the truth.' For a deconstruction of this image for digital ways of writing cf. Sevenant, *Met water schrijven*, particularly pp. 19–24.

83  At http://dc2.uni-bielefeld.de/dc2/tip/09_03.htm [accessed 16.01.07]

84  United States Patent Office, Patent No. 1.028.704 of 4 June 1912 for the 'Penholder' of May F. Gardner. An overview of the various procedures for the erasure of ink traces is provided by the Master's thesis of Stefanie Bieheim, *Der Tintenkiller. Techniken des Einschreibens and Auslöschens*, Dissertation supervised by Sonja Neef at the Faculty of Media, Bauhaus-University Weimar, Sommersemester 2006, pp. 8–19; quotation from Bieheim, *Der Tintenkiller*, pp. 16–19.

85  Mechanical erasing procedures, e.g. by blotting stone, erasing knife and eraser roll, are discussed by Bieheim in ibid. on pp. 8–16; the development of the ink eraser pen as a chemical process of erasure is traced by Bieheim on the basis of a consideration of the history of the technology through the patents, pp. 16–19.

85  Kaiserliches Patentamt (Imperial Patent Office), Patent No. 271913 of 28. September 1913 for the 'penholder with an arrangement for deleting mistakes in writing' of Heinrich Louis Steincke, pp. 35–44.

86  Johann Georg Krünitz, *Oekonomische Encyclopädie oder allgemeines System der Staats- Stadt- Haus und Landwirtschaft*, CLXXVIII (Berlin, 1841), Oeconomische Encyclopädie online, electronic complete text version from the Universitätsbibliothek Trier, at www.kruenitz1.uni-trier.de/ [accessed 5.12.2006], p. 580. The preparation of such secret inks is also described in the booklet on ink published by J. C. Wegener: *Neue Recept-Sammlung zu schwarzen, rothen, grünen und anderen Tinten* (Einbeck, 1830).

87  Krünitz, *Oekonomische Encyclopädie*, CLXXVIII, p. 584.

88  Ibid.

### Before a Photograph

1  Karin Schuller-Procopovici, 'Die Phantasien mit der Kamera notieren. Victor Hugos Portraits and Inszenierungen', in *Alles Wahrheit! Alles Lüge! (Sammlung Robert Lebeck)*, eds Bodo von Dewitz and Roland Scotti (Cologne, 1996), p. 80.

### 4 Fore-Word

1   Walter Benjamin, 'The Work of Art in the Age of Mechanical Reproduction' [1936], trans. Harry Zohn, in *Illuminations*, ed. Hannah Arendt (London, 1992), p. 212.

2   Georges Didi-Huberman, *Ähnlichkeit und Berührung: Archäologie, Anachronismus und Modernität des Abdrucks*, trans. Christoph Hollender (Cologne, 1999), p. 48.

3   Cf. Silvio A. Bedini, *Thomas Jefferson and His Copying Machines* (Charlottesville, VA, 1984), pp. 10–30; Wilhelm Eule, *Mit Stift and Feder. Kleine Kulturgeschichte der Schreib- and Zeichenwerkzeuge* (Leipzig, 1955), pp. 123–4.

4   Ibid., pp. 124–5.

5   Further technical application of the steel pen as a drawing instrument, for example by Senefelder in lithography (1796) is described by Eule in ibid., pp. 101–22.

6   See on this also Alfred Binet and Jules Courtier, 'Sur la vitesse des mouvements graphiques', in *Revue philosophique*, XVIII/1–6; 35 (1893), p. 664.

7   For the 'mimeograph', see Bedini, *Thomas Jefferson*, pp. 196–8, for the 'stylograph' ibid., pp. 154–7 and 160–64.

8   Nelson Goodman, *Languages of Art: An Approach to a Theory of Symbols* [1976] (Indianapolis, IN, 1988), pp. 113, 115, 114; emphasis in the original.

9   For example in George Bickham's *Universal Penman*, London 1733–41; cf. Michelle P. Brown, *The British Library Guide to Writing and Scripts* (London, 1998), pp. 84 and 87.

10   Goodman, *Languages of Art*, p. 113.

11   Benjamin, 'The Work of Art in the Age of Mechanical Reproduction', p. 214.

12   Goodman, *Languages of Art*, p. 114.

13   Walter Benjamin, 'The Work of Art in the Age of Mechanical Reproduction', in *Illuminations*, ed. Hannah Arendt, trans. Harry Zohn (London, 1992), p. 218.

14   Ibid., p. 218. This is how the title was translated by Harry Zohn in *Illuminations*, edited by Hannah Arendt (1968). See also the original subtitle of this book *Handschrift im Zeitalter ihrer technischen Reproduzierbarkeit*. Harry Zohn's translation has been adapted by Edmund Jephcott in *Walter Benjamin: Selected Writings*, vol. III, 1935–1938, pp. 101–122 under the title 'The Work of Art in the Age of Its Technological Reproducibility'.

15   See on this the observations from the perspective of media technology on the printing processes used for Leonardo da Vinci's leftwards-running and mirror-image handwriting: Sonja Neef, 'Zitat und Rahmen. Leonardo da Vinci's *Codex über den Vogelflug* digital', in *Kleine Erzählungen and ihre Medien*, eds Herbert Hrachovec, Wolfgang Müller-Funk and Birgit Wagner (Vienna, 2004), pp. 147–62; Michael Wetzel, 'Die Leonardo-Galaxis: Vom

Tafel- zum Monitorbild', in *Korrespondenzen. Visuelle Kulturen zwischen Früher Neuzeit and Gegenwart*, eds Matthias Bickenbach and Axel Fliethmann (Köln, 2002), pp. 75–88; also Robert Zwijnenberg, *The Writings and Drawings of Leonardo Da Vinci: Order and Chaos in Early Modern Thought* (Cambridge, 1999), pp. 83–4.

16   The inspiration for this inverted idea was given to me by my daughter Vera Neef, for which many thanks.

17   Karin Leonhard, 'Über Rechts und Links und Symmetrie im Barock', Lecture for the Workshop 'Topologie 2' organized by Stephan Günzel, Kolleg Friedrich Nietzsche, Klassik Stiftung Weimar, 22 March 2006. For a detailed discussion see the historic monumental work on the classification of shells by the English naturalist Martin Lister (born 1638 at Radcliffe, died 1712 as the personal doctor of Queen Anne in London) 'Historia sive synopsis conchyloriurn' 1685–93, 2 vols; see also Stefan Siemer, 'Die Erziehung des Auges. Überlegungen zur Darstellung von Natur in naturhistorischen Sammlungen in der frühen Neuzeit', in: *Zeitschrift für Kunst- und Kulturgeschichte im Netz, Sektion Bild Wissen Technik*, 1 (2001), pp. 1–12, at www.kunsttexte.de/download/bwt/siemer.pdf; [30.01.07].

18   Benjamin, 'The Work of Art', p. 237; my emphasis.

19   The dissociation of hand and writing, of writer and handwriting, had been conditioned for a long time not just by the technological methods of writing such as the polygraph and Watt's press but it has *always already* been inherent in any sort of writing. See on this for example Davide Giuriato's commentary on Walter Benjamin's handwritten letter to Siegfried Kracauer dated 5.6.1927, in which Benjamin illustrates such a dissociation between 'writer, writer's hand, writing instrument and what is written'. ('Einleitung', in *'SCHREIBKUGEL IST EIN DING GLEICH MIR: VON EISEN': Schreibszenen im Zeitalter der Typoskripte*, eds Davide Giuriato, Martin Stingelin and Sandro Zanetti (München, 2005) (Zur Genealogie des Schreibens 2), p. 18). Giuriato correctly demonstrates that Benjamin's letter was a reaction to Kracauer's 'Schreibmaschinchen' ('little typewriter'), and that the sensitivity towards the dissociation by the machine was revealed only as a logical response to the typewriter. The typewriter remediates handwriting still retrospectively.

20   *New York Gazette*, 6 July 1804; quoted in Bedini, *Thomas Jefferson*, p. 85.

21   *A List of Patents Granted by the United States, for the Encouragement of Arts and Sciences … from 1790 to 1828* (Washington, DC, 1828), p. 632, quoted in Bedini, p. 45. Other polygraph machines are described by Eule, *Mit Stift und Feder*, p. 104.

22   Bedini, *Thomas Jefferson*, p. 82.

23   Didi-Huberman, *Ähnlichkeit und Berührung*, p. 25.

24   Goodman, *Languages of Art*, p. 118.

25   Didi-Huberman, *Ähnlichkeit und Berührung*, p. 168; emphasis in the

original.

26 Wetzel, 'The Authority of Drawing: Hand, Authenticity, and Authorship', in *Sign Here! Handwriting in the Age of New Media*, eds Sonja Neef, José van Dijck and Eric Ketelaar (Amsterdam, 2006), p. 25; my emphasis.

27 Cf. Didi-Huberman, *Ähnlichkeit und Berührung*, pp. 138–41.

28 Goodman, *Languages of Art* p. 118.

29 Didi-Huberman, *Ähnlichkeit und Berührung*, pp. 167–8.

30 Jacques Derrida, *Of Grammatology* [1967], trans. Gayatri Chakravorty Spivak (Baltimore, MD, and London, 1976), p. 62

31 Didi-Huberman, *Ähnlichkeit und Berührung*, p. 160.

32 Cf. Michael Wetzel, 'Unter Sprachen – Unter Kulturen. Walter Benjamins "Interlinearversion" des Übersetzens als *Inframedialität*' (2002), at www.uni-konstanz.de/paech2002/zdk/beitrg/Wetzel.htm [accessed 11.10.2006].

33 Benjamin, 'The Work of Art', p. 216; my emphasis.

34 Walter Benjamin, 'A Small History of Photography' [1931], in *One-Way Street and Other Writings*, trans. Edmund Jephcott and Kinsley Shorter (London, 1997), p. 250; my emphasis.

35 'Semblabilité / similarité // Le meme (fabricat en série) // approximation pratique de la similarité. Dans le temps, un même object n'est pas le même à 1 seconde d'intervalle. Quels rapports avec le principe d'identité ?' Marcel Duchamp, *Notes*, ed. Paul Matisse (Boston, 1983), 7, p. 21 cf. Didi-Huberman, *Ähnlichkeit und Berührung*, p. 173.

36 Wetzel, 'Ein Auge zuviel. Derridas Urszenen des Ästhetischen', in Jacques Derrida, *Aufzeichnungen eines Blinden. Das Selbstporträt and andere Ruinen* (München, 1997), pp. 129–55 (Bild und Text)', pp. 135, 447.

37 'Le possible est un infra-mince', Duchamp, *Notes*, 1, p. 21

38 Didi-Huberman, *Ähnlichkeit und Berührung*, p. 190. Cf. Thomas Fechner-Smarsly, 'Blood Samples and Fingerprint Files: Blood as Artificial Matter, Artistic Material, and Means of the Signature', in *Sign Here! Handwriting in the Age of New Media*, ed. Sonja Neef, José van Dijck and Eric Ketelaar (Amsterdam, 2006)', pp. 200–1.

39 Walter Benjamin, *The Arcades Project* [1927–1940], trans. Howard Eiland and Kevin McLaughlin (Cambridge, MA, and London, 1999) p. 447.

40 Cf. Wetzel, 'Ein Auge zuviel', p. 149.

41 Didi-Huberman, *Ähnlichkeit und Berührung*, p. 25; Benjamin, 'A Small History of Photography', p. 248.

42 Benjamin, 'A Small History of Photography', p. 243.

43 Ibid., p. 250.

### Before a Hand

1 Siegmund Prillwitz, 'Fingeralphabete, Manualsysteme und Gebärden-sprachschriften', , in *HSK*, 10.2, p. 1625.

## 5 The Screen Saver

1  Daniel Paul Schreber, *Memoirs of My Nervous Illness* [*Denkwürdigkeiten eines Nervenkranken*, 1900–2], trans. Ida Macalpine and Richard A. Hunter (London, 1955), p. 118.

2  Vaslav Nijinsky, *The Diary of Vaslav Nijinsky: Unexpurgated Edition* [1919], trans. Kyril Fitzlyon (London, 1999), pp. 31–3.

3  The relevant leading lights of hypertext theory are well known: following Roland Barthes' model of the text as a web of quotations they include for example Georges P. Landow and Jay Bolter; the work of Espen J. Aarseth owes much to the concept of the rhizome in Gilles Deleuze and Félix Guattari; the work of Katherine N. Hayles and Donna Haraway focuses on cybernetics.

4  The effect of hypermedia, according to Bolter and Grusin, is based on a dual cultural desire: 'Our culture wants both to multiply its media and to erase all traces of mediation: ideally, it wants to erase media in the very act of multiplying them.' Jay David Bolter and Richard Grusin, *Remediation: Understanding New Media* (Cambridge, MA, and London, 1999), p. 5.

5  N. Katherine Hayles, *Writing Machines* (Cambridge, 2002), p. 25.

6  The way screen savers historically work is explained at www.technovelgy.com as follows: 'An electron shoots particles at the phosphor on the back of the screen, causing tiny points of light to appear, constantly varying the images prevents the screen phosphor from being permanently marked if the electron gun points at the same point of the screen.' ('Where Science Meets Fiction', www.technovelgy.com, [1.12.06])

7  Claus Pias, 'Digitale Sekretäre: 1968, 1978, 1998', in *Europa. Kultur der Sekretäre*, ed. Joseph Vogl (Zürich and Berlin, 2003), p. 236.

8  Ibid., p. 238.

9  Ibid., pp. 236–7.

10  Ibid., p. 237.

11  If one can believe the information on wikipedia.org, Palm is simply a development, if not downright plagiarism of Newton, a product arising from a dispute over a patent: 'The original Graffiti system was the subject of a lawsuit by Xerox, claiming it violated Xerox's patent relating to its Unistrokes technology (US Patent 5,596,656, granted in 1997). The Unistrokes technology was invented at the Palo Alto Research Center (PARC) by David Goldberg. Palm had a demonstration of Unistrokes from PARC before they created their Graffiti system. During the original case, a court ruled that Palm violated Xerox's patent and ordered them to discontinue use of the original Graffiti system in further versions of its Palm OS software, which Palm did. It replaced the original Graffiti system with a licensed variant of the Jot system from CIC, which Palm refers to as Graffiti 2 . . . Palm later appealed the original court ruling both on the

claim it violated Xerox's patent and as to the validity of the patent in the first place. An appeals court ruled in favour of Xerox with regard to the original ruling that Palm had violated its patent but referred the case back to the lower court to decide whether the patent was valid to begin with. In 2004, a judge ruled in favour of Palm, saying Xerox's patent was not valid on the basis that 'prior art references anticipate and render obvious the claim.' (http://en.wikipedia.org/wiki/Graffiti_(Palm_OS) [15.10.2006].

12   More recent writing recognition software meanwhile can handle more variety in handwriting by training the computer as in voice recognition programs, e.g. the tablet PC from Fujitsu-Siemens 2004 on which the manuscript of this present volume was written.

13   Cesare Lombroso, *Handbuch der Graphologie* (Leipzig, 1893), p. 16.

14   Cesare Lombroso, *Handbuch der Graphologie* (Leipzig, 1893), pp. 16–7.

15   Cf. Armin Schäfer, 'Lebendes Dispositiv: Hand beim Schreiben', in *Psychographien*, eds Cornelius Borck and Armin Schäfer (Zürich and Berlin, 2005), p. 250–9.

16   Alfred Binet and Jules Courtier, 'Sur la vitesse des mouvements graphiques' , in *Revue philosophique*, XVIII/1–6; 35 (1893), pp. 664–6.

17   Binet and Courtier, 'Expériences sur la vitesse des mouvements graphiques', in *Revue philosophique,* 37 (1894), p. 111. See also Binet, 'Une expérience collective, en séance, sur les relations entre l'écriture et l'intelligence', in *Bulletin*, 15 (1904), pp. 395–7, 'Note sur l'écriture hystérique', in *Revue Philosophique de la France et de l'étranger*, 23 (1887), pp. 67–70.

18   Lombroso, *Handbuch der Graphologie*, Part 1, pp. 13–118 (p. 66), Part 2, pp. 119–99. So-called 'criminal handwriting' soon became the speciality of Roda Wieser, who published on this until the end of the 1930s; cf. Schäfer, 'Lebendes Dispositiv', p. 246, fn. 22.

19   See for example Stephan Kammer, 'Graphologie, Schreibmaschine und die Ambivalenz der Hand', in *'SCHREIBKUGEL IST EIN DING GLEICH MIR: VON EISEN': Schreibszenen im Zeitalter der Typoskripte*, eds Davide Giuriato, Martin Stingelin and Sandro Zanetti (München, 2005) (Zur Genealogie des Schreibens 2), pp. 142–9.

20   Carlo Ginzburg, *Spurensicherung. Die Wissenschaft auf der Suche nach sich selbst* (Berlin, 2002), pp. 43–7; Simon A. Cole, *Suspect Identities: A History of Fingerprinting and Criminal Identification* (Cambridge, MA, and London, 2002).

21   Schäfer, 'Lebendes Dispositiv', pp. 245, 252–4, 256.

22   On the concept of free will in Nicholas of Cusa, see Robert Zwijnenberg, *The Writings and Drawings of Leonardo Da Vinci: Order and Chaos in Early Modern Thought* (Cambridge, 1999), p. 78. The original theological category of free will is reinterpreted from 1900 in the graphological epistemes, as for example in the case of Ludwig Klages, who discusses will in terms of the inhibition of drives ('*Antriebshemmung*')/the

inhibited driving force ('*Hemmtriebfeder*') (in *Sämtliche Werke, Volume 3: Philosophie III*, eds Ernst Frauchiger et al. (Bonn, 1974), pp. 704; 793–5; see also in the same volume the relevant chapter 'Zur Theorie und Symptomatologie des Willens', pp. 642–5; 'Die Triebe und der Wille', pp. 693–709; in addition the appendix at the end of the volume pp. 779–81; 792–8). Thanks to Arndt Himmelreich for this reference.

23  Nicholas of Cusa, *Dialogus de ludo globi/Gespräch über das Globusspiel*, 4:1–11, 5:4–5, 6:1–5.

24  A poetic exception to this is provided by the topos of lovers writing with the same handwriting, the archetype of this being Eduard and Ottilie in Goethe's *Elective Affinities*; cf. Jochen Hörisch, *Ende der Vorstellung – Die Poesie der Medien* (Frankfurt am Main, 1999), pp. 35–56.

25  Cf. Malcolm B. Parkes, *Pause and Effect: An Introduction to the History of Punctuations in the West* (London, 1992), (esp. p. 304); Paul Saenger, *Space Between Words: The Origins of Silent Reading* (Stanford, CA, 1997), (esp. p. 72–3.).

26  'x ex *N* non latissimo ductu sed aequè à latissimo recedente', Gerardus Mercator, *Literarum latinarum*, p. 158, my transcription.

27  'Typoi' means literally 'tracks'. This is pointed out by Vilém Flusser in *Die Schrift. Hat Schreiben Zukunft?* [1987], ed. Andreas Müller-Pohle, Edition Flusser, vol. 5 (Göttingen, 2002), in his chapter on book printing. He exemplifies the type of the letter case with the typoi or tracks of a bird that has walked along a beach. The word type then signifies 'that these tracks can be used as models to classify the bird who has passed by'. Unlike a fingerprint, the track of the bird gives no indication about the individual bird but only allows for its classification as a serial 'model' (cf. 'Exergue' in this book).

28  Heidegger, *Parmenides*, trans. André Schuwer and Richard Rojcewicz (Bloomington, IN, 1992), p. 81.

29  Sir Arthur Conan Doyle, 'A Case of Identity', in *The Penguin Complete Sherlock Holmes* (London, 1981), p. 199.

30  At www.mos.org/sln/Leonardo/write.html on the Leonardo-Right-to-Left website, one can (or at least one could on 5.11.06) have every key entry transcribed into Leonardo's left-running handwriting by online transmitter (cf. Sonja Neef, 'Introduction', in *Sign Here! Handwriting in the Age of New Media*, eds Sonja Neef, José van Dijck and Eric Ketelaar (Amsterdam, 2006), together with José van Dijck, p. 13f.). In addition, Leonardo's manuscripts and graphics are used repeatedly in Microsoft as 'image drivers', e.g. in the screen saver 'Leonardo da Vinci', Windows 98 (cf. Sonja Neef 'The W/Ri(gh)ting Hand, Leonardo da Vinci as Screen Saver', in *Travelling Concepts III: Memory, Image, Narrative*, ed. Nancy Pedri (Amsterdam, 2003), pp. 341–55). On the digital function converting illegible mirror writing into legible monitor writing (without any remainder), see Sonja Neef, 'Zitat und Rahmen. Leonardo da Vinci's

*Codex über den Vogelflug* digital', in *Kleine Erzählungen and ihre Medien*, eds Herbert Hrachovec, Wolfgang Müller-Funk and Birgit Wagner (Vienna, 2004), plus Neef, 'Die (rechte) Schrift und die (linke) Hand', in *Kodikas/Code. Ars Semeiotica*, 25 (2002), pp. 157–74.

31  John R. Searle, 'Reiterating the Differences: A Reply to Derrida', in *Glyph*, 1 (1977), p. 199; quoted in Jacques Derrida, 'Limited Inc. abc…', trans. Samuel Weber in *Limited Inc.* (Evanston, IL, 1988) p. 79. In this polemical essay Searle attempts a 'correction' of Austin's speech-act theory by accusing Derrida of confusing 'iterability' (as the characteristic that makes no decisive difference, at least not between writing and speech) with the 'permanence of the text', i.e. the quality of language that makes it possible to function even in the absence of the sender. Derrida answered 'Sarl's' polemic in the same year by return of post with a reply under the title of 'Limited Inc abc'. Cf. the summary by Gerald Graff, pp. 47–51.

32  Searle, 'Reiterating the Differences', p. 206.

33  Brian Rotman, *Signifying Nothing: The Semiotics of Zero* (London, 1987), p. 14.

34  Roland Barthes, '*Non multa sed multum*' [1982], in *Writings on Cy Twombly*, ed. Nicola del Roscio (Munich, 2002), p. 97.

35  Jacques Derrida, 'How to Avoid Speaking: Denials' [1987], trans. Ken Frieden, in *Languages of the Unsayable: The Play of Negativity in Literature and Literary Theory*, ed. Sanford Budick and Wolfgang Iser (New York, 1989), p. 4.

36  On the 'technique' of negative language use, see also the chapter 'Mystische Sprechweisen' in Sonja Neef, *Kalligramme. Zur Medialität einer Schrift. Anhand van Paul van Ostaijen's 'De feesten van angst en pijn'* (Amsterdam, 2000), pp. 169–79.

37  Peter Fuchs, 'Vom Zweitlosen: Paradoxe Kommunikation im Zen-Buddhismus', in *Reden and Schweigen*, eds Niklas Luhmann and Peter Fuchs (Frankfurt am Main, 1997), p. 54; see on this Fuchs, 'Von der Beobachtung des Unbeobachtbaren: Ist Mystik ein Fall von Inkommunikabilität?', in *Reden and Schweigen*, eds Niklas Luhmann and Peter Fuchs (Frankfurt am Main, 1997), pp. 70–100.

38  I have analyzed in detail the particular poetological implications of this pericope in relation to the concept of 'authorship' based on a close reading of Paul van Ostaijen's poem 'fatalisties liedje' in 'Handspiel' (pp. 241–7).

39  Bernard Siegert, *Auslassungspunkte. Vortrag an der Hochschule für Grafik und Buchdruck Leipzig* (Leipzig, 2003), p. 23f.

40  Schreber, *Memoirs*, p. 113.

41  Hayles, *Writing Machines*, p. 22.

42  Heidegger, *Parmenides*, p. 82.

43  Manfred Riepe, 'Ich computiere, also bin ich. Schreber – Descartes – Computer und virtueller Wahn', *Künstliche Spiele*, eds Georg Hartwagner, Stefan Iglhaut and Florian Rötzer (München, 1993), p. 222; cf. also Claus

Pias, 'Digitale Sekretäre: 1968, 1978, 1998', in *Europa. Kultur der Sekretäre*, ed. Joseph Vogl (Zürich and Berlin, 2003), p. 235.

44 Georges Didi-Huberman, *The Invention of Hysteria: Charcot and the Photographic Iconography of the Salpêtrière*, trans. Alisa Hartz (Cambridge, MA, 2003), p. 250.

45 Ibid.

46 Ibid., p. 279.

### 6 The Diary

1 This chapter is a revised version of the essay 'Authentic Events: The Diaries of Anne Frank and the Alleged Diaries of Adolf Hitler'.

2 Jacques Derrida, *Archive Fever: A Freudian Impression* [1995], trans. Eric Prenowitz (Chicago, 1998) pp. 8–9; italics by Jacques Derrida, my underlining.

3 Sigmund Freud, *Note on the Mystic Writing-Pad* [1925], in *The Standard Edition of the Complete Psychological Works of Sigmund Freud Vol XIX*, trans. John Strachey (London, 1961), p. 227.

4 Ibid., p. 229; my emphasis.

5 Plato, *The Theaetetus of Plato*, trans. M. J. Levett (Glasgow, 1977), 191 c,d.

6 Aristotle, *De Memoria et Reminiscentia* (Of Memory and Remembering), trans. J. I. Beare, in *The Basic Works of Aristotle*, ed. Richard McKeon (New York, 2001), 1: 450a 25–49; my emphasis. Cf. Bettine Menke, 'Mneme, Mnemonik – Medien (in) der Antike', in *Medien der Antike*, eds Lorenz Engell and Joseph Vogl (Weimar, 2003) (Archiv für Mediengeschichte), pp. 126–7.

7 During a fixation, between five and seven letters are perceived in focus in the centre of the fixation along with five to seven other ones in the direction of reading but out of focus in the periphery. Along with saccadic jumps in the direction of the text, backward jumps, called regressions, in the text also take place. There are three to five saccades per second. The act of reading thus implies a temporality whose speed is determined by the duration of the fixation, the length of the saccadic jumps and the number of regressions. Cf. Stefan Gfroerer, Hartmut Günther and Michael Bock, 'Augenbewegungen und Substantivgroßschreibung', in *Schriftsystem and Orthographie*, ed. Peter Eisenberg and Hartmut Günther (Tübingen, 1989), pp. 116–7.

8 Menke, 'Mneme, Mnemonik', p. 128; my emphasis.

9 Thomas Holl, 'Rechtsextremismus. Empörung über Bücherverbrennung', *FAZ*, CLV/1, 07.07.2006.

10 Sebastian Haffner, 'Das Gift der Kameradschaft', in *Die Zeit*, 21, 16.05.2002.

11 Israel Gutman et al., eds, 'Tagebücher', in *Enzyklopädie des Holocaust. Die Verfolgung und Ermordung der europäischen Juden*, vol. III [1990], pp. 1392–5 (Munich and Zürich, 1998).

12  In the case of British archives, the term 'official custody' illustrates this difference. This is defined by Sir Hilary Jenkinson in his *Manual of Archive Administration* (Oxford, 1922, p. 10) as the basic condition for public archives. A certified copy of a document from the body of the Public Record Office in London is accepted as being as valid as the original in any Court of Law, whereas for a document from the British Museum to receive this validation the judge would require the presentation of the original. Thanks to Eric Ketelaar.

13  Mieke Bal, 'Introduction', in *The Practice of Cultural Analysis: Exposing Interdisciplinary Interpretation*, eds Mieke Bal and Hent de Vries (Stanford, CA, 1999).

14  Krystzof Pomian, *Der Ursprung des Museums. Vom Sammeln*, trans. Gustav Rossler (Berlin, 1988), p. 14.

15  The pamphlet was distributed by Schönborn in Frankfurt in July, 1978; quoted in Teresien da Silva, 'Zur Echtheit des Tagebuchs'.

16  These involve the Stielau case in Lübeck (1960), the Roth case in Frankfurt (1977), the Schönborn case in Frankfurt and the Kunth case in Stuttgart (both 1979), and finally the Römer case in Hamburg (1993). A detailed overview of the protracted debate on the authenticity of this diary is provided by David Barnouw 'Aanvallen op de Echtheid van het Dagboek' (Attacks of the authenticity of the Diary) in *De dagboeken van Anne Frank*. 99–119. The latest 'incident' in Pretzien is of course not documented there.

17  Teresien da Silva, 'Zur Echtheit des Tagebuchs', http://home.arcor.de/annefrank/tagb_echth.htm. [15.12.2005]. English version: 'Denial of the Authenticity of the Diary', www.AnneFrankHouse.

18  The material concerning the scandal of the Hitler forgeries is immense. Numerous articles were published in newspapers worldwide as well as on the Internet (see http://fortunecity.com/dikigoros/schtonk.htm and www.sniggle.net/kujau.php; [both 19.03.03]). The story was later turned into a film (*Schtonk*, 1992, Dir.: Helmut Dietl), and there have been numerous academic studies on the subject in the fields of information and archival research; for an overview, see for example Günther Picker, *Der Fall Kujau. Chronik eines Fälschungsskandals* (Frankfurt am Main, 1992), and N. In 't Veld, 'De dagboeken van Hitler', in *Knoeien met het verleden*, eds Z. R. Dittrich, B. Naarden and H. Renner (Utrecht and Antwerp, 1984), pp. 176–89.

19  Thomas Walde, 'Wie Sternreporter Gerd Heidemann die Tagebücher fand', *Der Stern*, 18, 28.04.1983.

20  At www.sniggle.net/kujau.php [3.12.04].

21  According to Josef Henke, archivist of the Bundesarchiv (German Federal Archive), the process of exposing Hitler's diaries as fake can be divided into two phases. He defines the first phase as running from 5 April 1982 – when Thomas Walde and Leo Pesch from *Stern* first

contacted the Bundesarchiv – until 22 April 1983 – when *Stern* announced the discovery of the lost Hitler diaries. The second phase runs from 25 April 1983 – when three diaries were given to the Bundesarchiv for certification of their authenticity – until 6 May 1983, when the German Minister of the Interior declared the diaries to be forgeries, cf. Henke, 'Die sogenannten Hitler-Tagebücher und der Nachweis ihrer Fälschung. Eine archivfachliche Nachbetrachtung', in *Aus der Arbeit der Archive. Beiträge zum Archivwesen, zur Quellenkunde und zur Geschichte*, ed. Friedrich P. Kahlenberg (Boppard am Rhein, 1989), p. 289.

22 Ibid., pp. 310–4.

23 Charles Hamilton, *The Hitler Diaries: Fakes that Fooled the World* (Lexington, KY, 1991), p. 1.

24 Quoted in www.sniggle.net/kujau.php [7.08.03].

25 More precisely, the assessors identified perlon, also known as polyamide 6, in the bindings of the volumes dating from 1934, 1941, and 1943, as well as polyester fibres in the 1941 volume. Perlon was not produced until after 1943, and polyester not before 1953. Moreover, by means of ultra-violet irradiation, they discovered paper-bleaching agents in the paper from the 1941 and 1943 volumes, substances that were not used prior to 1945. Cf. Horst Czichos, *Was ist falsch am falschen Rembrandt? und Wie hart ist Damaszener Stahl? Wie man mit Technik Kunst erforscht, prüft und erhält* (Berlin, 2002), pp. 78–9, also Werner Franke, 'Papierbezogene Echtheitsprüfung der sogenannten "Hitler-Tagebücher"', in *BAM-Jahresbericht 1983*. Another flaw was that the diaries had a monogram on the front cover – which, moreover, turned out to be plastic – written in Fraktur and oddly composed of the letters 'FH' instead of 'AH'.

26 '. . . met aan zekerheid grenzende waarschijnlijkheid afkomstig van de producente van het vergelijkingsschrift, Anne Frank', H.J.J. Hardy, 'Samenvatting van de resultaten van het handschriftvergelijkend en document-technisch onderzoek van wat bekend staat als het dagboek van Anne Frank', in *De dagboeken van Anne Frank*, eds Harry Paape, Gerrold van der Stroom and David Barnouw (Amsterdam, 1990)', p. 164.

27 Nelson Goodman, *Languages of Art: An Approach to a Theory of Symbols* [1976] (Indianapolis, IN, 1988), p. 113.

28 James M. O'Toole, 'On the Idea of Uniqueness', in *American Archivist*, 57 (1994), p. 633.

29 Derrida, *Archive Fever*, p. 3; emphasis in the original.

30 This idea comes close to Michel Foucault's conception of the archive as 'a historical *a priori*', emphasizing '[i]t is not a question of rediscovering what might legitimize an assertion, but of freeing the conditions of emergence of statement, the law of their coexistence with others, the specific form of their mode of being, the principles according to which they survive, become transformed, and disappear . . . [I]n short, it [the historical *a priori* of the archive] has to take account of the

fact that discourse has not only a meaning or a truth, but a history.' (p. 127).

In *Das Rumoren der Archive. Ordnung aus Unordnung* (Berlin, 2002), Wolfgang Ernst summarizes this as follows: 'Foucault defines the *archive* as referring to neither the sum of all transmitted documents, nor to the institution of this transmission. Rather, it refers to the system dominating the appearance and the actual functioning of the utterances.'(p. 16). This connection between Derrida's and Foucault's concepts of the archive is only mentioned here in passing and further examination is required to appreciate them in more detail and in relation to their respective emphases.

31  Cf. Hardy, 'Samenvatting', pp. 125, 133, 139.

32  Manfred Bissinger, *Hitlers Sternstunde. Kujau, Heidemann und die Millionen* (Hamburg, 1984), p. 173.

33  Cf. Jaap Tanja, 'Anne Frank's Diaries in Facsimile' [2002], trans. from the Dutch by Frank van Pernis. http://www.annefrank.ch/images/content/ pdf/faksimile_d.pdf, [15.12.2006]; 'Anne Frank's Diaries in Facsimile', http://www.AnneFrankHouse.

34  For the wider cultural implications of this statement see Hillel Schwartz's monumental *The Culture of the Copy: Striking Likenesses, Unreasonable Facsimiles* (New York, 1998).

35  Bissinger, *Hitlers Sternstunde*, p. 227.

36  Marx's terms *commodity* and *fetish* form the epistemic foundation of a series of studies. Mieke Bal in 'Telling Objects: A Narrative Perspective on Collecting', in *The Cultures of Collecting*, eds John Elsner and Roger Cardinal (London, 1994), develops her concept of collecting by critically discussing the relevant theories of fetishism in terms of the epistemic development Freud-Marx-Lacan/Žižek (pp. 107–10); William J. T. Mitchell discusses – referring to Derrida's essay with the same title in *Diacritics*, 11 (1981), pp. 3–25 – the 'Economimesis' of the slave as commodity and the slave *narrative*-as-commodity following a Marxist approach (*Picture Theory: Essays on Verbal and Visual Representation* (Chicago and London, 1994) pp. 195–9). For the idea of fetishism as an archival drive, see Helen Wood, 'The Fetish of the Document: An Exploration of Attitudes Towards Archives', in *New Directions in Archival Research*, eds Margaret Procter and C. P. Lewis (Liverpool, 2000), pp. 20–48.

37  Henke, 'Die sogenannten Hitler-Tagebücher', pp. 309–310.

38  Hamilton, *The Hitler Diaries*, p. 12.

39  Bal in 'Telling Objects: A Narrative Perspective on Collecting', p. 104. Bal refers here to James Clifford, 'On Collecting Art and Culture', in *The Predicament of Culture: Twentieth-Century Ethnography, Literature and Art* (Cambridge, MA, 1988), pp. 215–51.

40  Cf. for example Eilean Hooper-Greenhill, who in *Museums and the Shaping of Knowledge* (New York and London, 2001) relates the question

'What is a Museum?' back to Foucault's concept of the order of things. According to this, the epistemic order of the museum is not so much related to an irrevocably 'true' or definitively 'rational' taxonomy than it is shaped by socio-cultural constructions; i.e. it arises in the end from domination and subjugation.

41   Derrida, *Archive Fever*, p. 2; my emphasis.

42   By 'semiophores' Pomian understands 'bearers of signs' (Krysztof Pomian, *Der Ursprung des Museums. Vom Sammeln*, trans. Gustav Roßler (Berlin, 1988), p. 81), for example museum objects but also grave goods or offerings made to the gods in the temple, i.e. devices (or media) serving to mediate between this world and the other, the visible and the invisible. In the *exhibite*d features of semiophores one can 'see an indication of something that is not there at the moment, possibly something also that is considered to be simply invisible. The visible features here serve as bearers of invisible relations; these are produced, in contrast to physical relations, not so much by the *hand* as by *perception* and *language*' (p. 84; his emphasis). For Pomian the authority of semiophores is accordingly based on their sacred function of maintaining a connection to the Empire of the Dead and of the Divine. This rhetorical position transforms the museum as a 'displayer' into a temple in the sense of an institution conceived of as making an invisible truth visible, it thus transforms it to a certain extent into an 'apparatus' for the production of authenticity. Pomian has extended the concept of semiophores from the museum to the archive (p. 16). For a critical re-interpretation of Pomian's concept of the museum and the archive in which historiography is conceived of less as statement than as performance, see Eric Ketelaar, 'The Power of the Past: Visibilities and Invisibilities in Archives, Libraries and Museums', keynote address at *Kildenes Makt*, a conference organized by ABM-Utvikling, Norwegian Archive, Library and Museum Authority (Oslo, September 2003).

43   Cf. for example James J. Sheehan, *Geschichte der deutschen Kunstmuseen. Von der fürstlichen Kunstkammer zur modernen Sammlung* [2000], trans. Martin Pfeiffer (München, 2002), pp. 59–66.

44   Bal, *Double Exposures*, pp. 3–4.

45   Walter Benjamin, 'The Work of Art in the Age of Mechanical Reproduction' [1936], trans. Harry Zohn, in *Illuminations*, ed. Hannah Arendt (London, 1992), p. 218.

46   Jean-François Lyotard, *The Differend: Phrases in Dispute* [1983], trans. Georges Van Den Abbeele (Manchester, 1988), pp. 3–4.

47   Ibid., p. 13.

48   The literature on the problem of traumatic recall is immense. Van Alphen in 'Symptoms of Discursivity: Experience, Memory, and Trauma' explains the difficulty of producing subjectivity in the experience of traumatic events because this would imply admitting

one's own responsibility and confessing one's own guilt. See also Mieke Bal's 'Introduction' in *Acts of Memory*.

49  W.J.T. Mitchell, *Picture Theory: Essays on Verbal and Visual Representation* (Chicago and London, 1994), p. 194. Mitchell does not develop his concept of the 'image-text' by reference to the trauma of Holocaust experiences, but by reference to the traumatic experiences of slavery. If I am here applying his concept to Holocaust experiences, in no way do I intend to equate these two historical fields because this would imply an unwarranted denial of the very specific quality of each of them.

50  William J. T. Mitchell, *Picture Theory: Essays on Verbal and Visual Representations* (Chicago, IL, and London, 1994), p. 194.

51  This is how Roland Barthes puts it in 'Cy Twombly or *Non Multa Sed Multum*' on that other 'scribble' in Twombly's *Untitled* images. (p. 88; emphasis in the original)

52  That writing to the same extent that it serves the memory, also promotes forgetting, has been a commonplace ever since the time of the ancient writings. And paradoxically we know about it through writing, i.e. through Plato's celebrated *Phaedrus* dialogue in which he has wise King Thamus comment on the invention of letters by Theuth as follows: 'You [Theuth] who are the father of writing, have out of fondness for your offspring attributed to it quite the opposite of its real function. Those who acquire it will cease to exercise their memory and become forgetful; they will rely on writing to bring things to their remembrance by external signs instead of on their own internal resources. What you have discovered is a receipt (pharmakon) for recollection (hypomnema), not for memory (mneme).' (Plato, *Phaedrus*, trans. Walter Hamilton (Harmondsworth, 1973), 275 D, p. 96) Once registered, mental notes can be erased since writing preserves what is to be remembered for a future present, in which what is memorized as the glyph of a memory trace can be summoned up again. And thus at the beginning of every note-taking there stands the erasure of memory.

53  'Ik zal hoop ik aan jou alles kunnen toevertrouwen, zoals ik nog aan niemand gekund heb, en ik hoop dat je een grote steun voor me zult zijn. Anne Frank. 12 juni 1942' (Anne Frank, *De dagboeken*, p. 197; trans. by B. M. Mooyart-Doubleday [adapted by Sonja Neef and Anthony Mathews] in David Barnouw and Gerrold van der Stroom, eds, *The Diary of Anne Frank: The Critical Edition* (Amsterdam, 1990), p. 177).

54  For the dialogical relationship between Anne and Kitty see Ton Brouwers, 'Anne Frank', in *Kritisch Literatuur Lexikon*, eds Ad Zuiderent, Hugo Brems and Tom van Deel (Amsterdam, 2002), pp. 7–8.

55  José van Dijck, 'Writing the Self: Of Diaries and Weblogs', in *Sign Here! Handwriting in the Age of New Media*, eds Sonja Neef, José van Dijck and Eric Ketelaar (Amsterdam, 2006), pp. 121–2.

56  Cf. Van der Stroom, 'De dagboeken, "Het Achterhuis" en de vertalingen',

pp. 69–71. This 'original copy' of her diary by the hand of Anne Frank herself added fuel to the fire of the debates about the authenticity of the diaries. For this reason, the Dutch *Rijksinstituut voor oorlogsdocumentatie* commissioned the elaboration of a historical-critical text edition containing all three versions of the diary – A: Anne's first version, B: her second version  and C: the final version that Otto Frank edited for publication. See Harry Paape, Gerrold van der Stroom and David Barnouw, eds, *De dagboeken van Anne Frank*,  English translation in 'The Diaries, *Het Achterhuis* and the Translations' in *The Diary of Anne Frank: The Critical Edition*, pp. 59–77.

57 'Stel je eens voor hoe interessant het zou zijn, als ik een roman van het Achterhuis uit zou geven . . . (Anne Frank, *De dagboeken*, p. 594, trans. by B. M. Mooyart-Doubleday in Barnouw and van der Stroom, *The Diary of Anne Frank: The Critical Edition*, p. 578).

58 When reading the image as text, the name Kitty invites us, for a change, to not only focus on what the diary *does not* tell us (because from the perspective of the annexe it is still in the future) but on what it *does* tell us. Brouwers, 'Anne Frank' (pp. 5–7), emphasizes that the main topic of the diary is the process of identity formation in the course of a young girl's awakening sexuality and the awakening self-consciousness of a novice writer. The diary also contains a multiplicity of literary, picturesque, and humorous short stories. Both this intimate and this comical dimension of the notebooks cause us to revise our view of Anne and protect her from being embalmed for ever in a two-dimensional, fixed image.

59 For an analysis of the politics of the gaze as an agent of power see Norman Bryson, chapter 5, 'Gaze and Glance' in *Vision and Painting: The Logic of the Gaze* (London, 1983). Specifically on the logic of the museum's gaze, see Bal, *Double Exposures*, especially chapter 8, 'His Master's Eye'.

60 Marianne Hirsch describes the belated memory of the Holocaust containing the second generation as a coded message from the first generation as 'postmemory': 'Postmemory characterizes the experience of those who grow up dominated by narratives that preceded their birth, whose own belated stories are displaced by the stories of the previous generation, shaped by traumatic events that they can neither understand nor re-create' ('Projected Memory: Holocaust Photographs in Personal and Public Fantasy', in *Acts of Memory*, eds Mieke Bal, Jonathan Crewe and Leo Spitzer (Hanover, NH, and London, 1990), p. 8).

61 [Sabine :] 'Het gaat hier maar door het achterhuis te zijn. Dat gaat nooit meer weg. Nooit meer. Het is voor altijd leeg hier. Dat is zo wreed, zo tragisch. . . . Eigenlijk wordt het elke dag opnieuw leeggehaald, dit huis. Iedere dag worden ze opnieuw opgepakt. En elke dag, elke morgen als ik hier kom, tref ik het huis leeg aan. Zijn ze weg, alweer. Een gruwelijke herhaling, net als in de hel . . . Alles wat voor altijd nooit meer is, vind ik eng' (Jessica Durlacher, *De dochter*, p. 13,

translation by Sonja Neef and Anthony Mathews).

62 Ernst van Alphen, *Caught by History: Holocaust Effects in Contemporary Art, Literature, and Theory* (Stanford, CA, 1997), p. 10.

63 Derrida, *Archive Fever*, pp. 16–7, cf. Eric Prenowitz, 'Translator's Note. Right on [à même]' [1996], in Derrida, *Archive Fever*, pp. 110–1 (italics by Derrida, my underlining).

64 Ibid.

65 Ketelaar, 'Writing Archival Machines', in *Sign Here! Handwriting in the Age of New Media*, eds Sonja Neef, José van Dijck and Eric Ketelaar (Amsterdam, 2006), p. 188; his emphasis. Cf. his 'Archivalisering en Archivering', inaugural address at the accession to the Chair of Archivistics at the University of Amsterdam (Alphen aan den Rhijn, 1998), p. 10.

66 Ketelaar, 'Archivalisation and Archiving', p. 55.

67 On the poetological differences between *blogging* and traditional, hand-written diary writing, see van Dijck, 'Writing the Self: Of Diaries and Weblogs'.

68 Derrida, *Archive Fever*, p. 10, original emphasis.

69 For a pejorative use of this neologism as an overall term for all the (hyper-) activities of museums, including a critical assessment of 'museum mania'(p. 14) and of a no less questionable 'museum phobia' (p. 17), see Andreas Huyssen, 'Escape from Amnesia: The Museum as Mass Medium', in *Twilight Memories. Marking Time in a Culture of Amnesia* (New York, 1995).

70 Jacques Derrida, *Archive Fever: A Freudian Impression*, trans. Eric Prenowitz (Chicago, IL, and London, 1998), p. 80.

71 Ibid., p. 79.

72 Ibid.

73 Ibid., pp. 76, 80, 79. Derrida writes 'en abyme' twice. The English translator has kept to the French wording (p. 39).

74 Ibid., p. 79.

### Before a Grave

1 Walter Benjamin, 'Weimar' [1927–1940], in Walter Benjamin, *Selected Writings. Vol 2 Part 1*, eds Michael Jennings, Howard Eiland and Gary Smith, trans. Rodney Livingstone (Cambridge, MA, and London, 2005), pp. 148–50.

2 Ibid., p. 149

3 Ibid., p. 150.

4 Lorenz Engell, 'Von Goethes Gartenhaus zu McGoethe. Eine kleine Ideengeschichte des Duplikats', in *Ausfahrt nach Babylon. Essais and Vorträge zur Kritik der Medienkultur* (Weimar, 2002), p. 231.

5 Albrecht Schöne, *Schillers Schädel* (München, 2002), pp. 17–21.

6 Ibid., pp. 5; 39.

7 Quoted in ibid., p. 14.

8 Ibid.

9 Indeed the competently executed dentistry has given rise to doubts as to the authenticity of the skull; cf. Kai Michel, 'Zwei Schädel, ach! . . . ruh'n in Weimars Gruft. Welcher gehört Schiller?', in *Die Zeit*, 19, 04.05.2005.

## 7 Tattooing

This chapter is a revised version of the article that appeared under the title 'Perfor/m/ative Writing: Tattoo, Mark, Signature'.

1 Jacques Derrida, *Monolingualism of the Other: or the Prosthesis of Origin*, trans. Patrick Mensah (Stanford, CA, 1998), p. 78.

2 Georges Didi-Huberman, *Ähnlichkeit und Berührung: Archäologie, Anachronismus und Modernität des Abdrucks*, trans. Christoph Hollender (Köln, 1999), p. 52.

3 Jacques Derrida, 'Signature Event Context', trans. Samuel Weber and Jeffrey Mehlman, in *Limited Inc.* (Evanston, IL, 1988), p. 5; my emphasis.

4 Ibid., p. 6.

5 Cf. Jane Caplan '"National Tattooing": Traditions of Tattooing in Nineteenth-century Europe', in *Written on the Body: The Tattoo in European and American History*, ed. Jane Caplan (London, 2000), pp. 156–73, also Stefan Oetterman, *Zeichen auf der Haut. Die Geschichte der Tätowierung in Europa* (Europäische Verlagsanstalt, 1994), pp. 58–74.

6 Not signing an artwork is nowadays rather unusual and is at most the practice in the field of anonymous craftwork. From the historical point of view the practice of signing works of art has become widespread since the Renaissance referring back to the culture of Antiquity and took place at about the same time as the introduction of techniques of reproduction; cf. Petra Hoftichová, 'Vorwort', in *Malermonogramme. vol. 1. 15–17. Jahrhundert*, trans. Rudolf Rada (Hanau am Main, 1988), pp. 3–10.

7 'The Penal Colony', in the *Penguin Complete Short Stories of Franz Kafka*, ed. Nahum N. Glatzer, trans. Willa and Edwin Muir (Harmondsworth, 1983), p. 140; it was first published in 1919 but it was written in 1914; see the editorial note on p. 469.

8 In his article on 'Handschrift und Tätowierung', in *Schrift*, eds Hans Ulrich Gumbrecht and K. Ludwig Pfeiffer (München, 1993) (Materialität der Zeichen: Reihe A, vol. 12), Alois Hahn goes as far as to see in graphology such an instrument of total surveillance as Foucault describes. Hahn argues that graphology contributes to institutionalizing 'the commissioning of the other'. In such a 'graphological panopticon' handwriting becomes a 'text allowing a collectively legitimated graphological reading of the identity of the victim of interpretation'. (pp. 215–6) Strictly speaking, not much can be objected to this paranoia. Historically, graphology was

at its height in the nineteenth century at the time when criminology and biological positivism took a common interest in the physiognomy of the – no less panoptically visible – facial features, the fingerprint and the hand-writing of criminals. These instruments of surveillance and identification, even if they have been largely superceded by iris and DNA analysis, still feature today amongst police forensic techniques.

9   An overview of this is provided by Oetterman, *Zeichen auf der Haut*, pp. 103–19; detailed case-studies can be found in the collection *Written on the Body*, ed. Caplan.

10   Cf. Alan Govenar, 'The Changing Image of Tattooing in American Culture, 1846–1966', in *Written on the Body*, pp. 214–5; Margo DeMello, *Bodies of Inscription: A Cultural History of the Modern Tattoo Community* (Durham, NC, and London, 2000), p. 50.

11   Friedrich Kittler, *Gramophone, Film, Typewriter*, trans. Geoffrey Winthrop-Young and Michael Wutz (Stanford, CA, 1999), pp. 277, 282.

12   Ibid., p. 277.

13   Ibid., p. 191.

14   Ibid., p. 283.

15   The sight of these spots prompts one to reach for a magnifying glass, and the observer's inspection becomes a dermatological inspection. In the nineteenth century the main interest of clinical research focused primarily on the connection between tattooing and syphilis. As regards the military milieu, James Bradley ('Body Commodification? Class and Tattoos in Victorian Britain', in *Written on the Body*, pp. 143–5) has proved this connection in the case of several European armies, and relevant medical publications also report this, cf. for example *Atlas der Hautkrankheiten*, Vienna 1856 (quoted in Stephan Oetterman, 'On Display: Tattooed Entertainers in America and Germany', in *Written on the Body*, p. 200). See also Caplan, '"National Tattooing"', and Oetterman, *Zeichen auf der Haut*, pp. 58–74. The pathological 'skin flowers' photographed in the 1930s by a French dermatologist using his patients are obscenely beautiful and were published by Gérard Lévy and Serge Bramly under the title *Fleurs de peau*.

16   Roland Barthes, *Camera Lucida: Reflections on Photography* [1980], trans. Richard Howard (London, 1984), pp. 26–8.

17   Cf. here Michael Wetzel's discussion of 'Ge/Spür' in 'Ein Auge zuviel. Derridas Urszenen des Ästhetischen', in Jacques Derrida, *Aufzeichnungen eines Blinden. Das Selbstporträt und andere Ruinen* (Munich, 1997) (Bild und Text), pp. 143–4.

18   For a discussion of 'clinical detail' in visual processes of reading (in the case of Proust's *À la recherche*) cf. Mieke Bal's chapter 'Optical Instruments', in her *The Mottled Screen: Reading Proust Visually*, trans. Anna-Louise Milne (Stanford, CA, 1997), pp. 69–78.

19   Luce Irigaray, *The Sex That Is Not One*, trans. Catherine Porter and Carolyn Burke (Ithaca, NY, 1985) p. 212.

20   DeMello, *Bodies of Inscription*, p. 44.

21   Cf. Oetterman, *Zeichen auf der Haut*, pp. 21–47.

22   The cultural technique of tattooing has been known in Europe since the Celts and was used in the most varied contexts, mostly however in ritual circumstances, for example by crusaders as also by Coptic Christians to incarnate their adherence to the faith. The *word* 'tattoo' was first brought to Europe by Cook who, along with the South Sea Islander Omai as a curiosity, also introduced a new discourse into the salons of Europe: a new way of talking about an ancient cultural practice which until that date had been called 'pointing', 'painting', 'engraving', 'pricking', 'marking', 'branding' or *compungere*. Cf. Oetterman, *Zeichen auf der Haut*, pp. 9–20.

23   Herman Melville, *Moby-Dick or, The White Whale* [1851] (London, 1962), pp. 50, 113, 114.

24   Juliet Fleming, in her brilliant article on 'The Renaissance Tattoo', in *Written on the Body*, pp. 61–82, discusses the act of naming by tattooing and the cultural norms that frame it. Depending on cultural norms and on practices of name-'giving', a tattoo can have various functions. Either it is 'a scandalously prosthetic act of naming — one that labels, rather than divines, the essence of a person or thing'. Or it may 'cause identity retroactively' (p. 82). The latter description indeed fits freely chosen, postmodern tattooing as a performative, drawing its power from a 'retroactive' repetition.

25   The idea that the proper name has a magic force (or spell) is discussed by Jacques Derrida in his chapter 'The Battle of Proper Names' (*Of Grammatology* [1967], trans. Gayatri Chakravorty Spivak (Baltimore, MD, and London, 1976), pp. 107–18). Against Lévi-Strauss's ethnological classification of the Nambikwara Native Americans as savage and 'without writing', because that society forbids the use of the proper name, Derrida argues that it is precisely knowledge about the 'magic spell' of the name, which consists in making the named one nameable and hence present even in their absence, that marks their culture according to the structure of *écriture*.

26   Derrida, *Of Grammatology*, p. 113.

27   Cf. DeMello, *Bodies of Inscription*, pp. 56–7; Tony Cohen, *The Tattoo* (Mosman/New South Wales, 2000), pp. 29; 52.

28   Quoted in DeMello, *Bodies of Inscription*, p. 57.

29   The rhetorical charge inherent in the question 'What's the difference?' has been demonstrated masterfully by Paul de Man in 'Semiology and Rhetoric' (in *Allegories of Reading: Figural Language in Rousseau, Nietzsche, Rilke, and Proust* (New Haven and London, 1979), pp. 9–10). He develops his concept of undecidability by making Archie Bunker ask his wife the 'difference' between the lacing over and lacing under of bowling shoes. A grammatical pattern such as the question: 'What's the difference?' can produce two different, mutually-exclusive rhetorical

structures: one that wants to know the difference and another that does not give a damn about the difference.

30   Cf. Donna Haraway's essay on the origin of the Natural History Museum in New York: 'Teddy Bear Patriarchy: Taxidermy in the Garden of Eden', in *Social Text*, ɪɪ (1984), pp. 20–64.

31   J. L. Austin, *How To Do Things With Words* (Oxford, 1962), p. 22; my emphasis.

32   Derrida, 'Signature Event Context', p. 17.

33   Judith Butler, *Bodies that Matter: On the Discursive Matters of 'Sex'* (New York, 1993), p. 12.

34   Derrida, 'Signature Event Context', p. 12.

35   Susan Benson, 'Inscriptions of the Self: Reflections on Tattooing and Piercing in Contemporary Euro-America', in *Written on the Body*, p. 242; my emphasis.

36   At www.tattooarchive.com/history/great_omi.htm [15.03.05].

37   Didier Anzieu, *The Skin Ego: A Psychoanalytic Approach to the Self*, trans. Chris Turner (New Haven and London, 1989), p. 9.

38   Ibid., pp. 40, 10.

39   I should like to thank my son, Jonas Neef, for this technical detail, being an expert on all things relating to Harry Potter and being, as a namesake of Jonah, also a specialist on questions to do with whales. His name is particularly apt since on close examination it turns out to be an exact anagram of his mother's name.

40   Melville, *Moby-Dick*, p. 202.

41   Irigaray, *The Sex That Is Not One*, pp. 217–8.

42   Derrida, 'Signature Event Context', p. 20.

43   Self-tattooing is widespread – in all periods – particularly in the case of imprisonment; see for example Abby M. Schrader, 'Branding the Other/ Tattooing the Self: Bodily Inscription among Convicts in Russia and the Soviet Union' in *Written on the Body*, pp. 174–92. The tattooing instruments, put together from a combination of a toothbrush, an electric razor and parts of a ballpoint pen, are worthy of note; see the Internet for relevant instructions on how to construct them.

### Before a Wall

1   I have Eric Ketelaar, who knows his city as well as his archive, to thank for pointing out this address.

### 8 Graffiti

This chapter is a revised version of the article that appeared under the title 'Killing Kool: The Graffiti Museum'.

1   Walter Benjamin, *The Arcades Project* [1927–1940], trans. Howard Eiland and Kevin McLaughlin (Cambridge, MA, and London, 1999), p. 175.

2   Marc Augé, *Non-Places: An Introduction to an Anthropology of Supermodernity* [1992], trans. John Howe (London and New York, 1995), pp. 86, 97; my emphasis.

3   Michel de Certeatu, 'Spatial Stories', in *The Practice of Everyday Life* [1980], trans. Steven Rendall (Berkeley and London, 1984), p. 117, emphasis in original.

4   Augé, *Non-Places*, p. 95, emphasis in original.

5   Ibid., p. 85, emphasis in original.

6   For documentation on the border within Germany, see Robert Lebegern, *Mauer, Zaun und Stacheldraht: Sperranlagen an der innerdeutschen Grenze 1945–1990* (Weiden, 2002).

7   Not until the end of 2006 were signs put up on the occasion of the sixteenth anniversary of the Fall of the Wall on the former Autobahn crossing points, i.e. on the A2, A4, A9, A20, A24, A71 and A73. They carry the words: 'Former border within Germany 1945–1990'. There is now also such a sign in Herleshausen. *Between* the crossing points, border archaeologists try in fact without success to find remaining traces of the unmarked death strip.

8   Jean Baudrillard, 'KOOL KILLER, or The Insurrection of Signs', in *Symbolic Exchange and Death*, trans. Iain Hamilton Grant (London, 1993), p. 24.

9   Ibid., pp. 76, 83.

10  The literature on graffiti styles is enormous. See, for example, Jeff Ferrell, *Crimes of Style: Urban Graffiti and the Politics of Criminality* (New York and London, 1993); Johannes Stahl, *Graffiti: zwischen Alltag und Ästhetik* (München, 1990); Beat Suter, *Graffiti: Rebellion der Zeichen* (Frankfurt am Main, 1988).

11  Baudrillard, 'KOOL KILLER', p. 34.

12  Ibid., pp. 82.

13  See Ferrell, *Crimes of Style*.

14  Baudrillard, 'KOOL KILLER', pp. 78, 79, 83.

15  Ibid., p. 26 (my emphasis).

16  Ibid., pp. 78–9, 83.

17  Ibid., pp. 80, 82.

18  Judith Butler, *Excitable Speech: A Politics of the Performative* (New York and London, 1997), pp. 72–3.

19  Mieke Bal, *Double Exposures: The Subject of Cultural Analysis* (New York and London, 1996), pp. 1–2; Bal's emphasis; also 'Introduction' to *The Practice of Cultural Analysis: Exposing Interdisciplinary Interpretation*, eds Mieke Bal and Hent de Vries (Stanford, CA, 1999), p. 5. For the analysis of 'apo-deiknymai' Bal refers to Gregory Nagy, *Pindar's Homer: The Lyric Possession of an Epic Past* (Baltimore, MD, 1990), pp. 217–20.

20  Bal, *Double Exposures*, p. 88.

21  The 'trade mark' of the Amsterdam School for Cultural Analysis (ASCA) founded by Mieke Bal is this example of graffiti.

22  Bal, *The Practice of Cultural Analysis*, p. 4.

23  Cf. Beat Suter, *Graffiti*, pp. 155–61.

24  Baudrillard, 'KOOL KILLER', p. 83.

25  On conceptual metaphors I refer to Lakoff and Johnson, *Metaphors We Live By*.

26  Jacques Derrida, 'Otobiographien – Die Lehre Nietzsches und die Politik des Eigennamens. 1. Unabhängigkeitserklärungen', in Derrida and Friedrich Kittler, *Nietzsche – Politik des Eigennamens: wie man abschafft, wovon man spricht* (Berlin, 2000), p. 14; trans. here by Anthony Mathews.

27  Paul de Man, 'Semiology and Rhetoric', in *Allegories of Reading: Figural Language in Rousseau, Nietzsche, Rilke, and Proust* (New Haven and London, 1979), pp. 11–2.

28  Baudrillard, 'KOOL KILLER', pp. 83, 76.

29  Bal, *The Practice of Cultural Analysis*, p. 3.

30  See Jacques Derrida's celebrated 'Parergon' chapter (in *The Truth in Painting* [1978], trans. Geoff Bennington and Ian McLeod (Chicago, 1987), pp. 37–82), in which he deals with the 'Parergon' that dictionaries mostly translate as '*hors-d'œuvre*', but also as 'accessory, foreign or secondary object', 'supplement', 'aside', 'remainder', in which he describes this superfluous thing as something which 'does not however stand simply outside the work [hors d'œuvre]', but also acts 'alongside, right up against the work [*ergon*]'.(p. 54)

31  Jacques Derrida, 'Otobiographies – The Teaching of Nietzsche and the Politics of the Proper Name', in Derrida, *The Ear of the Other*, trans. Peggy Kamuf (Lincoln, NE, and London, 1988), p. 8.

32  For an overview of the theological debate on the exegesis of this passage, see the discussion by Alexander Campbell, *Christian Baptism with Its Antecedents and Consequents*, [1851], at www.mun.ca/rels/restmov/texts/ acampbell/cbac/CBAC00.HTM [accessed 17.05.2006].

33  I owe this idea of graffiti as wallpaper to my student Frank Langer.

34  Heinz J. Kuzdas, *Berliner Mauer Kunst/Berlin Wall Art. Mit East Side Gallery.* Text by Michael Nungesser (Berlin, 1998), pp. 16–17; Rainer Hildebrandt, *Die Mauer spricht/The Wall Speaks* (Berlin, 1992), pp. 9–17.

35  Robert Musil, 'Denkmale' [1936], in *Nachlass zu Lebzeiten* (Reinbek bei Hamburg, 1962), p. 62.

36  Michel de Certeau, *The Practice of Everyday Life* [1980], trans. Steven Rendall (Berkeley and London, 1984), p. 124 (de Certeau's emphasis).

37  See, for example, *Le mur de Berlin. Vente aux Enchères à Monte-Carlo, Samedi 23 Juin 1990*.

38  See Angelika von Stocki, *Zerfall der Mauer/Fall of the Wall* (Berlin, 1995), p. 16; Kuzdas, *Berliner Mauer Kunst*, pp. 32, 40, 50, also www.berlin.de/mauergedenken [1.05.07]

39  Bal, *Double Exposures*, p. 57.
40  Ibid., p. 2

**9 Paralipomena**

1  Jacques Derrida, *Cinders*, trans. and ed. Ned Lukacher (Lincoln, NE, and London, 1991), p. 43.
2  Jacques Derrida, *Of Grammatology* [1967], trans. Gayatri Chakravorty Spivak (Baltimore, MD, and London, 1976), pp. 62–3.
3  Vilém Flusser, *Die Schrift. Hat Schreiben Zukunft?* [1987], ed. Andreas Müller-Pohle, Edition Flusser, vol. 5 (Göttingen, 2002), pp. 152–3.
4  Derrida, *Of Grammatology*, p. 46.
5  Michael Knoche, *Die Bibliothek brennt* (Göttingen, 2006), pp. 84–6.
6  Georges Didi-Huberman, *Ähnlichkeit und Berührung: Archäologie, Anachronismus und Modernität des Abdrucks*, trans. Christoph Hollender (Köln, 1999), p. 17; emphasis in the original.
7  Lászlo Moholy-Nagy, 'Produktion – Reproduktion', pp. 98–9, trans. by Frederic Samson in: Andreas Haus, *Moholy-Nagy: Photographs and Photograms*, pp. 46–7;  see also Kittler, *Gramophone*, pp. 46–47.

# Bibliography

Ackeri, Henrici, *Historia Pennarum. Pennae inclitissimi polyhistoris et consummatissimi theology. 10. Francisc. Buddei* (Altenburg, 1726)

Alphen, Ernst van, *Caught by History: Holocaust Effects in Contemporary Art, Literature, and Theory* (Stanford, CA, 1997)

——, 'Symptoms of Discursivity: Experience, Memory, and Trauma', in *Acts of Memory*, eds Mieke Bal, Jonathan Crewe and Leo Spitzer (Hanover, NH, and London, 1990), pp. 24–38

Andrews, Carol, *The Rosetta Stone* (London, 2003)

Anzieu, Didier, *The Skin Ego: A Psychoanalytic Approach to the Self*, trans. Chris Turner (New Haven, CT, and London, 1989)

Aristotle, *De Anima* (On the Soul), trans. J. A. Smith, in *The Basic Works of Aristotle*, eds Richard McKeon (New York, 2001)

——, *De Memoria et Reminiscentia* (Of Memory and Remembering), trans. J. I. Beare, in *The Basic Works of Aristotle*, ed. Richard McKeon (New York, 2001)

——, *Parts of Animals*, trans. A. L. Peck (London, 1937)

Assmann, Aleida, 'Pflug, Schwert, Feder. Kulturwerkzeuge als Herrschaftszeichen', in *Schrift*, eds Hans Ulrich Gumbrecht and K. Ludwig Pfeiffer (Munich, 1993) (Materialität der Zeichen: Reihe A, vol. XII), pp. 219–31

——, and Jan Assmann, 'Einleitung. Schrift-Kognition-Evolution. Eric A. Havelock und die Technologie kultureller Kommunikation', in Eric Alfred Havelock, *Schriftlichkeit. Das griechische Alphabet und die kulturelle Revolution*, ed. Aleida and Jan Assmann, pp. 1–35 (Weinheim, 1990)

Assmann, Jan, 'Die Ägyptische Schriftkultur', in *HSK*, x/1, pp. 472–91

——, 'Sieben Funktionen der ägyptischen Hieroglyphenschrift', in *Materialität and Medialität von Schrift*, eds Erika Greber, Konrad Ehlich and Jan-Dirk Müller (Bielefeld, 2002) (Schrift und Bild in Bewegung, vol. I), pp. 31–50

Augé, Marc, *Non-Places: Introduction to an Anthropology of Supermodernity* [1992], trans. John Howe (London and New York, 1995)

Austin, John L., *How To Do Things With Words* (Oxford, 1962)

Aydemir, Murat, 'Gossamer Thread: Textuality, Ejaculation, Proust', in *Travelling Concepts: Text Subjectivity, Hybridity*, eds Joyce Goggin and Sonja Neef (Amsterdam, 2001), pp. 43–54

Aydemir, Murat, *Images of Bliss: Ejaculation, Masculinity, Meaning* (Minneapolis, MN, 2007)

Bain, Peter, and Paul Shaw, eds, *Blackletter: Type and National Identity* (Princeton, NJ, 1998)

Bal, Mieke, *Double Exposures: The Subject of Cultural Analysis* (New York and London, 1996)

——, 'Introduction', in *The Practice of Cultural Analysis: Exposing Interdisciplinary Interpretation*, ed. Mieke Bal and Hent de Vries (Stanford, CA, 1999), pp. 1–14

——, 'Introduction', in *Acts of Memory*, eds Mieke Bal, Jonathan Crewe and Leo
Spitzer (Hanover, NH, and London, 1990), pp. vii–xvii

——, 'Memory Acts: Performing Subjektivity', in *Performance Research*, v/3
(2000), pp. 102–14

——, *Quoting Caravaggio: Contemporary Art, Preposterous History* (Chicago and
London, 1999)

——, *Reading Rembrandt, Beyond the Word Image Opposition* (New York and
Cambridge, 1994)

——, 'Telling Objects: A Narrative Perspective on Collecting', in *The Cultures of
Collecting*, eds John Elsner and Roger Cardinal (London, 1994), pp. 97–115

——, *The Mottled Screen: Reading Proust Visually*, trans. Anna-Louise Milne
(Stanford, CA, 1997)

——, *Travelling Concepts in the Humanities: A Rough Guide* (Toronto, Buffalo
and London, 2002)

——, Jonathan Crewe and Leo Spitzer, eds, *Acts of Memory: Cultural Recall in
the Present* (Hanover, NH, and London, 1990)

Barnouw, David, 'Aanvallen op de echtheid van het dagboek', in *De dagboeken
van Anne Frank*, eds Harry Paape, Gerrold van der Stroom and David
Barnouw (Amsterdam, 1990), pp. 99–119

Barthes, Roland, '*Non multa sed multum*' [1976], trans. Henry Martin, in
*Writings on Cy Twombly*, ed. Nicola del Roscio (Munich, 2002), pp. 88–101

——, *Camera Lucida: Reflections on Photography* [1980], trans. Richard Howard
(London, 1984)

——, *The Pleasure of the Text* [1973], trans. Richard Miller (London, 1976)

Baudrillard, Jean, 'KOOL KILLER, or The Insurrection of Signs', in *Symbolic
Exchange and Death*, trans. Iain Hamilton Grant (London, 1993), pp. 76–84

Bauer, Thomas, 'Arabic Writing', in *The World's Writing Systems*, eds Peter T.
Daniels and William Bright (New York and Oxford, 1996), pp. 559–64

Bedini, Silvio A., *Thomas Jefferson and His Copying Machines* (Charlottesville,
VA, 1984)

Benjamin, Walter, 'A Small History of Photography' [1931], in *One-Way Street
and Other Writings*, trans. Edmund Jephcott and Kinsley Shorter
(London, 1997), pp. 240–57

——, *The Arcades Project* [1927–1940], trans. Howard Eiland and Kevin
McLaughlin (Cambridge, MA, and London, 1999)

——, 'The Work of Art in the Age of Mechanical Reproduction' [1936], trans.
Harry Zohn, in *Illuminations*, ed. Hannah Arendt (London, 1992), pp.
211–44

——, 'Weimar' [1927–1940], trans. Rodney Livingstone, in Walter Benjamin,
*Selected Writings. Vol 2 Part 1*, eds Michael Jennings, Howard Eiland and
Gary Smith (Cambridge, MA, and London, 2005), pp. 148–150

Bennington, Geoffrey and Jacques Derrida, *Jacques Derrida* [1991], trans.
Geoffrey Bennington (Chicago and London, 1993)

Benson, Susan, 'Inscriptions of the Self: Reflections on Tattooing and Piercing in

Contemporary Euro-America', in *Written on the Body: The Tattoo in European and American History*, ed. Jane Caplan (London, 2000), pp. 234–54

Bergh, Thomas van den, 'Handschrift. Van krul tot hanenpoot', *Elsevier*, 21.10.2006, pp. 120–21

Bieheim, Stefanie, *Der Tintenkiller. Techniken des Einschreibens and Auslöschens*, Thesis supervised by Sonja Neef, Bauhaus-University Weimar 2006, Sommersemester 2006

Binet, Alfred, 'Note sur l'écriture hystérique', in *Revue Philosophique de la France et de l'étranger*, 23 (1887), pp. 67–70

——, 'Une expérience collective, en séance, sur les relations entre l'écriture et l'intelligence', in *Bulletin*, 15 (1904), pp. 395–7

——, and Jules Courtier, 'Sur la vitesse des mouvements graphiques', in *Revue philosophique*, xviii/1–6; 35 (1893), pp. 664–71

——, and ——, 'Expériences sur la vitesse des mouvements graphiques', in *Revue philosophique,* 37 (1894), pp. 111–12

Bischoff, Bernhard, 'Elementarunterricht und Probationes Pennae in der ersten Hälfte des Mittelalters', in *Mittelalterliche Studien 1* (Stuttgart, 1966), pp. 74–87

——, *Ein neu entdeckter modus scribendi des 15. Jahrhanderts aus der Abtei Melk* (Berlin, 1939)

——, *Paläographie des römischen Altertums und des abendländischen Mittelalters*, 2nd extended edn (Berlin, 1986) (Grundlagen der Germanistik 24)

Bissinger, Manfred, *Hitlers Sternstunde. Kujau, Heidemann und die Millionen* (Hamburg, 1984)

Boecker, Arne, 'Durchhalten mit Härte 2B', in *Die Zeit*, 30.07.2001

Boge, Herbert, *Griechische Tachygraphie und Tironische Noten. Ein Handbuch der mittelalterlichen und antiken Schnellschrift* (Berlin, 1973)

Bolter, Jay David, and Richard Grusin, *Remediation: Understanding New Media* (Cambridge, MA, and London, 1999)

Boswell, David, and Jessica Evens, eds, *Representing the Nation: A Reader* [1999] (New York and London, 2005)

Bradley, James, 'Body Commodification? Class and Tattoos in Victorian Britain', in *Written on the Body: The Tattoo in European and American History*, ed. Jane Caplan (London, 2000), pp. 136–55

Brekle, Herbert E., *Die Antiqualinie von ca. -1500 bis ca. +1500. Untersuchungen zur Morphogenese des westlichen Alphabets auf kognitivistischer Basis* (Münster, 1994)

——, 'Die Buchstabenformen westlicher Alphabetschriften in ihrer historischen Entwicklung', in *HSK*, x/1, pp. 171–204

Brokken, Jan, 'Schrijven is bijna niet kunnen schrijven. Harry Mulisch', in *Schrijven. Interviews met*, pp. 11–21; digitale bibliotheek voor de nederlandse letteren, 2002 [1980], at www.dbnl.org/tekst/brok002schr01_01/brok002schr01_01_0002.htm [accessed 22.07.2006]

Brouwers, Ton, 'Anne Frank', in *Kritisch Literatuur Lexikon*, eds Ad Zuiderent, Hugo Brems and Tom van Deel (Amsterdam, 2002)

Brown, Michelle P., *The British Library Guide to Writing and Scripts* (London, 1998)

Bryson, Norman, *Vision and Painting: The Logic of the Gaze* (London, 1983)

Burghagen, Otto, *Die Schreibmaschine. Illustrierte Beschreibung aller gangbaren Schreibmaschinen nebst gründlicher Anleitung zum Arbeiten auf sämtlichen Systemen* (Hamburg, 1898)

Butler, Judith, *Excitable Speech: A Politics of the Performative* (New York and London, 1997)

——, *Bodies that Matter: On the Discursive Matters of 'Sex'* (New York, 1993)

Campbell, Alexander, *Christian Baptism, with Its Antecedents and Consequents* [1851], at www.mun.ca/rels/restmov/texts/acampbell/cbac/CBAC00.HTM [accessed 17.05.2006]

Campe, Rüdiger, 'Schreiben im Prozess. Kafkas ausgesetzte Schreibszene', in *'SCHREIBKUGEL IST EIN DING GLEICH MIR: VON EISEN': Schreibszenen im Zeitalter der Typoskripte*, ed. Davide Giuriato, Martin Stingelin and Sandro Zanetti (Munich, 2005) (Zur Genealogie des Schreibens 2)

Caplan, Jane, '"National Tattooing": Traditions of Tattooing in Nineteenth-century Europe', in *Written on the Body: The Tattoo in European and American History*, ed. Jane Caplan (London, 2000), pp. 156–73

——, ed., *Written on the Body: The Tattoo in European and American History* (London, 2000)

Carstairs-McCarthy, Andrew, *The Origins of Complex Language: An Inquiry into the Evolutionary Beginnings of Sentences, Syllables, and Truth* (Oxford, 1999)

Certeau, Michel de, 'Spatial Stories', in *The Practice of Everyday Life* [1980], trans. Steven Rendall (Berkeley and London, 1984), pp. 115–30

Champollion, Jean-François, *Grammaire Égyptienne, ou principes généraux de l'écriture sacrée égyptienne (appliqué à la représentation de la langue parlée)* [1835], ed. Michel Sidhom (Paris, 1984)

Clark, Juan Manuel, *Füllfederhalter*, trans. Ingrid Ickler (Paris, 2005)

Clifford, James, 'On Collecting Art and Culture', in *The Predicament of Culture: Twentieth-Century Ethnography, Literature and Art* (Cambridge, MA, 1988), pp. 215–51

Cohen, Tony, *The Tattoo* (Mosman, New South Wales, 2000)

Cole, Simon A., *Suspect Identities: A History of Fingerprinting and Criminal Identification* (Cambridge, MA, and London, 2002)

Conan Doyle, Sir Arthur, 'A Case of Identity', in *The Penguin Complete Sherlock Holmes* (London, 1981)

Coulmas, Florian, *Über Schrift* (Frankfurt am Main, 1981)

Czichos, Horst, *Was ist falsch am falschen Rembrandt? und Wie hart ist Damaszener Stahl? Wie man mit Technik Kunst erforscht, prüft and erhält* (Berlin, 2002)

Dalgarno, George, *Didascalocophus, or; The Deaf and Dumb Mans Tutor* [1680] (Oxford and Menston, England, 1971) (English Linguistics 1500–1800, No. 286)

Daniels, Peter T., and William Bright, eds, *The World's Writing Systems* (New York and Oxford, 1996)

Dekeyser, Hannelore, 'Authenticity in Bits and Bytes', in *Sign Here! Handwriting in the Age of New Media*, eds Sonja Neef, José van Dijck and Eric Ketelaar (Amsterdam, 2006), pp. 76–90

DeMello, Margo, *Bodies of Inscription: A Cultural History of the Modern Tattoo Community* (Durham, NC, and London, 2000)

Denucé, Jan, 'Introduction', in *Mercator, Gerardus, 1512–1594: The Treatise of Gerard Mercator: literarum latinarum, quas italicas, cursoriasque vocant, scribendarium ratio (Antwerp 1540)*, ed. in facsimile by Jan Denucé (Antwerp and Paris, 1930)

Derrida, Jacques, *Archive Fever: A Freudian Impression* [1995], trans. Eric Prenowitz (Chicago, 1998)

——, *Aufzeichnungen eines Blinden. Das Selbstporträt und andere Ruinen* [1990], ed. Michael Wetzel, trans. Andreas Knop and Michael Wetzel (Munich, 1997) (Bild und Text)

——, *Cinders*, trans. and ed. Ned Lukacher (Lincoln, NE, and London, 1991)

——, 'Différance', in *Speech and Phenomena and Other Essays on Husserl's Theory of Signs*, trans. David. B. Allison (Evanston, IL, 1973), pp. 3–27

——, 'Fors. Die Winkelwörter von N. Abraham and M. Torok', in *Kryptonymie. Das Verbarium des Wolfsmanns*, eds Nicolas Abraham and Maria Torok (Frankfurt am Main, 1979), pp. 7–58

——, 'Heidegger's Hand (Geschlecht II)', trans. John P. Leavey Jr, in *Psyche: Inventions of the Other, Vol. II*, eds Peggy Kamuf and Elizabeth Rottenberg (Stanford, CA, 2007–8), pp. 42–3

——, 'How to Avoid Speaking: Denials' [1987], trans. Ken Frieden, in *Languages of the Unsayable: The Play of Negativity in Literature and Literary Theory*, ed. Sanford Budick and Wolfgang Iser (New York, 1989), pp. 3–70

——, 'Limited Inc. abc…', trans. Samuel Weber in *Limited Inc.* (Evanston, IL, 1988), pp. 29–110

——, *Limited Inc.* (Evanston, IL, 1988)

——, *Monolinguism of the Other: or the Prosthesis of Origin*, trans. Patrick Mensah (Stanford, CA, 1998)

——, *Of Grammatology* [1967], trans. Gayatri Chakravorty Spivak (Baltimore, MD, and London, 1976)

——, 'Otobiographies – The Teaching of Nietzsche and the Politics of the Proper Name', in Derrida, *The Ear of the Other*, trans. Peggy Kamuf (Lincoln, NE, and London, 1988), pp. 3–38; German version: 'Otobiographien – Die Lehre Nietzsches und die Politik des Eigennamens. 1. Unabhängigkeitserklärungen', in Derrida and Friedrich Kittler, *Nietzsche – Politik des Eigennamens: wie man abschafft, wovon man spricht* (Berlin, 2000)

——, 'Signature Event Context', trans. Samuel Weber and Jeffrey Mehlman, in
*Limited Inc.* (Evanston, IL, 1988), pp. 1–23

——, *The Truth in Painting* [1978], trans. Geoff Bennington and Ian McLeod
(Chicago, 1987)

——, and Lucette Finas, 'Avoir l'oreille de la philosophie. Entretien de Lucette
Finas avec Jacques Derrida', in *Écarts. Quatre essais à propos de Jacques
Derrida*, eds Lucette Finas, Sarah Kofman, Roger Laporte and Jean-Michel
Rey (Paris, 1973), pp. 303–16

'De school, 100 jaar geleden', in: *Basiskennis geschiedenis. 5. Vanaf de industriële
revolutie*, S. 811, http://people.zeelandnet.nl/gwpgabr/files/geschiedenis/
Reader%20%20BKN-GES-5%20%20Vanaf%20de%20Industriele%20
Revolutie.pdf [accessed 12.12.2006]

Dewitz, Bodo von, and Roland Scotti, eds, *Alles Wahrheit! Alles Lüge!
Photographie und Wirklichkeit im 19. Jahrhandert. Die Sammlung Robert
Lebeck*, on the occasion of the exhibition at the Wallraf-Richardz-
Museum, Köln, 30.11.199602.02.1997 (Amsterdam and Dresden, 1996)

Didi-Huberman, Georges, *Ähnlichkeit und Berührung: Archäologie,
Anachronismus und Modernität des Abdrucks*, trans. Christoph Hollender
(Cologne, 1999) (*L'Empreinte*. Paris, 1997)

——, *The Invention of Hysteria: Charcot and the Photographic Iconography of the
Salpêtrière*, trans. Alisa Hartz (Cambridge, MA, 2003)

Dietlein, Hermann Rudolph, *Wegweiser für den Schreibunterricht. Eine theoretisch-praktische Anweisung zur Begründung und Durchführung einer allseitig
naturgemäßen Schreiblehr-Methode, mit besonderer Berücksichtigung der
Volksschule, für Lehrer aller Schulanstalten, welche Schreibunterricht zu
ertheilen haben* (Leipzig, 1856)

Dijck, José van, 'Writing the Self: Of Diaries and Weblogs', in *Sign Here!
Handwriting in the Age of New Media*, eds Sonja Neef, José van Dijck and
Eric Ketelaar (Amsterdam, 2006), pp. 116–33

——, and Sonja Neef, 'Introduction', in *Sign Here! Handwriting in the Age of
New Media*, eds Sonja Neef, José van Dijck and Eric Ketelaar (Amsterdam,
2006), pp. 7–17

Domarus, Max, *Hitlers Reden und Proklamationen*, 2 vols (1962–3)

Drösser, Christoph, 'Schreiben im All', in *Die Zeit*, 10, 02.03.2006

Duchamp, Marcel, *Notes*, ed. Paul Matisse (Boston, 1983)

Durlacher, Jessica, *De dochter. Roman* (Amsterdam, 2000)

Eisenstein, Elizabeth, *The Printing Press as an Agent of Change: Communications
and Cultural Transformations in Early-Modern Europe* (Cambridge, 1980)

Eisler, Tobias, *Das aufs neue wohl zubereitete Tinten=faß: oder Anweisung, wie
man gute schwarze, buntfaerbige, auch andere curioese Tinten auf mancherlei
Weise zubereiten, auch wie man Gold, Silber und anderen Metallen aus der
Feder auf Pappier, Pergament and andere Dinge schreiben solle; nebst noch
andern zur Schreiberei gehoerigen noethigen and nuetzlichen Stuecken*
(Helmstaedt, 1733)

Eisler-Feldafing, Robert, 'Platon und das ägyptische Alphabet', in *Archiv für Philosophie*, 34 (1922), pp. 3–13 (Berlin, 1970)

Engell, Lorenz, 'Die genetische Funktion des Historischen in der Geschichte der Bildmedien', in *Mediale Historiographien*, eds Lorenz Engell and Joseph Vogl (Weimar, 2001), pp. 33–56 (Archiv für Mediengeschichte 1)

——, 'Von Goethes Gartenhaus zu McGoethe. Eine kleine Ideengeschichte des Duplikats', in *Ausfahrt nach Babylon. Essais und Vorträge zur Kritik der Medienkultur* (Weimar, 2002), pp. 231–43

——, and Joseph Vogl, 'Editorial', in *Mediale Historiographien*, eds Lorenz Engell and Joseph Vogl (Weimar, 2001), pp. 5–8 (Archiv für Mediengeschichte 1)

Erasmus of Rotterdam, 'De libero arbitrio. Hyperaspistis diatribae adversus servum arbitrium Martini Lutheri. Liber primus'. 'Erstes Buch über die Unterredung "Hyperaspistes" gegen den "Unfreien Willen" Martin Luthers' [1527], in *Ausgewählte Schriften*, Latin and German, vol. IV, trans., intro. and annotated by Winfried Lesowsky, pp. 197–673 (Darmstadt, 1995)

——, *The Collected Works of Erasmus. Vol. 85: Poems*, trans. Clarence H. Miller, ed. Harry Vredeveld (Toronto and London, 1993)

Erbach, Karl, *Lehrgang der deutschen Kurzschrift* (Darmstadt, 1938)

Ernst, Wolfgang, *Das Rumoren der Archive. Ordnung aus Unordnung* (Berlin, 2002)

——, 'Mit dem Gespür des Stil(ett)s: Klio in den Spuren von Atlantis (Historiograffiti)', in *Stil. Geschichten und Funktionen eines kultur-wissenschaftlichen Diskurselements*, eds Hans Ulrich Gumbrecht and K. Ludwig Pfeiffer (Frankfurt am Main, 1986), pp. 15–30

Eule, Wilhelm, *Mit Stift and Feder. Kleine Kulturgeschichte der Schreib- and Zeichenwerkzeuge* (Leipzig, 1955)

Faye, Emmanuel, *Heidegger – l'introduction du nazisme dans la philosophie: Autour des séminaires inédits de 1933–1935* (Paris, 2005) (Bibliothèque des idées)

Fechner-Smarsly, Thomas, 'Blood Samples and Fingerprint Files: Blood as Artificial Matter, Artistic Material, and Means of the Signature', in *Sign Here! Handwriting in the Age of New Media*, eds Sonja Neef, José van Dijck and Eric Ketelaar (Amsterdam, 2006), pp. 196–205

Ferrell, Jeff, *Crimes of Style: Urban Graffiti and the Politics of Criminality* (New York and London, 1993)

Fischer, Wolfgang Georg, and Fritz von der Schulenburg, *Die Mauer: Monument des Jahrhanderts* (Berlin, 1990)

Fleming, Juliet, 'The Renaissance Tattoo', in *Written on the Body: The Tattoo in European and American History*, eds Jane Caplan (London, 2000), pp. 61–82

Flusser, Vilém, *Die Schrift. Hat Schreiben Zukunft?* [1987], ed. Andreas Müller-Pohle, Edition Flusser, vol. 5 (Göttingen, 2002)

Foerster, Hans, and Thomas Frenz, *Abriss der lateinischen Paläographie* [1949], extended edition with additional chapter 'Die Schriften der Neuzeit' by Thomas Frenz (Stuttgart: Hiersemann, 2004) (Bibliothek des Buchwesens, vol. 15)

Foucault, Michel, *The Archaeology of Knowledge* [1972], trans. A. M. Sheridan Smith (London and New York, 2002)

Fraenkel, Béatrice, *La signature. Genèse d'un signe* (Paris, 1992)

Frank, Anne, [*De dagboeken van Anne Frank*, bronuitgave], text-historical critical edition by David Barnouw and Gerrold van der Stroom, in *De dagboeken van Anne Frank*, eds Harry Paape, Gerrold van der Stroom and David Barnouw (Amsterdam, 1990), pp. 189–736. English edition: *The Diary of Anne Frank: The Critical Edition*, trans. Arnold J. Pomerans and B. M. Mooyart (New York and London, 1989)

Franke, Werner, 'Papierbezogene Echtheitsprüfung der sogenannten "Hitler-Tagebücher"', in *BAM-Jahresbericht 1983*

Franzke, Jürgen, and Peter Schafhauser, 'Faber-Castell. Die Bleistiftdynastie', in Henry Petroski, *Der Bleistift. Die Geschichte eines Gebrauchsgegenstands. Mit einem Anhang zur Geschichte des Unternehmens Faber-Castell*, trans. Sabine Rochlitz (Basel, Boston and Berlin, 1995), pp. 331–60

Freitag, Egon, '"Wenn … eine vertraute Feder meine Worte auffängt." Schreibgeräte and kreatives Schreiben im 18. and 19. Jahrhandert', in *Werkzeuge des Pegasus. Historische Schreibzeuge im Goethe-Nationalmuseum*, ed. Egon Freitag et al., exh. cat., Stiftung Weimarer Klassik, 9 November–5 January 2003, designed and produced by Egon Freitag, Viola Geyersbach, Susanne Schroeder, ed. Reiner Schlichting (Weimar, 2003), pp. 937

Freitag, Egon et al., eds, *Werkzeuge des Pegasus. Historische Schreibzeuge im Goethe-Nationalmuseum*, exh. cat., Stiftung Weimarer Klassik, 9 November–5 January 2003, designed and produced by Egon Freitag, Viola Geyersbach, Susanne Schroeder, ed. Reiner Schlichting (Weimar, 2003)

Freiwirth, S., *Der Arzt für Hand und Handschrift oder S. Freiwirth's neuestes Lehrsystem, nach welchem sich ein jeder Schlechtschreibende ohne Lehrer in nicht mehr als acht Lektionen eine Fertigkeit im Schön-Schnellschreiben aneignen kann. Erster Theil: die deutsche Handschrift* (Leipzig, 1855)

Freud, Sigmund, 'Fetishism' [1927], in *The Standard Edition of the Complete Psychological Works of Sigmund Freud*, vol xxi, trans. John Strachey (London, 1961), pp. 379–89

——, 'Note on the Mystic Writing Pad' [1925], in *The Standard Edition of the Complete Psychological Works of Sigmund Freud*, vol xix, trans. John Strachey (London, 1961), pp. 227–32

——, 'Symbolism in Dreams' [1915]. Part Two: 'Dreams', Chap. 10, in *The Standard Edition of the Complete Psychological Works of Sigmund Freud*, vol xv, trans. John Strachey (London, 1961), pp. 149–69

Frizot, Michel, 'Die Lichtmaschinen an der Schwelle der Erfindung', in *Neue Geschichte der Fotografie*, ed. Michel Frizot (Cologne, 1998), pp. 14–22

Fuchs, Peter, 'Vom Zweitlosen: Paradoxe Kommunikation im Zen-Buddhismus', in *Reden and Schweigen*, eds Niklas Luhmann and Peter Fuchs (Frankfurt am Main, 1997), pp. 46–69

——, 'Von der Beobachtung des Unbeobachtbaren: Ist Mystik ein Fall von Inkommunikabilität?', in *Reden and Schweigen*, ed. Niklas Luhmann and Peter Fuchs (Frankfurt am Main, 1997), pp. 70–100

Gabelsberger, Franz Xaver, *Anleitung zur deutschen Redezeichenkunst* (Munich, 1834)

Gfroerer, Stefan, Hartmut Günther and Michael Bock, 'Augenbewegungen und Substantivgroßschreibung', in *Schriftsystem and Orthographie*, eds Peter Eisenberg and Hartmut Günther (Tübingen, 1989), pp. 111–35

Giesecke, Michael, *Der Buchdruck in der frühen Neuzeit. Eine historische Fallstudie über die Durchsetzung neuer Informations- and Kommunikationstechnologien* (Frankfurt am Main, 1998)

Ginzburg, Carlo, *Spurensicherung. Die Wissenschaft auf der Suche nach sich selbst* (Berlin, 2002)

Giuriato, Davide, 'Einleitung', in *'SCHREIBKUGEL IST EIN DING GLEICH MIR: VON EISEN': Schreibszenen im Zeitalter der Typoskripte*, eds Davide Giuriato, Martin Stingelin and Sandro Zanetti (München, 2005) (Zur Genealogie des Schreibens 2), pp. 7–20

Giuriato, Davide, Martin Stingelin and Sandro Zanetti, eds, *'SCHREIBKUGEL IST EIN DING GLEICH MIR: VON EISEN': Schreibszenen im Zeitalter der Typoskripte* (München, 2005) (Zur Genealogie des Schreibens 2)

Glück-Schmitt, Annette, 'Spiritus', in *Metzler Lexikon Sprache*, eds Helmut Glück (Stuttgart and Weimar, 2005), p. 608.

Goerwitz, Richard L., 'The Jewish Scripts', in *The World's Writing Systems*, eds Peter T. Daniels and William Bright (New York and Oxford, 1996), pp. 487–98

Goethe, Johann Wolfgang von, *Gedenkausgabe der Werke. Briefe und Gespräche*, ed. Ernst Beutler, 24 vols (Zurich and Stuttgart, 1948–71)

Goldberg, Jonathan, *Writing Matter: From the Hands of the English Renaissance* (Stanford, CA, 1990)

Goodman, Nelson, *Languages of Art: An Approach to a Theory of Symbols* [1976] (Indianapolis, IN, 1988)

Goody, Jack, *The Interface between the Oral and the Written* (Cambridge, 1987)

Govenar, Alan, 'The Changing Image of Tattooing in American Culture, 1846–1966', in *Written on the Body: The Tattoo in European and American History*, ed. Jane Caplan (London, 2000), pp. 212–33

*Graf von Faber-Castell. Collection 2004/2005*, brochure

Graff, Gerald, 'Summary of "Reiterating the Differences": John R. Searle's "Reply to Derrida"', in Jacques Derrida, Jacques, *Limited Inc.* (Evanston, IL, 1988), pp. 25–7

Greber, Erika, Konrad Ehlich and Jan-Dirk Müller, eds, *Materialität und Medialität von Schrift* (Bielefeld, 2002) (Schrift and Bild in Bewegung, vol. 1)

Gröning, Karl, ed., *Geschmückte Haut. Eine Kulturgeschichte der Körperkunst* (Munich, 1997)

Gumbrecht, Hans Ulrich and K. Ludwig Pfeiffer, eds, *Schrift* (München, 1993)

(Materialität der Zeichen: Reihe A, vol. 12)

——, and ——, eds, *Stil. Geschichten und Funktionen eines kultur-wissenschaftlichen Diskurselements* (Frankfurt am Main, 1986)

Gutman, Israel et al., eds, 'Tagebücher', in *Enzyklopädie des Holocaust. Die Verfolgung und Ermordung der europäischen Juden*, vol. III [1990], pp. 1392–5 (München and Zürich, 1998)

Haarmann, Harald, *Universalgeschichte der Schrift* (Frankfurt am Main, 1991)

'Haffner, Sebastian. Das Gift der Kameradschaft', in *Die Zeit*, 21, 16.05.2002

Hahn, Alois, 'Handschrift und Tätowierung', in *Schrift*, ed. Hans Ulrich Gumbrecht, and K. Ludwig Pfeiffer (Munich, 1993) (Materialität der Zeichen: Reihe A, vol. XII), pp. 201–17

Hamann, Johann Georg, *Writings on Philosophy and Language*, trans. and ed. Kenneth Haynes (Cambridge, 2007)

Hamilton, Charles, *The Hitler Diaries: Fakes that Fooled the World* (Lexington, KY, 1991)

Hanebutt-Benz, Eva-Maria, 'Gutenbergs Erfindungen. Die technischen Aspekte des Druckens mit vielfachen Lettern auf der Buchdruckerpresse', in *Gutenberg. Aventur und Kunst. Vom Geheimunternehmen zur ersten Medienrevolution,* Catalogue to the exhibition of the City of Mainz on the occasion of the 600th anniversary of the birth of Johannes Gutenberg, 14 April–3 October 2000 (Mainz, 2000)

Haraway, Donna, 'Teddy Bear Patriarchy: Taxidermy in the Garden of Eden. New York City, 1908–1936', in *Social Text*, II (1984), pp. 20–64

Hardy, J. J. 'Samenvatting van de resultaten van het handschriftvergelijkend en document-technisch onderzoek van wat bekend staat als het dagboek van Anne Frank', in *De dagboeken van Anne Frank*, eds Harry Paape, Gerrold van der Stroom and David Barnouw (Amsterdam, 1990), pp. 121–86

Hartmann, Frank, 'Techniktheorien der Medien', at http://homepage.univie.ac.at/Frank.Hartmann/Vorlesung/new/medien-technik.html [accessed 13.06.2006]

Havelock, Eric Alfred, *The Literate Revolution in Greece and Its Cultural Consequences* (Princeton, NJ, 1981)

Hayles, N. Catherine, *Writing Machines* (Cambridge, 2002)

Heidegger, Martin, *Parmenides*, trans. André Schuwer and Richard Rojcewicz (Bloomington, IN, 1992)

Henke, Josef, 'Die sogenannten Hitler-Tagebücher und der Nachweis ihrer Fälschung. Eine archivfachliche Nachbetrachtung', in *Aus der Arbeit der Archive. Beiträge zum Archivwesen, zur Quellenkande und zur Geschichte*, ed. Friedrich P. Kahlenberg (Boppard am Rhein, 1989), pp. 287–317

Hildebrandt, Rainer, *Die Mauer spricht/The Wall Speaks* (Berlin, 1992)

Hirsch, Marianne, 'Projected Memory: Holocaust Photographs in Personal and Public Fantasy', in *Acts of Memory*, eds Mieke Bal, Jonathan Crewe and Leo Spitzer (Hanover, NH, and London, 1990), pp. 3–23

Hoftichová, Petra, 'Vorwort', in *Malermonogramme. vol. 1. 15.17. Jahrhundert,* trans. Rudolf Rada (Hanau am Main, 1988), pp. 3–10

Holl, Thomas, 'Rechtsextremismus. Empörung über Bücherverbrennung', *FAZ*, CLV/1, 07.07.2006

Hooper-Greenhill, Eilean, *Museums and the Shaping of Knowledge* (New York and London, 2001)

Hörisch, Jochen, *Der Sinn und die Sinne. Eine Geschichte der Medien* (Frankfurt am Main, 2001)

——, *Ende der Vorstellung – Die Poesie der Medien* (Frankfurt am Main, 1999)

[HSK] Günther, Hartmut and Otto Ludwig, eds, *Schrift und Schriftlichkeit. Ein interdisziplinäres Handbuch internationaler Forschung*, vol. 10.1 and 10.2 (Berlin, 1994–6) (Handbücher zur Sprach- and Kommunikationswissenschaft)

Hugo, Victor, *Notre-Dame de Paris* [1831], trans. Alban Krailsheimer (Oxford, 1993)

Hunger, Herbert, 'Antikes und mittelalterliches Buch- und Schriftwesen', in *Geschichte der Textüberlieferung der antiken und mittelalterlichen Literatur. vol. 1*, eds Herbert Hunger et al. (Zürich, 1961), pp. 25–147

——, Otto Stegmüller and Hartmut Erbse, eds, *Die Textüberlieferung der antiken Literatur und der Bibel* (Munich, 1975)

Huyssen, Andreas, 'Escape from Amnesia: The Museum as Mass Medium', in *Twilight Memories. Marking Time in a Culture of Amnesia* (New York, 1995), pp. 13–35

Ifrah, Georges, *Universalgeschichte der Zahlen* (Frankfurt am Main and New York, 1991)

In 't Veld, N., 'De dagboeken van Hitler', in *Knoeien met het verleden*, eds Z. R. Dittrich, B. Naarden and H. Renner (Utrecht and Antwerp, 1984), pp. 176–89

Innis, Harold Adam, 'The Problem of Space', in *The Bias of Communication*, eds Harold Adam Innis, Paul Heyer and David J. Crowley (Toronto, 1951), pp. 92–131

Irigaray, Luce, *The Sex That is Not One*, trans. Catherine Porter and Carolyn Burke (Ithaca, NY, 1985)

Jenkinson, Hilary, *A Manual of Archive Administration* (Oxford, 1922)

Jennings, Margaret, 'Tutivillus: The Literary Career of the Recording Demon', in *Studies in Philology*, LXXIV/5 (1977), pp. 1–95

Jochems, Helmut, 'Schreiben in Gedankenschnelle. Wegleite durch eine terra incognita der Graphematik', in *New Trends in Graphemics and Orthography*, ed. Gerhard Augst (Berlin and New York, 1986), pp. 105–23

——, 'Stenographie', in *HSK*, 10.2, pp. 1604–8

Kaeppler, Adrienne, 'Hawaiian Tattoo: A Conjunction of Genealogy and Aesthetics', in *Marks of Civilisation*, ed. Arnold Rubin (Los Angeles, 1988), pp. 157–70

Kafka, Franz, 'In the Penal Colony' [1919], in *The Penguin Complete Short Stories of Franz Kafka*, ed. Nahum N. Glatzer, trans. Willa and Edwin Muir

(Harmondsworth, 1983), pp. 140–67

Kallir, Alfred, *Sign and Design: The Psychogenetic Source of the Alphabet* (London, 1961)

Kammer, Stephan, 'Graphologie, Schreibmaschine und die Ambivalenz der Hand', in *'SCHREIBKUGEL IST EIN DING GLEICH MIR: VON EISEN': Schreibszenen im Zeitalter der Typoskripte*, eds Davide Giuriato, Martin Stingelin and Sandro Zanetti (München, 2005) (Zur Genealogie des Schreibens 2), pp. 133–52

Kapr, Albert, *Fraktur. Form und Geschichte der gebrochenen Schriften* (Mainz, 1993)

Ketelaar, Eric, 'Archivalisation and Archiving', in *Archives and Manuscripts*, 27 (1999), pp. 54–61

——, 'Archivalisering en Archivering', inaugural address at the accession to the Chair of Archivistics at the University of Amsterdam (Alphen aan den Rhijn, 1998)

——, 'The Power of the Past: Visibilities and Invisibilities in Archives, Libraries and Museums', keynote address at *Kildenes Makt*, a conference organized by ABM-Utvikling, Norwegian Archive, Library and Museum Authority (Oslo, September 2003)

——, 'Writing Archival Machines', in *Sign Here! Handwriting in the Age of New Media*, eds Sonja Neef, José van Dijck and Eric Ketelaar (Amsterdam, 2006), pp. 183–95

Killius, Christina, *Die Antiqua-Fraktur Debatte um 1800 und ihre historische Herleitung* (Wiesbaden, 1999) (Mainzer Studien zur Buchwissenschaft)

Kittler, Friedrich, *Discourse Networks 1800/1900*, trans. Michael Metteer (Stanford, CA, 1990)

——, *Draculas Vermächtnis. Technische Schriften* (Leipzig, 1993)

——, 'Gleichschaltungen. Über Normen und Standards der elektronischen Kommunikation', in *Geschichte der Medien*, eds Manfred Fassler and Wulf Halbach (Munich, 1998), pp. 255–67

——, *Gramophone, Film, Typewriter*, trans. Geoffrey Winthrop-Young and Michael Wutz (Stanford, CA, 1999)

Klages, Ludwig, *Graphologie I. Sämtliche Werke, vol. 7*, eds Ernst Frauchiger et al. (Bonn, 1968)

——, *Philosophie III. Sämtliche Werke, vol. 3*, eds Ernst Frauchiger et al. (Bonn, 1974)

Knoche, Michael, *Die Bibliothek brennt. Ein Bericht aus Weimar* (Göttingen, 2006)

Koch, Peter and Sybille Krämer, 'Einleitung', in *Schrift, Medien, Kognition. Über die Exteriorität des Geistes* (Tübingen, 1997), pp. 9–26 (Probleme der Semiotik 19)

Krämer, Sybille, 'Friedrich Kittler – Kulturtechniken der Zeitachsenmanipulation', in *Medientheorien. Eine philosophische Einführung*, ed. Alice Lagaay and David Lauer (Frankfurt am Main and New York, 2004), pp. 201–24

——, 'Sprache und Schrift oder: ist Schrift verschriftete Sprache?', in *Zeitschrift für Sprachwissenschaft*, xv/1 (1997), pp. 92–112

Krohn, Wolfgang, 'Technik als Lebensform – Von der aristotelischen Praxis zur Technisierung der Lebenswelt', at www.cipa4u.net/fileadmin/iwt2003/PDF/tech_leben.pdf [accessed 6.01.2006]

Krünitz, Johann Georg, *Oekonomische Encyclopädie oder allgemeines System der Staats- Stadt- Haus und Landwirtschaft*, CLXXVIII (Berlin, 1841), Oeconomische Encyclopädie online, electronic complete text version from the Universitätsbibliothek Trier, at www.kruenitz1.uni-trier.de/ [accessed 5.12.2006]

Kuzdas, Heinz J., *Berliner Mauer Kunst/Berlin Wall Art. Mit East Side Gallery*. Text by Michael Nungesser (Berlin, 1998)

Le Collen, Eric, *Feder, Tinte und Papier. Die Geschichte schönen Schreibgeräts*, trans. Cornelia Panzacchi (Hildesheim, 1999)

*Le mur de Berlin. Vente aux Enchères à Monte-Carlo, Samedi 23 Juin 1990* (Galerie Park Palace, 1990)

Lebegern, Robert, *Mauer, Zaun und Stacheldraht: Sperranlagen an der innerdeutschen Grenze 1945–1990* (Weiden, 2002)

Leroi-Gourhan, André, *Gesture and Speech* [1964/5], trans. Anna Bostock Berger (Cambridge, MA, and London, 1993)

——, *Le fil du temps* (Paris, 1983)

——, *The Art of Prehistoric Man in Western Europe*, trans. Norbert Guterman (London, 1968)

Lévy, Gérard and Serge Bramly, eds, *Fleurs de peau: skin illustrations; the photographic word of a dermatologist in Lyon in the thirties*, trans. Paul Gould (Munich, 1999)

Lombroso, Cesare, *Handbuch der Graphologie* (Leipzig, 1893)

Luhmann, Niklas, and Peter Fuchs, *Reden und Schweigen* (Frankfurt am Main, 1997)

Lyotard, Jean-François, *The Differend: Phrases in Dispute* [1983], trans. Georges Van Den Abbeele (Manchester, 1988)

Mackenzie Owen, John, 'Authenticity and Objectivity in Scientific Communication: Implications of Digital Media', in *Sign Here! Handwriting in the Age of New Media*, eds Sonja Neef, José van Dijck and Eric Ketelaar (Amsterdam, 2006), pp. 60–75

Maier, Max, and Karl Lang, *Lehrgang der Deutschen Kurzschrift, bearbeitet nach der amtlichen Schriftkunde vom 30.01.1936* (Darmstadt, 1938)

Mainberger, Sabine, *Schriftskepsis. Von Philosophen, Mönchen, Buchhaltern, Kalligraphen* (Munich, 1995)

Man, Paul de, 'Semiology and Rhetoric', in *Allegories of Reading: Figural Language in Rousseau, Nietzsche, Rilke, and Proust* (New Haven and London, 1979), pp. 3–19

Marx, Karl, 'Fetishism of the Commodity and Its Secrets', in *Capital. Vol. I.* [1867], trans. Ben Fowkes (Harmondsworth, 1976), pp. 163–177

McLuhan, Marshall Herbert, *The Gutenberg Galaxy: The Making of Typographic Man* (London, 1962)

Melville, Herman, *Moby-Dick or, The White Whale* [1851] (London, 1962)

Menke, Bettine, 'Mneme, Mnemonik – Medien (in) der Antike', in *Medien der Antike*, eds Lorenz Engell and Joseph Vogl (Weimar, 2003), pp. 121–36 (Archiv für Mediengeschichte)

Mentz, Arthur, and Fritz Haeger, *Geschichte der Kurzschrift* (Wolfenbüttel, 1981)

Mercator, Gerardus, 'Literarum Latinarum, quas italicas, cursoriasque vocant, scribendarium ratio' (Louvain, 1540), Faksimile Nieuwkoop: Miland, in Arthur S. Osley, *Mercator: A Monograph on the Lettering of Maps, Etc.* (New York, 1970), pp. 121–76

Michel, Kai, 'Zwei Schädel, ach! … ruh'n in Weimars Gruft. Welcher gehört Schiller?', in *Die Zeit*, 19, 04.05.2005

Mitchell, William J. T., *Picture Theory: Essays on Verbal and Visual Representation* (Chicago and London, 1994)

Moholy-Nagy, Lászlo, 'Produktion – Reproduktion', in *De Stijl. Maandblad voor nieuwe kunst, wetenschap en kultuur*, ed. Theo van Doesburg, 57 (1922), pp. 98–9. English version trans. Frederic Samson, in Andreas Haus, *Moholy-Nagy: Photographs and Photograms* (London, 1980)

Musil, Robert, 'Denkmale' [1936], in *Nachlass zu Lebzeiten* (Reinbek bei Hamburg, 1962), pp. 62–6

Nagy, Gregory, *Pindar's Homer: The Lyric Possession of an Epic Past* (Baltimore, MD, 1990)

Neef, Sonja, 'Authentic Events: The Diaries of Anne Frank and the Alleged Diaries of Adolf Hitler', in *Sign Here! Handwriting in the Age of New Media*, eds Sonja Neef, José van Dijck and Eric Ketelaar (Amsterdam, 2006), pp. 23–49

——, 'Die (rechte) Schrift und die (linke) Hand', in *Kodikas/Code. Ars Semeiotica*, 25 (2002), pp. 157–74

——, 'Handspiel. Stil/us und rhythmische Typographie bei Paul van Ostaijen', in *'SCHREIBKUGEL IST EIN DING GLEICH MIR: VON EISEN': Schreibszenen im Zeitalter der Typoskripte*, eds Davide Giuriato, Martin Stingelin and Sandro Zanetti (Munich, 2005) (Zur Genealogie des Schreibens 2), pp. 235–54

——, *Kalligramme. Zur Medialität einer Schrift. Anhand van Paul van Ostaijens ›De feesten van angst en pijn‹* (Amsterdam, 2000)

——, 'Killing Kool: The Graffiti Museum', in *Journal for Art History. Special Issue 'About Mieke Bal'*, 30 (2007), pp. 418–31

——, 'M/Othering Europe. Or: how Europe and Atlas are Balancing Hand in Hand on the Prime Meridian – she Carrying the Alphabet, he Shouldering the Globe they are Walking on', in *Discerning Translations. Special Issue Visual Culture*, 6, eds Mieke Bal and Joanne Morra (2007), pp. 58–76

——, 'Perfor/m/ative Writing. Tattoo, Mark, Signature', in *Sign Here! Handwriting in the Age of New Media*, eds Sonja Neef, José van Dijck and

Eric Ketelaar (Amsterdam, 2006), pp. 221–36

——, 'The W/Ri(gh)ting Hand'. Leonardo da Vinci as Screen Saver', in *Travelling Concepts III: Memory, Image, Narrative*, ed. Nancy Pedri (Amsterdam, 2003), pp. 341–55

——, 'Zitat und Rahmen. Leonardo da Vinci's *Codex über den Vogelflug* digital', in *Kleine Erzählungen and ihre Medien*, eds Herbert Hrachovec, Wolfgang Müller-Funk and Birgit Wagner (Vienna, 2004), pp. 147–62

——, José van Dijck and Eric Ketelaar, eds, *Sign Here! Handwriting in the Age of New Media* (Amsterdam, 2006)

Neuhaus-Siemon, Elisabeth, 'Aspekte und Probleme des Schreibunterrichts', in *HSK*, 10.2, pp. 1240–48

Nicolai de Cusa (Nicholas of Cusa), *Dialogus de ludo globi/Gespräch über das Globusspiel* (1463), Latin-German parallel edition, eds Ernst Hoffmann, Paul Wilpert and Karl Bormann, based on the text of the critical edition trans. and intro. by Gerda von Bredow (Hamburg, 2000)

Nijinsky, Vaslav, *The Diary of Vaslav Nijinsky: Unexpurgated Edition* [1919], trans. Kyril Fitzlyon (London, 1999)

Oetterman, Stephan, 'On Display: Tattooed Entertainers in America and Germany', in *Written on the Body: The Tattoo in European and American History*, ed. Jane Caplan (London, 2000), pp. 193–211

——, *Zeichen auf der Haut. Die Geschichte der Tätowierung in Europa* (Hamburg, 1994)

Ong, Walter J., *Orality and Literacy. The Technologizing of the Word* (London and New York, 1987)

Osley, Arthur S., *Mercator: A monograph on the lettering of maps, etc. in the 16th century Netherlands with a facsimile and translation of his treatise on the italic hand and a translation of Ghim's 'VITA MERCATORIS'* (New York, 1970)

Ostaijen, Paul van, *Verzameld werk/Poëzie II. [VW2] Bezette stad. Nagelaten gedichten* (1928), ed. Gerrit Borgers (Amsterdam, 1979)

O'Toole, James M., 'On the Idea of Uniqueness', in *American Archivist*, 57 (1994), pp. 632–88

Ouaknin, Marc-Alain, *Mysteries of the Alphabet: The Origins of Writing*, trans. Josephine Bacon (New York, London and Paris, 1999)

Paape, Harry, Gerrold van der Stroom and David Barnouw, eds, *De dagboeken van Anne Frank*, Rijksinstituut voor Oorlogsdocumentatie (Amsterdam, 1990). English edition: *The Diary of Anne Frank: The Critical Edition*, trans. Arnold J. Pomerans and B. M. Mooyart-Doubleday (New York and London, 1989)

Palmen, Connie, *De erfenis* (Amsterdam, 1999)

Parkes, Malcolm B., *Pause and Effect: An Introduction to the History of Punctuations in the West* (London, 1992)

Peirce, Charles Sanders, 'The Icon, Index and Symbol', in *Collected Papers of Charles Sanders Peirce*, eds Charles Hartshorne and Paul Weiss, vol. II

(Cambridge, MA, 1932), pp. 156–73

Petroski, Henry, *Der Bleistift. Die Geschichte eines Gebrauchsgegenstands. Mit einem Anhang zur Geschichte des Unternehmens Faber-Castell*, trans. Sabine Rochlitz (Basel, Boston and Berlin, 1995)

Pias, Claus, 'Digitale Sekretäre: 1968, 1978, 1998', in *Europa. Kultur der Sekretäre*, ed. Joseph Vogl (Zürich and Berlin, 2003), pp. 235–51

Picker, Günther, *Der Fall Kujau. Chronik eines Fälschungsskandals* (Frankfurt am Main, 1992)

Plakins-Thorton, Tamara, *Handwriting in America: A Cultural History* (New Haven, CT, 1996)

Plato, *Phaedrus*, trans. Walter Hamilton (Harmondsworth, 1973)

——, *The Theaetetus of Plato*, trans. M. J. Levett (Glasgow, 1977)

Pomian, Krysztof, *Der Ursprung des Museums. Vom Sammeln*, trans. Gustav Rossler (Berlin, 1988)

Prenowitz, Eric, 'Translator's Note. Right on [à même]' [1996], in Jacques Derrida, *Archive Fever: A Freudian Impression* (Chicago, 1998), pp. 103–11

Price, Billy, *Adolf Hitler: The Unknown Artist* (Houston, TX, 1983)

Prillwitz, Siegmand, 'Fingeralphabete, Manualsysteme and Gebärdensprachschriften', in *HSK*, 10.2, pp. 1623–9

Riepe, Manfred, 'Ich computiere, also bin ich. Schreber – Descartes – Computer und virtueller Wahn', in *Künstliche Spiele*, eds Georg Hartwagner, Stefan Iglhaut and Florian Rötzer (Munich, 1993), pp. 219–32

Ronell, Avital, *The Telephone Book: Technology, Schizophrenia, Electric Speech* (Lincoln, NE, 1989)

Rotman, Brian, *Signifying Nothing: The Semiotics of Zero* (London, 1987)

Rühle, Gerd, *Das dritte Reich. Dokumentarische Darstellung des Aufbaus der Nation* (Berlin, n.d.)

Saenger, Paul, *Space Between Words: The Origins of Silent Reading* (Stanford, CA, 1997)

Salthouse, Timothy, 'Die Fertigkeit des Maschineschreibens', in *Spektrum der Wissenschaft*, 4 (1984), pp. 94–100

Schäfer, Armin, 'Lebendes Dispositiv: Hand beim Schreiben', in *Psychographien*, eds Cornelius Borck and Armin Schäfer (Zürich and Berlin, 2005), pp. 241–65

Schäffner, Wolfgang, 'Mechanische Schreiber', in *Europa. Kultur der Sekretäre*, ed. Joseph Vogl (Zürich and Berlin, 2003), pp. 221–34

Schanze, Helmut, ed., *Handbuch der Mediengeschichte* (Stuttgart, 2001)

Schmid, Anne, *Roms karolingische Minuskel im neunten Jahrhundert* (Hamburg, 2002)

Schmitt, Alfred, *Der Buchstabe H im Griechischen* (Münster, 1952)

Schneider, Karin, *Paläographie und Handschriftenkunde für Germanisten. Eine Einführung* (Tübingen, 1999)

Schnell, Ralf, *Medienästhetik. 20 Geschichte und Theorie audiovisueller Wahrnehmungsformen* (Stuttgart, 2000)

Schöne, Albrecht, *Schillers Schädel* (Munich, 2002)

Schor, Naomi, *Breaking the Chain: Women, Theory and French Realist Fiction* (New York, 1985)

Schrader, Abby M., 'Branding the Other/Tattooing the Self: Bodily Inscription among Convicts in Russia and the Soviet Union', in *Written on the Body: The Tattoo in European and American History*, ed. Jane Caplan (London, 2000), pp. 174–92

Schreber, Daniel Paul, *Memoirs of My Nervous Illness* [*Denkwürdigkeiten eines Nervenkranken*, 1900–2], trans. Ida Macalpine and Richard A. Hunter (London, 1955)

Schuller-Procopovici, Karin, 'Die Phantasien mit der Kamera notieren: Victor Hugo's Portraits und Inszenierungen', in *Alles Wahrheit! Alles Lüge! (Sammlung Robert Lebeck)*, eds Bodo von Dewitz and Roland Scotti (Cologne, 1996), pp. 77–94

Schulze, Johann Heinrich, 'Scotophorus (Dunkelheitsträger) anstatt Phosphorus (Lichtträger) entdeckt – oder merkwürdiger Versuch über die Wirkung der Sonnenstrahlen' (1727), *Neue Solidarität*, 47 (2003), www.solidaritaet.com/neuesol/2003/47/leseprobe.htm [20.11.2006]

Schumacher, Eckhard, 'Performativität und Performance', in *Performanz. Zwischen Sprachphilosophie und Kulturwissenschaften*, ed. Uwe Wirth (Frankfurt am Main, 2002), pp. 383–402

Schwartz, Hillel, *The Culture of the Copy: Striking Likenesses, Unreasonable Facsimiles* (New York, 1998)

Searle, John R., 'Reiterating the Differences: A Reply to Derrida', in *Glyph*, 1 (1977), pp. 198–208

Sevenant, Ann van, *Met water schrijven. De filosofie in het computertijdperk* (Antwerp, 1997)

Sheehan, James J., *Geschichte der deutschen Kunstmuseen. Von der fürstlichen Kunstkammer zur modernen Sammlung* [2000], trans. Martin Pfeiffer (Munich, 2002)

Siemer, Stefan, 'Die Erziehung des Auges. Überlegungen zur Darstellung von Natur in naturhistorischen Sammlungen in der frühen Neuzeit', in *Zeitschrift für Kunst- und Kulturgeschichte im Netz, Sektion Bild Wissen Technik*, 1 (2001), pp. 1–12, www.kunsttexte.de/download/bwt/siemer.pdf [30.01.07]

Silva, Teresien da, 'Zur Echtheit des Tagebuchs', http://home.arcor.de/annefrank/tagb_echth.htm. [15.12.2005]. English version: 'Denial of the Authenticity of the Diary', www.AnneFrankHouse

Sofri, Adriano, *Der Knoten und der Nagel. Ein Buch zur linken Hand*, trans. Walter Kögler (Frankfurt am Main, 1998)

Stahl, Johannes, *Graffiti: zwischen Alltag und Ästhetik* (Munich, 1990)

Stephani, D. Heinrich, *Ausführliche Beschreibung der genetischen Schreibmethode für Volksschulen* (Erlangen, 1815)

Stiegler, Bernard, *La technique et le temps. La désorientation* (Paris, 1996)

——, *La technique et le temps. La faute d'Épiméthée* (Paris, 1994)

Stingelin, Martin, 'Kugeläußerungen. Nietzsches Spiel auf der Schreibmaschine', in *Materialität der Kommunikation*, eds Hans Ulrich Gumbrecht and K. Ludwig Pfeiffer (Frankfurt am Main, 1988), pp. 326–41

Stocki, Angelika von, *Zerfall der Mauer/Fall of the Wall* (Berlin, 1995)

Stroom, Gerrold van der, 'The Diaries, *Het Achterhuis* and the Translations', in *The Diary of Anne Frank: The Critical Edition*, eds Van der Stroom and Barnouw Paape (Amsterdam, 1990), pp. 59–77

Strzyzewski, Jan, 'Lichtgestalt des deutschen Barocks: Johann Heinrich Schulze (1687–1744)', in *Neue Solidarität*, 47 (2003), at www.solidaritaet.com/neuesol/2003/47.htm [accessed 11.07.2006]

Suter, Beat, *Graffiti: Rebellion der Zeichen* (Frankfurt am Main, 1988)

Sütterlin, Ludwig, *Neuer Leitfaden für den Schreibunterricht* (Berlin, 1917)

Tanja, Jaap, 'Das Faksimile der Tagebücher von Anne Frank' [2002], trans. from the Dutch by Frank van Pernis. http://www.annefrank.ch/images/content/pdf/faksimile_d.pdf, [15.12.2006]; 'Anne Frank's Diaries in Facsimile', http://www.AnneFrankHouse

Tropper, Josef, 'Die nordwestsemitischen Schriften', in HSK, 10.1, pp. 297–306

Vergrote, Jozef, 'Clément d'Alexandrie et l'écriture égyptienne', in *Chronique d'Egypte*, 16 (1941), pp. 21–8

Vogl, Joseph, ed., *Europa. Kultur der Sekretäre* (Zürich and Berlin, 2003)

Walde, Thomas, 'Wie Sternreporter Gerd Heidemann die Tagebücher fand', in *Der Stern*, 18, 28.04.1983

Wankel, Hermann, ed., *Inschriften griechischer Städte aus Kleinasien, vol. 11.1. Die Inschriften von Ephesos.* 32: Arbeitsgemeinschaft für die Edition der Inschriften von Ephesos: Hermann Vetters, Dieter Knibbe, Reinhold Merkelbach, Helmut Engelmann (Bonn, 1979)

Watelet, Marcel, ed., *Gérard Mercator, cosmographe: le temps et l'espace* (Antwerp, 1994)

Wegener, J. C., ed., *Neue Recept-Sammlung zu schwarzen, rothen, grünen und anderen Tinten* (Einbeck, 1830)

Weingarten, Rüdiger, 'Der Computer als Schriftmuseum. Latinisierung von Schriften durch computertechnische Zwänge?', in *Materialität and Medialität von Schrift*, eds Erika Greber, Konrad Ehlich and Jan-Dirk Müller (Bielefeld, 2002) (Schrift and Bild in Bewegung, vol. 1), pp. 165–182

Welser-Ude, Edith von and Christian Ude, *Wand-art: farbige Fassaden-Fantasien* (Munich, 1992)

Wetzel, Michael, *Die Enden des Buches oder die Wiederkehr der Schrift* (Weinheim, 1991) (Acta Humaniora)

——, 'Die Leonardo-Galaxis: Vom Tafel- zum Monitorbild', in *Korrespondenzen. Visuelle Kulturen zwischen Früher Neuzeit und Gegenwart*, ed. Cologne Bickenbach and Axel Fliethmann (Cologne, 2002), pp. 75–88

——, 'Ein Auge zuviel. Derridas Urszenen des Ästhetischen', in Jacques Derrida, *Aufzeichnungen eines Blinden. Das Selbstporträt und andere Ruinen*

(Munich, 1997) (Bild und Text), pp. 129–55

——, 'The Authority of Drawing: Hand, Authenticity, and Authorship', in *Sign Here! Handwriting in the Age of New Media*, eds Sonja Neef, José van Dijck and Eric Ketelaar (Amsterdam, 2006), pp. 50–59

——, 'Unter Sprachen – Unter Kulturen. Walter Benjamins 'Interlinearversion' des Übersetzens als *Inframedialität*' (2002), at www.uni-konstanz.de/paech2002/zdk/beitrg/Wetzel.htm. [accessed 11.10.2006]

Windgätter, Christof, *Medienwechsel. Vom Nutzen und Nachteil der Sprache für die Schrift* (Berlin, 2006)

——, 'Und dabei kann immer noch etwas verloren gehen! – Eine Typologie feder- und maschinenschriftlicher Störungen bei Friedrich Nietzsche', in Giuriato, Stingelin and Zanetti, eds, '*SCHREIBKUGEL IST EIN DING GLEICH MIR: VON EISEN*', pp. 49–75

Wood, Helen, 'The Fetish of the Document: An Exploration of Attitudes Towards Archives', in *New Directions in Archival Research*, eds Margaret Procter and C. P. Lewis (Liverpool, 2000), pp. 20–48

Ziegler, Christiane, 'Préface de la nouvelle Édition', in Jean-François Champollion, *Grammaire Égyptienne, ou principes généraux de l'écriture sacrée égyptienne (appliqué à la représentation de la langue parlée)* [1835], ed. Michel Sidhom (Paris, 1984), pp. 1–13

Zwijnenberg, Robert, *The Writings and Drawings of Leonardo Da Vinci: Order and Chaos in Early Modern Thought* (Cambridge, 1999)